THE
TRADITIONAL
BOWYER'S
BIBLE

Volume Four

Steve Allely
Tim Baker
Paul Comstock
Steve Gardner
Jim Hamm
Mickey Lotz
Tom Mills
Dan Perry
Marc St. Louis
Jim Welch
Mike Westvang

THE LYONS PRESS
GUILFORD, CONNECTICUT
AN IMPRINT OF THE GLOBE PEQUOT PRESS

ACKNOWLEDGEMENTS

A volume such as this would be impossible without the efforts of many interested people. The authors would like to thank Dr. Bert Grayson, whose archery collection is housed at the University of Missouri Museum in Columbia, Missouri, and Don Geary, from Mt. Orab, Ohio. We are all richer for their generosity in sharing their amazing collections. Ken Villars, Marty Kreis, and Don Conrad kindly provided photographs. Hugh Soar not only provided photos of his exceptional collection, but also beautiful line drawings. Thanks also to Jen Mahoney for her fine line drawings. Dick Baugh, David Dewey, and Tuukka Kumpulainen provided technical expertise. Gary Davis is not only a gifted bowyer, but a generous bowyer, volunteering staves and bows for photographs. Dr. Errett Callahan offered his vast expertise, particularly on Ishi material.

Steven Bridges went far beyond the call of duty in laying out this volume, ably assisted by Tammy Miles. Donna Hamm (dubbed "Comma Momma" by some of the contributors) edited for grammar and punctuation, as she has every *Traditional Bowyer's Bible* volume.

And finally, the authors would like to thank Paul Brunner, for not being too tall.

Originally published by Bois d'Arc Press

First Lyons Press Edition ©2008

The Lyons Press in an imprint of The Globe Pequot Press

ISBN 978-1-59921-543-5

Library of Congress Cataloging-in-Publication Data is available on file.

Graphic design and layout by The Goldthwaite Eagle Press.
Printed in Canada

ABOUT THE AUTHORS

Steve Allely is an Oregon artist, flintknapper and bowmaker. He specializes in the subject of Native American archery, replicating Native American knives, bows, and arrows, particularly those used in the Far West. He has written about Native archery and has illustrated several books on the subject including the *Traditional Bowyers Bible Volumes 1-4* and *The Encyclopedia of Native American Bows, Arrows, and Quivers Volumes 1-2*. He has also made items for museum exhibits around the country, private collections, and has worked on exhibits for the National Park Service. Steve and his wife Susie make their home in Central Oregon. To contact him about artwork or replications, write: PO Box 1648, Sisters, OR 97759.

Tim Baker, like many others, first became interested in archery after reading about Ishi and the remarkable weapons he made. Upon reading the available archery texts it became clear to Tim there was a great deal of misinformation and confusion concerning wooden bow design. He decided the only way to acquire reliable information was to make every conceivable type of bow of every conceivable material while keeping complete statistics on each. By comparing stats, the qualities which produced superior bows slowly became apparent. Based upon his research, he has written articles on the design, construction and performance of wooden bows, contributed to all four *Traditional Bowyer's Bibles,* as well as teaching at primitive archery meets. Since *TBB 3* his efforts have largely been seen on natural-materials online archery forums, especially *PaleoPlanet's*. He can be contacted at 6609 Whitney Street, Oakland, California, 94609. Or on the primitive archery forum at PaleoPlanet.net.

Paul Comstock never used a hunting weapon he really liked until he started carrying a wooden bow. He earlier tagged whitetails and black bears using center-fire rifles, muzzleloader, shotgun, compound bow, and glass-laminated recurve bow. Since switching to wooden bows, he has abandoned modern hunting weapons entirely. His largest game so far with a wooden bow is a 300 pound black bear.

He began making wooden bows in 1984. From the outset, he began experimenting with woods other than yew and Osage orange, curious because the old bowmaking books ignored these woods almost completely. In 1988, he published the first edition of *The Bent Stick*, the first bowmaking manual to describe in comprehensive detail how to get the best results from some of North America's most common trees. Paul is also a co-author of all four *Traditional Bowyer's Bibles*. Paul sells *The Bent Stick* for $13.95, postpaid, and *Hit the Mark! Shooting Wooden and Primitive Bows* for $7, postpaid. He can be reached at P.O. Box 1102, Delaware, OH, 43015.

Steve Gardner was born and raised in the suburbs of Los Angeles, spending nearly every waking hour with his old lemonwood bow. As an adult, his lifelong interest in archery expanded to include making his own bows of natural materials. After many, many failures, he found George Tsoukalas' bow building site on the Internet, and immediately began producing shooters.

Since that time, he has made bows of every wood and every design imaginable, crafting thousands of bows in the process. In addition to becoming a world record flight shooter along the way, he has now come full circle, back to the basic longbow. His experience has convinced him that with proper design and sound techniques and materials, a longbow may well be the ultimate bow.

Jim Hamm, along with his wife, Donna, owns and operates Bois d'Arc Press. He has co-authored, edited, and published the *Traditional Bowyer's Bible* series, as well as other traditional archery books such as *Encyclopedia of Native American Bows, Arrows, and Quivers* (with Steve Allely), *Whitetail Tactics with Recurves and Longbows*, and *Ishi & Elvis*. Bois d'Arc Press titles have become perennial bestsellers among traditional archers around the world, and have been translated into Italian, French, and German. Jim has also written scores of magazine articles for publications as diverse as *Field & Stream, Primitive Archer,* and The Rocky Mountain Elk Foundation's *Bugle Magazine.*

Jim lives on his ranch in Central Texas, which he manages extensively for wildlife, and where he conducts a very limited number of guided bowhunts for whitetailed deer each year. Along with his two sons, Lee and Reed, he also teaches occasional bowmaking seminars. He can be reached through www.boisdarcpress.com, which also has a compete list of books, guided bowhunt details, and seminar schedules.

Mickey Lotz hails from rural southwest Ohio, where he lives with his wife Dianne on a small section of wooded land "teeming with deer and turkey". Thanks to a bowyer father, Mickey started a love affair with the bow and arrow at a very early age, which is still going strong after more than fifty years. He and Dianne have bowhunted over much of the U.S., Canada and Alaska, harvesting numerous big game animals of ten different species. They have two grown children, daughter Melissa, and son Brian (also a traditional bowhunter) and two grandchildren Jorie and Caden.

A bowyer, primitive arrowsmith and writer, Mickey has authored dozens of pieces for national and international publications. He holds the title of Associate Editor for *Primitive Archer Magazine.* His online Internet tutorials on making wood bows, cane arrows, trade points and stripping turkey feathers et al, have helped countless individuals get started in making their own traditional bowhunting equipment. Among his widely used innovations in this sport are the Floppy arrow rest, the Floppy quiver and the Floppy Bowyer's ruler.

Tom Mills was born and raised on Long Island, New York, and grew up with a keen interest in archaeology and anthropology. He relocated to southern California in 1988, where he shot store-bought fiberglass bows. The trajectory of Tom's archery future was suddenly and completely altered one day when he saw a short little stick bow, literally with the bark still on, at an archery tournament. From that moment forward, Tom set off on a course of learning everything he could about primal archery and other prehistoric skills, also becoming a flintknapper and atlatlist. Tom has also been a member of the World Atlatl Association for many years, serving for a time on the board of directors.

In 2000, Tom started PaleoPlanet.net - an on-line forum dedicated to discussion about all aspects of primitive technology. Now, this truly world-wide Internet community has nearly 2000 members from across America and over 30 countries around the globe. The largest and most active of these forums are those dedicated to primitive archery. Although Tom has a wide and varied interest in prehistoric archery in general, he is especially drawn to prehistoric European archery.

At age seven, **Dan Perry** began building bows from willow branches, and as a teenager graduated to building compound and recurve bows. In the 1970's, he learned to make sinew-backed Plains-style bows from Paul Mantz, of Blanding, Utah. In college at C.E.U., Dan was lab assistant for Professor Don Burge, an avid student of ancient archery and curator of the natural history museum. "Don taught me about bows," Dan said, "I would draw bow designs on the chalkboard and Don could tell me if the ideas were new. They never were." Burge also planted the seeds for Dan's interest in flight archery, in which he has become a recognized expert, holding numerous world records.

In 1985 Dan married Gwen Shakespear, who was patient enough to tolerate racks of drying sinew and sinew glue boiling in her pots. They have seven boys and one girl, and reside in Utah. Besides his skill at flight shooting, he is also is interested in violin making, faceting gems, falconry, fly rod building, and beekeeping.

Marc St. Louis is a self-taught bowyer from Northern Ontario, Canada. His father was involved in archery and instructed him in the art when he was a young boy. Marc has been making his own bows and arrows for over three decades using natural materials and techniques. He has produced record-breaking distance-shooting bows, war bows, hunting bows and historically-accurate bows. His bows are known worldwide for their high performance.

Marc has been interested in the performance aspect of natural material bows for many years and it was his interest in cutting-edge recurves that led him to his experiments on heat-treating. On the Internet and locally, he has been sharing his technique of making high-performance self-bows through heat-treating to both novice and accomplished bowyers for many years.

Marc St.Louis is a contributor to *Primitive Archer Magazine,* the *Bowyer's Journal* and an Administrator of the *Primitive Archer* message board.

Jim Welch, a Sioux/Mohawk Native American, was born in Redwood Falls, Minnesota. He can't remember a time when he didn't shoot a bow, and started making his own at age ten. Jim continued making wooden bows and has hunted with them ever since, taking whitetails in numerous states, two bull elk, and a one-ton bull buffalo. He has made and sold hundreds of wood bows over the years, from sinew-backed horse bows to recurves to long target bows, but prefers to teach someone the art rather than make a bow for them. He now hunts with the Eastern Woodlands bows of his ancestors, and especially likes making character bows from Osage orange.

Mike Westvang was born in western Washington state in 1951. He grew up in proximity to some great self bowyers but never laid eyes on an all wooden bow until he moved to Texas in 1998. That first day's visit to Rusty Craine's bow shop and working the back of an Osage selfbow was all it took. Mike and his son Jason have been building all natural bows ever since. In 1992, they created Dryad Bows and today build and sell fine bows to traditional archers throughout the world.

They can be reached at www.dryadbows.com or Dryad Bows, 231 Rambling Loop, Weatherford, Texas 76087.

DEDICATION

Y

This volume is for all of the grandpas
who make bows for their grandkids.
And in so doing, they pass along this wonderful art.

TABLE OF CONTENTS

SIGN OVER THE ENTRANCE
TO THE BOWMAKERS BAR

"When two or more wood bowmen find themselves together, whatever conversation ensues is largely veneer. Their most important communication is subterranean and wordless. It's a shared sense of the bow's mystery, of ties to an ancient, authentic world, of quiet kinship. Become a woodbow man and you join a band of brothers stretching back in an unbroken line to your 500th grandfather. A time when, unlike our present competitive world, your life and the life of those close to you depended on the sharing of knowledge, goods, and danger. Become a woodbow man and you see that ancient spirit resurrected, other bowmen offering you their secrets, their help, even wood and tools. And maybe more surprising, you note that without calculation or conscious will you yourself becoming such a person too. If this evokes even a whiff of primal familiarity then it's entirely proper that you step at least tentatively onto that ancient path: Make your first bow and see what happens."

OUT OF THE SHADOWS

Paul Comstock

Imagine a world where it is next to impossible to find out anything about wooden bows. In this world, many things we take for granted today do not exist. No contemporary books about wooden bows can be found. There are no Internet websites or message boards. You can search bookstores, bowhunting magazines, hunting catalogs and public libraries - and you can search for years - and find nothing about how to make a wooden bow. The vast majority of North American bowhunters know next to nothing about such bows, and have never seen one.

And any reference you could find about wooden bows, if you could find one anywhere, almost certainly would be exceptionally vague.

Such a world is not a fictional premise for a horror story. It actually existed. In all the articles I have yet read on archery history, no one has described this era. That's probably because most of us who remember it vividly would like to forget it.

The process of how this world came to be is chronicled in some of the vintage archery literature I own. One mentioned that the use of fiberglass in laminated bows was still in the experimental stage in the late 1940s, and noted that by 1954 most bows were using the material. More than a decade later, in the late 1960s, Osage staves were still advertised for sale. By the early 1980s, however, fiberglass had saturated the bowhunting and archery worlds. Wooden bows had all but disappeared - almost without a trace.

If you use and love wooden bows, I would like for you to stop a moment and imagine yourself in such a world. Think about this hobby and all it means to you - all the work you have done, all you have learned, all the excitement and pride and fellowship it has given you - and ask yourself what you would be missing (and if you are old enough, what you in fact missed) during such a dark time.

If you were interested in wooden bows and lucky, like I was, you would have found some decades-old literature that would have told you what you needed to start making wooden bows.

Or you might have met one of a small group of people - very few and far between - who were making wooden bows and dedicated to them. They were a virtual underground, and the vast majority of bowhunters across the continent didn't know they existed.

I was making wooden bows in 1984, and I knew no such people. I cared about wooden bows, but I had no proof anyone else did. None of my acquaintances, archers included, were particularly interested in what I was doing.

By early 1987, the story was still the same, and as far as I knew it would continue that way forever.

We know today, of course, that it wouldn't.

But imagine that somehow you and I - two people who had managed to make wooden bows - had made acquaintance in early 1987. After a few hours of excited jabbering about bows we had made and what we knew about them, we might have told each other long and mournful stories about the agonized and frustrating journey we had to take before gaining even the slightest proficiency in making wooden bows.

We might even have turned to the question of what it was going to take to create a widespread interest in wooden bows.

Had we done that, we could have decided it might happen gradually over 40 or 50 years. Or we might have agreed that if a national bowhunting figure - someone already well-known and well-respected, with a name recognized by hundreds of thousands - announced himself as a wooden bow devotee, a nationwide interest would begin almost overnight.

Such a development, we might have agreed, would attract the attention of thousands, lighting a fuse that would unite those active in the pursuit and lead to an explosion of activity, with wooden bows and information about them literally everywhere.

Let me say this: If we had reached such a conclusion, you would have suggested it, because I wasn't bright enough to imagine such a thing.

But it happened. And I can recall the exact day when I began to understand it was happening. It was the summer of 1987. I was sitting in my living room and opened a small package that arrived in the mail. Inside was a brand new, just-published book: *The Bowyer's Craft* by Jay Massey.

For a few years previous, I and a vast number of other hunters had known who Jay Massey was. We had seen his articles in national magazines, thrilled at the hunts he described and admired him for going afield with longbows and recurves.

And now I was sitting on my couch with his book in my hands, reading as Jay Massey told how to make bows, including wooden bows and sinew-backed bows.

Here was a national bowhunting celebrity who made his own wooden bows and was enthusiastic about them.

I could hardly believe my eyes. I read every word, from beginning to end, that day. I am sure that for many of us who bought Jay Massey's book that summer, one of the immediate results is we decided to follow his examples. Certainly many would make glass-laminated bows, also described in his book.

Others like me were interested in the wooden bows he detailed. I'd never used sinew backings before, but Jay Massey used them. During deer gun season that fall, I went to a processing plant and came home with about 80 deer legs. It took me an entire weekend to cut out all the tendons and start drying them; it kept me in sinew for years.

Within a few short years of *The Bowyer's Craft* being published, the wooden bow resurgence was full-blown and growing bigger every day. To me, this was no coincidence. I began to understand that Jay Massey did more than prove to me that wooden bows were important. He proved it to the mainstream bowhunting community of North America. Eventually I would learn there were other people making wooden bows who were active at the time I was working by myself. I came to know many of them personally. I admired all of the work they did and believe each made valuable contributions to the future of natural archery. Many sold bows, many gave them away, many provided hours of help to any novice who sought it. Some took steps to publicize what they were doing. I know each of these bowyers kept working despite days when they were sustained by nothing but blind determination. It is not my intention to besmirch in any way the stalwart work they did.

But none of us could pull wooden bows out of the shadows and into the national spotlight - with a single stroke - the way Jay Massey did.

Speaking for myself, I was inspired to write *The Bent Stick* after Jay Massey demonstrated to me wooden bows were worth writing about. Once I understood that, I wondered if anyone would be interested in the things wooden bows had shown to me. And other books on wooden bows also appeared soon after *The Bowyer's Craft*.

Almost as soon as I started selling my manual, Tim Baker wrote me a letter introducing himself. Baker knew practically everybody who was visibly active in making wooden bows. I got to know many of them, and one thing most had in common was they knew Jay Massey. If you were making wooden bows, he regarded you as a kindred spirit. An equal.

In 1989, I wrote to Jay and he replied with a three-page letter. He indicated that not everyone understood why he was using sinewed bows and homemade arrows.

"It seems the more basic and primitive one becomes in archery," he wrote, "the more his fellows look at him askance, even those who are shooting laminated longbows." Another paragraph read: "Actually, I've gotten so far out of the mainstream ... that I feel more comfortable hunting by myself much of the time. I spent two weeks hunting in Montana this September, and hunted strictly by myself."

He also wrote, "Some time ago I began to see that the only way to set archery back on track is to abandon everything modern, and go strictly primitive ... wood bows, wood arrows, stone heads where applicable and legal, or tied-on steel heads or handmade heads of steel, iron, copper, or bronze where they are not."

As I read such sentences, I began to understand the fearlessness it took for him to write *The Bowyer's Craft*. By writing it and living by his philosophy, Massey was taking a courageous stand. Instead of playing it safe and not making waves, he was putting his considerable reputation on the line. He was experiencing sacrifice on a personal level. Here was a hero worthy of the name.

Two men who knew Jay Massey well - including the years leading to *The Bowyer's Craft* - were Doug Borland and Dick Hamilton. They remember a man who was resolute in his personal ethics and his passion for crafting archery tackle.

Borland wrote to me that Jay was "not afraid to go against the grain to defend what he thought was right ... He was against the Trophy-Club mentality, abhorred bear-baiting and other image-tarnishing hunting methods and means, and was old school with a minimalist philosophy in everything he endeavored to achieve."

Borland added, "As you may know, Jay's passion leaned more towards the art and craft of traditional archery than the hunting itself. He would rather craft the perfect bow (or an imperfect one!) than kill the biggest animal any day!"

Hamilton remembers the conversations he had with Jay while Massey was writing *The Bowyer's Craft* and after it came out. "It sold quite a few copies," Hamilton recalled, and "I got the impression (Jay) hadn't expected it would sell that well."

If Massey was aware his book was changing the traditional archery landscape, he didn't show it, Hamilton said. "Not that it would have made any difference. He wrote it because he loved it. That's the reason he put it out," Hamilton said.

Hamilton also stressed that, "Jay was a man's man, a good woodsman and a dependable companion when things got rough."

In 1990, I first traveled to Michigan for the Great Lakes Longbow Invitational. Three years before, before *The Bowyer's Craft*, there was no national wooden bow scene. But now I saw at least a dozen people with wooden bows. It was during an

Paul Comstock, Jay Massey, Tim Baker, and Jim Hamm, Michigan, summer 1993.

evening at that event - when several future contributors were sitting around in chairs - that Jim Hamm proposed the first volume of the *Traditional Bowyer's Bibles*. I'm sure none of us that night could have quite envisioned what the series would evolve into, and that some of us would return to it now 16 years hence.

Two years after that invitational, I would return to the event and see more than a hundred people with wooden bows. By 1994, there would be virtually too many to count. Baker, Hamm and I told each other we were astounded to see such an explosion of interest. I also first met Jay at the 1990 invitational and saw him at a couple of events in the next few years. Like the rest of us, he marveled at the rapid popularity of wooden bows. Jay Massey would die too young in 1997. At a longbow event a couple of years before then, on what would be the last day I would see him, I made a brief and feeble attempt to tell him how important *The Bowyer's Craft* was.

We were standing by ourselves, and as I raised the subject I saw a look on his face that told me he didn't want to hear it.

I could only guess what he was thinking. After all, I was essentially a casual acquaintance. Perhaps he felt I was patronizing him. Perhaps he had a deep sense of modesty that would entertain no such idea. I let the subject drop. Now I wish I had pressed the issue. Now I feel that I had a chance to say something important to someone who did something profoundly important, and I bungled the job.

Yet in my imagination I can picture us having that conversation, and I can imagine him telling me I am wrong: That no individual is that important, that only an innate love for the challenge and frustrations and rewards that are wooden bows can lead thousands upon thousands to embrace them with such fervor.

And maybe I'd answer, Yeah, you're right. That's all true. But somebody had to be the first one capable of walking up and kicking the status quo in the head.

And if I am right, those endless thousands have Jay Massey to thank for delivering the kick.

BOW WOOD

Tim Baker

Using one wood exclusively is singing just one song, reading just one book, never leaving home. There is clear or subtle beauty in each species of wood, some wonderful attribute to discover, some unique property to employ or challenge to overcome. Each new wood is a new adventure.

Getting the best from each wood is simple, but the means not always obvious. Those experienced with one particular wood often get poor results when using another, and tend to blame the new wood. Only in recent years have comparative wood tests appropriate to wood bowmaking been done. These helped to devise design principles applicable to all woods. These tests and principles, detailed in the *TBB* series, enlarged on observations reported in *The Bent Stick*, Paul Comstock's important and instructive book.

Lacking such knowledge, bow cultures of the past, and later individual bowmakers, would embrace one design and one or a few woods. Others woods were assigned to lower status or no status whatever. For the first time in history, and surely prehistory too, individual bowmakers can now make equally effective bows of scores of woods and of many different designs.

When working different woods it's often useful to have an understanding of the generic anatomy of wood.

ANATOMY OF WOOD

Wood is formed only by the cambium, a microscopically thin layer of living cells between bark and wood. Once formed, the wood cell wall undergoes no further change in cell type, dimension or thickness. The cell wall is built mainly of strong, long-chain molecules of cellulose, typically about 50%, fortified by lignin, typically about 25%, the remaining 25% being largely non-structural tissue. In essence, cellulose provides tension strength, lignin compression strength.

As the tree grows, inner portions of the trunk are no longer needed to bring water and nutrients to the leaves and are transformed into heartwood. Sapwood becomes heartwood as the tree creates and deposits various chemical and mineral extractives in the cells. Sapwood is generally not resistant to fungi. Any decay resistance a species may have is largely due to various organic compounds residing in heartwood which are toxic to fungi.

Sapwood from many thin-sapwood trees can be compression-weak compared to the heartwood, yet one year later when extractives have been infused into the inner sapwood ring, that sapwood, now heartwood, is a different creature. Of several dozen species of bow woods tried so far, every heartwood serves well in both tension and compression. Mechanical properties of sapwood and heartwood on thick-sapwood trees don't vary much in most species.

Many hardwoods are softer/less dense than many conifers; "broadleaf" more accurately distinguishes the two.

Tom Mills hauling a eucalyptus branch in for questioning. The present number of wooden bowmakers is counted in the tens of thousands. And a large percentage of them are adventurous bowmen, always on the lookout for some previously unmentioned bow wood to try. Hardly a week goes by without someone announcing a fine bow made of a new "non-bow wood" species. The scope of this exploratory realm of natural archery is new. It has never existed before at anything near this level, and is one of the larger areas of satisfaction for this era's natural archery devotees.

In hardwoods, conduction and support are performed by large-diameter, thin-walled cells called pores. Hardwood is therefore called porous wood; softwood is called non-porous wood. In oak, pecan, elm, ash, locust and Osage, for example, the pores are concentrated in the early wood. These are ring-porous woods. Cherry, maple, and birch, for example, have evenly distributed pores and are called diffuse-porous woods. In semi ring-porous wood such as black walnut and persimmon the pores are larger in the early wood, becoming smaller toward the latewood, with no distinct transition boundary.

Annual rings: If ring-porous hardwood rings are thin (many rings per inch) balsa-like early wood will often occupy a high percentage of each annual ring. Such wood will be light and weak and not useable for normal-weight bows at normal widths/lengths. In normal-growth ring-porous trees early wood equals about 15% of ring width, more or less for different species. Hickory can be less than 10%. Ash often more than 20%. For a given species, the larger the percentage of early wood the wider or longer the bow limb must be, all else equal. Unnaturally wide rings may also be less dense and weaker. If unhappy with a tree's surface ring structure then explore

Typical early-wood/late-wood ratios for white ash. Such ratios are the principle predictors of density in ring-porous woods. Eyeing such ratios in a known wood will indicate which staves can yield strong, narrow or short bows, or weaker, wide or long bows.

deeper, where the wood may be thicker-ringed and denser. Unlike hardwoods, the more rings per inch in conifers the denser the wood.

Late summer-growth wood from a ring-porous species is denser than that wood's average density. So bow backs of such wood will be stronger than if of same-density diffuse-porous wood - if the ring-porous growth ring is thick enough for its dense latewood to assume a good portion of the tension load. The back surface of diffuse porous wood is not especially denser.

Fifty percent of a limb's tension work is done by just 10% of limb thickness. If close-ringed, surface late wood is too thin to carry its needed share of the tension load and the bow can break in tension, because only pithy early wood is underneath it to accept its share of load. A related observation: If ring-porous wood is used at a biased angle, as is common with board staves, it behaves like diffuse porous wood, in that no level is denser than another.

Grain: The word "grain" can mean different things, so the term has no value when used without context. If used without further explanation here it will mean the longitudinal cells, the principle fibers that constitute wood.

All wood is dead: Heartwood is dead wood. Sapwood is too. Everything under the cambium is dead, in the sense that that no new cellulose or lignin is being formed. Heartwood is old dead wood, but unless discolored by decay or compromised by insects, weathering or physical trauma it's as sound as if new. Decades-old wood can be fine to use for bows, whether from the inside of a tree, basement storage pile, or old doors or flooring.

Age and density: The ring-count/density relationship seems to apply to all distinct-ring conifers, less so to conifers with little or no distinction between early and late wood. For example, eastern yellow pine, yes; eastern white pine less so. Fir and yew are in the distinct-ring group. But possibly this means juniper and eastern red cedar are in the less-so group.

There may be much more to this. For example, different species have different life spans, so does wood progressively become denser per year, or per a species' maturity profile? Surely the ratio of late to early wood is still important, but how important? And how does this change with tree age? We still have much to learn about bow wood.

Experienced and respected yew harvesters and bowmakers of the past reported that fine-ringed yew was best; others felt that ring width was not all that important, color being the deciding factor. Possibly this conifer-age insight can resolve the two views. On average, thick-ringed conifer wood is less dense than fine-ringed. That's why, for example, fine-ringed yew is preferred over coarse-ringed.

But the ring-thickness, wood-density connection has layers to it: It seems that tree age has more to do with wood density than ring width itself: Young, distinct-ring conifers such as fir produce relatively low-density wood; older mature trees produce the densest wood. In other words, same-age younger wood tends to be of equally low density whether fast or slow growing, while mature wood is denser whether fast or slow growing. Since mature trees tend to be closer ringed, this may be the root of the general thicker-is-weaker rule.

Hundred-year-old fir doors may be denser simply because the old-growth wood had been allowed to live long enough to generate dense wood. Whereas most new fir is harvested before that phase of its growth. There are likely more layers to this story still.

Slow-growing close-ringed ring-porous hardwoods have low density and are weak, due to the high percentage of porous early growth. But that's not so much the case with non ring-porous hardwoods such as maple.

One limb of the described 70 lb red oak bow by Steve Gardner. On a particular redoak stave's SG, an identical design can safely yield 40 lb to 80 lb bows. Similar density ranges exist for most ring-porous woods, less so for diffuse-porous woods. Note the straight but slightly out-of-parallel ring path. This is about the safe angle-of-violation limit for this design.

A thick-ringed red oak board bow by Steve Gardner is D-tillered, flat belly, 71" long, 1 3/8" at widest, fairly pyramidal in design, so just 1" wide at midlimb. The bow pulls 70 lbs at 28", with 1 3/8" resting stringfollow. He chose an especially dense piece of red oak for this heavy-per-width bow. If English-warbow length and width this bow would easily match their 100 lb-plus weights.

Reaction wood: For trunks to straighten themselves once moved from vertical, or to prevent branches bending down from their own weight, hardwood trees lay down tension-strong, cellulose-rich **tension wood** on the top side of trunks and branches. Conifers lay down denser and thicker-ringed, higher lignin content **compression wood** on the bottom side. Wood with high lignin content is especially strong in compression. The little-studied two-wood bows of extreme northern Eurasia, the Saami bows, for example, were bellied with pine compression wood. Related to this, most conifer species produce inadequate bow wood. But the bottom, compression side of horizontal branches can be sinew-backed, yielding first-class results.

Conifer compression wood contains little cellulose so is weak and brittle in tension. Compression wood shrinks or expands with MC changes 10 times or more than normal wood. Tension wood contains more cellulose than normal wood, so is espe-

Reaction wood, tension wood from the top side of branches or leaning trunks, will often dry reflexed. If a bow limb is all tension wood, low in lignin, much of the reflex will surrender in compression. Half-splits of saplings often dry with similar reflex.

cially strong in tension. Tension wood also shrinks and expands with MC changes more so than normal wood. The tension-wood side of a split stave will often dry into reflex. Hardwood reaction wood rings are not always eccentric as in conifers, so it's important to mark the upper side before felling. If the top of such staves are not centered at bow back much twisting and warping will occur.

Branch wood: Even vertical branches, containing no reaction wood, are often denser and stronger than trunk wood.

False growth rings, 'monthly rings': When working down the backs of some woods, Osage, black locust, and sometimes elm, for example, less distinct but recognizable layers can be seen, as if the tree put down monthly rings within the annual ring. Don't be confused; when the real annual ring appears you'll know it.

Decay: If wood is kept dry it will stay strong for hundreds, even thousands of years. Wood is degraded mainly by fungi, hardly ever by bacteria. Early stages of infestation are marked by bluish gray discoloration. For wood to decay the temperature must be between 40° F and 105° F. There must be 20% air volume in the wood. Above 30% MC, wood is protected, its cells now filled with water instead of air. Below 20% moisture content, decay fungi again can no longer grow.

Some decay resistant woods: Exceptionally resistant: Black locust, Red mulberry, Osage. **Highly resistant**: Black cherry; the junipers; burr, gambel, Oregon white, and white oak; sassafras, black walnut; yew. **Moderately resistant**: Honey locust, tamarack, Douglas fir, swamp oak.

The best bow wood: When designed and tillered appropriately all bow woods perform about the same and have similar durability, but woods do vary considerably in other ways. Each bowyer will assign a different order, but as a starting point, here is one suggested order or preference when selecting bow wood:

Cost, or availability
Beauty
Difficulty harvesting
Difficulty drying
Difficulty preparing
Difficulty working
Durability

Availability is at the top of my personal list. Howard Ludington, from Illinois, once signed off with: "We in the land of many trees." He and others fortunate enough to live in hardwood-rich areas can't sympathize enough with we poor Californians.

WOOD AND MC

Few products of man or nature are as appealing as the quiet, disinterested beauty of a wooden bow. But don't be confused. A wooden bow is only death in repose. Strong wooden bows poach elephants in Africa, pin steel-armored knights to their saddles, kill the largest, most ferocious bears mid-charge, and toy-like versions turn great, noble bison into graceless heaps. But only because we do one thing to our bow wood. We dry it well.

A bow can be made from dripping green wood, but if tillered to 50 lb it will shoot as if 25 lb. Wood with a high moisture content is less likely to break. But wet wood is heavy, springs back slowly, and takes enormous set. On the other hand, if wood is too dry it becomes brittle and shatters.

At a given girth, whether debarked or not, whether sapwood is removed or not, every stave of every wood species has a temperature and RH at which it can safely dry.

Ideal moisture content (MC): Each wood species no doubt has its own particular ideal moisture content, given a certain climate. Tension-weak/compression-strong woods like black cherry are safer in damper climates, tension-strong/compression weak woods in drier climates. This is well demonstrated for hickory, where at 6% its cast dramatically improves while retaining tension safety and reduced set. For most woods the best tradeoff point between safety and efficiency is about 10%, with 8% as a good rule-of-thumb minimum and 12% a maximum. At 6% or below most woods become too brash. Above 12% they become too limp, sluggish and prone to set.

"Curing" wood: Any wood can be safely dried over a period of months or years. Any wood can also be dried to highest quality in just days. There are dangers and benefits to both approaches.

This is an important issue. Think of the thousands of poor saps in decades past who never had the satisfactions we're all having now, simply because they'd been sold the Dark Trinity of archery: Only a certain few woods will make decent bows; boards won't make decent bows; wood must be long-cured to make decent bows. All along this was just superstition disguised as prudence. Any time one of these three archery-damaging myths tries to soak back into fashion it should be challenged vigorously with counter examples.

Drying dangers: The main dangers when drying wood are fungal decay, insect infestation, checking, warping, twisting and internal crushing of wood cells - associated with drying too fast per girth.

Wood checks when its exterior dries and shrinks faster than its interior. The shrinking exterior surface wood can also crush damp, still-soft interior wood cells. Uneven surface drying and non-symmetrical cross-sections, along with too-fast drying, causes wood to warp, especially small-dimension staves.

Surface, and even deeper wood, can both decay and become riddled with insect tunnels if allowed to stay wet inside, especially in warm weather, and most especially if resting on the ground. Much good bow wood is lost in woodpiles.

When new to all this I visited a friend in N. Florida who owned some forestland. We felled several perfect logs of maple, elm and mulberry. A treasure trove for a Californian. We laid them out with worshipful care on the soft, damp soil beside his house. He would ship them to California when time allowed. Problem is, time spins thousands of times faster for bugs and fungi than for humans. Once the logs arrived removing the bark was a breeze, because a complex ecosystem had been chewing it loose for about 1000 bug years. It was no longer bow wood. Even the mulberry.

Reducing logs to split staves allows them to quickly drop to decay and bug-safe MC levels. Especially if the bark is removed. Depending on the relative humidity (RH) and wood species the exposed back and ends of green staves should almost always be coated with paint, glue, wax or such to prevent checking.

Once reduced to near bow thickness there is no interior, so to speak, so the stave is largely immune to all forms of drying damage. And being so thin it will now dry in days instead of months or years. This quickest way to dry wood can also be the safest. This is one of the most useful pieces of bowmaking information. And is essentially how bow staves were dried in the beginning, and through time, until recent centuries where bows were largely made by professionals with long pipelines of seasoning wood.

Quick-drying staves - unforced: Fell and split a tree into staves. Take one of these and pull or work the bark free. Floortiller the stave just as if making a finished bow. But keep the stave at least two-inches wide its full length - this to quell any lateral warping impulses as it dries. The more uniform in thickness its cross-section the less it will want to warp.

Tiller until the green bow will bend two inches when pushed with about 25 lb of force against the grip (for a 50 lb bow). This will not cause set, but will tell you how far the stave can be safely thinned. This 25 lb will almost double when the stave is dry, leaving plenty of stiffness for finish tillering.

Rest the stave horizontally, with spacers of some sort beneath it, allowing air to move freely over all surfaces. Place the stave in air close to 50% relative humidity. In damp areas this may be high up in the kitchen, or near the floor of the basement in dry areas. A humidity meter will pinpoint the best location. The warmer the air the faster the stave will dry. A fan blowing evenly over the stave, or any gentle flow of air, will shorten drying time considerably, just as with clothes on a line.

Under unusually fast drying conditions the stave may try to warp. If so, tie it down on a 2" by 4" or such, with spacers beneath it. Or place it in cooler or damper air.

A side benefit of quick drying is that the stave is reduced while green, and green wood is far easier to work. If time allows, reduce all staves to near bow thickness. Or place unworked staves where they can dry slowly enough for their girth. **A floortillered stave can dry as much in two days as a bark-on split stave may dry in many months, and even years if an unsplit log.**

Equilibrium moisture content (EMC, or MC). Wood responds to changes in humidity and loses or gains water as RH drops or rises. For a given RH level a balance is eventually reached at which wood no longer gains or loses moisture.

Since a floortillered green stave can drop below 20% in as short as one day, and since wood can't decay at all once below 20% MC, it's good to debark and floor tiller staves of wood which are not decay resistant, especially in warm, moist climates. Any coating applied to the back to slow drying must later be worked off, taking the pristine surface with it. Quick drying solves this problem also.

Once way to preserve felled wood is to place it under water. England's Hadrian's Wall has yielded relatively sound waterlogged wood almost two thousand years old. If you have prime felled logs, but no time for processing, just submerge them in a pond or such until you do. The deeper the better. Colder water and low-oxygen water aid preservation.

How to weigh up to four-pound staves on a two-pound scale: Set one end on the scale, support the other end, the stave horizontal, and double the indicated weight.

Drying time: Once thinned as described, and placed in room-temperature 50% RH air, **a stave will reach 10.5% MC in about ten days, about 9% several days later.** 10.5% is usually close enough for finish tillering. In air of 40% RH a floortillered stave will reach 9% in about ten days, 8% several days later. Short bows have thinner limbs, floortillered staves drying quicker than thicker-limbed longer bows.

Your personal moisture content: Dry a stave to a moisture content matching the humidity in which the bow will be stored. Otherwise the finished bow will gain or lose draw weight over time as it adjusts to its home RH.

Drying by postage scale: Two of the most valuable tools a bowmaker can own are a humidity meter and a low-weight scale. If the air's RH is known, and the chart, to follow, is consulted, you can know how dry your stave will eventually be - but not WHEN it will reach that point. A scale will say exactly when: Weigh the drying stave every day or so with a five-pound or lighter scale. For convenience write each day's weight on the belly. **The stave is dry when it has lost NO weight for one-third of the time it's been drying.** Scale monitoring is only effective for staves of near floortillered thickness. Thicker wood dries too slowly for weight changes to register accurately. If only twice as thick the eventual belly may not be fully dry for two or three months. If four times as thick it can easily need a year.

The scale's dial should be large enough to clearly show the needle's movement between ounce marks. **The last few percentage points of moisture content take two-thirds of total drying time.**

A floortillered stave will weigh up to about 50 oz if dripping-wet green. Too heavy for a two-pound scale. But it needn't be weighed for the first few days, by which time it will have fallen below two pounds. To weigh it green put one end on the scale, support the other parallel to the ground, and the scale will display half the stave's weight.

Humidity meters. One of the most valuable tools a bowmaker can own. Note the differing readings. Reaction times are slower for conventional meters, on the right, but no batteries are needed. These analog meters are rugged, inexpensive and pay for themselves many times over in saved wood and bows. It's good to keep one everywhere staves are drying and bows are stored.

To force dry or not: There are several interacting factors here: **Does the species like to check?** Some woods split if you just look at them wrong, plum and fruit cherry for example. **Is the humidity high or low?** Wood is much less likely to split in higher humidity air. **Wind speed.** Moving air dries wood surfaces faster. **Present moisture content.** If MC is high, and if the surface wood dries quickly, therefore shrinking faster than inner wood, the resulting difference in stress makes checking almost inevitable. Nearly dry wood can handle quick-drying well. **Stave width.** Inner wood can also dry more quickly on a narrow stave, so it shrinks in width at nearer the same rate as surface wood. **Stave thickness.** Nearly-bow-thin staves, in a sense, have no inner wood to dry slower than outer wood, so differential stresses are much reduced.

In a drying box, a dripping green floortillered stave in 100° F and 40% relative-humidity air will reach 10% moisture content in about five days. It's heading for just under 8%, which lets it reach 10% more quickly. It would reach 8% in a few more days, if allowed. **Again, higher temperature largely shortens drying time, relative humidity largely determines final moisture content.**

Drying boxes are convenient if a dry stave is needed during high-humidity season. Or if a dry season's RH is just high enough so that it takes a very long time for a stave's MC to creep down to tolerable levels.

Controlling humidity: A humidity meter will aid in maintaining optimum RH when drying staves and storing dried staves and finished bows. Do this by opening vents in the early stages of drying, letting damp air out. And later, by closing vents, and adding wet rags or green wood if needed.

Moisture escaping from drying wood raises RH in the box. On the other hand, heating the air lowers RH. Relative humidity can easily drop below 30%, taking the wood below, and possibly well below, 6% MC, where most become dangerously brittle.

High heat and very low RH can cause even thin wood to occasionally check and warp. The RH of the air must be known in order to know the moisture content a stave is heading for. Drying wood in a drying box without a humidity meter inside is like driving a car without a steering wheel.

Heat source: The box's heat source can be solar, light bulbs, a crock pot, or an electric heater. Light bulbs work well for small to medium-sized boxes. Often an electric heater's thermostat won't allow plus-90f temperatures. A cheap no-thermo-stat heater, with low, medium, and high settings, will reach desired temperature in a larger box. If the box's floor is combustible the heater can rest on a large cookie sheet.

A few one-inch vent holes should be evenly spaced in or near the floor and ceiling. Only the top holes need be adjustable, and this can be done simply by placing move-able slats over them. A small fan inside the box speeds drying and promotes unform drying. Point the fan away from the wood.

In open air **a floortillered green stave loses about 25% of its weight in one day, 35% in three days**. Free water leaves the stave so quickly during this phase there is really no point in putting it in the drying box. In fact, it's safer not to. In room-tem-perature, 50% RH air, a near bow-thin stave will drop from dripping wet to about 14% in less than a week. At 50% RH the wood is aiming for just under 10% MC. It will reach about 11% in another few days. That last 1% can take quite awhile. But this 1% can generally be ignored. A drying box is most useful for going from 15% MC or so to dry. Largely because the target moisture content can be lowered. For example, if aim-ing for 10% MC, reachable at 55% RH, adjust RH to 40% and the wood will think it's reaching for just under 8% and will run down to 10% more quickly.

If air is hot and damp outside the box then box temperature must be elevated many degrees higher to lower internal RH. If low enough RH can't be reached con-sider using a **dehumidifier**. Or dry staves during the least humid time of the year, seal them well, and store them in the lowest RH air available.

If air is cold outside the box then heat inside the box will cause box RH to drop far below outside RH. Once the bulk of a stave's water has departed, box **RH can then fall dangerously low**, even into the teens. Vents, wet rags or fresh green wood are easy remedies. Percentage-wise, more wood is wrecked in drying boxes than any other way. All avoidable with a $15 humidity meter.

A low-budget box: One corner of a basement can be made into an effective wood drying chamber for just a couple of dollars. The floor, ceiling and two walls of the basement can be the floor, ceiling and two walls of the chamber. Just tape or staple plastic from ceiling to floor for the other two walls. From eye-hooks in the ceiling, hang wires to trapeze-like cross pieces, one, two or three deep. A 3 by 7-foot space with three levels of hangers will hold about 30 floortillered staves. Place the hangers about 10", 20", and 30" from the ceiling. Put a space heater or dehumidifier on the floor.

A stay-wet box: Sometimes the drying process must be slowed, as some woods will check or crack unless dried very slowly. If natural conditions would dry the stave too quickly, and if you'd like to keep the stave's back pristine and uncoated, raise the humidity in the box to 90% or even higher, then slowly decrease this in safe incre-ments over time. Even Osage can be debarked and dried without its sapwood check-ing. **Again, surface wood must be prevented from drying appreciably faster than inner wood.** Safe drying techniques all have this as a goal.

The thicker the wood the slower it must dry: The higher the temperature, or the lower the humidity, or the faster air moves over the wood, the faster a given thickness of wood will dry. Dense wood should be dried more slowly than lighter wood to avoid checking, warping and cell crushing. Heartwoods must dry more slowly. Heartwood contains extractives, giving wood not just color but density. Heartwood cannot shrink as fast or as much as sapwood.

Drying time: A stave can season for twenty years and still be too wet, if local RH is too high. A stave drying in 65% RH, for example, could not fall below 12% MC in a thousand years. But worse, it can take a very long time to creep down through the last few percentage points of MC to that 12% mark. It might be at 14% when tillered and take far too much set. Wood aiming for 10% and reaching 12% is not as bad off as wood aiming for 12% and reaching 14%. When stuck with high RH it's more important to take the extra time to let wood get as close to equilibrium as possibly before tillering.

Bark is almost waterproof: Typical year-old, sealed, split staves will be about as damp under the bark as quick-dried staves after three days. Floortiller green staves ten days or so before making a bow, as per Quick-Drying, above, and they will be ready when you are.

Low RH or high heat or strong wind can wreck thick wood. Unless wood is reduced to near bow thickness, or coated heavily, the bark might as well be left on. Coat the ends and the sides too, if conditions are severe.

De-barked sapwood on thin-sapwood species, such as black locust and Osage, dries far more quickly than heartwood, usually checking almost immediately and everywhere, the checks often diving deep into heartwood. For this reason sapwood on such species is usually laboriously removed. But if allowed to dry at an unnaturally slow rate, as in artificially controlled humidity, such staves will dry unchecked, and considerably faster than with bark intact. The underbark sapwood surface can then become the bow's pristine bow back. As with yew, such sapwood is lighter than heartwood, somewhat lowering limb mass and raising cast. Such drying is an art in itself.

Other eager-to-check woods can be wrapped in sized paper or perforated plastic, or kept in an almost-sealed tube, or in a "stay-wet' box (described earlier) where humidity can be kept first at 90%-plus. Then gradually lower the humidity via ventilation.

Should wood check from poor drying it may still be useable, if the checks are not too deep and don't run off the side of the limb. Fill checks with glue. If severe use glue-saturated fine sawdust. And possibly back the bow. Back checks are safer than belly checks: The back is being stretched and narrowed; only if back checks run off the side of the limb will they want to peel free, endangering the back. Under compression, belly checks tend to expand sideways, weakening the limb.

Stopping checks that have started: Immediately douse the checking surfaces with water and keep it wet until surface wood is saturated. Then dry the wood slowly. The stave might then be wrapped loosely in plastic, with small vent holes. Or the temperature might be lowered, or the stave placed in higher RH air until later stages of drying.

Air-drying irony: Air-dried staves often show more checking, cracking, twisting and compression damage than lumber staves, all avoidable using above information.

Curing kerfs: Speed drying and prevent full-diameter logs from checking, and causes a log to split true and easily. Make full-length straight cuts with a Skill saw where the log would otherwise be split into staves. This technique is especially useful for drying wood with the bark left on. As long as the log is straight-grained, saw

Curing kerfs can save the life of large-diameter boles. Each kerfed section shrinks as if a small-dimension sapling — more quickly and with reduced checking danger. This brings special peace of mind when drying prized wood such as the pictured debarked yew.

cutting will yield more staves per tree than more-damaging wedge splitting. If the log has more than slight twist it's good to split the log in half, in order to read the twist. Blind kerfing on such logs can cut through future limbs at some angle, violating fibers and endangering the future bow. Staves split from such a log will have some amount of twist, but if not too severe it can be heat-straightened or tolerated.

Hidden checks: Quickly dried surface wood shrinks and checks. When later split and reduced the inner wood then dries and shrinks also, causing the surface checks to close. Later, if dried further and quickly, they can open up again.

Forcing a stave into reflex while drying: Such staves are just pretending. Most of this reflex will pull out when strained, especially in main working portions of a bow limb. Staves which are steamed or heat-bent into reflex do better - steam-bending temperatures let cellulose plasticize somewhat, assuming a true altered position. Staves that grow naturally reflexed do better still.

Rehydrating wood: If a stave is too dry reduce it to near bow thickness and place it in destination RH air for a ten days, or a few more if patience allows. Wood is stiffer when dry, so don't determine proper limb thickness based on floortiller resistance while too dry.

Drying and rehydrating rates: It's easy to test the rate at which water moves in and out of wood. Just weigh the sample each day, as per Drying by Postage Scale, earlier.

Equilibrium MC differences: At 50% humidity, Hoadley (*Understanding Wood*) reports the limit of difference in EMC between woods at about 2.3 points, or for example, about 8.1 MC to 10.4 MC. At 70% humidity this gap is about 11.2 MC to 14.3 MC. To know this gap for any two particular woods is difficult, requiring oven drying and weighing of samples - when measuring small differences in MC, meters are fooled by extractives and such. Woods with high extractive contents have slightly lower equilibrium moisture content than low-extractive wood.

Do light woods have a moisture absorption problem? Or one could as properly ask: Do dense woods have a moisture retaining problem? All wood, no matter how light or dense will reach nearly the same MC in a given RH environment. So the question becomes: How quickly do light and dense woods respond to high and low RH?

If unsealed, less dense woods lose moisture more quickly. So if exposed to very high RH for days at a time, unsealed or poorly sealed low-density bows will lose drawweight and take more set than denser woods. But there's this too: Once at a too-high MC light woods dry back to original MC faster. So dense-wood bows are out of service for a longer time, light-wood bows go out of service quicker. If both dense and light-wood archers treat their bows appropriately this seems to be a different-but-equal issue. If bows are well sealed the issue largely become moot.

Moisture content and stiffness: When wood becomes very dry, it becomes stiffer and stronger in compression, but its tension strength doesn't rise in lockstep, increasing the chance of tension failure. Woods like hickory, elm and white oak do well at very low MCs; others explode if not backed with low MC- tolerant materials.

Temperature and strength: Depending on the species, wood strength rises and falls with its temperature, by about 3.5% for each 10 F°. Bow weight drops when shooting in the summer heat and rises in the winter cold. Just as with MC, it's good to design and tiller a bow for conditions of intended use. Too-cold bows can mimic too-dry bows, breaking when too stiff. Low winter humidity combines these dangers.

Wood taken to temperatures of 200° F and higher will be permanently weaker by one or a few percentage points, depending on time and temperature. Same-temperature dry heat bending is slightly less damaging than steam bending. But it's easy to overheat without steam's automatic temperature ceiling of 212° F.

Heat or steam-bent wood is weaker by about 10%, or more, depending on the severity of the bend, temperature, and time spent at that temperature.

The MC of wood dried at about 212° F will always be up to 2-percentage points lower than air-dried wood. This is useful information for humid-weather bowyers. I imagine that heating an already air-dried stave to high temperatures would have the same effect.

Measuring MC: The MC of wood is the ratio of the weight of water in a given piece of wood to the weight of the wood when it's oven dry. The MC of a stave can be measured by cutting off a portion, weighing it carefully, then placing it in a 212° F oven for sufficient time to completely dry the sample. Weigh it again, then calculate the initial MC percentage. For example if a 550-grian sample of wood weights 500-grains once dried, it starting MC was 50/500 or 10% MC.

Moisture meters: Electrical-resistance, prong-type moisture meters cost about a day's pay, are convenient to use, and are moderately accurate if used with care and insight.

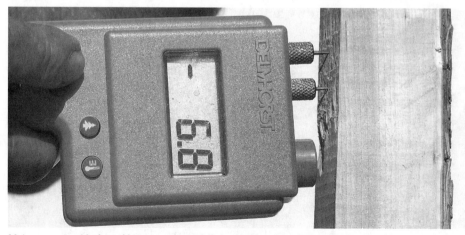

Moisture meters. Much used by some, purposefully ignored by others. Delicate and informed use is required or grossly inaccurate readings can result. Instant MC readings can be a large plus if accurate. The humidity-meter and low-weight scale method of drying, mixed with experience, may be the most precise way to know the MC of a drying stave,

Different woods yield different meter readings, and supplied correcting charts are incomplete and imperfect. Even readings from same-species staves of equal MC can be off by a few points, possibly due to minerals in the soil during growth or differences in density. Worse than that, often a reading taken with prongs parallel to the grain will give one reading, a different reading when placed at 90-degrees, with no way of knowing which, or if either orientation is correct unless indicated in the meter's instruction manual. For example, a maple stave just read 8.1MC with the grain, 7.0 across the grain. Hickory: 9.9 with, 9.2 across. red oak: 7.6 with, 6.0 across.

But the greatest metering errors are due to uneven dampness on and in the stave. If just the very surface is somehow moist the meter reads high. If the surface is bone dry, but underwood is damp, the reading will he high. It might read 10% while the surface, the wood that does the work, might be 5%, causing the bow to break. There are many such scenarios in which the stave and meter outsmart us. Common sense is the best protection here. A more certain way to know the moisture content of wood is to know the relative humidity of the air surrounding it.

A moisture meter will never read below about 13% if the air rests at 70% RH. So even when using a moisture meter a humidity meter is also needed. A humidity meter is about the most useful tool a bowmaker can have.

Humidity meters are inexpensive - as low as ten-dollars. Without one your bows may be taking large set, or breaking, without you knowing why. A humidity meter aids bowmaking in other large and subtle ways.

For a fairly good check of a meter's accuracy set it outside in the shade on a steady-conditions day, give it an hour or more to acclimate, note the indicated RH. Then check with the local weather bureau for RH in your area at that time. If the meter is off just tape new numbers on its face. Such recalibrations works best when first done at say, 30% RH, than again in at say, 70% RH. It's good to keep a humidity meter everywhere you dry or store wood and finished bows.

Equilibrium Moisture Content of Wood at Given Relative Humidity and Air Temperature Fahrenheit

0	30	40	50	60	70	80	90	100	110	120	130
						Temperature					
5	1.4	1.4	1.4	1.3	1.3	1.3	1.2	1.2	1.1	1.1	1.0
10	2.6	2.6	2.6	2.5	2.5	2.4	2.3	2.3	2.2	2.1	2.0
15	3.7	3.7	3.6	3.6	3.5	3.5	3.4	3.3	3.2	3.0	2.9
20	4.6	4.6	4.6	4.6	4.5	4.4	4.3	4.2	3.0	3.9	3.7
25	5.5	5.5	5.5	5.4	5.4	5.3	5.1	5.0	4.9	4.7	4.5
30	6.3	6.3	6.3	6.2	6.2	6.1	5.9	5.8	5.6	5.4	5.2
35	7.1	7.1	7.1	7.0	6.9	6.8	6.7	6.5	6.3	6.1	5.9
40	7.9	7.9	7.9	7.8	7.7	7.6	7.4	7.2	7.0	6.8	6.6
45	8.7	8.7	8.7	8.6	8.5	8.3	8.1	7.9	7.7	7.5	7.2
50	9.5	9.5	9.5	9.4	9.2	9.1	8.9	8.7	8.4	8.2	7.9
55	10.4	10.4	10.3	10.2	10.1	9.9	9.7	9.5	9.2	8.9	8.7
60	11.3	11.3	11.2	11.1	11.0	10.8	10.5	10.3	10.0	9.7	9.4
65	12.4	12.3	12.3	12.1	12.0	11.7	11.5	11.2	11.0	10.6	10.3
70	13.5	13.5	13.4	13.3	13.1	12.9	12.6	12.3	12.0	11.7	11.3
75	14.9	14.9	14.8	14.6	14.4	14.2	13.9	13.6	13.2	12.9	12.5
80	16.5	16.5	16.4	16.2	16.0	15.7	15.4	15.1	14.7	14.4	14.0
85	18.5	18.5	18.4	18.2	17.9	17.7	17.3	17.0	16.6	16.2	15.8
90	21.0	21.0	20.9	20.7	20.5	20.2	19.8	19.5	19.1	18.6	18.2
95	24.3	24.3	24.3	24.1	23.9	23.6	23.3	22.9	22.4	22.0	21.5
98	26.9	26.9	26.9	26.8	26.6	26.3	26.0	25.6	25.2	24.7	24.2

(left axis label: Humidity)

In time you'll develop a sense of how fast water moves in and out of wood of different dimensions in air of different dampness and temperature. A humidity meter alone will then say with good-enough accuracy the moisture content of your staves, blanks, and bows.

Keeping bows at ideal MC: Should local humidity not favor bow health, finished bows can be kept in a cabinet with adjustable vent holes, and either a heat source or container of water inside. And an easily visible humidity meter. With a little trial and error, inside humidity can be kept hovering at about target RH of, say, 50%. Once at chosen moisture content, three coats of marine spar varnish or similar will keep wood bows stable for weeks, or many days at a time, even in worst weather.

SELECTING BOARD STAVES

The main hurdle when board bow making is proper board selection - making sure the board is as mechanically sound as if split from the surface of a tree. There are dozens of ways in which a board can be dangerously different from a split tree stave. And a good-sized book could be filled noting these and explaining how to avoid such boards. But forget all that. You don't need to know dozens of negatives features to avoid; you only need look for one, just one, positive feature to approve.

Only a perfectly straight tree can yield a perfect board stave. Imagine a straight board milled from a tree which had a wavy or arched surface. It's clear that the board's surface fibers must be violated. Its fibers - the material which makes the bow strong and safe - approach the back surface in places at sharp angles, where they can be peeled away from each other rather than accept full tension strain. There is a very good chance an unbacked bow from such a board would fail. So when searching for a board stave choose one milled parallel to the surface of a straight, untwisted tree.

Doing this is simplicity itself, because the exposed ring lines on the face of such a board **will necessarily be perfectly straight from one end of the board to another.**

If these exposed ring lines are curved or have waves, V's, kinks, islands, bow-legs, or any shape at all other than perfectly straight from one end of the board to the other the tree was twisted, wavy or lumpy and the board's fibers are violated, severed, and already broken, so to speak. The more the rings stray from perfectly straight the greater the fiber violation, the greater the chance the bow will break.

The single positive feature to look for: Look at the face (the future bow's back) of board after board and simply choose one with perfectly straight ring lines running from one end to the other. No waves, no kinks, no islands, no V's, no knock-knees, no nothing. Just perfectly straight ring lines from end to end. This is so simple no photos or drawings are needed.

A monkey could be trained to do this. Even a dog might be. But you'll screw up the first few times, because you won't be able to keep yourself from having complicated thoughts. So here's your IQ test: If you come back from the hardwood store with a perfectly straight-ringed board stave the very first time then you score way low. Please don't have children.

But after a few trips you'll learn to control you higher brain functions and accept how simple the job is. **Straight ring lines on the face of the board from one end to the other.**

Viewed from its butt end, the board can be edge-ringed, bias-ringed or flat-ringed. All that matters is that ring lines on the face of the board, the future back of the bow, are straight.

Stare at this picture while saying: 'straight rings from one end of the board to the other.' Keep at it until the idea is cauterized into your brain's surface as by a branding iron. Then march to the lumber stacks, zombie-like, repeating that mantra. Do this and there's a fifty-fifty chance you'll arrive back home with a useable board stave your very first attempt. Otherwise there's almost no chance - that big brain of yours will somehow get in the way.

Don't bother looking at the ring lines on the side of the board. They can look terribly violated yet the board still be a perfect stave - the why of this is explained farther on.

Advanced class: If a board has perfectly straight ring lines from one end of the board to the other, and if those ring lines are perfectly parallel with the edge of the board, any ring lines that appear on the side of the board will also be perfectly straight and parallel from on end to the other.

But if ring lines on the face are even a bit out of parallel with the edge of the board this will cause ring lines on the side of the board to run downhill at a sharp angle, giving the illusion of a terribly violated board. This is only illusion. The board can still be a perfect bow stave because its fibers are perfectly parallel with the bow's back. If the edge of the board is trimmed, making it parallel with the ring lines on the board face, the ring lines on the side will magically become parallel too. So don't look as the ring lines on the edge of the board when prospecting.

Advanced, advanced class: Ring lines on the face of a flat-ringed board can have a bit of wave to them, even though the fibers in the wood are perfectly sound and unviolated. But as boards move from flat ringed to bias-ringed to edge-ringed this becomes progressively less true. In other words, any waviness at all on an edge-ringed board is signaling severe fiber violation, so this board should be rejected. The same minor waviness on a bias-ringed board reveals only slight fiber violation.

On a flat-ringed board such waviness is almost unavoidable and means nothing. An insignificant angle of fiber violation is at work. This can be demonstrated by scraping such a board, carefully exposing the full original surface of the tree. That surface will be almost perfectly smooth, at no point deviating from board-flat by more than an insignificant angle.

Do the same test on a bias-ringed board having equally wavy ring lines on its face. The exposed original tree surface will be quite undulating. To make that surface board-flat its surface fibers would be cut through at dangerous angles.

With flat-ringed boards some ring line waviness is almost inevitable, and is not indicative of dangerous fiber violation. The degree of meandering seen here is completely tolerable.

Ring lines on the face of an edge-ringed boards can look almost perfectly straight while surface fibers are dangerously violated. The narrow side of an edge-ringed board can be thought of as a very narrow but thick flat-ringed board. So judge it that way. If ring lines aren't as acceptably straight on its narrow 'face' then move on to the next board.

Other board flaws: When standing before the stacks our eyes are hungry. We want each board we appraise to be a choice stave, and this gives us biased eyes, which often don't see what they should. Australian bowmaker David Clark once wrote that "pin knots in the timber yard revealed themselves to be cyclones of twisted grain when polished at home." Maybe one in ten of otherwise perfect boards will have some physical flaw, a depth charge waiting to explode.

With a grownup's eye, check each board for drying checks, signs of decay, warp, twist, pin knots, and sunken surfaces (a type of drying damage). Surface knots on split staves are almost always OK, because the tree was smart enough to elevate the wood in compensation. Boards ignore the tree's engineering wisdom. The back surface of a bow is under several hundred pounds of tension. The angle of fiber violation is severe around a decapitated knot, even a pin knot. If such a board is selected by mistake a backing serves as depth charge neutralizer.

It's good to cruise the stacks every couple of week so as to build up a supply of A-grade staves. Then you can stand in front of such B-grade boards and not feel the torture of temptation. Your life will be torture if you can't walk away from the wrong board, or the wrong girl.

In time you'll develop a feel for the allowable angle of fiber and ring violation for various woods. Some are more tolerant than others. Hickory, white oak, pecan, elm and maple, in that order, for example.

If new to board bowmaking, this might be a good time for a fair warning: Be careful making board bows. After a while you won't be able to have a meal in public. You'll be too busy examining how the growth rings run in all the red oak trim.

The bowmaker's lumberyard creed: Leave the stacks neater than you found them.

Tropical boards: With the rare exception of woods such at teak, tropical woods usually have no discernible growth ring to use as guide to the wood's fiber path. All can look well, especially the darker species, but when examined closely anomalies in the fiber path might be found, caused by branches or such that rested above or below the board when in the tree. Before using such wood unbacked, it's useful to examine every inch of the future back with a 5X glass. This can save much heartache. Assuming otherwise sound wood, decent tiller and low set, when those dense tropicals break it's almost always due to grain anomaly.

Dangerous woods: Some woods contain substances harmful to us. Breathing their dust can lead to serious health problems. All bow woods haven't been studied, but it's presently clear that some cause one or more of the following: allergic skin reactions, headaches, eye inflammation, nausea, fatigue, hay fever, asthma, coughing and more severe respiratory diseases, cardiovascular illness, and there are reported cancer links.

Someone making a few bows, or using hand tools only, should have little concern. Multi-bowmaking and bandsaw use is another story. This is no doubt an extreme example: During a four year period I bandsawed 2000 or more staves of scores of woods in a basement with only fair ventilation using cheap masks during peak dust episodes. Over time my lungs seemed to close down to half volume. Breathing was labored and somewhat painful. I felt half poisoned all the time. I knocked off for a few months, then installed a big fan to draw out the dust-laden air. I used better masks and the fan on high speed when making dust. From then on I worked upwind in about a 2-mph dust-free airflow.

That saved my bowmaking life.

During later stages of that peak bandsawing period one of my favorite heart arteries shut down, almost ending any future bowmaking, and breathing. No way to know if or how much all that dust had to do with this.

Given incomplete knowledge in this dust/danger area it seems best not to breathe wood dust at all if possible, and very little at most. Fortunately, it's quite easy to arrange this. Simply work outside, upwind of any dust making.

If this isn't possible, a quiet $20 fan blowing air out a shop window replaces the shop's entire volume of air every few minutes. The bad air is gone! No need for much slower, much less effective physical or ion filters.

The bandsaw can be the real lung killer, so split, shave and scrape instead if good ventilation is not possible. If none exists, it's not much work to frame out a new window in a garage, basement or shop wall. Make it at least the size of 20-inch fan.

Some wood toxins are cumulative, taking years to cause damage. Hardwoods, especially the dense tropicals, are more likely to offend than softwoods. Risk increases with fine dust, and the duration, frequency and density of exposure. Here are a few of the woods requiring caution:

Beech: Cancer of eyes, nose, throat. Leaves, bark, and wood dust.
Black locust: Nausea. Leaves and bark.
Elm: Irritant; eyes and skin. Wood dust.
Goncalo Alves: Eyes and skin. Wood and wood dust.
Hemlock: Respiratory cancer. Wood dust
Myrtle: Respiratory. Leaves, bark, wood dust.
Olivewood: Eyes, skin, respiratory. Wood and wood dust.
Padauk: Eyes, skin, respiratory. Wood and wood dust.
Purpleheart: Nausea. Wood and wood dust.
Sassafras: Respiratory. Wood dust.
Black Walnut: Eyes and skin. Wood and wood dust.
Wenge: Eyes and skin. Wood dust.
Willow: Respiratory. Wood, bark, wood dust.
Teak: Eyes, skin, respiratory. Wood dust.
Yew: Direct toxin; heart, eyes, skin. Wood and wood dust.

Bow wood commonly found as lumber: Ash, black walnut, black cherry, Douglas fir, hickory, maple, pecan, oak, poplar, ipe, teak, ramin, purpleheart, paduak, goncalo alves, wenge, Brazilian cherry, zebrawood.

PROPERTIES OF PARTICULAR WOODS

An earlier version of the below list was once divided into non bow woods, borderline bow woods, and true bow woods. But those distinctions had to go because serviceable bows are now being made from too many of those non and borderline woods. And because there can be such large variation in mechanical properties within a species. A species with an average density of .60 SG, for example, can range from .45 SG

Phil Gershwin shooting El Pescado, his dedicated red oak fishing bow. Made from a red oak board when first leaning the craft. From the number of red oak board-stave bows in present use, future paleoanthropologists might assume this wood was especially valued by us. The truth is more prosaic: Boards are an inexpensive way for beginners to learn the ropes, and there are lots of beginners now, and red oak is simply the most common dense wood sold at our ubiquitous home-repair centers. We might be making similarly off-base assumptions regarding wood preferences of our ancient kin.

to .75 SG. Density distribution follows a similar curve as height in humans: extreme differences are rare, moderate differences are more common, with relatively small differences among the majority.

There are over 75,000 species of trees and large shrubs in the world from which hunting-weight bows can be made. Below are just a few of the most commonly known, and a few less commonly known.

It's important to note that for most of the newly emancipated light woods draw weight must be low, or the limbs considerably wider or longer. For starting dimensions consult the Design Rule Of Thumb, pg. 115.

At 1.5" by 72" by 28" draw length, .40 SG wood can yield safe and efficient up-to-50 lb bows if 'D' tillered. A useful approach is to begin at 1.5" wide and 80" or so long, D-tillered to 50 lb. Then retiller shorter and shorter until the bow takes about 1.5" of set.

The following derives from personal SG and wood tests, tested bows, published wood properties, and reports from other bowmakers. This information is provisional, but is at least a close approximation. Room won't allow but a partial list of the world's near countless bow wood species. Some woods likely too light for common use are listed here also, largely to signal which to avoid.

ACACIA, Over 1000 species. **Black,** *Acacia melanoxlyon,* About .60 SG. Australian native. In US, mainly California, Georgia, Florida, Hawaii. Diffuse-porous. Golden brown heartwood. Steambends well. Often found growing enticingly pipe-straight in clusters. The wood is somewhat brittle though. Treat as if about .50 SG unless backed, as with rawhife, or carefully decrowned, it being one of the few woods needing decrowning.

ALDER, Red, *Alnus rubra,* .41 SG; **Gray,** *A. incana,* .47 SG.

ALMOND, *Prunus dulcis,* about .67 SG.

APRICOT, *Prunus armeniaca,* About .67 SG.

APPLE, *Malus spp.* About 68 SG. Tends to check and warp when drying, so extra care needed here. Often grows twisted. Otherwise makes fine bows.

ASH, Black, *Fraxinus nigra,* .49 SG. The lightest ash; weak in compression, and brittle. This is the ash Indians pounded apart for basket weaving. Less than one-inch thick sapwood. Wood from two separate logs took much more set than expected even though width-adjusted for density; **Green,** *F. pennsylvanica,* .56 SG; **Oregon,** *F. latifolia,* .56 SG; **Blue,** .58 SG; **White,** *F. americana,* .59 SG. White is our heaviest ash. Almost all sapwood. Oregon looks and behaves almost identically to White.

ASH, European, *Fraxinus excelsior,* .61 SG.

ASPEN, Quaking, *Populus tremuloides,* .38 SG. The most widely distributed tree in North America. **Bigtooth,** *P. grandidentala,* .39 SG.

ASPEN, European, *Populus tremula,* .45 SG.

AVOCADO, *Persea Americana Mill,* about .70 SG.

BALDCYPRESS, *Taxodium distichum,* .46 SG.

BAMBOO, Over 1000 species. For generic properties see Backing Bamboo in *Design and Performance Revisited.*

BASSWOOD, *Tilia americana,* .37 SG. Basswood, as in bast wood - inner bark makes good rope and cordage. Related to the denser European Lime.

BAY, California laurel, Pepperwood, Oregon Myrtle, *Umbellularia californica,* .57 SG. Diffuse-porous. Strong spicy odor to freshly exposed wood. A West Coast native found from Oregon to San Diego. Primitive technologist Joe Dabill prefers upright shoots from fallen but living trees for staves.

BEECH, American, *Fagus grandifolia,* .64 SG. **European,** *Fagus syvatica,* .64 SG.

BEEFWOOD, see **Massaranduba**.

BIRCH, Paper, *Betula papyrifers,* .55 SG; **European (Silver),** *B. pendula,* .59 SG; **European (White),** *B pubescens,* .59 SG; **Yellow,** *B. alleghaniersis,* .62 SG; **Sweet/Cherry/Black,** *B. lenta,* .65 SG. All birches are diffuse-porous. Lighter species somewhat brittle in tension, and often fretting in compression.

BLACK LOCUST, *Robinia pseudoacacia,* .69 SG. Always has two or three sapwood rings, unless a hybrid. Relatively low in compression elasticity. A flat-back design is fine, but a crowned-back, wide-belly design is ideal, as from a smaller diameter limb or trunk. This wood is more likely to fret and chrysal, especially if the belly

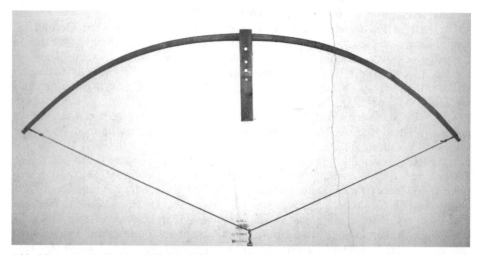

A black locust bow by Mark Lansiink of the Netherlands; 120 lb at 28"; 71" ntn; 1.42" wide; .98" thick, 18 rings per inch but thin early wood; flat belly, slightly crowned back; especially dense wood; 1.5" set. Along with dense wood and a flat belly almost hypnotically perfect D-tiller accounts for this bow's low set and fretless belly. Textbook design and tiller for this textbook wood.

is rounded, but here there is variation between trees. Nature loves bowmakers. She knows it's hard to tiller a bow for best safety and speed, so she gave us black locust as teacher. If a black locust bow develops clusters of frets in one or a few small areas this is locust's way of telling us we haven't tillered the bow well. The fretted areas were put under greater strain, the unfretted areas loafing. Someone may think they've tillered a bow perfectly, but in the case of locust, the bow will actually tell if they have or not. A well tillered bow will either have no frets, or have small frets spread along almost the entire length of the working limb. If a locust bow is tillered perfectly and still develops frets, this is locust's way of saying we haven't designed the bow properly for its weight, length, draw, and the particular properties of the stave. The locust stave is a classroom.

BLACKTHORN, *Prunus spinosa*, 87 SG. Plum family; tart sloe berries; Full of thorns. Native to Europe, West Asia, N. Africa.

BLUE BEECH - See Hornbeam.

BOXELDER, a maple, *Acer negundo*, .46 SG.

BRAZILIAN CHERRY, Jatoba, *Hymenaea courbaril*, .91 SG. Steambends well.

BRAZILWOOD, Pau-Brasil, Pernambuco, *Caesalpinia echinata*, about .98 SG.

BUCKEYE, Yellow, *Aesculus octandra*, .36 SG.

BUCKTHORN, Cascara Buckthorn, Cascara, Chittam, *Rhamnus purshiana*, .52 SG. Largest of the buckthorns, small tree, Pacific Northwest, orange-red wood. Treat as if medium density birch. Good bows reported by Oregon bowmakers.

BUTTERNUT, *Juglans cinerea*, .38 SG.

BUTTONWOOD, Button Mangrove, .85 SG. Found in tidal lagoons of Florida.

CALIFORNIA NUTMEG, *Torreya californica*. A somewhat less-dense cousin of yew. It behaves like lower-density yew. As with yew, the sapwood is useless in compression. Working this wood releases a pleasant spicy aroma.

CASCARA, See Buckthorn.

CATALPA, Northern, *Catalpa speciosa*, .41 SG.

CEDAR, Atlantic white, *Chamaecyparis thyoicles*, .32 SG; **Port Orford**, C. *lawsoniana*, .43 SG; **Alaska**, *C. nootkatensis*, .44 SG. Cedars are brittle, and among the worst bow wood candidates. As with other low-density conifers there is always the rare piece of old-growth heartwood or compression wood substantially denser/ stronger than average. When choosing any conifer choose old-growth, high-percentage latewood if possible.

CEDAR, Northern White, *Thuja occidentalis*, .31 SG; **Western red**, *T. plicata*, .33 SG. Western Red Cedar, not related to Eastern Red Cedar, a Juniper. Very light, very brittle. **Yellow**, .44 SG.

CHERRY, Several dozen species. **Sweet Cherry**, *Prunus avium L.* About .66 SG; **Bitter Cherry**, *Prunus emarginata*. About .66 SG. From Oregon to San Diego; **European Wild Cherry**, *Prunus avium* .65 SG; **Common Chokecherry**, *Prunus virginiana*, about .65 SG. Common across N. America except far north and south. **Western Chokecherry**, *Prunus virginiana var. demissa*, .65 SG. Shrub or small tree. Along the coast from Oregon to Southern California, and east of the Sierras, used by the Paiute Indians for arrows and bows; **Eastern**, *P. virginiana var. virtiniana;* **Hollyleaf, Evergreen**, *Prunus ilicifolia*, about .93 SG. No, that SG is not a typo. A chaparral shrub on coast ranges from Sonoma to San Diego counties. Used for bows by central-coast Indians.

CHERRY, Black, *Prunus serotina*, .50 SG. Diffuse-porous. Tallest of all the cherry trees, to 100-feet tall, and straight. Common as lumber. A "bright" wood, taking little set, and probably having less hysterisis/returning less sluggishly, than about any other common bow wood. Cherry is brash, almost too touchy for bow wood unless backed, but once made, a cherry bow is unusually sweet and fast shooting. If the stave tree was smaller than about 4" in diameter and bow limbs wider than 2" it's best to decrown or back with a low-stiffness wood or other material. A thin, properly applied rawhide backing makes cherry about as safe as any unbacked wood. On the other hand, Paul Rodgers, near Berkeley, California, made a lumberyard board version, 58" by 1 5/8", 55 lb at 28". It's still shooting after several years of stocking Paul's freezer, still surprisingly straight-limbed and fast. Sapwood takes more set in compression than heartwood. For a long time my favorite bow was a flat-bellied D-tillered cherry heartwood bow, backed with thin rawhide. About 74" long by 1.5", narrow outer limbs and tips, elliptical tiller. It released so sweetly the bow hand could hardly feel it go off. I love black cherry.

CHESTNUT, American, *Castanea dentate*, .43 SG.

COTTONWOOD, Black, *Populus trichocarpa*, .35 SG; **Eastern,** *P. deltoids*, .40 SG.

CREPE MYRTLE, *Lagerstroemia:* Several species. Estimated about .75 SG. A tough, elastic wood. Dogwood-like.

DESERT WILLOW, *Chilopsis linearis*, .61 SG. Not a willow. Used as bow wood by Southwest Indians.

DOGWOOD, Flowering, *Cornus florida*, .73 SG; **Pacific,** *C. nuttallii*, .75 SG. Tough, strong wood. Will endure large set before breaking, similar to hickory, but non ring-porous. Takes more set per mass that other woods. Like hickory, it possibly performs better in dry climates. Due to its high breaking strength and high set it lends itself to a narrower crowned back, as from small diameter saplings or limbs. Some dogwoods, particularly roughleafed and red osier, make excellent arrowshafts and were preferred by American Indians when available.

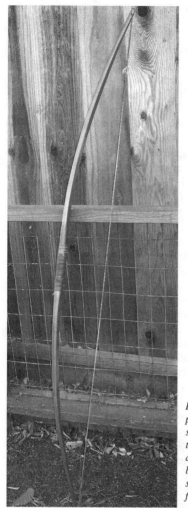

Black cherry has wonderful bow wood properties, especially in compression. But great care must be taken if unbacked versions are to survive, unless quite long. However, there's always the unruly stave that breaks the rule. This unbacked 58" anomaly pulls 55 lbs at 28", and has been pulling that weight for years of active hunting. Made by Paul Rogers from a board stave, it's 1 5/8" wide, with a slightly slimmer grip, is mildly D-tillered, and still shows quite low string follow.

EBONY, *Diospyros spp.,* .90 SG.

EASTERN RED CEDAR, *Juniperus virginiana,* .48 SG. An exceptional bow wood if handled appropriately. It's a juniper, not a cedar, having berries instead of cones. Purple-red heartwood. Redcedar is quite elastic per mass. Somewhat weak in tension. Again, a thin rawhide backing makes it as tension safe as any wood. As with other junipers and yew, it's well matched to sinew, the backing riding higher above the neutral plane for greater leverage, the wider ribbon of sinew holding the bow in greater reflex. An all sapwood bow is possible, but sapwood takes considerably more set than heartwood. The boundary between sapwood and heartwood can suddenly plunge several growth rings from one area or spot to another, possibly more so than any other wood. Knot-free lumber staves are almost impossible to find, more so than about any other wood. Knot-free wood is best found growing in dense shelter or with one side hard against another tree.

ELDERBERRY, several species. *Sambucus velutina*, variable .40 - .60 SG. Southwestern US. Young limbs are light and brittle, with large pithy centers. A lower-density elderberry bow must be longer, lower weight, shorter drawn or sinew backed. Extra low bracing helps too, as with all borderline wood. Trunk wood is denser. Dr. Bert Grayson has made relatively strong bows of a denser species found in Oregon, and surely other places too. Denser, better-bow elderberry is also reported by European bowyers. Dry a stave of it, heft it and decide if it's as dense as wood you're used to. Or oven dry a piece and float it in water. If it sinks deeper than its mid point it's heavier than .50 SG and will make a bow in the normal-dimension range. Elderberry is superior wood for the drill and base when making handrill fires.

ELM, English, *Ulmus procera*, .49 SG; **American,** *U. americana*, .50 SG; **Sippery,** *U, rubra*, .53 SG; **Wych,** *U. glabra*, .60 SG. Throughout much of Europe. In Scandinavia it is the most common elm. In England it was thought of as best of the "other woods". **Rock,** *U. thomasii*, .63 SG; **Cedar,** *U. crassifolia*, .64 SG; **Winged,** *U. alata*, .66 SG. All elms are excellent bow woods. Elms are especially strong in tension compared to compression, like a lighter brother to hickory. As with the hickories, elms hold up in overstrained designs. Elm almost never breaks. It dries quickly, works easily, and takes low set if the belly is properly flat, long or wide. It shoots smoothly, due to is low outer limb mass. Its tension strength allows highly crowned backs, so small diameter saplings can be used. These make excellent English-tillered bows (D-bows), with fairly narrow limbs, the grip as part of the working limbs. Sapling longbows with crowned backs outperform other designs. After figuring in all the big-picture pros and cons of all woods, elm may rate the highest. Occasionally I ask this question of bowmakers who have deep experience with many woods: "If you could only use one wood for the rest of your life, what would it be?" Then through their faces their brain can be seen at work, thoughts bouncing back and forth like that shiny metal ball in a pinball machine. When the ball has finally run its course, more than for any other wood the answer is, "elm."

EUCALYPTUS, Over 600 species. Large density variation within and between species. **Spotted Gum,** *Eucalyptus maculate*, weighs in at about 1.0 SG while others, especially young trees, are quite light and brittle. **Blue gum, Red Gum, and Grey Gum** grown in California for timber and furniture were reported to match the strength of hickory and white oak. Sub 100-year old trees are reportedly far less dense than when older. California-grown eucalyptus tends to be twisted, leaving clues to this in the bark. Less twisted when grown undercover or closely together and away from wind. High water content. Must be dried slowly and carefully. The only eucalyptus I've tested was small diameter saplings and limbs of an unidentified species grown in the San Francisco Bay Area. .65 SG. Stiff, but took early set, chrysaled badly, and broke earlier than almost all tested woods. This particular wood would have to be wider or longer per mass to make a durable bow. Australian bowyers report good results from various species, staves often in the 1.0 SG range.

FIR, Balsam, *Abies balsamea*, .36 SG; **White,** *A. concolor*, .37 SG; **Noble,** *A. procera*, .38 SG; **Pacific Silver,** *A. amabilis*, .38 SG; **California Red,** *A. magnifica*, .39 SG; **Norway,** *A. alba*, .43 SG.

FIR, Douglas, *Pseudotsuga menziesii*, .48 SG. As with other conifers, look for heartwood boards or trees with a high percentage of dark latewood in the rings, 50% or more if possible. The darker the dark portion the better. Especially dark latewood usually comes from fine-ringed, old-growth wood, more frequently seen in old doors and beams at salvage yards. Such dense fir can perform like mid-weight white ash.

Bay, fremontia, toyon, and California walnut. Four superb hunting bows from four California native species, none commonly known as bow wood, all recently discovered, or re-discovered, for that use. But any part of the world not artic-like or true desert holds similar rewards for the bow wood prospector. If you can find decent new bow wood in California you can find it anywhere.

FREMONTIA, Flannelbush, *fremontodendron californicum*. Below .40 SG. Tom Mills: "It's much lighter than even juniper. Much lighter!" A crowned-back flat-bellied hunting-weigh bow of it by Tom seems about to float from your hands yet holds together and takes essentially no set, despite its approximately .65 SG design. I'm always ranting that all woods are equal, but this one has me excited. Sorry there was no time for more testing before completing this chapter. Saplings are used for arrow shafts. Inner bark makes especially strong cordage.

GONCOLO ALVES, *Astronium fraxinifolium,* .79 SG. Tropical. Dark red brown with brown to black stripes. An especially pretty bow wood. Extremely difficult to steam bend. My crowned-belly bow fretted fairly easily. Flat-belly versions were fine.

GUAVA, Strawberry, Purple, Pineapple, *Psidium cattleianum Sabine,* about .90 SG. South Florida and Hawaii. Red-blond to dark red-brown. Manny Padroni of Hawaii recently intoduced this dense, beautiful wood to the archery world. It dries and heat-bends easily. Many fine self and backed bows now reported. Unlike thousands of other brush and tree species still silently waiting to be revealed as bow wood, someone decided to try this one.

HACKBERRY, *Celtis occidentalis*, .53 SG. Similar in looks and mechanical properties to elm. Steam bends especially easily.

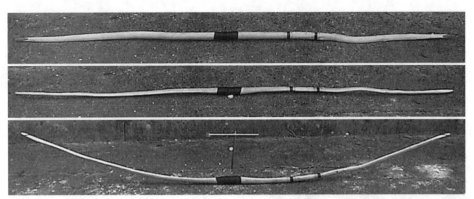

*Hawthorn bow by Bruno Corbeau of France; 70 1/2" long; from a 1 5/32" diameter branch stave; 47 lb at 28".
Transverse knots on the narrow belly threatened to chrysal, so Bruno opted for longer length than otherwise
needed with this very dense, strong wood.*

HAWTHORN, *Crataegus spp.* About .83 SG. **English,** *Crataegus laevigata.*

HAZEL, Hazelnut, *Corylus spp.* About .58 SG. A bush or low tree. Fifteen species, most in Asia, Europe, N. Africa. **California Hazelnut, California Hazel, California Filbert,** *Corylus cornuta.* Occurs from central Ca. to British Columbia. **Common Hazel,** *C. avellana,* native to Europe and Asia. Many sound bows reported.

HEMLOCK, Eastern, *Tsuga Canadensis,* .40 SG; **Western,** *T. heterophylla,* .44 SG.

HICKORY, Shellbark, *Carya laciniosa,* .69 SG; **Shagbark,** *C. ovata,* .72 SG; **Mocknut,** *C. tomentosa,* .72 SG; **Pignut,** *C. glabra,* .75 SG. **Nutmeg Hickory,** *Carya myristiciformis,* .60 SG; **Water Hickory,** *C. aquatica,* .62 SG; **Pecan,** *C. illinoensis,* .66 SG; **Bitternut Hickory,** *C. cordiformis,* .66 SG. Pecan and hickory are often sold under the same label in yards. Due to their extreme strength in tension the hickories are about the hardest bows to break and unless at least moderately violated, never need backing. Hickory is used for backing other bows. Is it a myth that hickory likes to soak up water? At equal RH all woods reach near equal MC. Might it be that hickory is simply poor in compression at typical MC compared to most other woods? Or that it's so strong in tension it overpowers it's own belly?

HOLLY, American, *Ilex opaca,* .56 SG; **European,** *I. aquifolium,* .68 SG.

HONEYLOCUST, *Gleditsia triacanthos,* .66 SG. Slightly less dense than black locust. One of the prettier woods. Its sapwood is about twice as thick as that of black locust. Thorns grow on both trunk and branches. A sapwood-only bow is OK if longer or wider.

HONEYSUCKLE, *Lonicera spp.,* About .85 SG. Northern hemisphere. Over 100 species, most in Asia, about 20 native species each in Europe and North America.

HORNBEAM, (American), Blue Beech, Musclewood, Ironwood, *Carpinus caroliniana,* .70 SG. Usually twisted, winding and gnarly, but makes a fine bow when a decent stave is found. Diffuse-porous. **(European),** *C. betulus,* .78 SG. Europe and England. Often described as "the hardest of woods", it was used in the past for axles, wooden screws and moving mechanical parts.

HORSECHESTNUT, *Aesculus hippocastanum,* .45 SG.

HOPHORNBEAM, Eastern, *Ostrya virginiana,* .70 SG. Diffuse-porous. Can be treated as if a somewhat heavier maple.

Jim Iwanski chronographing Steve Gardner's hophornbeam war bow, Steve ready to check length of draw. 140 lb. at 28", 72" ntn, 2" at the fades, 10" stiff handle and fade area, 38 oz. mass. Tillered using Steve's Mass Formula.

Ken Villars checking tiller on, for him, a lightweight hophornbeam D-bow; 85 lbs at 30", 74" ntn, the center one-foot is 1-1/4" wide, 1" wide at midlimb, 1-1/2" string follow. The excellent stave from Ontario, Canada's Marc St. Louis.

IPE, Brazilian Walnut, *Tabebuia spp.*, 1.00 SG. Sometimes more dense than water. Tropical. Resistant to decay and insects. Usually in board form, usually requiring backing. Makes especially narrow, beautiful bows. As with other high-density woods, outer limbs must be especially narrow for low handshock and high performance.

JUNIPERS, .40 to low .50 SG, depending on species, growth condition and individual trees. All junipers make good bows. **Alligator Juniper,** *Juniperus deppeana,*

A random sampling of juniper surfaces. Maybe one in fifty trees will allow a clear-enough, safe-enough, long-enough stave. Maybe one in twenty if sinew-backed. But the search is worthwhile. Juniper is an especially pleasant to work, light, elastic wood. A favorite for sinew-backing.

possibly the densest. Junipers are somewhat weak in tension, often benefiting from a light backing. Sinew-backed juniper is an especially sweet-shooting combination. As is true of wood in general, the denser the juniper the shorter or narrower a bow can be per given weight and draw. The hardest part of making a juniper bow is finding a long-enough, straight-enough stave. Rather than felling the whole tree, Indians would sometimes score and pry out a juniper stave from clear, straight areas of a tree. The tree grows new wood over such scars. Sometimes several staves were harvested over the decades from the same place on the tree. Two short staves can be spliced together at the grip. Ishi's people used mountain juniper branches before the axe arrived. Saplings and branches two inches in diameter or less work fine, especially if sinew-backed. Inner bark can sometimes be confused with surface sapwood, leading to broken backs.

KENTUCKY COFFEETREE, *Gymnocladus dioicus,* .60 SG.

KOA, *Acacia koa,* .60 SG. Hawaii.

LABURNUM, *Laburnum spp.,* 84 SG. Dense, elastic wood. Chocolate brown. Poisonous wood dust. Was well regarded as bow wood in northern Europe and Britain in the past. Several excellent laburnum bows have been recently been reported by modern European bowyers.

LARCH, European, *Larix deciduas,* .53 SG. **Western,** *L occidentalis,* .53 SG. Also see Tamarack.

LEMONWOOD, *Degame* .67 SG. One of the icon woods of archery. At one level, it's disappointing to discover it's just another wood, no better or worse. About the weight of pecan, not as strong in tension, taking a touch less set per width. Heartwood is stronger than sapwood. Based on personal bend tests, if back fibers are much violated it will break like any other wood. Lemonwood will possibly tolerate a somewhat greater angle of violation, but this wood generally grows so straight the problem seldom arises.

LIGNUMVITAE, *Guaiacum spp.,* 1.14 SG. "Ironwood" (one of the many so called). Heavier than water. I've made one bow from its sapwood, density estimated at .85 SG. A Standard Bend Test yielded 1/4" of set when bent 3" to 38 lb. Osage yields about 3.5" at 34 lb. A slight thickness adjustment would have them testing about the same. An Osage-design bow took near zero set.

LILAC, Syringa, *Syringa spp. Syringa vulgaris,* about .82 SG. Diffuse-porous. One of the densest woods in Europe, where it is native. Now common in US. Care needed while drying to avoid splitting. May be brittle at low MC. Several good bows reported. Tuukka Kumpulainen, of Finland: "Lilac is the strongest and most elastic bow wood in both tension and compression that I have used to date. Get syringa vulgaris if you can. That's the true bow lilac and the one that is native to Southeastern Europe (now cultivated throughout the temperate world). The secret to good lilac staves is to seek out old, overgrown gardens where the surrounding vegetation forces lilacs to grow taller, straighter and less twisted."

LIME, European, *Tilia vulgaris,* .48 SG, denser cousin of American Basswood.

LINDEN, American: See Basswood.

LOCUST - See Black Locust, Honey Locust.

MADRONE, Pacific Madrone, *Arbutus menziesii,* .65 SG. Somewhat brittle in tension. Rawhide would help here. Some have reported shorter madrone bows breaking even when lightly sinewed. But as with all such woods, appropriate cross-section, limb width/length, and good tillering will yield a durable bow.

MAGNOLIA, Southern, *Magnolia grandifora,* .48 SG. Diffuse-porous.

An image from our Stone Age past. Tuukka Kumpulainen of Finland and his lilac bow, 53" long and pulling 60"@23" - a semi-pyramid D-bow just 1 1/8" wide at its handle and only 7/8" wide at mid-limb. Pipe-straight when just unstrung (original natural reflex of one inch). An example of what lilac is capable of. A fashion note: All clothing is generic Stone Age garb. All self-braintanned buckskin - leggins, breechcloth, shirt and quiver.

MAHOGANY. Mahogany and wood sold as mahogany is usually quite light and brittle. Some samples reach .50 SG, and even above. **African Mahogany,** *Khaya spp.,* 63 SG, and **Central American Mahogany,** *Swietenia spp.,* .58 SG, for example. If made wide or long enough a decent bow can be coaxed from the lighter varieties. As usual, it's mainly a matter of the density of the particular stave.

MAPLE, Silver, *Acer saccharinum,* .47 SG; **Bigleaf,** *A. macrophyllum,* .48 SG; **Red,** *A. rubrum,* .54 SG; **Norway,** *A. platanoides,* about .57; **Black,** *A. nigrum,* .57 SG; **Vine,** *A. circinatum Pursh,* about .60 SG. John Strunk discovered the good qualities of this strong, elastic wood. He notes that when felling staves it's important to indicate which side faced the sky, This is important because vine maple usually leans as it grows. As a result the top, tension side of the limb is stronger. Even more so than with other branch staves, if a vinemaple bow's back is made of side wood it will twist during tillering - an important consideration when ordering staves. With sky-side at the back, the stave will usually dry into several inches of reflex, which vine maple is well able to handle. As with other strong-in-tension woods, there can be an advantage to crowned backs. The crowned back has less mass, and being narrower, stretches farther, doing more work, reducing belly strain, all resulting in greater arrow speed.. **Hard, Sugar, or Rock,** (the same wood) *A. saccharum,* .63 SG. **Field,** *A. campestre,* .66, Much of Europe and southern England. All maples are diffuse-porous.

MASSARANDUBA, Brazillian Redwood, Beefwood, *Manilkara bidentata,* 1.0 SG. Dark plum red, fades to silver gray if not UV protected. Similar to, but usually straighter-grained, than Ipe. Good self and backed bows reported.

MESQUITE, Honey Mesquite, *Prosopis glandulosa,* .77 SG.

MOUNTAIN MAHOGANY, *Cercocarpus betuloides,* about .90 SG. Very heavy, hard, tough, wood. "Doc" Safford of S. California reports good results with this wood. Occurs in far western states, especially in high semi-deserts.

MOUNTAIN LAUREL, Spoonwood, *Kalmia latifolia,* .68 SG. to 30-feet tall. From Maine to N. Florida.

MULBERRY, Red, *Morus rubra,* .66 SG. A very distant cousin of Osage. A mulberry bow should be about 25% wider than Osage, all else equal. As with locust and Osage, sapwood can be left on the back if the wood is felled and dried before sapwood decay or insect damage begins. **White/Fruitless** (male trees are fruitless), *Morus alba,* .62 SG, many excellent bows reported. All sapwood, all heartwood, or mixed. Ken Villars and I once tillered a naturally reflexed, ultra knotty and wavy stave, wincing at every tiller check. But it survived to full tiller, shot fast, and is still shooting.

OAK (Red), **California Black,** *Quercus kelloggii,* .57 SG; **Southern Red,** *Q. falcate,* .59 SG; **Black,** *Q. velutina,* .61 SG; **Northern Red,** *Q. rubra,* .63 SG.

OAK (White), **Bur,** *Q. macrocarpa,* .64 SG; **Chestnut,** *Q. prinus,* .66 SG; **Post,** *Q. stellata,* .67 SG; **Scarlet,** *Q. coccinea,* .67 SG; **White,** *Q. alba,* .67 SG; **Oregon White,**

Note the reflex held by this knotty white mulberry bow. I'd never used less-dense white mulberry, so with its high crown and abundant knots I turned my head and winced at each tiller check, other bowmakers looking on, ready to be highly amused. It just had to blow, but it didn't, and is still shooting three years later. Only a thin center band of heartwood shows on its flat belly. 64" ntn, 1 5/8" at grip, 1 1/2" at midlimb, flat belly; 48 lbs at 25". D-bow tiller. 2 3/4" initial reflex, presently holding 2" reflex. From 4.5" diameter branch, well dried to about 6% MC. Grown in well-watered lawn and desert weather.

Q. garryana, .69 SG; **Swamp White**, *Q. bicolor*, .70 SG; **Live**, *Q. virginiana*, .85 SG. Our heaviest oak, and the only non-ring-porous oak. **Tanoak** - see Tanoak.

White oak is about as close to unbreakable as wood gets. In my bend tests it breaks after hickory. Bows I've made of unidentified species of white oak boards took large sets without much excuse. On the other hand, I haven't been able to break a bow made from this wood. One was steamed into 6" of reflex. When tillered it took 7" of set, standing at one inch of string follow at 55 lb, and equaled the cast of any bow of equal follow. Of several white oak bows, from several different trees, the one that stayed the straightest was fine-ringed, with high-percentage early growth. Quite strange. Some report less set in their white oak bows, others report similar set. Apparently different sub-species here. White oak is extremely strong in tension. As a backing material it stands about even with hickory. White oak boards are usually Q. alba, but all white oak species appear in the white oak piles. To identify white vs. red oak use about a 10-power loupe: pores of the redoaks are clear; those of white oaks obstructed with ty-loses, which is the reason wine barrels are made of white oak.

OAK, European, *Quercus robur*, .62 SG.

OCEANSPRAY, *Holodiscus discolor*, .81 SG. Dense, strong wood. A bush, to just over 15-feet tall, known as ironwood by S. British Columbia Indians, and made into bows, arrows, spear shafts, and fire-hardened digging sticks. Found as far south as central California and east to Montana.

OLIVE, *Olea europaea L.*, .91 SG. Checks easily while drying. Difficult to find straight, unflawed staves. The oldest known bow from the Near East is a 6000 year old setback-in-the-handle selfbow made from an olive branch. Irony unintended.

ORANGE, *Citrus spp.*, About .64 SG. Other citrus species weigh about the same.

OSAGE ORANGE, *Maclura pomifera*. At about .82 SG, Osage is the heaviest common native North American wood, except occasionally for live oak. It seems that

Cutting the Mother of all Osage trees, growing west of Ft. Worth, TX. This exceptionally straight, clean tree yielded three dozen staves, as well as numerous sets of billets. (Don Conrad photos)

Good things come in small packages too. This five-inch diameter pipe-straight Osage tree was split into quarters.

The picture on the left was taken seven years ago when a heavy branch tore portions of this Osage tree free. Well, Indians stripped Juniper staves from living trees, allowed the wound to grow over, then stripped another stave from the healed wound. So I waited. And waited. The picture on the right shows the reward for seven years of waiting. Zero! Recently I learned that broadleaf trees don't heal as many conifers do.

light yellow Osage is less dense, weaker, takes more set, and is more brittle, but has slightly better cast if it holds together. For equal safety, less-dense Osage should be a little wider or a little longer than denser, darker Osage. Staves having a low percentage of early wood are also heavier and stronger. Osage is easily heat or steam bent. Everything else being equal, Osage will make the narrowest bow of all common US woods. For Osage to equal the cast and low handshock of lighter woods its outer limbs and tips must be proportionately narrower. Osage becomes brittle at low MC.

PADAUK, *Pterocarpus spp., .*67 SG. Diffuse-porous. Tropical. Tested samples were somewhat brittle in tension, but this may not be typical.

PALM, Black palm. About .90 SG. Extremely dense. Black Palm is the palm most commonly used for bows. Palm is not wood in the normal sense. Related to grass and bamboo, it doesn't grow by adding a new ring each year, gradually increasing in diameter. Instead it exudes upward like bamboo, or animal horn. And somewhat like bamboo, it is denser at its surface, gradually becoming less dense moving toward its center. As with bamboo, set can be reduced by using its outer surface as belly. I've seen bows from Amazonia reversed in this manner. Generally found in areas of high humidity, these bows are also unusually long in order to prevent set. Once dry, palm will serve for any design.

I have a 50 lb. black palm bow, which even at 75" long and 1" wide is only 1/2" thick at midlimb. Very stiff wood. This bow was made and used by the Bari people of the South American rainforest. It took many monkeys from many trees for many years in extremely high humidity. In our drier climate the bow gained weight, so was retillered. It still has only 3/4" of follow. The bow is more than a foot taller than its maker. The wood is dark and dense and heavy, about .90-plus by the feel of it, so heavy its outer limbs must be unusually narrow to avoid handshock. Hardwood yards sometimes stock palm, but seldom surface wood, so density/strength/elasticity will vary per its place in the tree. Adjust limb width per density.

PEACH, *Prunus persica,* about .68 SG.

PEAR, *Pyrus ssp., .*73 SG.

PECAN - See Hickory, Pecan.

PERSIMMON, *Diospyros virginiana,* .74 SG. Interlocking grain. Semi-ring-porous. Very attractive with an off-white sapwood back and dark belly. Tested samples and bows took slightly more set per mass, but strength in tension allowed corrective reflexing. Due to density and interlocking grain persimmon was once used for such diverse purposes as weaving shuttles and golf club heads.

Joe Prince was brand new to bowmaking. He'd heard that when choosing a board stave straight ring lines were all that mattered. So he bought the straightest-ringed board he could find. The board was white pine. Not knowing that a decent bow couldn't be made of white pine, he made a decent bow of white pine. He did glue on a paper-thin pecan-veneer backing (visible in the near-handle closeup. 40 lbs at 27", 73" ntn, 2.5" wide at the grip, pyramid front view. He calls it the Pinosaurus.

PINE, Eastern White, *Pinus strobe,* .35 SG; **Sugar,** *P. lambertiana,* .36 SG; **Western White,** *P. monticola,* .38 SG; **Ponderosa,** *P. ponderosa,* .40 SG; **Lodgepole,** *P. contorta,* .41 SG**; Red,** *P. resinosa,* .44 SG; **Scots,** *P. sylvestris,* .45 SG; **Loblolly,** *P. taeda,* .51 SG**; Shortleaf,** *P. echinata,* .51 SG; **Southern Yellow, Georgia, Longleaf,** *P. palustris,* .57 SG; **Slash pine,** *Pinus elliotti,* .60 SG. Up to .65 in older trees of *Pinus elliotti var. densa,* popular name: Dade County (Florida) Pine. Slash Pine grows in the SW United States.

PLUM, Wild plum, *Prunus Americana,* .73. Much of the US. Shrub to small tree; often twisted and gnarly. **Domestic Plums,** *Prunus domestica,* dozens of varieties, about .68 SG. **Purple Leaf Plum,** *P. cerasifera,* about .69 SG. All plum species are about the same density. My favorites are the Purple Leaf plums. This volume's cover photo is of a Purple Leaf plum bow, with its bark left on the back. Beautiful wood, red

Purple plum branch bows, bark left on. Even 5/8" diameter branches will make short, hunting-weight "Indian" bows. There is something unexplainably endearing about these elemental little weapons, and bigger versions too. I've made countless bows over the years but these just won't leave my hands.

For an especially appealing bow back the bark can be left on many small-diameter staves of various species. Young bark is elastic, and can endure the mild stretching felt by a bow back. Older surface bark on somewhat thicker staves can be sanded down to younger bark. The pictured bow tip is plum, lightly sanded, then linseed oiled to a dull gleam.

to purple leaves and red-purple-brown bark. All plum species are among the most difficult woods to dry without cracking and checking. After felling, if not making a bow immediately, leave the bark on and seal the ends with two or three coats of paint or glue, or a paraffin dip. A day or two might be needed for the ends to dry enough to hold paint, but don't wait too long. If making a bow right away, remove its bark the first day or so while it will pull off freely (if during the growing season). A dull table knife helps. If winter-cut, or once semi-dry, bark must be worked off with sharp tools. This is more work and often leaves a marred back. You might want to leave the bark on smaller diameter branches and saplings. It makes a beautiful back, especially Purple Leaf. On all but the smallest diameter staves, plum bark will crack when drawn unless the more brittle outer layers are sanded down, leaving the more supple but still plum-colored young bark. This is especially needed on older branches. When the finished bow is oiled, young Purple Leaf bark turns a rich, near-black plum. Short 30 lb. bows can be made from branches as small as 5/8"; 40 lb from 3/4; 50 lb from 1", and on up. If the bark is left on the entire branch drying can take a couple of years. Better to floor tiller the bow, keeping it full width for full length to avoid lateral warping. Coat exposed wood with carpenter's glue and it will be dry in a couple of months. If the bark is removed, immediately floor tiller the branch, keeping it full width for full length. The wood will be so thin it likely won't check or crack (unless in very low humidity air) and will be dry in ten days or so. Narrow branches make long, narrow bows. Wider branches can make shorter, wider bows.

Denser woods are preferable, but when none are available appropriately designed sub .50 SG woods can become serviceable target or hunting-weight bows. This .41 SG black poplar D-bow draws 50 lb at 30". At 1.5" by 76", it weighs a mere 17 ounces. I made this bow to win an argument with a lightwood-phobe, but bravely let Steve Gardner take the first live shots, just in case it blew.

Learning that he'd done the impossible with pine, Joe Prince nevertheless became more conservative, stepping up in wood density. To poplar. 45 lbs, otherwise the same specs as for the Pinosaurus. Decorative backing made of printed "T-shirt material."

POPLAR, Yellow, *Liriodendron tulipifera*, .42 SG.

POPLAR, Balsam, *Populus balsamifera*, .34 SG; **White,** *P. alba* .36 SG; **European, Black,** *Populus nigra*, .39 SG. The tree is rare in the US but the wood is imported in quantity. **Grey,** *P. canesceris,* .40 SG, Durable long, wide, lower-weight bows have been finessed out of poplars, especially with easy-stretch backings such as rawhide. Although, again, there is the rare exception: Steve Gardner has a 60" board-stave recurved poplar bow, 50 lb at 28". My favorite poplar bow, also from a board, is 80" by 1.5" by 40 lb, ELB tillered. Just 7/8" of just-unbraced set.

Tom Mills and I posing with twin privet and red oak D-bows. Privet is a wild shrub in southern California. Tom decided to try it as bow wood. It seems identical in mass and behavior to red oak, prompting the photo. Privet has an appealing bone white look, especially attractive when polished to a gleaming surface.

PRIVET, *Ligustrum vulgare,* about .65 SG. European, now scattered across the US. A bush to 15-feet tall. Makes attractive bone-white bows. Test bows show unusually low set.

PURPLEHEART, *Peltogyne spp.* .82 SG. Diffuse-porous. Tropical. Usually from heartwood boards. Purpleheart has the compression elasticity of perhaps .70 SG wood, fretting more easily than other woods. Pretend the stave is hophornbeam to be safe. Or, even more carefully than with other woods, execute thickness taper so that no portion or the limb is overstrained - perfect tiller per front-view shape, and no local or general dips or rises. Purpleheart is strong in tension so needs no backing IF the back grain is straight and sound. But a flawless-looking purpleheart back will often have small fatal knots or grain kinks difficult to see given its dark close grain. A couple of my early purplehearts blew due to such hard-to-see back knots. Now I always carry a small 5-power glass when buying dark wood. A sharp sheetmetal scraper is useful too, board often being too rough to read. A thin hickory backing looks good on this dark tropical wood. Hickory or such applied in Perry-reflex fashion protects the belly as well as the back.

RAMIN, *Gonystylus macrophyllum*, .59 SG. Diffuse-porous. Often found in the form or dowels and tool handles. Smaller pushbroom handles handy for kids bows, larger handles good for 50 lbs.

REDWOOD, *Sequoia sempervirens*, .38 SG.

ROSEWOOD, Honduras, *Dalbergia latifolia,* .90 SG.

ROWAN, Quicken, Mountain ash, *Sorbus aucuparia,* .61 SG. Other *Sorbus* species spread over temperate regions, especially in western China. A small tree native to north and west Britain and northern Europe. Mentioned in a beautiful little book, *British Woodland Trees*, written in the 1940's by H. I. Edlin. The heartwood is reddish brown and tough. The fruit makes an edible jelly. Used by the British in past centuries. Several current European bowmakers have reported good result with European rowan. Oregon bowmakers have used the American version, *Sorbus americana*.

RUSSIAN-OLIVE, *Elaeagnus angustifolia L.* Not an olive. Has edible olive-like fruit.

SASSAFRAS, *Sassafras albidum,* .46 SG. Tends to break on its back before taking cast-robbing set. Sassafras will become a fast, smooth bow if handled carefully. D-tiller makes the handle area work, letting about 20% more wood store energy. At 1.5" wide and 74" or so long, with narrow outer limbs, it will be a durable, sweet-shooting bow. As with other tension-weak woods, a crowned belly will offer some protection by causing the belly to compress more, the back stretch less. If backed with light rawhide then length or width can be reduced to that of a bow of typical .55 SG wood. The belly can then be flat for less set. All the sassafras I've seen has been thin-ringed, with a high percentage of early growth. This wood was thought well of in earlier times. Possibly better growing conditions allowed thicker-ringed, denser, stronger, more elastic wood. Possibly such wood still grows today. If given a choice select staves with thicker growth rings and low-percentage early wood. Sassafras is especially easy to work.

SERVICEBERRY, Juneberry, Shadbush, *Amelanchier spp.,* .75 SG. A bush, to 15'. Brown wood, reddish brown heartwood with red streaks. Several species, one species also in Europe and Asia. Used for bows by American Indians. Several strong bows made by modern 'primitive' bowmakers. Has been used for snowshoes and fishing rods

SCOTCH BROOM, *Cytisus scoparius*. About .66 SG. European. Also known as Irish Broom and English Broom. Invasive in eastern and western US. A yellow-flowering bush that grows along the roadways of northern California. It's like countless other such plants in that, at first glance, it seems more like a useless weed than the makings of a first-class bow. There are scores of such unsung shrubs waiting to sling arrows as well as the known woods if just given a chance. If any size at all it tends to be twisted and gnarly. This wood likes to check when drying, so treat it like plum. Use trunks as narrow as 3/4" in diameter for short bows. Two too-short trunks spliced together at the grip will often yield a useable-length bow. This is often the only way to get a scotch broom bow. The high crown will be safe, the resulting low mass only improving cast. The narrower the limb the longer the bow should be. But sub 48", even 36", self staves make evil little "Indian bows".

SILVERBELL, *Halesia Carolina,* .48 SG. Southeast U.S. To 25-feet tall.

SNAKEWOOD, *Piratinera quiannsi,* 1.0-plus. Very dense tropical wood. Thought highly of in the past, it was once harvested in southern Florida and still may possibly grow there.

SPRUCE, Sitka, *Picea sitchensis,* .40 SG; **White,** *P. glauca,* .40 SG, **Black,** *P. mariana,* .40 SG; **Red,** *P. rubens,* .41 SG; **Norway,** *P. abies,* .42 SG.

SUGARBERRY, *Celtis laevigata,* .51 SG. Treat as if a lighter elm.

SUMAC, Staghorn, *Rhus typhina,* .47 SG.

SWEETBAY, Laurel Magnolia, .48 SG.

SWEETGUM, *Liquidambar styraciflua,* .52 SG. Diffuse-porous. Good bows reported, and that a crowned belly often frets. Also that it warps while drying. Best reduced to near-bow thickness and restrained.

SYCAMORE, *Platanus occidentalis,* .49 SG. Diffuse-porous. Easy to work and makes a fast, sweet shooting bow. **London Plane,** *P. acerifolia,* .55 SG.

SYRINGA, *Philadelpus spp.,* about .75 SG. A dense, light yellow, diffuse-porous wood. A preferred bow wood of Northwest Indians. Saplings as small a 1" diameter yield 50 lb., low-set bows.

TAMARACK, a Larch, *Larix Laricina,* .52 SG. Several good bows reported.

TANOAK, *Lithocarpus densiflorus,* .65 SG. Semi-ring-porous.

TEAK, *Tectoria grandis.* From about .55 SG to about .65 SG. Teak that I've tested, and bows made from same, were somewhat brash. But this is from a small sample of just three teak boards. Oily, extremely rot resistant. Has a husky old-leather aroma.

TOYON, California-Holly, *Heteromeles arbutifolia.* To 20-feet tall. Not a true holly. Often seen as chaparral, to 4000-feet. Hollywood, California may or may not have been named after this small tree. Central CA, to Baja. Fairly brittle, but good bows have been made from it. White flowers in clusters, bright red berries, evergreen. Was used by Chumash Indians for bows, the berries for food - after processing.

TREE-OF-HEAVEN, *Ailanthus altissima,* .52 SG. To 80-feet. Introduced from Asia to Europe then to most of US except northern central states.

TULIPWOOD, Brazilian, *Dalbergia fructescens var. tomentosa,* .86 SG.

TUPELO, Black Gum, *Nyssa sylvatica,* .51 SG. Diffuse-porous.

TROPICAL WOODS, Space only allowed listing a few of the most often used. But there are scores more, most of above average SG. Note: More than for our temperate species, tropical woods can vary greatly in SG within a species, sometimes 15 points above or below their average.

WALNUT, Black, *Juglans nigra,* .55 SG. Semi-ring-porous, easy to work, elastic for its mass, similar in performance to cherry, but more tension-safe. Will try to chrysal where cherry won't. A wonderful, overlooked bow wood. Bows can be all sapwood or all heartwood, or mixed, sapwood taking a bit more set in compression. The off-white sapwood can be worked down to 25% or so of limb thickness, creating appealing contrast with the almost black belly. Very high heartwood extractive level, so as with similar woods, it may be more resistant to water absorption. It's reported not to warp with rising and falling humidity, possibly for this reason. **Southern California Walnut,** *Juglans californica,* about .55 SG; **Northern California Walnut,** *Juglans hindsii,* about .55 SG.

Black walnut is an all-round near perfect wood for midweight bows. It's especially attractive, and works even more easily than yew. It can yield character bows with the best of them, back and belly, as shown above. Due to its low SG, normal-dimension outer limbs release with a pleasant absence of hand shock. If a thin layer of off-white sapwood is left on the back, such bows are not just beautiful, but strikingly beautiful.

WALNUT, (European), *Juglans regia,* .56. Design as per Black. Not as pretty, but makes a nice bow.

WENGE, *Millettia laurentii,* reported as .88 SG, but that I've tested averaged about .70 SG. Ring-porous African hardwood. Common in imported woodyards. Oils to a rich near-black. Looks impressive with a white hickory or rawhide back. When worked, wenge dusts up badly on its back, causing wood backings to pop off unless cleaned unusually well before gluing. The wood seems somewhat oily. Of possibly 100 boards observed, all were fairly thin ringed, but with even thinner earlywood. Wenge is more brittle in tension than other same SG woods. It won't allow the same degree of back fiber violation or as much overbending before breaking. A .70 SG bend test sample took 1/4" of set when bent 3.5" at 24.5 lb. An average of three Osage tests yielded 3.5" at 34 lb. So, at equal thickness, Osage and the tested wenge were equally elastic, but wenge would have to be about 30% wider for equal drawweight at equal set. This is based on just one wenge test, but comports with wenge bows I've made.

WILLOW, *Salix spp.* Most species below .40 SG. **Black,** *Salix nigra,* .39 SG; White, *S. alba,* .40 SG. As with many very light woods, a bow can be obtained by making very wide or long limbs, or low drawweight or drawlength, or as some Western Indians did, by deflexing the limbs, at the cost of lower cast per drawweight, but higher cast per stave.

WITCH HAZEL, *Hamamelis virginiana,* .60 SG. To 30-feet. Eastern half of US. Native. Also variants in Japan and China.

YEW, (Pacific), *Taxus brevifolia,* .64 SG. A touch lighter than *T. baccata,* more likely to sprout branches from sun-lighted surfaces. Otherwise near identical.

YEW, (European) *Taxus baccata,* .66 SG. As with other conifers, thin-ringed yew is denser, darker and stiffer than thick-ringed. The best yew staves suffered during their lifetimes, judged by their 50 to over 100 rings per inch. The densest yew, about (.80 SG) I've seen was harvested by bowyer Roy King from the face of an English

Kerf curing is about the only way to dry large bark-on boles with moderate speed. Leaving the bark on prevents small drying checks that can plague some small-dimension woods even in cool, high-humidity conditions. Many non-yew country bowyers wonder how bark of the illusive yew looks. Here's a photo, kerfs spaced to place knots away from limb sides.

chalk cliff. Most low-elevation yew, especially 'tame' landscape yew, well fed and watered, is thick-ringed, low density, and needs to be wider per drawweight. The longer the bow the higher the safe weight per width. The sapwood on such pampered yew is usually very thick, and since sapwood is weak in compression it will have to be worked down to no more than half of limb thickness.

Most landscape yew is **Irish yew,** *T. baccata fastigiata*, usually barrel-shaped and covered in small or large branches and pins wherever sunlight hits the bark. Some rare interior branches will yield usable character staves. 'Tame' Irish yew is wretched bow

Tame, well-watered front yard Irish yew. Note that branchlets forms everywhere sun strikes a limb, making it useless as bow wood. Still, if new to bowmaking, and thinking yew the only decent bow wood, and if desperate for a stave of it, pitiful would-be bowmakers have been seen groveling through the outer maze for less-pin-covered inner branches of this usually weaker, thick-ringed wood.

wood but, "secured by acts resting between larceny and a bad pruning job," this is the very first wood I ever worked when first smitten with wooden bowmaking, so I can't help having good feeling for it.

Yew sapwood is strong and elastic in tension but takes enormous set in compression. Heartwood is elastic in both tension and compression. The back of a heartwood-only yew bow is safe. Sapwood/heartwood will bend a little farther before breaking, but would have to be far overstrained for this margin to come into play. Sapwood is lighter than heartwood, this giving a sapwood/heartwood version a slight cast advantage. Knowing that heartwood is tension-safe allows the use of inner splits of yew as selfbow staves.

Due to its low bend resistance and high elasticity, yew can be narrower and thicker than any other wood, save possibly juniper. Only yew will make a same dimension and weight old English warbow. Horn nocks are not just for show. Yew is soft, and bowstrings can eat into the nocks on especially heavy bows having narrow strings. From one point of view, the more hoary and wild a yew stave, the better. Yew bows full of pins and even untouched twigs, a few yew leaves waving in the breeze ... such bows look ancient and full of mystery.

A character-rich yew limb. Sometimes a stave can have a little too much character to safely allow a long, narrow design. A wider, shorter flatbow from the same stave can be fully safe.

If sapwood is the correct thickness, and the stave too dry to peel bark free, try this: Begin tillering with the bark on, if strained fairly evenly, cracks will begin appearing every couple of inches in the bark. By 1/3 bend, bark will be popping up all along the limb, making removal by hand and dull knife quick and effortless, leaving a pristine textured back.

Save thick-sapwood staves for longbows. Long, narrow limbs are thicker, allowing proportionately thicker sapwood. At the same angle of fiber violation, fine-ringed yew will display more violated ring lines than thick ringed yew. This can look more dangerous, but the angle of fiber violation is what counts most.

ZEBRAWOOD, *Microberlinia brazzavillensi,* about .68 SG. Striking looks, maple-like properties.

A bowstave explosion. Purple leaf plum in this case. Many, maybe most, deciduous species will sprout such shoots once felled at near ground level. Maple, ash, plum, dogwood, chestnut, oak, hazel, elm, Osage, birch, cherry, and hophornbeam, to name a few. This is an ancient process called coppicing. Growth is extremely rapid, useable-diameter staves harvestable after as little as three years. The pictured plum staves are seven years old and have been useable for a couple of years. Occasional pruning of branchlets insures knot-free bows. New staves can be harvested every few years, practically forever.

SUGGESTED REFERENCES

Bruce Hoadley's *Understanding Wood,* and *Identifying Wood* are the most valuable books on the subject I've encountered. The USDA's *Wood Handbook* is next.

The best single aid to identifying North American trees may be the *National Audubon Society Field Guide to North American Trees.* Two volumes: Eastern Region and Western Region. It funnels the reader directly to an identification using pictures of leaves, bark, nuts, flowers, cones and fruit. Half the book is descriptive and general-information text.

HEAT-TREATING BOWS

Marc St. Louis

Like many others, I had heard reports that some North American natives preferred the wood from fire-killed trees for making their bows. Further, those rumours supported the idea that wood that had been subjected to fire - whether by forest fire or the application of heat directly to the wood - made superior bows. Primitive man also used fire to harden wood points for hunting when making arrows. In addition, bowyers in the early part of the last century used dry heat to correct set and to make improvements on their bows. Several years ago, I decided to do some experiments based upon the use of dry heat on bow wood.

Those experiments revealed a couple of things: how the use of dry heat could affect the shape of the wood, and how well the wood would retain this shape after being made into a bow. I was also interested to see if heating the belly would harden the wood and make it more resistant to compression. In many cases, wood is weaker in compression than in tension, so if heat-treating worked, it would make a more balanced bow. Not having any information or data to go by or even any idea how much heat was needed to produce the desired results, I based the tests on what I expected from an exceptional bow.

I had made many high-performance bows, most of which were highly-reflexed short static recurves with a sinew-backing, so I was familiar with the performance potential of wood bows. Sinew-backed bows could be temperamental, though, and were prone to humidity problems. I was interested in finding an alternative method of making high-performance bows without the negatives associated with a sinew-backing, thus making them simpler to make and more stable in humid environments.

EXPERIMENTS

The first bow I heat-treated was an elm static recurve that was already in progress, a relatively short bow for the intended draw length. I had been making recurved bows shorter over the years, and that bow was one of the shortest unbacked static recurves I had ever made. The bow had an overall length of 65", and the static recurves left the working part of the limbs considerably shorter than the intended draw length of 28". Consequently, the elm bow was taking a moderate amount of set while tillering, in other words, more than I liked. I therefore came up with the idea of reverse-bracing it, and suspending the bow one limb at a time over a hotplate. For reverse bracing, the tips were grooved on the belly side so the string would not slip off the end when drawn up tightly. Then, strong twine was looped around both tips in these grooves, and the string was tightened, drawing the bow into some reflex at the same time. I inserted a dowel between the two strings and started to twist it like a tourniquet. I did it in this way because I wanted to increase the reflex in the limbs as I heat-treated it, but did not want to release the tension on the string while the bow was hot. All I would

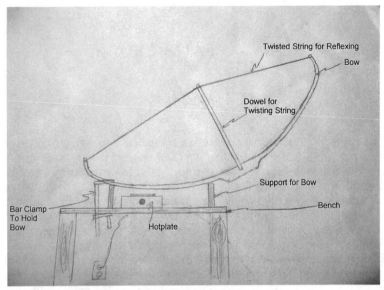

The original set-up to heat-treat the belly of a reflexed bow.

have to do was keep twisting the string and that would shorten it, thereby adding the reflex I wanted when I wanted it. I devised a relatively stable method of holding the bow in place and propped it up about 4" away from the burner.

I turned the hotplate on as high as it would go and watched and waited, keeping a pot of cold water nearby. I was concerned about the back of the bow getting too dry, so it was my intention to brush some water on the back when I was finished heat-treating that section. After about fifteen minutes there were light wisps of smoke coming from the wood, and the belly turned a dark brown. The wood also gave off a rather pleasant aroma. The back of the bow was hot enough that I could only lay my hand on the wood for a second or two, so I brushed some water on the back, which immediately started to steam. I removed the bow from the heat and adjusted the tension of the string by twisting it up with the dowel inserted between the twine, sighting down the limb at the same time to check the emerging shape. I did it in this manner because I wanted to get a uniform reflexed shape to the limb. This was a fairly simple method that I used initially, but since I was not sure exactly what to expect, I was not prepared to invest a great deal of time and energy.

I then repositioned the bow over the hotplate and started on another section of the limb. I noticed that as the wood was being tempered, the belly portion of the limb actually shrank from the heat, leaving the back wider than the belly. This seemed rather strange at the time, but I was too involved with the procedure to give it much thought. I repeated brushing water on the back, reflexing, and tempering until the whole limb was done, a process that took about two hours.

Once the one limb was heat-treated to a fairly uniform colour and nicely reflexed, the bow was removed from the heat source and allowed to cool down. It was then flipped end for end, and the same procedure repeated for the other limb. In total, the bow was reflexed several inches, and the colour of the belly wood turned from pale white to a dark brown.

Once both limbs were tempered and reflexed, the bow was put aside in my basement, where the relative humidity (RH) was fairly high, so that it would hydrate back up to equilibrium moisture content (MC). Even with the water brushed on the back, I knew that the tempering process had dried the wood down to a level that could pose problems for the back.

After leaving the bow several days, I started to work again. The edges of the limbs were squared off, and the belly was lightly scraped. This was when I noticed that not only had the belly shrunk in width, but also had become slightly concave as if the heat had drawn in the belly of the limb. Careful examination of the limb from the side showed there was a slight discoloration of the wood to nearly half way through the limb's cross-section. This indicated that the heat had made a change in the wood up to at least that depth. The shavings of wood coming from the belly also seemed to have a crisper texture, which indicated a harder, denser wood. I clamped the bow sideways in my wood vise and started working the limbs by applying pressure to the tip. I had to use my vise, since I couldn't hang onto the bow because of the reflex; the bow would try to twist out of my hand. That little trick I had learned from making a number of highly-reflexed sinew-backed bows.

There seemed to be a definite increase in draw weight, and bending the limbs well past brace height hardly made any difference in the reflex. The wood had a springier feel to it, and the limbs returned to their heat-treated reflexed shape as soon as I released them. That was my first experiment with tempering wood and the initial results were starting to impress me. The process of tillering the bow turned out to be a source of amazement; the limbs just did not want to take any appreciable amount of set. I went on to tiller this bow to 50# at a 28" draw, where it kept at least 50 percent of the reflex I had heated into it. It was very fast: I chronographed this bow at nearly 180 fps with a 10 grain per pound (GPP) arrow. It was stable and shot like a bow at least 10# heavier in draw-weight. The self-backed elm bow gave nothing away in performance

Flexing one limb of the heat-treated bow.

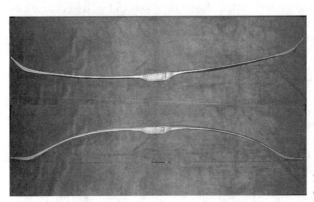

The first attempt at heat-treating, the elm bow unstrung and strung.

to the high-performance sinew-backed reflexed recurves I had made in the past. It was much easier to make and much more stable on high humidity days. Even now, years later, after having shot many arrows with this bow, I can report that it still holds a substantial reflexed profile when unbraced.

After such a resounding success with elm, I decided that my next experiment would be with Eastern hop hornbeam (HHB), and the HHB bow I heat-treated was also a static recurve. Both elm and HHB are good bow woods, and they are easily available here in this part of Canada, so it's only natural that these two wood species would be the basis of my initial experiments. With this HHB bow, I decided to start heat-treating after I had the static recurves bent in, and after the floor-tiller stage rather than a nearly finish-tillered bow. Once again, using the same method I had used for the first bow, I tempered the HHB bow, reflexing it several inches at the same time.

I again noticed a shrinking of the belly, indicating that something was being forced from the wood. Now, since the wood had been seasoned for several years and was very dry, I knew the shrinkage was not from moisture leaving the wood. Air made up a portion of wood cell structure, and the higher the density of the wood, the less air there was in the cells. Since the wood I was using was from trees with a moderate density (compared to the high-density tropical species), the only conclusion I could

Heat-treating made the belly concave. Note the dark colour of the treated white-wood limb.

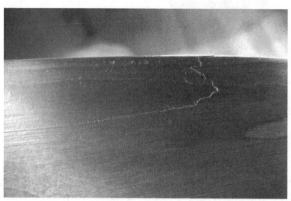

Compression fracture in the belly of the hop hornbeam bow.

reach was that the high heat was forcing some of this air out. If that were the case, then the end result would be a higher density on the belly side of the bow. The higher density could account for the increase in strength of the bow limbs since, generally speaking, as the density of the wood goes up, so does its compression strength.

This led me to go further with the experiments with this HHB bow, as I thought that perhaps an increase in heating time would yield better results. Subsequently, I decided to heat the limbs on this bow until they started to turn black. The same method was used to temper and reflex this bow as was used previously. Once I was done, the bow was again left in my basement for a suitable amount of time to let it hydrate back up to equilibrium MC. I tillered this bow, once again using the same method as the original elm bow. It also retained more than 50% of the several inches of reflex I introduced. Performance was spectacular, but unfortunately the bow began to fail not long after finishing it. The failure was in the form of large fractures that started to develop on the belly. That was when I learned that some heat-treating was good, but too much was not.

All of the work to that point had been with static recurves, since they were my favourite style of bow. But I also liked flat bows, and pyramid bows were my favourite style of those, so it was only natural that I would try the method on one. HHB was the wood of choice for the next experimental bow. The stave that was chosen was very nice and clean with a bit of character in the form of a mild S-bend at one end. The stave was cut down to 64", and the shape roughed out to 1 7/8" wide tapering to 1/2" wide at the tips. There was some natural reflex, about 1", but both tips were deflexed. I didn't care for the deflex and decided to take it out during the heat-treating process, so after floor tillering, I started tempering the bow. I had by that time bought a heat gun and had made my first basic form (caul) which made reflexing, removing deflex, and taking out twists much easier. The bow was tempered and the deflex in the tips removed. Before tillering, the bow started with 4" of reflex. Once again, it was put aside to re-hydrate. Then, it was tillered to 28" where it pulled 53 lb. Though being relatively short for the draw length, it still retained nearly 2" of reflex.

Enthused by the heat-treating results, I decided, as a further experiment, to temper the belly of a HHB bow I made many years before. This was a flat bow with shallow static recurves, and also a bit of set, having been used for one hunting season. The bow had been well worked in and followed the string about 1". The length of the bow

The heat gun in use, showing heat gun holder in place, with the bow reflexed by use of the caul. Note the darkened limb at left, which has already been treated.

was 67" and before heat-treating, its limbs were 2" wide, and the draw-weight measured 52 lb @ 28". The performance of the bow had been tested at the time it was built, and shot a 500 grain arrow about 170 yards or 150 fps, which was pretty standard. Since this exercise was simply to see what changes heat-treating would induce on its own, no reflex was introduced to the bow; it was heat-treated in its existing shape.

One limb was clamped in a wood vice, belly up, while the other limb was being tempered. A heat gun was used on the high setting, and the bow tempered from handle to tip. I proceeded to temper the limbs using basically the same methods I used before.

I had discontinued brushing water on the back and switched to brushing a natural sealant on the hot belly of the limbs. The sealant was a homemade varnish made of spruce gum and turpentine. I have also used tung oil and linseed oil, although I find the linseed oil to be less effective. I prefer the spruce gum for its ease of availability, and it costs nothing - a plus for me. Any type of varnish is flammable, and should only be used with proper ventilation or used outside.

The limbs were heat-treated a dark brown, and some spruce varnish was brushed on the hot limbs after each section of limb was tempered. Surprisingly, the heat removed some of the set, returning the limbs to nearly their original straight profile. The limbs again became somewhat concave from the heat.

After tempering, the bow was put in the washroom where the humidity was between 40% and 50%, monitored by a RH meter. This was to make sure the bow's MC

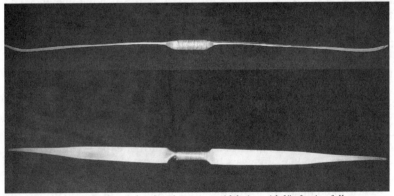

Heat-treating an existing bow, a hop hornbeam pyramid design with 1" of string follow.

returned to the equilibrium content it had before heat-treating.

Roughly two weeks later, I tested the limbs by flexing them in the same manner as floor tillering. It was quite apparent during this first flexing that there was a noticeable increase in strength. Bracing the bow also showed that draw weight had increased substantially. This added stiffness resulted in increased string tension, which I had found to be important in high performance bows. The bow was pulled back a few times to test for flexibility, and then the string was removed. The limbs did not take any set at all, so it was determined that the tempering was not a temporary phenomenon, and that flexibility of the wood was not compromised by the heat.

The bow had been well tillered before the tempering process, and heat-treating the limbs did not change that. Using a bow-scale, the bow was tested for draw weight. At 25", the bow already pulled 50 lb. At 28" of draw length, draw weight jumped from the original 52 lb to 60 lb. In all, the bow gained a full 8 lb of draw weight by tempering alone. It did not take any set in the testing process, with the limbs bouncing back straight after being unbraced. The increased draw weight coupled with the limbs not reclaiming any set brought performance up substantially.

The next process in this test was to tiller the bow back to the original draw weight. Tillering by narrowing the bow's limbs was the method used, and this would reduce mass and improve performance further. The bow was clamped sideways in a vice at the handle, and a small hand plane used to narrow the limbs. Tillering the bow back to the original draw weight was simply a matter of reducing limb width from the original 2" with a more aggressive width taper. This was done in small increments, with the fine-tuning to the tiller mostly in the outer limbs, until the bow drew its original 52 lb at 28". What did this mean for performance? The bow shot a standard 500 grain arrow more than 180 yards, indicating that heat-treating alone had yielded an additional 10 yards, or an additional 6-8 fps. Shooting that same standard arrow through a chronograph, the bow was averaging 156 fps with highs of 160 fps.

One last experiment was conducted to provide proof of the benefits of heat-treating and to test the idea of using natural means for the process. A relatively clean and straight white ash stave was selected, and the idea was to make a native style D bow

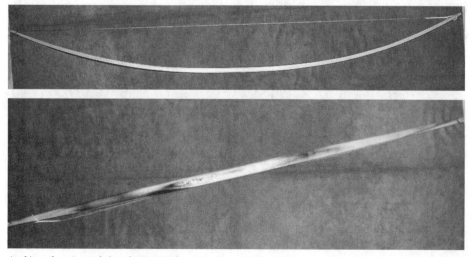

A white ash native-style bow heat-treated over coals.

with it. Though white ash was not a superior wood, it was reputed to be one of the species used by the natives of this continent where fire hardening was practiced. The stave was reduced to rough bow dimensions of approximately 64" long by 1 1/4" wide using hand tools of steel. This piece of wood had a natural reflex of more than 2", much of it in one limb, so I decided that no additional reflex would be introduced.

A hardwood fire was built and allowed to burn down to coals, after which the bow was held by hand, belly down, about 12" away. Starting from the tips, it took about one-half hour for the heat from the coals to temper one limb of the bow, as the fire pit was only large enough to do half of one limb at a time. After one-hour total tempering time, the whole bow had been heat-treated. It lost a bit of reflex during the process, but still had about 2" before tillering was started. As was done previously, once the bow was tempered, it was put aside for several days to allow it to hydrate back up to equilibrium moisture content. Then, after a few days, the bow's shape was cleaned up to 64" long by just over 1 1/8" wide. It was carefully tillered to a 28" draw length where it pulled 55 lb. Even after repeated pulls to full draw, the bow still held 1" of the initial reflex, making it apparent that this method works.

As it turned out, elm and HHB, two of the best wood species I have available locally for making bows, also showed the best results from heat-treating. Elm was

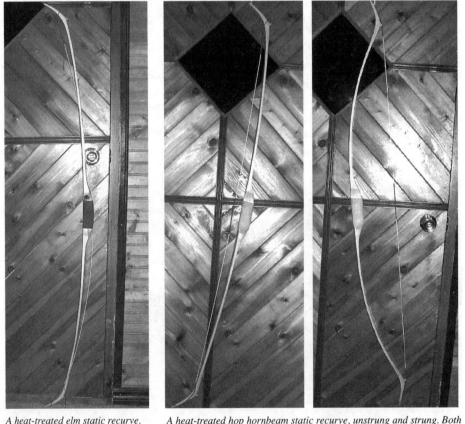

A heat-treated elm static recurve.   *A heat-treated hop hornbeam static recurve, unstrung and strung. Both of these 60# unbacked bows shot an arrow 190 fps.*

high in tension strength, and the wood elastic enough to work well in high-stress designs. HHB was a very elastic wood that lent itself well to a narrow design, though not quite as strong as elm in tension. I have had the occasional tension failure with heat-treated HHB, but when everything held together, the performance was astounding. The performance from such heat-treated recurves could exceed that of most modern glass bows. I have had more than one such bow in the 50 lb to 60 lb range shoot a 10 GPP arrow at more than 185 fps with a 28" draw. In fact, I have had two such bows with draw weights of between 55 lb and 60 lb shoot at more than 190 fps with arrow weights of 10 GPP on a 23" power stroke.

Tempering the belly wood of these two species allowed a bow of any design, from high-performance recurves to the venerable ELB. In fact, several years ago, I made a copy of an English war bow of very high draw weight with HHB that was a very narrow design for a whitewood bow. That bow was just over 1 1/4" in width, 74" long, and pulled more than 100 lb @ 32". I heat-treated about 3" of reflex into the bow after the floor tiller stage, and it kept about half the reflex after tillering and shooting it many times. I sent the bow overseas to a friend in the Czech Republic, since I couldn't use it to its full potential anyway, and it is still shooting today.

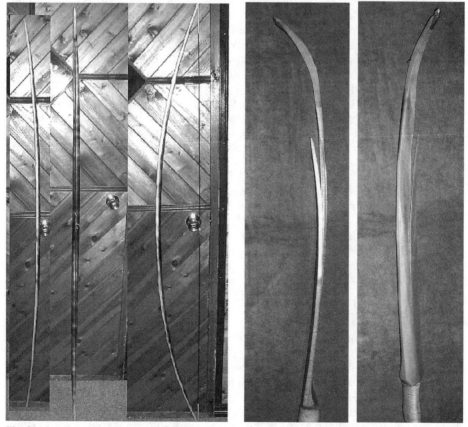

This hop hornbeam English warbow drew 100#.

A tension failure in a black locust static recurve.

WOOD

When heat-treating a bow, one can expect to retain at least 50% of any reflex introduced during the tempering process. Of course, this assumes the bow in question was properly tillered and not over-stressed when tillering. In addition, the wood seems to become slightly more tolerant of humidity changes, which can be an important benefit for whitewood bows.

Most any wood will benefit from heat-treating, but as the density of the wood rises, the benefits decline. Tempering the high-density tropical wood species does not seem to improve them at all. The benefits of heat-treating Osage are not as dramatic as those of a less dense wood such as black locust. Low quality Osage, on the other hand, does reap a substantial benefit from a tempering process. The little amount of heat-treating I have done with yew suggests it is also at the top of the list.

In other cases, the increase in compression strength can exceed the tension strength of the back, and a tension failure is the result. This is the case with some black locust I tried. The bows were highly reflexed static recurves and, after heat-treating, the back became the bow's weakness. These failures were not of a violent nature, but occasionally small cracks would develop during tillering. On the other hand, when these highly reflexed BL bows did stay together, they were very fast. A lower stress design would be the way to go with BL.

Mixed results were also the case with red oak. I experienced a violent failure with a highly stressed red oak recurve that I tempered, with the failure tension-related. The bow literally exploded in my hands, so I now shy away from red oak in highly stressed designs. Simple flat bows work well with this method, though, and I have made a few tempered red oak flatbows.

White ash is another wood species that has shown less than spectacular results. Though I have not had any failures with white ash, I also have not been able get a white ash bow to hold any appreciable amount of introduced reflex, especially in a static recurve design. Black cherry is another wood species that performed poorly. The low elasticity of the wood does not lend itself well to heat-treating, and chrysals are the result.

Of the wood species I have tried heat-treating, this is how I rate them.

Elm and Hop Hornbeam: These two are by far the best in my list and rated Excellent.

Black Locust: Also rated as Excellent but with restrictions. I have had tension failures with heat-treated Black Locust.

Yew: Very Good
Maple: Very Good
Osage: Good
White Ash: Good
Red Oak: Good
Black Cherry: Poor

Reports received from other reputable bowyers are that hickory, a wood that doesn't grow where I live, also responds very well to heat-treating and should also be rated as excellent. White oak is another species of tree that doesn't grow up here, but has been used by some with easy access to it. It also responds very well to heat-treating, and should be rated as excellent. Many of the North American species considered as white wood seem to respond quite well to heat-treating.

METHODS AND TOOLS

My methods of tempering have changed over the years from the reverse-bracing and a hotplate. I now use a special caul for reflexing; in fact, I have two different cauls, and now use a heat-gun as a source of heat. For the heat-gun, I made a jig that sits atop the limb. This jig holds the heat-gun firmly and is adjusted to keep the nozzle about 4 inches from the wood. It is also adjustable for angle so I don't have to hold it, since it generally takes at least five minutes of continuous heat on the high setting for the tempering process. The last thing I use is a number of adjustable screw-type clamps.

For the caul, I use a short 2X4 of spruce about two feet long with a shallow curve cut in, and it is also narrow enough (approx. 1" wide) to accommodate narrow bow limbs, which protects the back from charring. Heat from the gun can bounce off of a wide form and be redirected under the bow, charring its back. I certainly don't consider this to be good for the back of the bow and have had minor problems develop from a charred back. The other caul I made from a 2X8, and it is a little bit more elaborate. I use this one less often as it is made specifically for extremely reflexed bows.

Always make sure the wood is very dry before heat-treating. When wet wood is heat-treated, pressure from the water pushed ahead of the heat can create small splits in the belly of wood; I've seen this happen on more than one occasion with HHB and Osage. This is not a serious problem and will not compromise the bow's function, but is more of an aesthetic issue, as applying sealant to the bow afterward can be a bit annoying. The dry heat can also cause problems when reflexing the wood. If trying to introduce too much reflex in the limbs, lateral cracks can open. This is a product of the surface wood getting too dry. The use of oil can help, but there is still a limit to the amount of reflex that can be induced with dry heat. I generally do not use oil on the belly when tempering wood, but I do brush on a home-made varnish of spruce gum

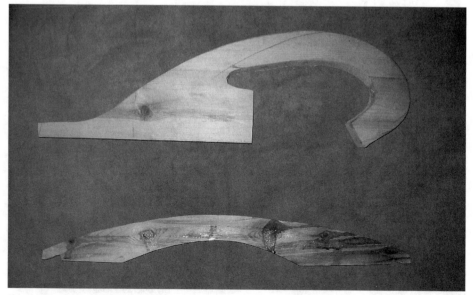

Two cauls, or forms, for heat-treating.

and turpentine on the hot wood. Naturally, this is applied to the belly, with the thought that perhaps the gum will be drawn into the wood as the limb cools, thereby having the compound benefit of more moisture resistance and increased compression strength.

Here is a process for heat treating and reflexing:

1. Start out by clamping the reflexing form in a vice.

2. Then clamp the very dry blank, belly up, by the limb tip on one end of the form using an adjustable screw-type clamp.

3. Use another adjustable screw-clamp to reflex the limb by clamping the blank down to the other end of the form at the handle end.

NOTE: Keep a supply of shims of different thicknesses handy. The bowyer may find that one is needed between the bow and form to correct a jog in the wood or to add a bit more reflex in a particular spot.

4. Once the correct amount of reflex is added, position the jig with the heat-gun over the bow-blank starting at the tip end.

5. Turn the heat-gun on the high setting, and direct the heat at the limb tip.

6. One may note that after roughly five minutes, the wood will give off a pleasant aroma and turn brown from the heat. (For those interested in numbers, I measured the heat at the surface of the wood with a candy thermometer, and it registered about 400 degrees Fahrenheit.) At this time, move the jig.

7. Move the jig up the limb a couple of inches towards the handle, carefully adding more reflex by screwing down the clamp and proceed with the tempering.

Side-view. Shims used to adjust placement and degree of reflex.

8. As the next section of the limb is being tempered, a natural varnish can be brushed on the area just tempered (I used my homemade spruce gum varnish). Other natural sealers can be used, but any flammable finish should ONLY be used outdoors. Modern finishes should NOT be used, as these are highly flammable and also quite often contain plastics, and the high heat could produce toxic fumes.

9. Continue the whole process and make sure to sight down the limb from both sides to check the reflex. If needed, add a shim between the limb and form at the appropriate place.

10. If the limb has any twist, this is the time to remove it. There are several ways to do this, here are a few I have used:

If the twist is isolated in one particular spot on the limb:

When that area is ready to be heated, grab the other limb by hand and twist it in the opposite direction, keeping a steady pressure. As the spot heats up, the wood will give as it starts to plasticize. Twist more than needed, because the limb will spring back a bit after it is released.

If the whole limb is twisted:

Clamp a screw-clamp to the opposite limb for leverage and gradually twist the limb being heated straight by applying steady pressure. Tie the clamp down with string using a fixed amount of twist in the opposite direction. Another method for applying steady pressure is to add weight to the end of the clamp, so there is constant pressure in a twisting motion applied to the limb. The bowyer may add or remove weight as needed.

Regardless of the method chosen to correct twist, careful monitoring is needed at this stage.

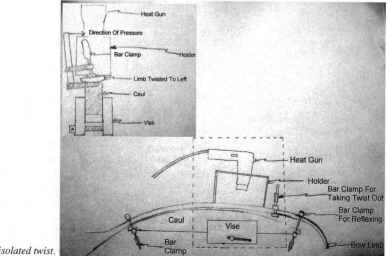

Straightening isolated twist.

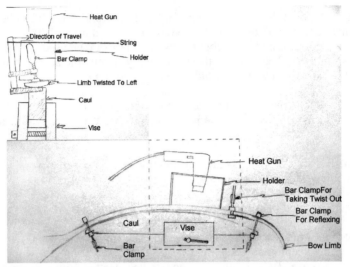

Straightening an entire limb with a twist.

NOTE: When correcting a twisted limb on a recurve, allowances must be made according to the amount of twist being removed. Therefore, if the limb is twisted to the left, as the limb is straightened, the tip will pivot towards the left. It is prudent to make the tip wide enough so that when the limb has been straightened, the tip will still line up with the centre of the bow when it has been narrowed for finishing. This will make the recurve track properly.

11. Continue the heat-treating process until the whole limb has been tempered and sealed with the varnish.

12. Let the blank sit for an hour or so in the form to cool down.

13. Once the blank has cooled, remove it from the form and examine it carefully, sighting down the limbs for areas that may need to be touched up.

14. Flip the blank around and repeat the same process for the other limb.

As a side note, I have found that if the bowyer needs to stop for any reason, resuming the tempering process where it was halted will not affect the outcome. Also, if it is necessary to make some corrections after the bow has been tempered, then this also will not have any adverse effect on the end result. I have even re-tempered a bow with good results. If the bowyer does need to re-temper a section of limb, the internal moisture must be allowed to equalise before further tillering. The heat moves the internal moisture of the wood; the area just tempered becoming relatively dry, and stiff, and moisture content in the adjacent areas becoming higher than normal. Bending the limb with this higher moisture content can induce set.

A bowyer can make heat-treated bows of a much narrower profile than an untreated bow. Also, reflex the bow when heat-treating even if it's by a small amount.

Dry heat can also be used to temper the static recurves on a bow after they have been steam bent, and this can reduce the mass of the limb tips. This process is best performed with a heat gun.

A. Make sure the recurves have dried quite well from the wet heat-bending process.

B. Each recurve will be done individually. Secure the recurve in its present shape, otherwise the dry heat will try to straighten it out.

C. Once secured, apply heat to the recurve, heat-treating it long and deep until the surface wood is almost black. Since these recurves are non-bending, a heavy tempering here will do no harm.

D. Reduce the thickness to the depth of the thinnest part of the bending limb, and it will still maintain the recurves.

NOTE: Heat-treating and reducing the mass of the tips is advantageous for those wishing to use lighter arrows than normal, as light tips reduce handshock. This can also be beneficial to those wanting to make bows to compete in flight archery.

Important facts to remember:

• When heat-treating, the wood needs to be very dry or checks and splits can develop in the belly.

• A long heating time is preferable so the tempering penetrates deeply rather than a quick surface tempering; a quick surface tempering will do little to improve the wood and generally will not last. This is important if also trying to reshape the wood, as a continuous temperature of at least 350 degrees fahrenheit is needed to plasticize the wood.

• Let the wood return to equilibrium moisture content before flexing the limbs.

• A well-tillered and heat-treated bow should retain at least 50% of any reflex introduced.

• The increased compression strength of the belly wood will put more strain on the back. Tension-stong wood species, such as elm, hickory, and HHB are therefore better candidates for heat-treating.

• A good rule of thumb when tempering: brown is good, black is bad.

• A heat-treated bow can be made as much as 30% narrower than a bow that has not been tempered.

• There are some wood species that do not benefit from heat-treating as much as others. As density of wood goes up, the benefits of heat-treating go down.

Since I performed my initial experiments, many people have begun heat-treating their bows. The feedback from this process is all positive, with the general consensus of many expert bowyers being that the process transforms whitewood bows. In effect, bows made from the better second-string wood species such as HHB or elm can exceed the performance of the higher density wood species. The process can be used to make very high performance bows, improve the performance of simple flatbows, or even to revitalise older bows. The tempering process reduces mass, thereby increasing performance. The reshaping of the wood and adding reflex increases string tension, which also improves performance. The plasticizing of the wood from the high heat seems to increase a bow's resistance to moisture incursion, which is always a concern with whitewood bows. The uses of heat-treating are many and have proven to be a winning combination in the flight-shooting world as well as in hunting and target shooting.

A COPPER AGE BOW

Tom Mills

They say "hindsight is 20/20." This may be true in some instances, but when looking back across thousands of years, 20/20 vision only goes so far. It's a bit like looking through a powerful pair of binoculars held the wrong way - the point of interest is a mere speck out in the distance, and detail is seriously lacking. At best, our view of the past is blurry and vague, mostly based on evidence gathered in the way of artifacts. These artifacts take the form of tools, weapons, objects of art, and the remnants of dwellings. In our attempt to understand these ancient tools, we draw inferences from these artifacts, make educated guesses about how they were made, and do our best to deduce their use and function.

As modern humans, our view is colored by our modern sensibilities and our modern experiences. So rarely, if ever, are the artifacts themselves sufficient to tell the whole story. One means of gaining a better understanding is to make replicas of these tools and put them to use. Of course, this can't tell everything there is to know about the particular tool, but it may bring about a closer understanding of its capabilities.

With certain irony, my inspiration for making a Copper Age bow originated in a "Computer Age" internet discussion forum in a conversation about the possible advantages of copper tools over stone tools.

Initiated by Tim Baker, the discussion raised many questions: "Was copper too soft to make a useful woodworking tool? If not, would it rival or surpass stone as a material for shaping wood? Could copper be more easily fashioned into the specific shapes best suited for such tools than stone? What about Otzi's copper axe ... was it a weapon or was it a woodworking tool?"

What finally pushed me away from my keyboard and out to the workshop was when Tim declared:

"It would be fascinating to learn of the quality of these tools and to what extent this copper technology influenced bow design and construction..."

To me, the first question to be answered, the larger question, was whether or not copper (a soft metal) would even work as an edged tool to shape wood. My few experiences with copper told me that it was much too soft to make a viable woodworking tool - and I expressed that view on the discussion forum. If my hunch proved true, the other questions would be irrelevant. It seemed clear that unless I relied on the research and experimentation of others, first-hand experimentation would be the best way to find the answers to these questions.

Before this mini-journey into the realm of experimental archaeology, I had only the faintest knowledge of the period of time identified by pre-historians as The Copper Age. I had a vague notion that the Copper Age fell somewhere between the Stone Age and the Bronze Age, but did not know much else.

My initial research revealed that the Copper Age began at different times in different places roughly between 6,000 and 3,500 years ago.

DATE (B.C.)	NAME	LOCATION	WOOD/TYPE	Reference
9,500	Stellmoor Bow	Hamburg, Germany	Pine - fragments only	Insulander, 2000
7,000	Holmegaard Bows	Denmark	Elm - Flatbows - 70.75" and 60.5"	Becker, 1945; Clark 1963
7,000	Veretye Bow	NW Russia	Pine/Spruce	
6,000	Blak Bow	Denmark	Elm? - Slightly flatened oval 55-59"	
6000	Vis bow	Russia	Pine	Burov 1980
5,500	Vedbaek Boldbaner Bow	Denmark	Elm - 76.4"	"Vedb kbogen", ISBN 87-87113-27-9, P72 ff
5,500	Ringkloster Bow	Denmark	Elm - 60.5" flat/oval	

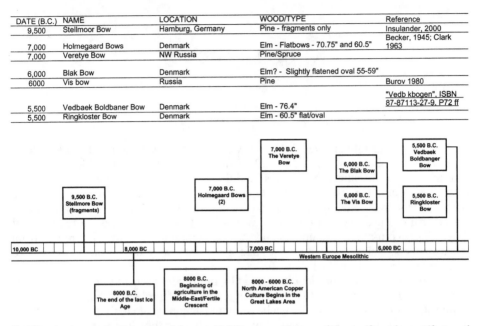

To follow is a proportional timeline of the past 12,000 years, with some of the significant bow artifacts and events placed in a time context. With each segment of the timeline is more information on the individually listed items.

The Copper Age is also referred to as the "Chalcolithic" – a term derived from the Greek words "Khalkos" (meaning copper) and "lithos" (meaning stone). It's funny, but when we talk of these various periods of time, there is a tendency for us to imagine artificial divisions in our minds, as if there are distinct beginning and ending points between these "ages." The truth is, however, that there are no distinct lines, and tool industries tend to blend into one another over time and space, like feathered edges of color in the evening sky.

The Copper Age – or Chalcolithic – is a perfect example of such a blending of industries, a transition between the Stone Age and the age of metals. Tools made of wood, stone, bone, and antler would have shared the stage with copper tools. In fact, they would have been the leading characters with copper the new and upcoming star. We can see this throughout the archaeological record, in burials like the Amesbury Archer, whose grave contained copper knives and wrist guards alongside flint arrowheads. Or with Otzi, the "Ice Man" of the Alps, who carried a copper axe, a flint knife, and flint-tipped arrows.

The Copper Age doesn't fall squarely within the accepted three-age system (the Stone Age, Bronze Age, and Iron Age), because it is difficult for pre-historians to identify a distinct transition from the use of copper to the use of bronze (the latter of which is a combination of copper and tin). More importantly perhaps, and for our purposes here, the question of when the Copper Age began is further frustrated by geography, as the answer changes a great deal from place to place. Generally speaking, similar to the so-called "agricultural revolution" that preceded it, the Copper Age spread outward from the "Fertile Crescent" – the area present day Europeans think of as the Near-East or Middle-East and areas in and around present day Turkey.

Timeline chart:

- 5,300 B.C. Tybrind Vig Bow
- 4,900 B.C. Hardinxveld-Giessendam Bow
- 3,800 B.C. Egolzwil Bows
- 3,800 B.C. Feldmeilen Bow
- 4,000 B.C. The Bodman Bow
- 4,000 B.C. Rotten Bottem Bow
- 4,000 B.C. Cave of the Warrior Bow
- 4,000 B.C. Bercy Bow
- 3,750 B.C. Douanne Bow
- 3,750 B.C. Burgaschisee-Sud Bows
- 3,700 B.C. Thayngen Bows
- 3,650 B.C. Robenhausen Bow
- 3,600 B.C. Neiderwill Bows
- 3,300 B.C. Hauslabjoch Bow (Otzi's Bow)
- 2,900 B.C. Hazendonk Bow
- 3,150 B.C. Seefeld Bows
- 3,100 B.C. Mozartstrasse Bows
- 3,100 B.C. Horgen-Scheller Bows
- 3,000 B.C. Muldbjerg Bow
- 3,000 B.C. La Neuveville Bow
- 3,000 B.C. Nidai Bow
- 2,800 B.C. Meare Heath Bow
- 2,750 B.C. Utoquai Bows
- 2,700 B.C. Sarnate Bow
- 2,700 B.C. Robenhausen Bow
- 2,650 B.C. Seefeld Bows
- 2,600 Stadskanaal Bow

Timeline axis: 5,000 BC | 4,000 BC | 3,000 BC

Western Europe Neolithic
European Copper Age - Chalcolithic

- 5000 B.C. Agriculture Begins in North/Western Europe
- 3200 B.C. Stonehenge Started
- 2700 B.C. 1st Egyptian Pyramid

DATE (B.C.)	NAME	LOCATION	WOOD/TYPE	Reference
5,300	Tybrind Vig Bow	Moesgaard Museum Aarhus Denmark	Elm - Flatbow	Journal of Danish Archaeologu, vol. 4, 1985
4900	Hardinxveld-Giessendam Bow	Archeologisch Instituut, Leiden.	Elm - Broken/incomplete. Defined grip, wide limbs	J.N. Lanting, B.W. Kooi, W.A. Casparie and R van Hinte
4,000	Bodman Bow	Rosgarten Museum Konstanz, Germany	Yew - D cross section - well defined grip 61" long.	Clark, 1963
4,000	Rotten Bottem Bow	Moffat, Scotland	Yew - Longbow	Sheridan 1993
4,000	Cave of Warrior Bow	Near East, Cave Burial - N/W of the Dead Sea	Olive	http://www.amnh.org/exhibitions/cave/bow.html
4000	Bercy Bow	Bercy, Paris, France	Yew	
3,800	Egolzwil Bows	Schweizerisches Landesmuseum, Switzerland	4 Yew bows - all fragments - all "D" cross-section.	Junkmanns, 1996; Clark 1963
3800	Feldmeilen	Switzerland	Yew	Junkmanns, 1996
3750	Douanne Bow	Switzerland	Yew	Junkmanns, 1996
3750	Burgaschisee-Sud Bows	Switzerland	Yew	Junkmanns, 1996
3700	Thayngen Bows	Museum zu Allerheiligen, Schaffhouse, Switzerland	Yew	Junkmanns, 1996
3650	Robenhausen Bow	National Museum, Zurich, Switzerland	Yew	Junkmanns, 1996
3600	Niederwil Bows	National Museum, Zurich, Switzerland	Yew	Junkmanns, 1996, Clark 1963
3,300	Hauslabjoch Bow	Sudtiroler Archaologiemuseum, Italy	Yew - Otzi's bow - "D" cross section 71.6" - likely an unfinished bow	Junkmanns, 1996 and Baker, Baugh and Brizzy 2006)
3150	Seefeld Bows	Kantosarcheologie Zurich, Switzerland	Yew	Junkmanns, Strahm, Bleuer
3100	Mozartstrasse Bows	Kantosarcheologie Zurich, Switzerland	Yew	Junkmanns, Strahm
3100	Horgen-Scheller Bows	Kantosarcheologie Zurich, Switzerland	Yew	Junkmanns, Strahm
3,000	Muldbjerg bow	Danisches National Museum, Denmark	Elm - 63"	Clark, 1963
3000	La Neuveville Bow	Switzerland	Yew	Junkmanns, 1996
3000	Nidau Bow	Switzerland	Yew	Junkmanns, 1996
2900	Hazendonk Bow	Rijksmuseum van Oudheden, Leiden,	Yew - Fragment, handle area showing a defined grip, wide limbs.	J.N. Lanting, B.W. Kooi, W.A. Casparie and R van Hinte
2800	Meare Heath Bow	Meare Heath, UK	Elm - Flat Bow approx. 74"	Comstock
2750	Utoquai Bows	Kantosarcheologie Zurich, Switzerland	Yew	Junkmanns, Strahm, Bleuer
2,700	Sarnate Bow	Latvia	Ash - flatbow 56.7" long, 2" wide	L. Vankina - "Torfyanikovaya stoyanka Sarnate" - "Sarnate bog settlement"
2700	Robenhausen Bows	Bernisches Historisches Museum, Berne, Switzerland	Yew - several fragments - "D" cross section.	Junkmanns, 1996
2650	Seefeld Bows	Kantosarcheologie Zurich, Switzerland	Yew	Junkmanns, Strahm, Bleuer
2,600	Stadskanaal Bow	Drents Museum, Assen	Yew - Complete. Narrow limb, "D" cross section, no defined grip. Length: 67.3" max width: 1"	J.N. Lanting, B.W. Kooi, W.A. Casparie and R van Hinte

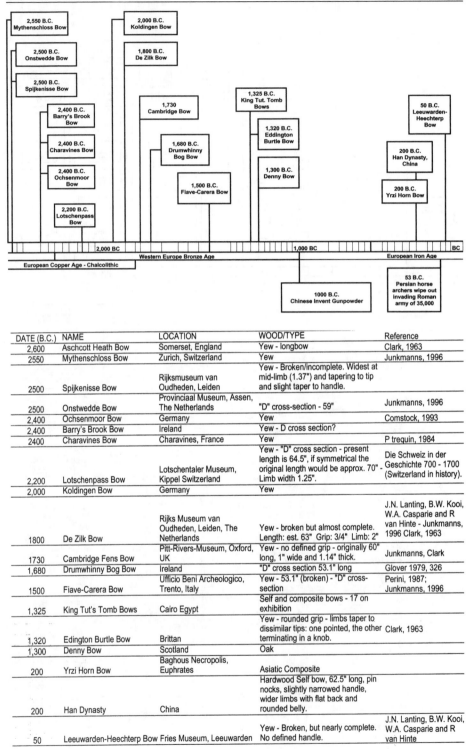

DATE (B.C.)	NAME	LOCATION	WOOD/TYPE	Reference
2,600	Aschcott Heath Bow	Somerset, England	Yew - longbow	Clark, 1963
2550	Mythenschloss Bow	Zurich, Switzerland	Yew	Junkmanns, 1996
2500	Spijkenisse Bow	Rijksmuseum van Oudheden, Leiden	Yew - Broken/incomplete. Widest at mid-limb (1.37") and tapering to tip and slight taper to handle.	
2500	Onstwedde Bow	Provinciaal Museum, Assen, The Netherlands	"D" cross-section - 59"	Junkmanns, 1996
2,400	Ochsenmoor Bow	Germany	Yew	Comstock, 1993
2,400	Barry's Brook Bow	Ireland	Yew - D cross section?	
2400	Charavines Bow	Charavines, France	Yew	P trequin, 1984
2,200	Lotschenpass Bow	Lotschentaler Museum, Kippel Switzerland	Yew - "D" cross section - present length is 64.5", if symmetrical the original length would be approx. 70" - Limb width 1.25".	Die Schweiz in der Geschichte 700 - 1700 (Switzerland in history).
2,000	Koldingen Bow	Germany	Yew	
1800	De Zilk Bow	Rijks Museum van Oudheden, Leiden, The Netherlands	Yew - broken but almost complete. Length: est. 63" Grip: 3/4" Limb: 2"	J.N. Lanting, B.W. Kooi, W.A. Casparie and R van Hinte - Junkmanns, 1996 Clark, 1963
1730	Cambridge Fens Bow	Pitt-Rivers-Museum, Oxford, UK	Yew - no defined grip - originally 60" long, 1" wide and 1.14" thick.	Junkmanns, Clark
1,680	Drumwhinny Bog Bow	Ireland	"D" cross section 53.1" long	Glover 1979, 326
1500	Fiave-Carera Bow	Ufficio Beni Archeologico, Trento, Italy	Yew - 53.1" (broken) - "D" cross-section	Perini, 1987; Junkmanns, 1996
1,325	King Tut's Tomb Bows	Cairo Egypt	Self and composite bows - 17 on exhibition	
1,320	Edington Burtle Bow	Brittan	Yew - rounded grip - limbs taper to dissimilar tips: one pointed, the other terminating in a knob.	Clark, 1963
1,300	Denny Bow	Scotland	Oak	
200	Yrzi Horn Bow	Baghous Necropolis, Euphrates	Asiatic Composite	
200	Han Dynasty	China	Hardwood Self bow, 62.5" long, pin nocks, slightly narrowed handle, wider limbs with flat back and rounded belly.	
50	Leeuwarden-Heechterp Bow	Fries Museum, Leeuwarden	Yew - Broken, but nearly complete. No defined handle.	J.N. Lanting, B.W. Kooi, W.A. Casparie and R van Hinte

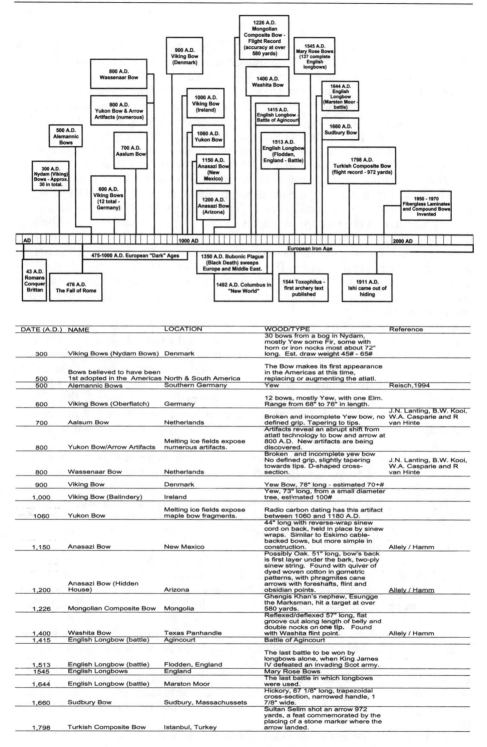

DATE (A.D.)	NAME	LOCATION	WOOD/TYPE	Reference
300	Viking Bows (Nydam Bows)	Denmark	30 bows from a bog in Nydam, mostly Yew, some with horn or iron nocks most about 72" long. Est. draw weight 45# - 65#	
500	Bows believed to have been 1st adopted in the Americas	North & South America	The Bow makes its first appearance in the Americas at this time, replacing or augmenting the atlatl.	
500	Alemannic Bows	Southern Germany	Yew	Reisch, 1994
600	Viking Bows (Oberflatch)	Germany	12 bows, mostly Yew, with one Elm. Range from 68" to 76" in length.	
700	Aalsum Bow	Netherlands	Broken and incomplete Yew bow, no defined grip. Tapering to tips.	J.N. Lanting, B.W. Kooi, W.A. Casparie and R van Hinte
800	Yukon Bow/Arrow Artifacts	Melting ice fields expose numerous artifacts.	Artifacts reveal an abrupt shift from atlatl technology to bow and arrow at 800 A.D. New artifacts are being discovered.	
800	Wassenaar Bow	Netherlands	Broken and incomplete yew bow No defined grip, slightly tapering towards tips. D-shaped cross-section.	J.N. Lanting, B.W. Kooi, W.A. Casparie and R van Hinte
900	Viking Bow	Denmark	Yew Bow, 78" long - estimated 70+#	
1,000	Viking Bow (Balindery)	Ireland	Yew, 73" long, from a small diameter tree, estimated 100#	
1060	Yukon Bow	Melting ice fields expose maple bow fragments.	Radio carbon dating has this artifact between 1060 and 1180 A.D.	
1,150	Anasazi Bow	New Mexico	44" long with reverse-wrap sinew cord on back, held in place by sinew wraps. Similar to Eskimo cable-backed bows, but more simple in construction.	Allely / Hamm
1,200	Anasazi Bow (Hidden House)	Arizona	Possibly Oak. 51" long, bow's back is first layer under the bark, two-ply sinew string. Found with quiver of dyed woven cotton in gometric patterns, with phragmites cane arrows with foreshafts, flint and obsidian points.	Allely / Hamm
1,226	Mongolian Composite Bow	Mongolia	Ghengis Khan's nephew, Esungge the Marksman, hit a target at over 580 yards.	
1,400	Washita Bow	Texas Panhandle	Reflexed/deflexed 57" long, flat groove cut along length of belly and double nocks on **one tip**. Found with Washita flint point.	Allely / Hamm
1,415	English Longbow (battle)	Agincourt	Battle of Agincourt	
1,513	English Longbow (battle)	Flodden, England	The last battle to be won by longbows alone, when King James IV defeated an invading Scot army.	
1545	English Longbows	England	Mary Rose Bows	
1,644	English Longbow (battle)	Marston Moor	The last battle in which longbows were used.	
1,660	Sudbury Bow	Sudbury, Massachussets	Hickory, 67 1/8" long, trapezoidal cross-section, narrowed handle, 1 7/8" wide.	
1,798	Turkish Composite Bow	Istanbul, Turkey	Sultan Selim shot an arrow 972 yards, a feat commemorated by the placing of a stone marker where the arrow landed.	

So keep in mind the fact that while the "Copper Age" might have begun in the Middle-East between six and eight thousand years ago, it didn't arrive in Western and North Europe until sometime afterward. We are focusing upon these limited areas of Europe because they are where the majority of ancient bow artifacts happened to have been found (simply due to the preservative environments of alpine lakes and peat bogs that occur in those regions - not because they weren't being used elsewhere). So, as we consider the possible effect the use of copper tools might have had on bow design, it is necessary to keep in mind the fact that copper tools likely were not prevalent in North/Western Europe until about 5,000 years ago.

Prehistoric humans living in proximity to naturally occurring surface copper would have been the first to discover the metal and begin to make use of it. The distinction between this early experimental use and later copper industries is a rather blurry line as well. The oldest known copper artifact is an oval shaped pendant found in Shanidar Cave in Northern Iraq, and it's estimated to be 10,700 years old. But this non-tool use of copper most certainly represents only experimentation with this metal, and not the beginning of a true copper culture. These first people to work with copper shaped it by hammering and grinding. The actual melting and casting of copper didn't come about until considerably later - and in some cultures, not at all. The smelting of copper from ore arose even later.

Interestingly, the North American continent was home to a rather ancient Copper Age culture - specifically in the region surrounding the Great Lakes, where "native copper" (i.e., naturally occurring surface copper) was and is quite abundant. Here evidence of the use of copper goes firmly back 6,000 years and continues right up into historic times. There is little or no solid evidence that indigenous Americans were smelting copper in North America at any point in time, however. Instead, like the first copper workers elsewhere in the world, these folks were making use of raw copper, and shaping it into various useful tools through a combination of hammering and heating.

Copper is an interesting metal in that it can be cold-hammered to manipulate its shape and physical properties. Hammering copper makes it harder and more tool-worthy. This is called "work hardening." Too much work hardening, and copper becomes brittle. This brittleness can be overcome (and shaping continued) by heating the metal to soften it again, a process called "annealing." Depending on the complexity of the item being made, the metal worker would go through many cycles of hammering and annealing.

Aside from jewelry and other decorative items, these copper-working artisans were making tools such as axe blades, adz blades, knives, arrowheads, spear points, etc. Archaeological evidence suggests that these items likely found their way via trade routes to people as far away as the east coast of the North American continent, from present day New York down to Florida.

After some consideration, I decided to make an adz for this experiment rather than an axe. Axe blades were more complicated to make and to set in a handle. I reasoned that making an adz blade was well within the capabilities of any prehistoric copper worker (an adz blade is simply a flat bar of copper with one end sharpened), whether he was working raw copper or smelting and casting the blade. I also was familiar with using an adz for various other woodworking projects, and knew first hand the utility of the tool.

Making the copper adz blade was quick work. As this was not an experiment in making copper tools – but rather an experiment in using them – I had no qualms about

The copper blade was set in a slight recess in the hardwood handle, and was held firmly in place by a combination of the leather wrapping and the small wooden wedge.

A front view of the adz showing the hammer blows on the work-hardened copper, and the flared cutting edge.

using modern tools in constructing the adz. I cut a 1.75 wide x 7" long blank out of 1/8" thick sheet copper. Hammering in a cutting edge served the dual purpose of both shaping and work-hardening the business end of the blade. To avoid problems with the blade bending in use, I concentrated many hammer blows down its center, creating a work-hardened "spine" the length of the blade. Some final shaping and sharpening with files and a sharpening stone was all that was necessary to make the blade ready. The blade was hafted in the handle with a simple but effective lashing strategy, employing a wooden wedge to create a strong friction fit.

Testing the copper adz on a tough elm stave. On the first pass, a quick series of shallow and precise cuts were made in the side of the stave, and then removed in an ensuing pass of the adz. This is a time-tested reduction strategy when using an axe or adz to carve and shape wood. The copper adz passed the test with flying colors.

I tested the copper adz on a partially seasoned elm stave. Elm is a tough wood, and I figured that if the copper blade held up to the elm, it would handle any hardwood. Keep in mind that Stone Age and Copper Age woodworkers most certainly worked with green wood (i.e., freshly cut, wet wood) for the majority of their woodworking needs. Even present-day, hand-tool-wielding woodcarvers and wood turners understand the benefits of working green wood.

The copper adz stood up to the test, handling the elm wood remarkably well. I had been afraid the blade would deform under the stress of repeated strikes against this tough wood, but that wasn't the case. As I'd hoped, the worked-hardened spine kept the blade from deforming.

There was one slight problem. I had initially created a single-bevel cutting edge as with a chisel, or most modern steel adz blades. The single-bevel didn't work very well with the copper. It created too fine an edge and tended to deform. I adjusted the edge to a double bevel, like an axe, with the cutting edge centered in the mass of the blade. This was all the adjustment needed.

Inspired by this success, I brought the experiment to its logical conclusion and fashioned a complete bow using only the copper adz and other stone and antler tools that would have been available to a Copper Age bowyer.

My tool-kit, like that of a Copper Age or Chalcolithic woodworker, was comprised primarily of Stone Age tools (those made of stone, bone, wood, and antler). Copper would have been the new guy on the block, the literal cutting edge of technology of the time.

I used a small diameter log of California walnut for this project, obtained from local tree-trimmers. The log was about 8' long and had a rather severe dogleg on one end. I utilized a basalt axe to trim this end from the log, thus simulating the felling of the sapling.

My plan was to fashion a fairly wide, flat, roughly man-tall bow, where most all of the wood would be removed from belly of the bow. Little work would be needed on

The Stone axe/celt used to trim the stave to length.

Reducing the log to size was easily accomplished using the hafted stone axe.

Antler wedges doubled as chisels when attempts at splitting the stave went awry.

the back; I would simply remove the bark and use the first layer of wood as the bow's back.

I trimmed the log to size (approximately 6') and attempted to split the log using several antler wedges. The grain of the log was spiraled slightly, and the splitting didn't work as planned. This seemingly unfortunate situation held a silver lining, as it led to my discovery of the utility of the antler wedges as chisels. Using a length of branch as a mallet, I proceeded to chisel wood from the belly of the bow stave. The antler chisels proved extremely useful, as they removed a lot of wood when needed and were also quite precise where precision was necessary.

Once finished with the chisel work, the belly of the stave was a bit ragged. I began working with the copper adz to clean up the belly and to continue reducing the overall thickness the stave. The copper adz made short work of this process. It only took a few minutes to clean up the belly and arrive at a fairly consistent thickness for the length of each bow limb. About half way through the process, I ran the sharpening

After a few minutes of work with the adz, the front-face profile of the stave was taking shape.

View down the back of the stave. The front-face profile was a bit closer to finished dimensions.

Using a sharp stone flake to carefully remove the still-green bark from the stave.

stone across the cutting edge of the copper blade, bringing it back to its original degree of sharpness.

Although the copper blade held up well, it was clear that a thicker blade would function better. At only 1/8" thick, the blade was a bit too springy, causing the blade to vibrate slightly when in use. A thicker, heavier blade would have made a more solid tool.

Even though the belly of the bow was clean and somewhat regular, there was still considerable thickness to remove before the stave would begin to bend. I decided to create the rough front-face profile of the bow by narrowing the tips of the bow limbs. With limbs and tips narrowed close to final dimensions, it would be easier to reduce the thickness of the limbs. The copper adz worked extremely well for this shaping procedure, as it allowed careful and precise removal of wood.

After this initial shaping of the bow limbs, I returned to reducing the belly of the stave with an eye towards getting each limb bending evenly. Again, I used the copper adz to do this. As I progressed in removing wood evenly from both limbs, I periodically tested and observed the evenness of the bend by bending the bow against the ground. I was able to bring the stave to floor tiller using only the copper adz. In effect, I used the adz as a modern bowyer might use a spokeshave - to bring the limb to near final dimension. The adz felt good in the hand - I generally held it close to the blade and took easy and well controlled swings. With each chopping motion, the blade would slice off another bit of wood, like taking small bites from an apple.

The tool marks left by the adz were reminiscent (if a bit larger in size) of the tool

Otzi's yew bow, showing distinct tool marks.

The belly of the stave, showing the adz tool marks.

A right-angle break on stone or glass makes an excellent scraping tool – in this instance, to remove the tool marks left by the copper adz.

marks on Otzi's unfinished bow, and not unlike those left by someone using a knife to whittle a piece of wood – only larger in scale.

I planned to cease work shortly as the wood was still "green" and needed further time to dry. Before setting it aside, I removed the bark using two razor-sharp flint flakes. As the wood directly underneath the bark was to be the back of my bow, I was careful not to damage this layer of wood. It helped to use a smaller flint flake to remove the bark around the knots. The wet/green bark was easy to remove with the flint tools. With many staves, the bark can literally be peeled off in one piece, but not so with this branch, so I proceeded with caution.

Before retiring this stave for a final bout of drying, I decided to clean up the tool marks on the belly. This work went very quickly using a couple of stone scrapers. A right angle break on flint makes for a scraper as efficient as any modern, steel cabinet scraper. I even experimented with hafting one of these scrapers in a simple wooden handle. The handle provided increased leverage and a more comfortable grip.

After approximately two weeks of drying, the stave was ready for final floor tillering. My previous bout of floor tillering had brought the stave extremely close to where it needed to be for an initial stringing - so much so that it only took a matter of minutes of scraping with the stone scraper to make the bow ready.

I cut the string nocks using a small stone "saw" (a serrated flake of flint set in a wood handle with pine pitch adhesive). A linen bow-string was quickly made - with a "Flemish" loop at one end and bowyer's knot on the other.

Tiller was near perfect on the first, low brace stringing. The limbs bent evenly and there were no terribly stiff spots and no hinges. The areas near the tips and the handle on both limbs were a bit stiff, so the bow was immediately unstrung and scraping renewed in those areas. As work continued, the tillering work progressed with the helpful eyes and expertise of some bowyer friends. Those in the group who had never seen a stone scraper in action were predictably impressed with how well it worked.

When tillering was nearly complete, I began to narrow the outer limbs further in the

The final check of floor-tiller immediately prior to the first stringing of the bow.

Using a stone "saw" to cut string nocks.

An experiment in hafting a stone scraper in a simple, split-stick handle. The handle provided a comfortable grip and allowed the increased power and control of two-handed operation.

The author using his body and the ground to hold the stave steady while using the hafted scraper. A pad of rolled up leather for protection and comfort made this a fairly effective holding device.

The first stringing of the bow, and tentative pulls to test the initial tiller.

Part of any Copper Age bowyer's tillering bag of tricks. Especially useful with character areas, as the shadow tends to average out small idiosyncrasies and give an overview of the true bend.

Using a stone scraper to make fine adjustments to the tiller.

A Stone Age or Copper Age woodworker could employ much more leverage bringing his work to the tool, rather than the tool to the work. This large rock functioned a bit like a Paleolithic belt-sander.

hope of making a faster shooting, more efficient bow. This was primarily accomplished using the stone scrapers. The scrapers left some chatter marks and a less than perfect surface, so I used a fairly large and heavy boulder as a makeshift "rasp" to clean up the outer limbs. It is amazing how much more efficient it is to shape a bow by rubbing it on an immovable rough rock than it is the other way around (i.e., rubbing a handheld rock on a bow limb). Within a few minutes, I succeeded in cleaning up the bow tips. With the mechanical aspects of the bow effectively completed, I decided to add a decorative touch to the bow by staining it with red ocher earth pigment. Interestingly enough, prehistoric Europeans apparently had the same affinity for red-ocher as Native Americans and numerous other cultures around the globe. Over the pigment finish, I applied a rubbed on, beeswax finish as a moisture barrier.

The final dimensions of this bow are: 63" total length, 2" at widest (out of the handle) tapering from about mid-limb in fairly straight lines to 5/8" nocks. The draw weight is 50# @ 27".

Many of our museums hold objects made by our Paleolithic ancestors using only the stone, bone, antler, and wood tools available to them. We marvel at their ability to create such things - such beauty - using these so-called "primitive" tools. Try as we might, we can only view these objects (and the tools and methods used to create them) through our modern eyes and through the filter of our present-day experience. To our sensibilities, stone tools and early metal tools will always seem crude and substandard. At best, we might momentarily suspend our 21st century knowledge, and imagine a time where stone tools were literally the cutting edge of technology.

Shooting the finished bow.

As modern humans, we take metals for granted. We can try, but we really can't imagine a world without metals. We are surrounded by metals, and our tool-kits are chock-full of metal tools. We know that these substances originate in the earth, we know how to extract them, and we know how to bend them to our will. We combine them into different alloys, and recombine them again. Although some of us dabble here and there trying to get a feel for using stone tools, it is the rare individual who might gain even a small fraction of understanding of these ancient tools that our ancestor's possessed. With this reality in mind, it would be rather presumptuous of us to try and make too general a conclusion from this small experiment.

That said, it appeared to me that copper would have been a fantastic addition to our ancestors' tool kits. The use of the copper adz allowed for the careful and accurate removal of wood - the equivalent of a modern bowyer's drawknife and spoke-shave rolled together into one tool.

It is more difficult to precisely and predictably shape stone tools. A fresh edge on a flint tool is extremely sharp and very useful. The thinner the edge, the sharper it is, but the less durable it becomes. For all but master flintknappers perhaps, it is very difficult to consistently fashion stone tools with the proper geometry for the job at hand. Also, stone can't be re-shaped, re-sharpened, or re-configured for other uses as easily and consistently.

Copper tools can be shaped, reshaped and adjusted to particular needs. The cutting edge on a copper tool will never be as sharp as an untouched fracture plane on a piece of flint or obsidian, but it can be consistently re-sharpened and reused over and over again. Surely, the initial benefits of copper over stone were probably small and tenuous at first. But it was an overall technological advance - an advance that ultimately ushered us into the Bronze Age, the Iron Age, and from there all the way forward to the present Computer Age - where I sit typing these words.

I propose that the answer to Tim's initial query: ("...to what extent this copper technology influenced bow design and construction") is not to be found in the success or failure of this small experiment. Instead, I believe the answer was in front of us all along. It lies in the collective knowledge of researchers of prehistory, in our museums, and in our libraries.

Due to our interest in archery and bowmaking, it is natural for us to look for answers to these questions by looking first to the history and prehistory of archery itself - specifically to archaeological evidence concerning what is known about the design and construction of ancient bows. Looking in this direction, however, we are disappointed to find that there are insufficient examples of prehistoric bows to make concrete determinations about the evolution of their design. To make matters worse, the relatively few examples of ancient bows that have been turned up do not show any marked difference between those made with stone tools, and those made in the Copper, Bronze, or Iron ages. In fact, the older artifacts tend to be wider flat bows (i.e., Holmgaard), which are more difficult to make regardless of the tools used.

Despite the paucity of evidence of ancient archery, perhaps we do have sufficient data to answer the question posed by this experiment; we just need to look at it from a different perspective in order to understand and appreciate what our ancestors were capable of.

Looking back in the past for answers to one question is a bit like looking at a dim star in the nighttime sky. As star-gazers will tell you, it is often best not to look directly at the star that interests you, but instead, focus your gaze just slightly to one side or another, using your peripheral vision to view the target of your inquiry. If we do this with Tim's question, and look just to the right and left of our interest in archery related woodworking, we'll see clues everywhere.

And then the answer becomes apparent.

The tool kit used to construct a Copper Age bow.

Well before the advent of the bow and arrow, our stone tool wielding ancestors were quite accomplished woodworkers. The physical act of carving a bow - even wide, flat bows - would have been child's play for them in comparison to the other objects they were making. All over the globe, our Stone Age ancestors were engaged in much more difficult woodworking projects: making sea worthy watercraft (from dugout canoes, to plank canoes), building various dwellings, carving decorative items from wood, antler, bone, and ivory. The examples are endless. So, fashioning a bow of any design would have been well within the reach of a man using only stone tools. Metal tools might be easier to make than stone tools, easier to re-sharpen, and perhaps easier to learn to use, but it is doubtful that in and of themselves metal tools contributed to design improvements in ancient archery.

A few years ago I stood in a museum in the South-West of France - Muse d' Mas d'azil. On the third floor, inside a small glass case sat one of the world's oldest and most beautiful spear-throwers. Carved from reindeer antler with stone tools some 13,000 years ago, the well-executed sculptural image of a young ibex stared back at me through the glass. Gazing at this ancient piece of functional art, the reality of our Paleolithic ancestors' capabilities became crystal clear; the man who created this beautiful sculpture wasn't constrained by the make-up of his tools; his only constraints were the limits of his imagination and the strength of his determination.

THE MASS PRINCIPLE

Steve Gardner

The development of the Mass Principle was a lengthy, not-so-simple process of elimination. Almost from the first bow, I became intent upon what makes a bow perform the way it does, never dreaming that it would be several thousand bows later, and years of time invested before arriving at a consistent formula.

I decided several years ago that there must be some simple rule to follow that could give predictable results. But like many simple things in life, they are often so obvious we fail to see them: we trip over them, we pick them up and set them out of our way, and we even use them but fail to see their full potential.

This was what mass was like for me. I always knew how important the effects of mass and mass placement were on performance, as detailed in the Design and Performance chapter in *TBB 1*. But the Mass Principle remained elusive. I did, however, measure mass; one of many things I measured and catalogued on bows as a matter of course.

As the research continued, I noticed fairly quickly that I could sacrifice a little stored energy and make up for that by reducing mass. From that point on, I began a process of attaching values: a value for bow length, a value for draw weight, a value for reflex, a value for draw length, and a value for working limb to draw length ratios. The Mass Principle is a by-product of connecting the dots of these measurements.

A group of pyramid bows I was comparing when the Mass Principle first started coming together. The species ranged from very light woods like poplar, to red oak, maple, elm and dense tropical bulletwood. All of these bows weighed between 15.5 oz and 16.5 oz., but with very different dimensions. My biggest clue in bringing the theory together came when comparing these bows as I had to tiller them differently to avoid taking set.

Below is a chart for two styles of bows, a standard longbow with a typical 8" stiff handle and riser section and also the bendy handle bows, which include the English longbow designs. The stiff handle design will be on the left of the slash (/) and the bendy handle will be on the right of the slash mark, (/). The mass projections are for a standard 50# bow. Below the tables are explanations on how to adapt it for various design and weight changes.

MASS TABLE FOR 50# BOWS
8" stiff handle/bendy handle   (Expressed in ounces)

Draw Length	24"	26"	28"	30"	32"
Bow Length					
58"	15.5/9.5	16.5/10.5	17.5/11.5	18.5/12.5	19.5/13.5
60"	16/10	17/11	18/12	19/13	20/14
62"	16.5/10.5	17.5/11.5	18.5/12.5	19.5/13.5	20.5/14.5
64"	17/11	18/12	19/13	20/14	21/15
66"	17.5/11.5	18.5/12.5	19.5/13.5	20.5/14.5	21.5/15.5
68"	18/12	19/13	20/14	21/15	22/16
70"	18.5/12.5	19.5/13.5	20.5/14.5	21.5/15.5	22.5/16.5
72"	19/13	20/14	21/15	22/16	23/17
74"	19.5/13.5	20.5/14.5	21.5/15.5	22.5/16.5	23.5/17.5
76"	20/14	21/15	22/16	23/17	24/18

Directions: To modify table for lesser or greater draw weights and designs:
A. Add or subtract 1 oz. for each variance of 5# draw weight.
B. Add or subtract .75 oz's for each 1" of stiff handle and fade variance.
C. Add 1 oz. for each 2" of induced reflex.
D. Draw length equal to one working limb length has a zero value, add 1 oz. for every 2" that draw length exceeds working limb (working limb measurement always starts from the handle fades or where the limb starts bending, and ignores stiff tips).
E. On the ELB designs calculate them out as normal and then multiply the answer by the following factors: 100# X .9 90# X .92 80# X .94 70# X .96 60# X .98
F. Perry-reflexed bows reduce mass by up to 10%.

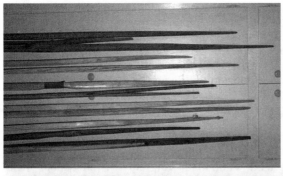

English longbow designs built specifically to test the mass principle. They ranged in weight from about 100# to 35# and are made from a wide range of wood densities. All of these bows performed very consistently between about 168 fps and 172 fps using 10 grains of arrow per pound of bow weight. This was a very enlightening test as it confirmed the importance of using the right density of wood for the draw weight and length of an ELB. It also convinced me that the Mass Principle worked perfectly for bend through the handle bows.

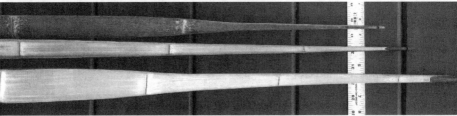

Bamboo-backed flight bows. Top to bottom: jatoba 50#, bulletwood 50#, jatoba 80#. The bow in the middle was clocked at 192 fps at 27" draw using a 500 grain arrow and drawing 52# at that time. This is on a par with the very best modern fiberglass recurves. Per some discussions with Tim Baker regarding width of inner limbs and comparing them to my mass theory, my flight bows now have more mass than ever before, all of the mass is where they are bending in the inner limbs, outer limbs are scary narrow. Very small sacrifices in performance would make these same bows durable, extended-life shooters by simply adding a little mass to the outer limbs. These are basically slightly reflexed versions of Tim's bow shown in TBB Volume 3, page 88. If made slightly more conservative they could be expected to shoot around 184 fps.

MASS AND WIDTH

As an ardent follower of the primitive archery online groups, one of the most common questions I see asked is: "How wide should I make my bow?"

There is no single factor when working with wood that can accurately predict dimensions that will produce good performers. I feel predetermined width is the least accurate of them all. Evidence shows that the most accurate single predictor of performance is mass.

Sal Ochoa reducing mass by removing wood from the sides.

A given amount of energy stored in a bow will require a specific amount of wood, or mass, no matter what the species. The Mass Principle operates under the assumption that for bowmaking purposes all wood is equal. Be assured that if bows from different woods are finished at the same mass, and have maintained the same unstrung side-view profiles, they will shoot about the same. So an Osage bow, a hickory bow, and an ash bow, as examples, will all have the same mass at a given design and draw weight, with the ash being widest, then the hickory, and the Osage the narrowest.

A specific mass target should dictate the width of the bow rather than letting the width dictate the mass.

It's a good idea to start thinking about width in the same way we think about thickness, it is adjustable and tunable and just as important in assuring the success or failure in making a bow of quality.

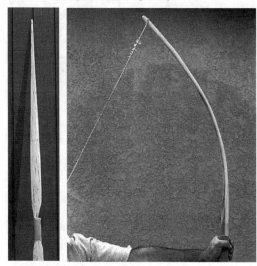

Purposely overbuilt 50#, 72" long, hop hornbeam flatbow, 28 oz. mass. Test was to see if an overbuilt bow could maintain performance of a lighter mass bow if tiller shape conformed to the front-view shape. Outer 13" remained stiff, center 16" remained stiff with a very small bending area mid limb. By in-putting numbers into the mass formula for a 32" draw to account for the stiff tips and a 16" stiff center, projected mass for a bow tillered this way was 28 oz., This bow shot a 500 grain arrow 171 fps drawing 28". A normal tillered bow of this length would have a projected mass of about 22 oz.

MASS AND TILLER

Consider all four sides of a bow and how they relate to each other, or, to think of it another way, the front view shape of the bow should reflect the tiller shape. On a pyramid-shaped bow where each limb bends in an arc of the circle, the thickness remains pretty much constant for the length of the limb. On any bow where the limbs are parallel on the sides, the thickness should gradually decrease the full length of the parallel. This simple concept can be applied to any style bow, English longbows, American flatbows, pyramid bows, Indian bows, and all other designs, as well. It is perfectly all right to intentionally deviate from this guideline, but recognize that mass will be higher and performance will suffer proportionately.

I would never suggest that all bows be built for maximum performance alone, but I do suggest that each design be optimized for all attributes, including performance. One of the biggest and most misunderstood fallacies about controlling mass is that this requires under-building bows. Nothing could be further from the truth. Often, average bows will be under-built near the fades and over-built mid-limb. The Mass Principle is all about putting wood where it is needed.

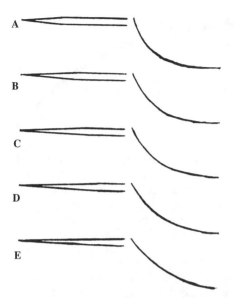

Five examples of limbs with decreasing parallel sides. Note how the tiller of the bow follows the parallels out toward the tip. This is what mass logic is all about, simply making the tiller agree with the front-view shape of the bow.

Example E: Arc of the circle tiller.

This tiller is for pyramid bows, and is a true arc of the circle for each limb. A pyramid bow has a straight width taper from the fades to the tips, and many times such a bow will have little or no thickness taper.

Jim Iwanski's arc of the circle tiller for pyramid-style bows; both 70" long and 70#, both with mass of 22 oz.

Example C:

This tiller is used on an English longbow or D-style bow with a bending handle. It is not an arc of the circle, as such a handle would bend too much and cause the bow to kick unmercifully. The handle bends less than the limbs, and so is slightly flattened.

With this style, particularly in longer lengths, it is important that the density of the wood be compatible with the draw weight, draw length, and bow length. For example, a bow 72" long, drawing 50#, with a dense wood over .80 specific gravity might become so narrow the limbs begin to twist, or become unstable. The same tiller and parameters might be perfect for a bow of 70# with the same wood.

The 72" 50# bow can be made by modifying the tiller as shown in the next example, or by simply using a lower specific gravity wood since this design is ideal for long moderate weight bows of ash, hickory, maple, or elm. In either case, the bow will reach target mass and still maintain a high level of performance.

Jaroslav Petrina drawing a 69" warbow he made from his native Czech yew, 90# @ 30". Perfect tiller for such an English longbow/D bow design - when drawn, working handle area bends slightly.

Example A: Elliptical Tiller

This design is for a narrow-handled, wider-fade bow, with parallel limbs such as an American flatbow or a Sudbury Indian bow. A 66"ntn 50# straight stave bow of this type should come in between 19.5 oz. and 21 oz. depending on how near the fades it first starts bending. I normally use the 10" figure for handle and fades on the chart, which would make the bow 21oz.

Jon Lopez with his first bow made with the Mass Principle, a bamboo-backed ipe, 70" long and 70#. Parallel limbs for 2/3 of their length called for elliptical tiller.

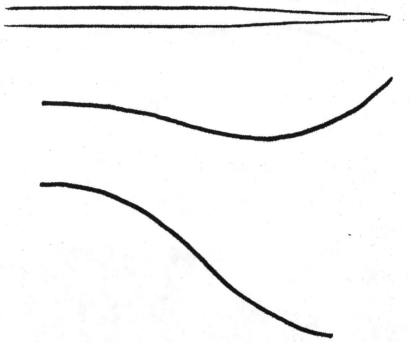

Above is an example of an reflex/deflex designed bow, which carries about the highest mass of any of the bows but also stores about the most energy. This particular example shows about 3" of reflex, also it is stiff out of the fades and the last 12" of limb is relatively stiff. All of the bending takes place mid-limb so it is necessary to carry the parallel limbs out to where the limbs stop flexing. It is also necessary to allow a little extra wood in the stiff outer limb as the high early draw weight of this design will try to torque the limbs sideways and break them off. With 50# @ 28" draw for a 64" bow of this design, I would figure the chart as follows: 12" stiff handle and fades, 32" draw to account for the stiff tips, 4" reflex, and 50# draw weight for a net target mass of 26 oz. Designs such as this are often made using the Perry Reflex principle of glued on backings, so deduct up to 10% mass. This particular bow with a hickory or bamboo backing would be around 23.5 oz.

IMPLEMENTING THE MASS PRINCIPLE

When laying out a new bow, the bowyer usually has a specific design in mind, whether an English longbow, a Cherokee flatbow, or a Holmegaard. The designs are almost limitless.

Past experience, or published dimensions on a historical bow, can be used to determine a starting width. The more experience a bowyer has the closer he may be to proper dimensions at the beginning. If unsure, the bowyer should err on the side of leaving the bow a little wide, then he will have plenty of room to zero in on target mass weight. Just remember that a lot of wood can be removed from the sides and have little effect on the draw weight but a large effect on total mass, while very little wood removed from the belly can have a great effect on the draw weight and relatively little effect on mass. (On a related note, Tim Baker has a method for starting dimensions that goes like this: For a 65" bow that is 2" wide at the fades, the specific gravity of the wood will equal a safe projected draw weight).

Once the bow is laid out and reduced to desired starting dimensions, proceed to remove wood from the belly, keeping it even on both sides and symmetrical in relation to the front-view shape. Periodically, as wood is removed from the belly, stop and floor tiller the bow. When a point is reached that a hard push to the floor gives a little flex, it is time to weigh the bow to determine total mass and re-evaluate the starting dimensions a bit. Only a couple additional ounces of wood removed from the belly will make a huge difference in the stiffness so it is a good idea to begin removing any excess mass from the sides at this time.

Let's suppose the bow is a 66" long, 50# @ 28", hickory bow. The formula calls for 19.5 oz. The bow is showing a weight of 29 oz. of mass at this point, so there are 10 oz. to go. Do not remove all of this 10 oz. immediately; remove maybe 5 oz. of wood by scraping and shaping the sides of the bow only. Now floortiller the bow again; is it still far too stiff? If so, do a little more belly shaving and get the bow bending a little more but try to keep it at least 20# heavy at this point. Weigh the bow again; maybe it dropped one more ounce and is now 4 oz. heavy. Shave a bit more from the sides, maybe about one more ounce. Floortiller again, to check the bend. There are now only 3 oz. to go, 1 1/2 oz. on each limb, so proceed with tillering. Remove wood from the belly, then check the draw weight, where the bow might draw about 22" at the desired 50# of draw weight. At this point, there may be only a little more than 1 oz. of wood left to remove. Set needs to be monitored very closely from here on out. Draw weight should be carefully reduced by a little side tillering and a little belly tillering, then

A beautiful example of a Holmgaard design made by Juri Voijola, elm, 62" long, 44# @ 27". Notice how quickly the limbs start to bend right into the fades, for a tiller such as this I would use a 6" figure for handle and fades instead of 8", this bow came in at 15.5 oz. No allowance was made for stiff outer limbs as they are actually working a bit. Projected mass for this bow would have been 16.5 oz. Lowering the mass in the outer limbs and a relatively small handle contributed to a streamlined, well-executed version of this ancient design.

A maple bow ready for first floor-tillering.

Using a spokeshave to remove wood from the belly of a maple bow.

regularly check the draw length at the desired draw weight. As the final draw length approaches, smaller and smaller amounts of wood can be removed from sides and belly, until the bow reaches final mass, draw weight, and draw length.

Being exactly on mass is not critical, especially when you first begin using the Mass Principle, just being in the vicinity should provide good performance. Trying to go too far under the formula will often overstress a bow, increase string follow, and place the bow in jeopardy.

Measuring mass as a bow progresses through the tillering stages can be compared to a model who places a book on her head and practices walking. It simply forces a bowyer to use good tillering techniques.

ADVANCED TECHNIQUES

When working with a design that uses unusual tillering configurations such as extended stiff tips or fades, some mass logic will need to be applied to compensate and arrive at an intended target mass.

For example, I like to think of stiffer than normal inner limbs as extended handle and fade areas and make small adjustments to the handle and fade calculation. If I am making a bow with unusually long stiff tips I will be asking the inner limb to do a little more bending. This is equivalent to making a bow with a longer draw length so I may add 2 inches or so of draw length to my calculation.

Another important concept is the longer the working limb area the narrower and thicker - thereby reducing mass - the wood can be. This is something to consider when laying out a bow. As a general rule of thumb, the bending, or working portion, of each limb approximately equals draw length. This is especially true for shooting hunting weight arrows between 9 and 11 grains per pound of draw weight. Heavier arrows may call for a little longer working limb and lighter arrows tend to like a little shorter working limb.

Ken Villars, right, evaluating progress on meeting projected mass. In the past, he has had problems with hickory bows taking too much set and having excessive handshock.

Ken's finished bow, back, belly, side-view, and braced. By carefully controlling mass, 70" long, 95# bow finished at 33 oz., and yielded a sweet shooter.

When a bow is extra long or has longer than normal working areas it is a good idea to use more elliptical tillers, or whip-tillers, as this tiller style bends progressively more as it gets further from the handle. This is a good reason for using parallel limbs on a bow, as long as the tiller reflects this front-view shape.

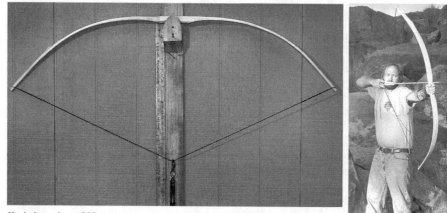

Ken's bow shot a 900 grain arrow an impressive 174 fps. With parallel limbs for much of their length, the bow called for a highly elliptical tiller.

The English longbow and the D bow, both bendy handle designs, have the lowest mass of all bows. A pyramid design generally has the lowest mass for stiff-handled bows. Traditional English longbows have design parameters that should be followed regarding ratio of thickness to width. Without modifying the tiller it would be nearly impossible to use these ratios and make bows lighter than the original 80+ pound bows. Longer bows of light draw weight made from medium dense woods will need to be very elliptical in tiller, while heavier draw weights will be more circular in tiller to maintain the dimensions required.

When working with different densities of woods some designs will appear not to work with the formula. For example, it may appear difficult to make a longbow with a dense wood and a light draw weight with an arc of the circle tiller narrow enough to reach the projected mass weight. But what the formula is saying is that these are not ideal design parameters for the chosen wood. A lightweight longbow with a dense wood can be made and made to shoot well, by lengthening the stiff handle and riser section, in effect making it elliptically tillered, or whip-tillered. The projected mass will go up enough to allow for narrow but stable limbs and also assure good performance.

Becoming familiar with the process makes adjustments and variations easy to calculate. Suppose the bowyer is building a 66" bow with an 8" stiff handle and fades, but wants to use an extreme elliptical tiller. In a case like this, telling the formula that the stiff handle and fade section is longer than it really is compensates for the extended near handle wood that is "semi" stiff. Using some logic and creativity in applying the Mass Principle helps in fine-tuning.

HOW MOISTURE AFFECTS THE PRINCIPLE

As work progresses on a bow, the scale will tip me off as to the condition of the wood. If a stave is too high in moisture or too low in moisture, the Mass Principle will allow detection early in the tillering process. Inferior specimens of wood will also be quickly exposed and exceptional specimens - those that will allow us to push the limits if we choose - will become obvious.

High Moisture

It will simply be impossible to make target mass with a bow too high in moisture: the mass will remain too high and the draw weight will fall quickly. If floor-tiller stage is reached and the mass is far above what it should be or the draw-weight is dropping too quickly, high moisture is almost a certainty. Refer to wood drying principles in the *Bow Wood* chapter to quickly dry a roughed-out stave, then proceed as normal.

Low Moisture

A moisture content too low will be reflected in the opposite: the bow will appear to be coming in far below projected mass. Bows like this can suddenly fail in tension.

Certain woods like hickory, for instance, are known to perform well in very dry conditions, but other woods like Osage, red cedar, and maple need to have the moisture content within workable limits. For the most part, the formula works well with woods between 7% and 10% moisture content. Refer to *Bow Wood* for further information on preferred moisture content for different woods.

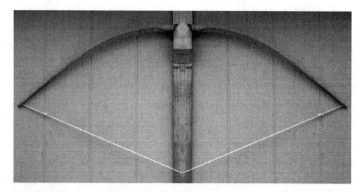

World record broadhead flight bow, Osage, 62" long, 50# @28". Notice the extreme bend right out of the handle and the long stiff limb areas. This bow weighed 17 oz. but would have performed better and taken less set at 20 oz. This bow should have been figured with an 8" stiff handle and fades, 32" draw to account for the extra stiff limbs, and added in 2" of reflex which was lost due to set. This bow shot 178 fps for 500 grains when fresh but after breaking-in dropped to 172 fps. The extra 3 oz. would have kept this bow in its fresh state.

WHEN AND HOW TO DEVIATE FROM THIS PRINCIPLE

The when and the how should be approached from different angles.

The **when** involves a bowyer setting higher goals for himself in performance, such as in flight shooting or in maximizing chronograph speed, in which case he may want to experiment with lighter mass than outlined above. It all depends on what the bowyer wants to accomplish. The difference between a high-performance bow and an average performing bow are only a few fps, an almost imperceptible difference in normal shooting situations. The average bow can be expected to be safe, dependable, and consistent with normal climatic changes where a high performance bow will make sacrifices in some or all of these areas. Pushing these limits means taking some calculated risks.

A lot of bowyers nowadays simply have more bows than they can shoot anyway, so they may as well enjoy experimenting with different designs. To such a bowyer, I encourage pushing the limits to the best of his ability.

The **how** involves reading the wood, the quality of the wood, and the bowyer applying his knowledge of a particular species and the amount of set or lack of set the bow is taking.

Reducing mass by reducing the sides of a 35# bamboo-backed ipe English longbow design.

The same bow braced. This competition flight bow weighed only 11 oz., and shot well over 200 fps through the chronograph using a 225 grain arrow.

For a flight-shooter, just a few fps can make the difference between setting a new record and just participating. I tend to push the limits on most all of my bows; the limiting factor is always the same: how much set the bow has taken. As a flight-shooting bowyer I tend to get my wood a bit dryer than a hunter/target-shooter so I therefore expect less set, but I also have smaller margins for error.

A very dry bow will take less set than a bow with a more moderate MC before it breaks. Most of the time when I am approaching 1" of set I start to consider the possibility of sudden catastrophic failure. The Mass Principle is geared toward normal MC readings of around 7% to 10%.

If a bowyer chooses to push the limits a bit, the first step lies in getting the wood down to around 6% moisture content. There is no advantage to going any lower as the failure rate will vastly increase. At 6% MC, mass may be reduced by as much as 10%. Risks of failure will go up to some degree, as well, but I feel it is worth it if high performance is the goal. I have several high-performance bows that have shot faithfully for several years with no noticeable change. For such bows, I don't like to depend on moisture meters as much as I do a controlled environment.

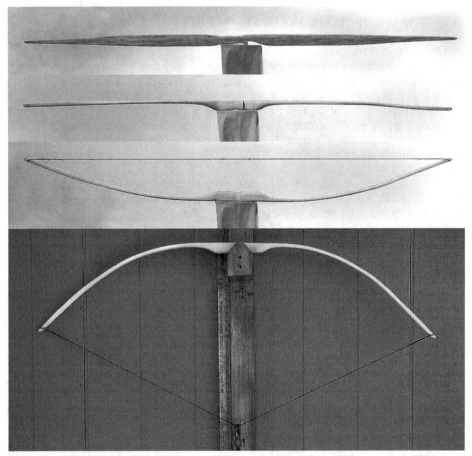

Maple bow, 55# @ 22". Note the stiff outer limbs. With a mass of 23 oz., it shot 550 grain arrows 172 fps.

PEAKING AND TWEAKING

Peaking and tweaking is an old term that the CB radio operators used when adjusting their CB's for maximum performance. I think it also fits well for bowers. **Peaking** is simply getting the maximum performance out of bows and **tweaking** refers to the process we go through to accomplish this.

These procedures are usually performed after the bow is basically finished and we have determined that the wood used on the bow has still more potential. Sometimes it will mean almost redesigning the bow, other times; it will simply be a matter of a few adjustments. Either way, it is a lot of fun and a great learning experience with each and every bow, even those taken past the breaking point.

The tweaking methods used:

Wood Removal

Let's suppose that a specimen of wood has reached its equilibrium moisture content. The bowyer is well along in the bow's progress, say within 4" of target draw length, and he can see the bow has shown no perceptible signs of stress, manifested either in set or loss of early draw weight. This would be a good candidate to start reducing the mass even further than outlined in the above chart by side tillering, always closely monitoring the condition of the wood after exercising and drawing to its intended draw-length.

Trapping is another form of wood removal and is a term used to describe giving a bow a trapezoidal cross-section, or one that is narrower on the back than on the belly. Since most woods are stronger in tension than in compression, trapping a bow does not compromise safety but further reduces mass.

Often with a bow of sufficient length that has shown little or no signs of taking a set, I will consider trapping.

Heat Treating

The most common form of peaking I do is heat-treating. For instance, I will take a finished bow that came in right at target mass that displays a healthy 1 1/2" of set right after shooting. I will heat-treat the limbs as outlined in Marc St. Louis' *Heat-treating Bows* chapter, slightly reflex them, then simply do some side tillering to lower the draw weight back down to the original, sometimes dropping my total mass by as much as 10%.

Very often I have turned less than stellar bows into very good performers by heat-treating the bellies.

PERFORMANCE: WHAT IS ATTAINABLE, REASONABLE, AND REPEATABLE?

Performance claims among bowers has always been an area of great dispute, and for good reason; there are just too many variables. As mentioned by Tim Baker in an earlier edition of *TBB*, perfectly honest bowers will make false but well-intentioned claims of speed. As a flight shooter, I have spent countless hours shooting before a chronograph and have, to some extent, perfected my release and know how to get the most out of a bow. It would do archery no good whatsoever for me to compare my chrono readings with a casual archery hunter who practices for accuracy.

I have spent a considerable amount of time watching archers shoot through a chrono and then shot the very same bows and gotten very different readings. Up to a 10 fps difference is not unusual. Obviously, a poor release will not accurately reflect a bows' performance anymore than an active flight shooter's release will, so I conducted my tests under the following conditions. I tried to keep my string weight at approx. 3 grains per pound of draw weight and used linen string. I tested the bows at 10 grains of arrow weight to 1# of draw weight. I marked the arrows with tape at desired draw length and drew the tape to the back of the bow, paused, then released with a relaxed bow hand.

I also don't think it is fair to report speeds of bows that were fired "fresh" - not broken in yet - or speeds from bows that self-destructed after a dozen or so shots. Bows that were too unstable to hold a string for continuous shots also did not qualify for mention. We will only talk about bows that can be carried afield with confidence and reliability.

In my opinion, a bowyer should expect a 50# selfbow made from any decent piece of properly dried wood to shoot 164 fps or better, up to about 172 fps. Managing the mass on a bow and proper tillering alone will accomplish this. Wood-backed bows and Perry-reflexed bows can expect consistent performance of about 168 to 176 fps, and will carry a little less mass.

These performance numbers are for very good bows, but by using the Mass Principle, anyone can build very good bows consistently. Since going public with the Mass Principle, I have seen a growing number of bowyers adopt it and was pleased with how quickly and easily it was adapted into their tillering programs.

Hopefully, as more bowyers experiment with this principle further improvements will be made. A big part of the challenge in bow building is one of discovery, and there are lots of new discoveries still to be made.

TURTLE BOW

Jim Hamm

In the original three *Traditional Bowyer's Bibles* volumes from the early 1990's, we repeatedly made the claim that dozens of hardwoods were virtually identical in performance, if only the bows were properly designed for the individual wood species. We felt this information and how to implement it would open up new bowmaking avenues, though the groundbreaking ideas naturally met some scattered resistance. Then, in 1999, on one of the traditional archery forums on the Internet, discussions evolved about the relative merits of different bow woods, which led, inevitably, to bow design. Few of us knew each other then, and with the faceless limits of the Internet, some of the discussions quickly degenerated into full-contact arguments.

There were two camps. First, there were the "Osage is the only true bow wood" adherents, who fervently believed any other wood species was inferior, end of story. Then, there were those who had read the three *Traditional Bowyer's Bibles* (or *TBB's*, as they had become known), and were fashioning excellent bows from a wide variety of hardwoods. In the interest of full disclosure, I have to reveal that I was firmly in this second camp, though Osage is my wood of choice and one of my chief pleasures is fashioning a really gnarly yellow stave into a fine bow. Hundreds of cyber witnesses, however, were in neither camp, but simply weren't sure what was truth and what was pure dogma, what was bedrock fact and what was ego. Finally, after we had circled the same rhetorical tree a dozen times with still no resolve, someone, out of frustration, suggested we all get together in a central location and test the various theories, an idea that met with wide approval.

Keith Bishop from Marshall, Missouri, kindly offered to ramrod and organize the entire event, scheduled for July of 1999. And thus Mojam, or Missouri Selfbow Jamboree, was born. It would be a *High Noon* wood bow shootout.

Though the original idea was to conduct exacting tests to resolve those nagging bow questions, a spirit of innovation also surfaced. A Hatchet Bow Contest was sponsored for the best bow using no tool but a hatchet, not even a nock file.

An old-time Clout Shoot was organized, the object being to shoot into a large target placed flat on the ground over a hundred yards away.

I conceived of a Turtle Bow Contest, and the rules were simple. The bow had to draw 50# at 28", and the maker of the bow that shot the slowest through the chronograph would win a premier Osage stave. My reasoning was that in order to make a really slow bow, you had to understand what made a fast bow, and do just the opposite, so I thought the good-natured contest would be instructive. Besides, I figured that having accidentally made some real dogs over the years, if I really put my mind to it I could make a canine of epic stature...

Word of the Mojam gathering spread. Folks arrived with trade goods such as bow staves, rivercane, dogwood and phragmites arrowshafts, flint and obsidian, literally pickup loads of raw materials from all over the country. Many of the participants on

Tim Baker demonstrated turning flax fiber into fine bowstrings (Marty Kreis photo).

either side of the wood species/bow design arguments were wary, at first. But as the campground filled, any ruffled feathers over the earlier bow-related arguments were soon downplayed as informal introductions were made, bows were admired, tents were set up, kids played, adult beverages were sampled, and wood shavings began flying. A couple of people had gone so far as to haul their bandsaws to the gathering, which were set up under a roofed, open-sided structure perfect for bowmaking.

Gary Davis, a fine bowyer with vast experience from Michigan, and Tim Baker, of *TBB's* Design and Performance fame, were prevailed upon to set up shop in the covered bowmaking area. Over the course of the long weekend, they helped dozens of beginners make their first bows, offered sage advice to those with detailed bow questions, used their practiced eyes to help tiller difficult staves, and, perhaps best of all, made kid's bows as fast as they could. Those bandsaws were humming eighteen hours a day, and Gary and Tim were kept so busy I doubt if either of them got more than a few hours of sleep a night.

On the second morning, the formal testing of bows began, and everyone was encouraged to bring their bows for detailed analysis. *High Noon*, Mojam style, had arrived, and a crowd of bowyers soon gathered in anticipation of the tests, wanting to see how their favorite bows and woods stacked up.

For each bow, Tim Baker, Joe Mattingly, and I recorded the data. Tim and I were *TBB* authors, and so (along with Paul Comstock) were buglers in the 'design is everything' revolution. Joe, one of the most fair-minded men I've ever known, leaned toward the Osage school of thought, and was asked to assist for the sake of balance. We carefully recorded a bow's overall length, mass, draw weight, draw length, string weight, mid-limb width, string follow, and any additional notes such as recurve, first bow, sinew-backed and so forth. The same 500 grain arrow was used for all the tests

A few of the bows from across the country lined up for testing (Marty Kreis photo).

Tim Baker, Jim Hamm, and Joe Mattingly measured and recorded stats for each bow (Marty Kreis photo).

through the chronograph. A draw marker was placed on the arrow for each bow's specific draw length, so the bow couldn't be inadvertently short-drawn or overdrawn. Each bow had to be shot cleanly, or pass the muster of the critical onlookers at least three times, and then the speeds were averaged and recorded.

In addition, we documented one further refinement. The number one hundred added to a bow's weight is considered average speed. For example, a 48 pound bow shooting an arrow 148 fps (feet per second) is average (48# plus 100 equals 148). We noted any speed above or below this baseline as + or – in the FPS Above Weight column. This is the critical test of a bow's performance, particularly as compared to other bows of different weights and other designs, and the chart is arranged from best to worst in this category. (We know now, eight years and many thousands of tested bows later, that

MOJAM BOW TEST DATA

Name	Wood	Draw Weight	FPS	Bow Length	Bow Mass (Oz.)	String Follow	String Material	String Mass (Grains)	Midlimb Width	FPS above weight	Backing	Comments
Baker	Pecan	47 @ 28"	164	76.25	25	0.75	Linen	180	1.38	17		1/2 heartwood, sapwood
Baker	Pecan	45 @ 28"	161	68	21	1.00	Linen	200	1.50	16		
Mattingly	Osage recurve	57 @ 28"	173	67.25	23	0.00	B-50	150	1.31	16		Recurve, 4"
Poindexter	Osage w/bamboo	58 @ 27"	174	65	24	1.25	B-50	180	1.25	16	Bamboo	Perry reflex 1.5"
Baker	Bl. Walnut w/hickory	47 @ 28"	165	65	17	0.75	Linen	130	1.25	15	Hickory	Perry reflex, 3/4"
Baker	Pecan board	50 @ 28"	164	65.5	21	0.50	Linen	200	1.88	14		
Baker	Pecan	66 @ 28"	180	62	24	1.00	Linen	190	1.13	14		
Baker	Hickory	53 @ 28"	167	72	27	1.00	Linen	160	1.25	14		
Strubberg	Osage	54 @ 28"	168	59	18	0.50	B-50	110	1.06	14		New, broke later, low mass
Baker	Pecan	71 @ 28"	184	62	25	1.00	Linen	190	2.00	13		
Baker	Hickory stave	51 @ 28"	163	67	24	0.88	Linen	200	1.63	12		
Mattingly	Osage recurve	52 @ 28"	164	67.5	24	0.25	B-50	180	1.50	12		
Baker	Cherry w/pecan back	39 @ 28"	150	67.75	17	0.38	Linen	150	1.63	11	Pecan veneer	
Baker	Hickory	47 @ 28"	158	61	21	1.25	Linen	130	1.88	11		Pyramid
Cook	Osage recurve	50 @ 28"	161	64	22	2.00	B-50	190	1.50	11		
Davis	Osage recurve	55 @ 28"	166	60	24	0.00	B-50	165	1.63	11	Sinew/rawhide	
Flood	Hickory w/bamboo	46 @ 28"	157	70	21	2.25	NA	170	1.25	11	Bamboo	
Hamm	Osage	51 @ 27"	162	66	21	(2.25)	B-50	210	1.38	11		2.25" reflex
Humphry	Osage	60 @ 28"	171	65	28	2.00	B-50	110	1.25	11		
Mattingly	Osage	65 @ 28"	176	67.75	28.5	0.50	B-50	160	1.50	11		
Winters	Osage recurve	60 @ 29"	167	61	21	1.38	B-50	160	1.38	11		
Baker	Cherry w/linen back	48 @ 28"	158	67.25	18	0.63	Linen	190	1.31	10	Linen cloth	
Mattingly	Yew	45 @ 28"	155	73.75	22.25	0.50	B-50	190	1.25	10		
Baker	Pecan board	70 @ 28"	179	61	27.5	0.75	Linen	200	2.50	9		
Keller	Osage	60 @ 28	169	66	29	1.50	B-50	190	1.69	9		
Lippert	Osage	60 @ 25"	169	54	23	0.50	B-50	140	1.25	9		Round back, flat belly
Wagner	Osage	42 @ 28"	151	63	23	1.75	B-50	160	1.50	9		Slightly rounded belly
Warner	Osage recurve	48 @ 28"	157	65	24	1.75	B-50	170	1.50	9		Slightly rounded belly
Baker	Bl. walnut w/pecan	51 @ 28"	159	72	20	1.00	Linen	200	1.25	8	pecan veneer	
Hamm	Yew	46 @ 28"	154	72.5	25.5	0.25	B-50	195	1.88	8		
Watson	Osage w/hickory back	50 @ 28"	158	70	29	1.88	B-50	160	1.38	8	Hickory	Round belly
Baker	Pecan board	45 @ 28"	152	68	21.25	1.00	Linen	190	1.50	7		
Baker	Elm stave	45 @ 28"	152	75	23	(1.00)	Linen	240	1.13	7		
Mattingly	Hackberry	55 @ 27"	162	64.75	25	1.00	B-50	160	1.75	7		
Scifres	Osage	55 @ 26"	153	56.5	20	(1.50)	B-50	120	1.50	7	Sinew	
Steffen	Osage recurve	45 @ 27"	152	61.75	20	(0.75)	B-50	160	1.50	7		Recurve, 5"
Baker	Pecan	48 @ 28"	154	64	15.5	0.75	Linen	210	1.75	6		
Baker	Pecan	44 @ 28"	150	60	17	0.75	Linen	190	1.50	6		slight recurves
Baker	Maple recurve	40 @ 28"	146	67	23	0.50	B-50	135	2.00	6		Recurve, 2 1/2"
Hamm	Hickory board	50 @ 28"	156	69	25	1.75	B-50	200	1.75	6		
Baker	Cherry w/pecan	59 @25"	164	54.5	17	0.75	Linen	180	1.75	5	Pecan veneer	Pyramid
Hamm	Osage	45 @ 29"	150	74	29	1.00	B-50	260	1.25	5		
Hamm	Osage	45 @ 29	150	74	27	1.50	B-50	230	1.13	5		Whip-tillered
Jones	Hickory recurve	48 @ 28"	153	64.75	24	0.00	B-50	155	1.75	5		3" reflex
Long	Osage w/bamboo back	44 @ 28"	149	67	18	(0.50)	B-50	190	1.00	5	Bamboo	Perry reflex
Poindexter	Osage	66 @ 27"	171	65.5	31	1.75	B-50	175	1.50	5		
Steffen	Osage	52 @ 27"	157	65	26	2.25	B-50	205	1.25	5		Round belly, whip-tillered
Steffen	Black Locust	42 @ 27"	147	60	18	0.25	B-50	150	1.38	5		
Swank	Osage	51 @ 28"	156	70.5	35	1.50	B-50	220	1.00	5		Takedown snake bow
Unknown	Maple w/hickory	50 @ 28"	155	68	24	2.50	B-50	130	1.50	5	Hickory	
Damm	Osage	58 @ 25"	162	64	28	0.00	B-50	180	1.50	4		New bow
White	Elm	48 @ 28"	152		25	1.25	B-50	210	1.75	4		
Holmer	Osage	42 @ 29"	145	70	27	1.25	B-50	140	1.00	3		
Sneyers	Hickory	44 @ 27"	146	67	28	3.25	B-50	210	1.38	3		
Van Petten	Osage	45 @ 28"	148	70	20	0.00	B-50	190	1.00	3		Round belly
James	Osage	53 @ 27"	155	64.75	25	0.75	B-50	190	1.56	2		
Melville	Osage	50 @ 26"	152	66	27	0.75	B-50	210	1.50	2		
Bare	Yew w/sinew	52 @ 27"	153	67	23	0.50	B-50	175	1.38	1	Sinew	
Jones	Osage sapling w/sapw.	44 @ 28"	145	71	25	(1.50)	B-50	195	1.38	1		Bend in Handle
Jones	Osage	42 @ 28"	143	72	25	1.25	Linen	260	0.88	1		Round belly, round tiller
White	Ash	55 @ 28"	156	67	26	2.25	B-50	260	2.00	1	Snakeskin	
Holmer	Osage	56 @ 29"	156	65.5	28	2.00	B-50	180	1.63	0		Heavy tips, second bow
Lotz	Hickory	46 @ 28"	146	66	26	1.00	B-50	225	1.75	0		
Sarren	Osage	47 @ 27"	147	63.5	20	0.75	B-50	195	1.44	0		
Steffen	Osage	50 @ 27"	150	65	24	2.25	B-50	195	1.38	0		Round belly
Spears	Osage	55 @ 26"	154	65	25	0.38	B-50	200	1.13	-1		New, rounded belly
Walchuk	Red Oak	39 @ 28"	138	70	20	2.50	B-50	160	1.25	-1		First bow
Lotz	Purpleheart w/hickory	37 @ 27"	135	70.5	24	1.38	B-50	185	1.25	-2	Hickory	Round belly
Smith	Osage w/hickory back	31 @ 27"	129	66	21	1.13	B-50	210	1.31	-2		Edge-ringed Osage
Strubberg	Osage	28.5"	148	62	27	1.00	B-50	220	2.00	-2		
Lotz	Osage	44 @ 28"	141	65	26	2.75	B-50	220	1.75	-3	Rawhide - Boar	
White	Hickory	39 @ 28"	136	69.75	30	2.50	B-50	230	1.88	-3	Rawhide	
Humphry	Hickory	56 @ 28"	153	64	28	3.50	B-50	200	1.75	-4		Wide tips
Melville	Osage	38 @ 26"	134	66.5	23	2.50	B-50	240	1.13	-4		
Smith	Hickory	40 @ 28"	136	66	23	1.25	B-50	180	1.50	-4		First successful bow
Smith	Hickory	51 @ 28"	147	67.5	27	1.25	B-50	170	1.75	-4		
Steffen	Hickory	54 @ 27"	149	70	27	2.50	B-50	190	1.69	-5		
Dickerson	Osage	56 @ 25"	150	66	24	0.00	B-50	170	1.75	-6		New
Kreis	Cherry w/hickory	48 @ 28"	142	68	23	2.00	B-50	180	1.50	-6	Hickory	
Snyder	Osage	45 @ 27	139	66.5	24	0.50	B-50	210	1.38	-6		
Grubb	Osage	45 @ 27"	138	63.25	26	(1.00)	B-50	175	1.88	-7		
Grubb	Hickory	57 @ 27"	150	66.75	32	2.25	B-50	230	2.38	-7		Very wide tips
Sneyers	Hickory	43 @ 27"	136	61	22	3.50	B-50	200	1.50	-7		Rounded belly
Kreis	Vine Maple	58 @ 28"	150	68	23	3.00	B-50	200	1.50	-8		
Steffen	Hickory	40 @ 27"	131	68	23	1.25	B-50	185	1.69	-9		

using the same 500 grain arrow for different weight bows proportionally handicaps lighter bows and improves the numbers for heavier bows. Ideally, bows should be tested with 10 grains of arrow weight and 3 grains of string weight for each pound of bow weight, ie: a 50# bow would shoot a 500 grain arrow and 150 grain string, a 40# bow would shoot a 400 grain arrow and 120 grain string, etc. With that in mind, individual bows in the Mojam tests can be fairly compared with others of similar draw weight).

In all, we measured and tested eighty-five bows made by thirty-six different bowyers. Fourteen different species of wood were represented with many additional combinations of hickory, rawhide, sinew, and bamboo backings. This is, to my knowledge, the largest testing of wooden bows ever conducted under controlled conditions with oversight by witnesses. On the accompanying graph, we have listed all of the relevant data.

The results gave us a unique window into the truths of bowmaking, in particular shining a bright light on the disputed points. They also yielded a couple of surprises.

First of all, the tests clearly showed that the woods such as pecan, walnut, hickory, and cherry held their own against the Osage. The whitewood bows largely out-shot the Osage bows of equal weight, not because they are superior woods, but because their designs were closer to optimum for the specific gravity of the particular wood species. As the *TBB's* had preached, scores of woods, including Osage, are essentially equal if designed properly. Matching the design to the wood species, by making the bow long enough and/or wide enough, was proven to be far and away more important than the wood species itself.

It should also be noted that the best bows were not some "toes over the edge of the cliff" short-lived specialties, but weapons that would measure durability in decades. Most were longer bows well above 65" in length, which would yield smooth draws with little stack. Only a couple of the top bows were really short, both at 62", and they drew a hefty 66# and 70# respectively. These short bows were made wider, up to 2" at midlimb, so there was plenty of wood to carry the load for durability.

Bows with rounded bellies performed surprisingly well, in spite of their higher than average string follow, which robs speed. Though slower than the rectangular cross-sections, the better than expected performance was due to the reduced mass of a rounded belly. So, in effect, the slightly lower mass helped cancel out some of the increased string follow of a rounded belly.

Another surprise was the performance of the recurves. Only the two very best recurves made by Joe Mattingly, a highly skilled bowyer, were in the top twelve bows. This illustrates that it is easy to make a recurve that is actually slower than a straight-stave bow, not to mention the far greater difficulty and time in constructing one.

So what had started out as a cyber argument had magically morphed into a valuable, instructive meeting for testing, which benefited bowmakers everywhere. Just as importantly, the participants, who before had been little more than images on a computer screen to each other, had also become friends and colleagues.

And the Turtle Bow contest?

Well, since I had sponsored the event, I was urged by the competition to test my bow first. The laughter started as soon as I brought it out, for it was, in a word, hideous. My masterpiece was an eight foot long full-sized Osage stave still sporting the bark, weighing nearly twenty pounds, with a bow fashioned out of the middle three feet. It resembled nothing more than two nail kegs connected by a broomstick.

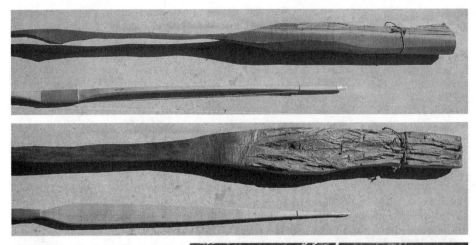

The Turtle Bow, the slowest bow in the history of archery, along with one of the bows which shone most brightly during the tests. These two are a reverse-study in bow design: The excellent pecan bow was designed by Tim Baker, and is the highly refined extension of the ancient Holmegaard and Andaman Island bows: very light tips, minimal string follow, fast, accurate, virtually no hand shock, with the width of the bow adjusted for the density of the wood species. The Osage Turtle Bow, on the other hand, had massive tips, all of the bend was near the handle, lots of string follow, and the large string was made from nylon, which is both heavy and highly elastic. Both bows drew 50# @ 28", but the Baker bow shot an arrow 164 fps, the Hamm bow about 150 fps less than that. His bow may have been faster, but mine was uglier.

The Turtle Bow in action. Note that the only thing in focus is the arrow, as it was moving slower than anything else, including leaves. It wouldn't register through the chronograph, thus the "flight" shooting, but we estimated the 50# bow's arrow speed at 10-15 fps (Marty Kreis photo).

I sauntered up to the chronograph, drew the beast, and released the arrow. It didn't have hand shock, it was more akin to body shock, like a belly-flop from a high dive. The chronograph never blinked. Not wanting to show fear, I tried again. Still nothing.

So we adjourned to the shooting range to try for distance. With huge effort - it's not easy holding a log at arms-length - I drew and launched the arrow at a 45 degree angle. I should have brought a yardstick for measuring. The arrow wobbled about twenty feet, hit point first, and fell over. You could throw an arrow further.

The onlookers, when they could finally get their breath, insisted I shoot again. To a man they said it was among the funniest things they had ever seen. I managed to shoot twice more, to growing guffaws, before giving out completely. The other competitors unanimously agreed that when it came to making a really awful bow, I had no equal, that I had made the slowest bow in the entire history of archery.

They conceded on the spot.

DESIGN AND PERFORMANCE REVISITED

Tim Baker

Chronographs, draw-weight scales, F/D curves… many wonder what in the world such equipment has to do with primitive bowmaking. But it's more than proper to use these devices now because we're all bow orphans. If we'd been born into an intact bow culture we'd have grow up knowing all we needed to know to make perfect bows for our needs. But we're bow orphans, so we have to make up for lifetimes, even scores of lifetimes, of lost tradition. We have to make several generations' worth of bows to know what a decent bow is and how to make it. And worse, we have to unlearn false traditions. We can't do this unaided. If we hope to accomplish this in one lifetime we must operate at least partly in research mode, or some do, so they can pass this information on. Others are concerned about bandsaws and other shortcuts, feeling that moisture meters, humidity meters, drying boxes and the like have no place in natural archery. Those people have sound instincts. But, again, we're bow orphans.

And what about the apparent obsession with ever-faster bows? At root this is a valid concern. It's not all that important if a bow shoots a few fps faster or slower. That's not the reason archery is so rewarding. An eternal dry search for greater speed can only lead to discontentment. But. If the search itself is seen as a hunt, a quest, a separate activity, where once having left the 'lab' the archer can pick up a quite ordinary bow and be happy, then it's a proper course.

It's proper for a few to use chronographs, scales and meters, tracking down the reasons for bow speed, and speed with safety, comfort and accuracy. Because once this learned or re-learned information spreads, as it has been spreading, the routine,

The perils of letting others use the "lab's" chronograph, and the perils of using other's arrows when testing. Actually, this chrono was 15 years old and had faced death before countless shooters. Such a bad misread had to happen eventually. The shooter felt just as you could imagine, and replaced this vintage machine with the latest bells and whistles model. The owner of the loose-feathered arrow felt even worse, with no need, really. The feather base was snipped off, the quill pulled through, and shooting continued.

I won't inform on this 20-year-old bow's maker, a well-published archery maven, whose present bows in no way resemble the above. This was a common profile not too long ago. Starting at about the same time as and largely the result of the TBBs, a growing awareness began of the benefits of lower outer limb mass and appropriate tiller shape per bow length and front view shape.

casually-made bows of others will improve, as they have been improving. Due to the shared results of this other hunt, present typical bows have less handshock, are less likely to break, are more accurate, and will shoot around 10 fps faster than typical bows of several years ago when the present wood bowmaking explosion began.

So don't disparage too harshly those who seem obsessed with speed. They aren't. They're simply hunters tracking game, hoping to bring the goods back to camp for all to share.

Archery and Bowmaking are only Cousins

The above concerns are usually expressed by archers rather than bowmakers. Bowmaking is a discreet realm unto itself, with its own separate goals, challenges and satisfactions. A bowmaker can be content while rarely casting an arrow. The thrill of the hunt an archer feels is completely analogous to the thrill of the hunt a bowmaker feels pursuing ever more interesting and effective bow designs. The fact that archers may benefit from these efforts is a smaller and separate satisfaction. Archers and bowmakers are only cousins.

DENSITY

In its entire 10,000-plus year history archery's most liberating development occurred over the last 20 years. Sparked by Paul Comstock's *The Bent Stick,* the nearly endless wood types of this and other continents are suddenly available to us.

A simple observation shows why this is possible:

Whether as a bough or a bow, a thin enough limb of any wood will bend to the shape of a drawn bow without breaking or taking excessive set. At a given width this limb will have a certain draw weight. Double this width and draw weight doubles too. This means that any wood, if reduced to its own particular safe bowlimb thickness, can make a low-set, durable bow of any draw weight simply by altering limb width.

With sufficient trial and error this idea alone could lead to design proficiency with all woods, but knowing the following speeds the process.

A bow stores energy by stretching and compressing wood. The more wood available for stretching and compressing the more energy a bow can store. But the bow doesn't measure 'more' by the volume of a piece of wood, only by the amount of *wood in the wood.* A wood's density, or specific gravity (SG), is effectively the measure of the amount of wood in the wood. Low-density wood needs more volume to enclose the same amount of wood, to store the same energy, so a limb of low-density wood must be wider. Wider instead of thicker because wood fibers in different woods can only be stretched or compressed a similar percentage of length before failure, and limb thickness determines that percentage.

A Design Rule of Thumb

For safety and low set in a straight-stave self bow: At 65" long and two inches wide, with 6" of net non-working handle area, poundage will equal the wood's specific gravity: Cherry, 50 lb; pecan, 66 lb; live oak, 82 lb. Woods lighter than .50 SG often need a bit more length. For higher or lower poundage adjust limb width in proportion to weight change, assuming a rectangular cross-section. Shorter bows will be wider, longer bows narrower. Until a good sense of needed adjustment is acquired, begin substantially wider or longer and let Steve Gardner's Mass Principle be a guide to more precise dimensions.

Most woods don't have published SG numbers, especially some new potential bow wood you've discovered. And many staves within a species can be significantly more or less dense than average. Here's a way to measure a particular stave's SG.

Determining SG at Home

From the stave to be tested, fashion a uniform cross-section sample about one-half inch in diameter by a few inches in length (preferably a length conveniently divisible by 10). With a pencil make marks at, say, 4, 5, 6, 7, and 8-tenths of its length. Dry the sample in an oven at 212f for several hours, or if a grain scale is available, until it loses no more weight. Even one-pound postage scales are not accurate enough for this use. If using a grain scale weigh the sample every hour or so after the first three hours. When the sample has lost NO, absolutely NO weight for an hour, it's dry.

Float the sample upright in a narrow container of water, making certain the sample is perfectly free to find its level. If four-tenths of the sample floats above water the wood is .60 SG, and so on.

Depending on humidity levels, an air-dried sample can float considerably deeper than if completely dry, seeming to be pecan-dense, for example, when only birch-dense. That's quite a difference when deciding how to lay out a bow. Readings from even wetter wood are pretty meaningless. White pine, .35 SG, can easily float at .80 SG or higher if wet enough. Microwave drying is probably best done with many 20-second periods in the oven and one minute breaks. Otherwise wood cells can explode and the wood scorch and smoke. A grain scale is needed here.

Determining Tension vs Compression Strength

Some wood species are inherently better in compression or tension. So when using unfamiliar wood a simple over-the-knee bend test of a limb-thick dried sample, combined with density, will not just put you in the design ballpark, but in the correct row. If the sample breaks in tension before taking moderate set it's tension weak compared to its compression strength - overbuilding, backing or reverse-trapping (a crowned or narrowed belly) is in order. If it takes moderate set before breaking normally it has typical wood properties. If it takes very large set before breaking it's extra strong in tension compared to its compression strength - trapping is in order. See *TBB 1*, p. 103 for tension break photos.

LAYOUT

Once a certain bow length and wood type is decided on, as well as proper width for that wood and length, then all else can essentially be condensed into a short bowmaking genome, an elemental mantra, which if followed assures bowmaking success.

The Mantra: Make inner limbs wide or long enough for virtually no set. Make midlimbs wide enough for little set. Make outer-limbs and tips narrow enough for lowest possible mass.

A couple of notes on tiller shape complete the picture. If a limb's front-view shape is triangular then even thickness along the length of the limb results in near perfect arc of a circle tiller, with all portions of the limb feeling about equal strain. Some slight elliptical tillering may still be in order, to prevent inner-limb set from projecting out to large string follow.

The more a limb's front-view shape changes from triangular to parallel the more elliptical the tiller must be. Such limbs are thicker near the grip and thicker wood can't bend as far without failing.

Tiller shape is also affected by bow length. Due to changing string angles short bows stack less if tillered to bend more near the grip, thus requiring wider near-grip limbs. In all cases the outer reaches of the limb should be relatively stiff; this explained further on.

Whip tillering reduces the amount of wood available for storing energy and shortens the bow during the draw, both leading to lower stored energy. Per the 74" Pecan, discussed later, apparent elliptical tiller is proper for very long bows of normal draw weight, draw length, and arrow mass.

In general, though, the longer the bow the more elliptical the tiller, unless high draw weight or long draw length requires near-grip wood to store its share of energy.

The master examples of shortbow tiller are Ishi's bows, and many short Pacific Coast bows. They let the grip work too, for purer circular tiller compared to same-length stiff-handled bows. They were wide bows, the handles also wide for our tastes, but narrowed compared to the main limbs (see combination Ishi-pyramid bow, pg. 125).

Where Energy is Stored in a Bow Limb

Engineer David Dewey computed the numbers for several dissimilar bow designs. The percentage of energy stored in the outer 20% of limb length averaged about 6%.

Here's the breakdown for a uniform-stress D-longbow:
Inches from center - energy
  0 — 7" 30%
  7 – 14" 27%
14 – 21" 22%
21 – 28" 15%
28 – 35" 6%

The fact that so little energy is stored in the outer limbs frees us to design stiff, narrow, light outer limbs, reducing limb vibration/energy loss both directly and indirectly. (see Limb Vibration pg. 140)

Design and Taste

When using lower SG wood a given draw weight bow might be too wide for some tastes. Making a longer bow is the answer. But at a certain draw weight, many woods would be both too wide and too long for taste or function. This is where denser woods are needed.

When fairly new to bowmaking, or given uncertain materials, make bows wider and longer than assumed necessary. If set is unusually low at desired draw weight and length then limb mass is too high. Narrow and shorten the limbs bit by bit until moderate set is reached at intended draw weight. Only light touch-up tillering will be needed as shortening proceeds.

Arrow Weight

For a given weight bow, heavy arrows need high energy storage, light arrows need high dry-fire speed (dry-fire speed is explained starting at the bottom of page 83, *TBB 3*).

Limb Corner Rounding Test

Black poplar, .41 SG. Perfectly rectangular section, 1.5" wide and 3/4" thick at grip. Parallel width for 1/4 of limb, then straight taper to 1/2" nocks. Elliptical tiller. Mass = 17.1 oz. 38 lb draw weight. Tested at 25.5" draw (this is a 50 lb at 30" bow). Back and belly corners were rounded, creating oval sides, the center 1/2 of back and belly width kept flat. Bow mass dropped to 15 oz and poundage to 33 lbs, draw weight falling roughly in step with limb mass.

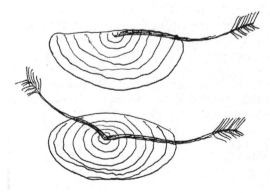

Flat is usually best, but a crowned belly is called for when the stave is a small-diameter sapling or branch having a good-sized pin sprouting out at 3 or 9 o'clock. On a flat belly such pins can run across the surface from the core outward, reducing belly strength by nearly half at that point. The same pin on a crowned belly can only occupy an area slightly larger than pin diameter.

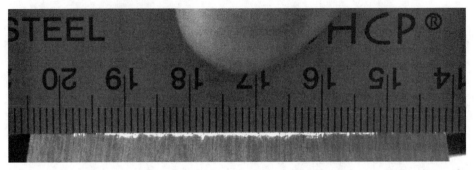

What the Poisson effect might mean for bow design: When rectangular limbs are bent, concaving elevates the back edges, placing them under greater strain. A very slight convex arching of the unbraced back should cause the drawn back to rest flat, with uniform strain across its width, the tension-safest condition. At least a good rounding of the back edge seems called for, especially with tension-weak woods.

Poisson Effect

Two 2.25" by about 1/2"-thick slats. One of rectangular section. The other sawn to a V-section, 1/8" thick at each edge and a 1/2" wide crown left at belly center. 15" of each was placed hanging over a bench edge, 5" resting on the bench, secured by C-clamps. A metal straight edge resting across the sample width, with hard light behind it, displayed a perfectly straight razor-thin perforated line of light. The straight edge was resting about 4" past the table edge. When the rectangular sample was bent downward like a drawn bow limb a distinct concave arc of light appeared under the straight edge. When the 'crowned' belly sample was bent the same a distinct convex pattern of light appeared. About 1/32" at the deepest in each case.

The concave result with the rectangular sample is normal Poisson effect. I don't know if the reverse effect on the 'crowned' sample has a name. Different woods show the Poisson effect to different degrees. For narrow limbs the effect is likely too small to consider. The belly was convexed into a slight "D", roughly matching the back's concave cupping. This seems to argue for creating slight concavity here, so that at full draw the belly would be flat again, for maximum compression resistance. But except for especially wide limbs simply leaving the belly perfectly flat should be good enough.

Of course these are all baseline considerations: Given the different tension and compression properties of different woods, accommodations would be made accordingly.

Trapezoidal Sections

Since wood is normally so much stronger in tension than compression, back wood on a rectangular-section bow does less work than belly wood. A trapped bow would not only gain by back mass reduction, it would gain again by forcing tension wood to do more stretching, storing more energy with reduced mass. A double plus. If more work is being done by the back then less need be done by the belly. Belly wood is then less strained, and takes less set, or can be a touch narrower, for more mass savings. A triple plus.

But, a bow is still a bow until its back breaks, so it's generally safer to avoid trapping. However, it's clear that in many cases trapping is a proper option, if done skillfully. The above triple benefit may tip the scale for many. For most though, especially if desiring safety over a few more fps, flat or nearly flat backs are better.

Crowned staves of most woods safely yield faster bows, and trapped backs can too. Properly trapped backs can even be safer, there being more working width at the point of greatest strain. Engineer David Dewey calculated safe strain levels for this redoak's back and belly wood, and trapped the back accordingly. The resulting bow performed especially well, and with a prudent margin of safety.

Reverse Trapping

If made to dimensions that yield normal set, tension-weak woods, black cherry, for example, are in danger of their backs breaking. If extra care is taken to avoid back fiber violation, and extra tillering care taken to insure uniform limb strain, then a normal-design black cherry bow will hold together, becoming one of the sweetest-releasing, fastest shooting bow woods of all. At only about .50 SG, its back needs to be the width of most other .50 SG woods to be safe. But its belly can be ".65 SG narrow," so to speak, a reverse trapezoid, narrower on the belly than the back. If a stave's back is unsafe for species or other reasons, reverse trapping, or a crowned belly, will increase safety.

Heat Trapping

As MC falls to low levels belly wood become stiffer, back wood not rising in strength to match it. In effect, the back is trapped, though not geometrically. A truly trapped bow would more be more and more likely to fail as RH falls to increasingly lower numbers.

Decrowning

Decrowning is seldom required. Wide limbs made from small-diameter staves obviously must be decrowned, to keep draw weight manageable. Otherwise only especially tension-weak wood or suspect back surfaces benefit.

DESIGN INGREDIENTS APPLIED

Enhanced Andaman-Holmegaard Designs

First presented on pages 47 and 88 of *TBB 3*, versions of this design likely yield the fastest possible straight bows. The principle: Outer limbs store little energy (see Where is Energy Stored in a Bow Limb, earlier) so there is little cost in tillering them to imperceptible bend. Benefits of resulting vibration suppression are explained on pg. 140. Such stiff limbs also allow narrowest/lightest possible outer limbs, for additional performance benefits. See "The Flax Plant as Teacher," for further limb-lightening ideas.

Advantages of these designs were broadly explained on various on-line archery forums, but until fairly recently they were rarely made. The design is becoming more

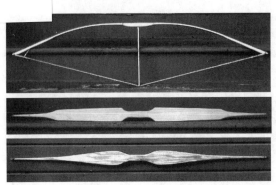

Even if not so extremely executed, lessons learned from these enhanced Andaman-Holmegaard designs can be applied to every bow.

popular now. Dan Perry, of this volume's flight shooting chapter and of Perry Reflex fame, recently won its divisions world flight record using a well-executed Andaman-Holmegaard bow.

The Andaman-Holmegaard can be shrunken or stretched to extremes. For example, the 76" straight stave bow on page 122, a simple stick of pecan lumber, its design alone letting it out-perform all yew, Osage, Perry reflexed, sinew-backed, and re-curved contenders at the MoJam several years ago (see the first MoJam bow test stats, pg. 110). Adjusted for differences in arrow and string mass, this bow shot 169 fps; it and related designs were the three fastest contenders. Next below this group was an Osage recurve.

The Andaman-Holmegaard, pictured below, is begging to be pulled into large re-flex, only its wide working area sinewed. This might be the fastest possible sinew/wood bow. Sinew is twice as heavy as bow wood, and since it's not needed on the outer limb for performance or protection it makes sense to keep sinew off the outer limb. Sinew can be feathered to zero thickness a few inches into the barely bending portion of the limb. The ends of such feathered sinew will not try to lift when strained. Since wood of these dimensions can't break unless it first bends, such barely-bending outer limbs need no backing protection, assuming the wood is sound.

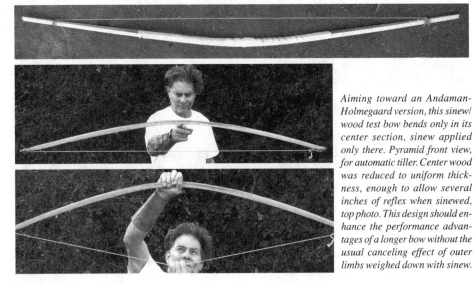

Aiming toward an Andaman-Holmegaard version, this sinew/wood test bow bends only in its center section, sinew applied only there. Pyramid front view, for automatic tiller. Center wood was reduced to uniform thickness, enough to allow several inches of reflex when sinewed, top photo. This design should enhance the performance advantages of a longer bow without the usual canceling effect of outer limbs weighed down with sinew.

A Composite Longbow

If the Andaman/Holmegaard bow's main bending portions were thinned and pulled into 15" or more reflex, horn placed on the belly of just that working area, with sinew above, it might be the fastest possible hunting-weight natural-materials bow.

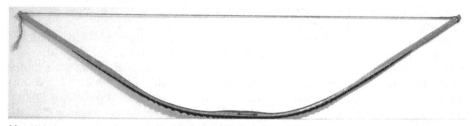

Most Asiatic composites have substantial siyahs, which create stability problems unless well reinforced. The extra mass of siyahs and required wider/thicker outer limbs results in middling cast in hunting-weight versions. This narrow-limbed prototype A-H composite longbow had the combined good features of a longbow and an Asiatic composite. Shown strung backwards, to maintain reflex as sinew dried. Note how wood thickens as horn thins on belly side. Later models will be wide and flat in the near-grip bending area, allowing greater reflex. Best wooden self bows presently about equal the cast of hunting-weight composites, often out-performing them. At circa 60 lb and lower weights it's hoped this design will well outshoot both.

The bow's 12" of reflex being wrestled through 19" of tip travel to brace position. The great looking gemsbok grooves were left raised, in order to see how much punishment such horn geometry could take before failing. We half expected the bow to blow while being braced, but it stayed in one piece.

The red oak core was tillered to bend evenly and to this tiller shape, but adding sinew was a bit more of a random process. Putting the sinew on three layers of same-size, evenly-spaced bundles aided uniformity. Still, it was surprising that tiller needed no adjustment. Sinew was recycled from an earlier experimental bow. It was applied in one session, and dried for three weeks in about 50% RH. Most of the compression work was being done by narrow, deep valley portions of the horn. Hard to believe it held up at this draw length. Its low 36 lb draw weight helped.

Easier to make than conventional composites, just the near grip portion of the pic-tured 3/4"-wide narrow prototype is horn/wood/sinew. Bending only occurs there, with the horn and sinew feathering out to zero by mid limb, wood thickening to match. The outer limb is very narrow, stiff, and light. In the top photo, previous page, limbs rest at 12" of reflex. The design idea: high energy storage via large reflex, permitted by horn/sinew, with stiff, light, outer limbs for speed.

Being just 3/4"wide in the bending area, and almost as thick, and with that much reflex, some lateral warping was inevitable. If the outer limbs had been left extra wide they could have been made to track true by narrowing the outbound side. Without that option the bow was instead shortened 10 inches, to create width for such narrowing. That went well, but the bow was then too heavy for the corrugated horn, and at its next full draw it began surrendering at one of the deeper grooves, visibly crushing the core. It didn't blow, but lost its even tiller and punch. Before this, it out-shot any circa-60 lb or lower traditional composite I've yet encountered. Bad light prevented chronographing, so no precise speeds are available. This design has good potential, and for a composite is quite easy to make. The next model will be a version of the extreme Andaman Island/Holmegaard design, as on page 88 of *TBB 3*, made with 15" or more reflex, with the same stiffness for most of limb length, and extremely light outer limbs. Horn ridges will be flattened next time.

A Stretched-out Andaman-Holmegaard

Before heading to the MoJam Shootout this bow had launched countless arrows, skied down hillsides, been thrown out of trees, and even after the worrisomely high Missouri humidity it still holds only 3/4" of string follow. In short, good design will yield high speed with equally high safety and durability. It is, of course, a *Mantra* bow.

Very long bows can be sluggish if tillered incorrectly. Front-view shape is impor-tant here for mass reasons, but complementing subtleties of tiller are as important. To get the most out of this design each portion of the limb is tillered as if a separate type of bow: Grip - Stiff, non-bending. The center two-feet of this bow is virtually stiff, bending well short of taking set, yet accounting for a few inches of tip movement during the draw, causing main-bending portions to take less set than otherwise. This portion largely serves to lengthen the bow in order to achieve a low string angle for low stack/high energy storage. Mid-inner limb - Only working enough to take insig-nificant set. Set here would project out to large tip deflection (string follow). But this area needs to bend all it can, short of taking significant set, so that the mid and mid outer limbs take as little set as possible. Mid limb - The bow has to bend a lot some-where, and this is the best place. Set is taken here where it has less distance to project out to tip-measured string follow. Eiffel Tower outer limbs: this portion actually sweeps

The pecan MoJam test bow. Essentially it's TBB 3's Andaman-Holmegaard, stretched out to 76". This is an extremely fast, smooth drawing, sweet-shooting, durable and accurate design.

Quarter-inch wide tips are too narrow for conventional nocks. A stepped tie-on nock, weighing just 10 grains, was used on the pecan A-H bows. The step helped prevent wear on the narrow tips. These nocks could be glued in place, but tying allowed nocks to be moved, for micro-tiller adjustments in the field, or raising and lowering of draw weight.

inward, becoming narrower than an already narrow straight-line pyramid design. Being so narrow, this wood is thicker than nearby gripward portions of the limb, therefore it does not bend as much as otherwise. Tip - Extremely narrow, non-bending needle tip.

It may seem that too much emphasis is being made in these pages on narrower, stiffer, lighter outer limbs. It seems this way only because not enough emphasis has been given to these design features in the past. This is simply where the physics leads.

An 80" Sister Version

From the same board as the above 76" pecan: *The Mantra* applies here, too: Inner wood is wide or long enough to take no set, the midlimb wide enough to take little set, the outer limbs narrow and stiff for low moving mass and reduced vibration. Regardless of bow length, this is the formula for sweet shooting, durable, high-cast bows.

At 80" a bow is quite stable and accurate and has a pleasantly stackless draw. With their 80" the old English Warbow makers bought poundage and draw length. This 80-incher bought low set and narrow, stiffer outer limbs. A bow of this length and design is ideal for target shooting and 'normal-arrow' flight shooting. It's too long for comfortable hunting for many. It too is just a stretched out version of the shorter A-H bow, above.

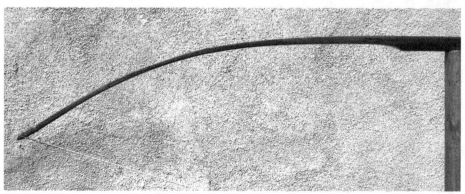

Note long, stiff center section, giving this 80 " bow a whip-tillered appearance. The near-grip "limb" looks like limb wood, but barely bends. In effect, the bow's center 18" is barely bending grip wood. Put another way, it's a normal length bow with stiff extra length spliced in at the grip. This allows the low inertia of a short bow with the low stack and high energy storage of a long bow.

The bow was designed and tillered for a 28" draw at 48 lb. Steve Gardner chronographed it at 30.5" and 54 lb and recorded a well-witnessed 191fps, using a semi flightshooter's draw and release. A slower draw and release would yield about 180 fps. Before being stressed at 30", 28" at 48 lbs and a more normal release yielded 174 fps at 10-grains. A least that's the best I could get out of it.

Shame on us for taking pleasure from this, but several fiberglass guys had drifted over while we were chronographing the 80-incher. They launched a few arrows, with patronizing body language, intending to show us what glass would do next to wood. The sputtering comments of disbelief as our same-poundage pecan outshot their glass pretty much made our day.

We were tempted to say, "Yeah, that's all we can get out of those $6 boards, but the $8 versions are pretty good." But that would just be wrong. We probably should have mentioned that Steve holds a mantel full of world flight records.

The bow: Pecan, board, heartwood, some sapwood showing on one edge. Bias-ringed. About 12 rings per inch, about 10% early wood. Rectangular section. 9% - 10% moisture content. 80" tip to tip, 79.25" ntn. 160-grain linen string. 500-grain arrow. Braced 5" from the back. 1-11/16" at the fades; 1-1/4" midlimb. Straightline

An Andaman-Holmegaard, mid-limbs a touch too wide for best speed, to provide "canvas" for the alligator gar design. This particular bow is stiff-handled, a red oak board stave, perfectly flat back and belly, 64" ntn. 2.5" wide at the fades, 2" wide where it begins to sweep into an Eiffel Tower shape, tie-on nocks 1/4" wide, 1/2" wide 6" from the nock, 53 lb at 28"; 172 fps with a 10-grains/lb arrow, normal draw speed, no hold time and clean release. The bow weighs 24 oz., most of that up near the grip and is slow moving. Most of the bend is in the inner one-third, almost none beyond that. Symmetrical tiller.

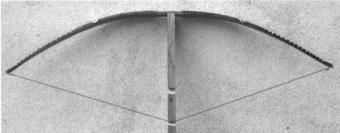

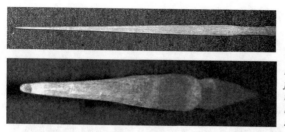

Views of a roughed-out 68" Andaman-Holmegaard. From a bird's-eye view it's difficult to see the subtle Eiffel-Tower outer limb. A nock to nock view shows the outer limb narrowing more severely than a straight-line taper.

taper to 1/4" nocks. Tie-on back nocks. The bow's long length yields a pleasant no-stack draw, gaining only about 2 lb of weight per inch at full draw. Before shooting, the bow showed 3/4" of set. After testing, just-unbraced set was 1". Two hours later: 7/8", all this indicating an extremely understrained bow.

Only two such bows were made. The design was not fine-tuned and idealized. Tinkering would squeeze a few more FPS, while maintaining durability and its other good features.

For Andaman-Holmegaard designs to be efficient outer limbs must be narrower than normal outer limbs, not just narrower than its extra wide inner limbs. Some replications of this design are wide enough near the grip, but have outer limbs no narrower than typical, so perform no better than typical designs.

A Combined Ishi-Pyramid Bow

Here's a moderately simple design, moderately easy and quick to make, and an exceptionally good performer, especially for a mid-length, mid-drawlength bow. Red oak board stave, 60" t/t, 59-1/4" ntn, 57 lbs at 23"; braced 4.5" from belly; 5" handle 1 5/8" wide, slightly-working Ishi-like handle and fades; 8" total handle/fade length; limb 2" at widest, straight line width taper aiming to a point at tips - a true triangle; 1/2" wide 5" from tips - the last 2" kept 1/4" wide for tie-on nocks; perfectly rectangular section, near circular tiller (stiffish handle area) the last 5" essentially stiff; just-unbraced set, 3/4", resting set, 5/8"; estimated MC: 9%; 16 oz. mass weight. 75-grain string; shot a couple of dozen times before final chronographing; 560-grain arrow = 172fps; 226fps with 220-grains. Steve Gardner shooting; draw and release time about 2 seconds, the last several inches drawn quickly. A typical linen string would weigh about 125 grains, bringing that speed to about 170 fps. Judging by its low set and lack of weight loss during the shooting session, draw weight or fps per pound should not fall significantly over time. The grip is too wide for most tastes. If narrowed to 1 1/4", with needed reduced bend in the handle area, performance and set would be about identical if the bow was a couple of inches longer.

Reasons for its high performance: Pure pyramid front-view shapes yield very light outer limbs. Its slightly working handle and fades reduce strain and set elsewhere, and benefit string angle slightly. Though small, that slight handle area bend yields a couple of inches of tip movement. Almost arc-of-circle tiller, except for the grip area. Several inches of near-tip stiffness slightly aids string angle and lowers vibration. Fairly low brace and short draw yielded unusually small set - meaning the wood is only lightly strained, the wood not broken down. The handle and fades were reduced along with the rest of the bow during the tillering process, so that their slight bending could have their effect on proceeding draw weight and tiller shape. That slight amount of handle bend can't be accurately judged by the eye, only felt in the hand. The triangle part of

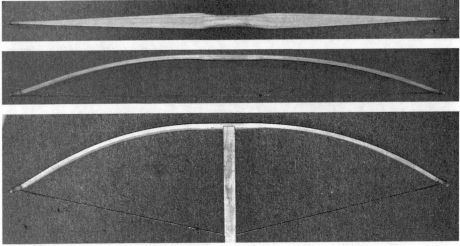

The combined Ishi-pyramid bow. Steve Gardner and I combined have tested over 5000 bows. This 57 lb at 23" red oak board bow is the fastest straight self-bow either of us has ever tested at this draw length.

the design is courtesy of Hickman and Klopsteg from the 1930's. The working grip and fades are from Ishi.

Possible improvements: The stave was perfectly sound and straight-ringed on the back, so substantial trapping would have been possible, saving mass and taking some load off the belly. The outer third of each limb could have been Eiffel-Towered a bit and left a touch thicker for lower moving limb mass.

A 27 lb. Kid's Bow

Red oak, medium density. Flat back, square sides, very slightly crowned belly; 27 lbs at 24"; 70" ntn; 1 1/16" grip/widest; 3/4" wide 18.5" from nocks; 5/8" wide 15" from nocks; 1/2" wide 10" from nocks; 3/8" wide 6.5" from nocks. Tips sharpened to points, linen wrap-on collar nocks. A D-bow with extremely narrow and light outer limbs. Resting string follow: 1 1/8". Mass: 13.25 oz. 163 fps with a 296-grain arrow, 160-grain string (6-grains/lb)]. 166 fps estimated with a 3-grain string. The best I could get was 156 fps.

The 27 lb kid's bow, front view and tiller profile, veteran bowyer Tom Mahr at the helm. Very light outer limbs. Possible improvements: Wider near-grip wood for lower follow, this giving the outer limb an Eiffel-Tower look. The outer limbs could have been stiffer, and trapped for lower moving mass.

For lightweight bows to be efficient their outer limbs must be proportionately narrower and thinner, sometimes becoming too narrow to allow side-groove or pin nocks. One option is to sharpen the tip belly to a fairly steep angle and wrap on a Life-Saver shaped collar of flax, sinew or such, lightly soaked with glue. Tiny loops fit over these.

A "Black" Oak Bow

A 55" 40 lb at 24" red oak D-bow, shot 188 fps with 300 grains, slash draw and release; 176 fps with a 2-second draw and release. 1 1/8" at grip/widest, 1/2" nocks, 5/16" midlimb; 1 1/8" follow; 11.5oz mass; 150-grain string. "Black" oak because it's painted black.

The Mantra*: Make inner limbs wide or long enough for virtually no set. Make midlimbs wide enough for little set. Make outer-limbs and tips narrow enough for lowest possible mass.*

But short bows need a slightly different mantra: Inner limbs bend more, so set will be taken there with no more cost to string follow than for midlimb set on long bows.

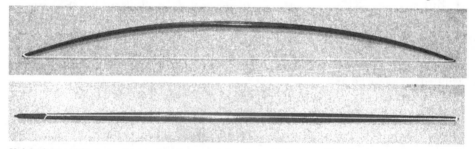

Unless designed for a short draw, short bows must bend more in the inner limb, far more so than long bows. Whip-tillered shorter bows become shorter in tip-to-grip length during the draw, increasing string angle at full draw, increasing stack and reducing energy storage even further than typical for shorter bows. So mid and outer limbs should bend a little less, inner limbs a little more.

Horn-Sinew Composites

Good hunting-weight straight selfbows outshoot most present hunting-weight Asiatic composites. Occasionally an expensive imported composite will appear at a woodbow meet where bows are being chronographed. It's a difficult moment, because we know our simple wood bows will outshoot the composite, and know its owner doesn't know this, and that he doesn't want to know this. We try to avoid the comparison. Possibly the best hunting weight composites from the past would outshoot same-weight best wood bows by a few fps. The potential is there.

Inaccurate performance mythology surrounds horn-sinew composites. This can give woodbow makers and archers groundless genus envy. It's good to counter such myths. They're probably due to the great distances gotten by Turkish and similar flight bows

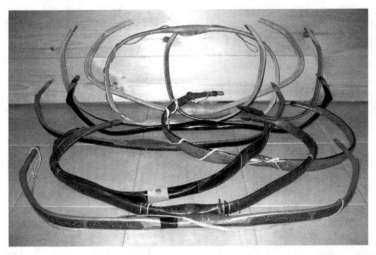

Some of the style and poundage composites made and tested by Asiatic composite scholar Adam Karpowicz. Due to faithfulness to original materials, designs and construction techniques, and rigorous testing procedures, there may be no better person past or present to compare the capacities of Asiatic composites to wooden selfbows. Adam concludes that best composite flight bows and heavier "war" designs out perform best wooden selfbows, but that in sub-60 lb weights the two are comparable. He explains this by noting that outer limb weight needed to insure limb stability is similar in both lighter and war-weight designs.

shooting lightweight arrows, and heavy composites warbows do outshoot heavy wood bows.

Except for research, curiosity, tradition, or esthetics no one in the know would make or buy a hunting-weight version. They're orders of magnitude more effort to make and maintain, and bring home no more meat than a sapling that's been properly whittled for a few hours.

When all factors are calculated, simple, ancient, primitive wood bows are the best choice for roving, hunting, and target shooting, the normal uses of bows by typical archers.

It's worth noting that horn composites which equal good woodbow normal-use performance are the antithesis of primitive bows; they could only and would only be made by complex advanced civilizations. Meanwhile, the simple, noble, easy and quick to build, effortless to maintain, primitive wooden bow casts a thousand arrows for every one cast by elaborate horn and sinew; archers voting with their arrows.

The Case For Symmetrical Tiller

On a 60" bow, for example, the center of the handle will be at 30". Bow limbs are of equal length and have identical tiller shape. On a tillering board the belly is supported at the 30" mark, the string contacted at a point dead square to that. When drawn, the bow hand's center of force is placed exactly at the 30" center point, preferably at the crotch formed by the base of the thumb and first finger. The 'V' center of force against the string is placed square to this. At brace and during the draw all forces and strains are mirror-image identical in each limb. A perfectly symmetrical bow in all measures.

The arrow rests about 5/8" above dead bow center. Because there are two fingers below the arrow and one above, the center of force on the string is below the arrow, exactly even with bow center.

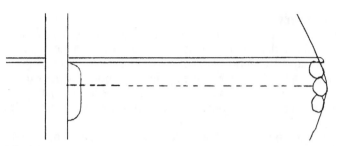

The dashed line makes contact at bow center where the hand's center of force rests, and at the center of force against the string with three fingers under the arrow.

At the instant before release there is perfect symmetry of forces and strains. The arrow is resting 5/8" or so above bow and string center, so after release, as the string drives the arrow forward, and at string impact, forces are therefore not in perfect balance. There is no way to have all forces perfectly balanced both during the draw and after release, without shooting through a hole in the hand and the bow. Symmetrical tiller seems the best compromise.

Should a bow be too heavy for shooting with a small pressure point a lower-in-the-hand grip would be needed. A three-fingers-under draw would return balance. Not a comfortable choice for some. The other option is a somewhat asymmetrical bow. Shooting with three fingers under puts the arrow nock closer to the eye, reducing parallax, increasing aiming accuracy at most wood bow hunting distances.

A symmetrical bow has the following advantages:
- With perfectly symmetrical tiller as the goal, the eyes know exactly how to match proper tiller in both limbs. Tillering is easier, faster, better.
- The bow can be reversed: A bow always shoots better from one side than the other. It can be reversed again if different arrows favor such.
- Tiller can migrate over the life of a bow; the option of reversing the bow can be useful in such cases.
- With moving mass and travel distance equal in both limbs, string impact will more likely be simultaneous, more impact energy transferred to the arrow.
- If a bow does not shoot well the bowmaker doesn't have a floating variable to weigh when trying to improve performance of future bows.
- With an asymmetrical bow there is no way to know when any of the features of one limb correctly complement the other limb - if one limb is made shorter/stiffer there is no way to know precisely how much shorter or stiffer to create a proper match to the longer limb, so such a limb will necessarily either be over-strained or carry more mass than needed; if one limb is shorter yet is pulled to equal bend it will be overstrained unless made wider; if one limb is made wider, different masses are being propelled forward at release, yielding discord at impact; if one limb is shorter but stiffer/pulled to lesser bend, that limb is not storing as much energy as it would if same-length, unless made narrower.

I can't imagine building a sailboat with the keel one-inch off-center then arranging ballast to compensate. Beauty is usually right, in boats, bridges, nature, and design of bows.

On the other hand, asymmetrical bows have fed and protected countless numbers over the eons. With ballast properly adjusted an off-center keeled boat will transport its cargo well enough.

Straightbow vs Recurve

Part of the reason we make bows of wood rather than glass is our attraction for their elemental, uncomplicated, primordial nature - and the idea that these simple and most ancient machines can perform the wonders they do. This is most strongly felt for the most ancient and simplest of all bows, the straight self bow. The idea that these most primitive weapons, fashioned with no more than sharpened stones, can perform as well or better than later more complicated and difficult to make upstarts is especially appealing.

The accuracy of a long straight bow is legendary. Their durability is unmatched. And if scraped to a certain shape they can outspeed almost all contenders. I personally have yet to see a self-wood recurve equal the speed of a best-design self longbow. Recurves store more energy, so at first thought they should shoot faster. Here are some the reasons this is usually not true.

Recurves slam home harder, so they need heavier strings. Recurves initially accelerate slower and arrive home faster, generating more energy-absorbing string stretch and limb vibration during that most critical stage of energy transfer. Outer limb and recurve area must be heavier to withstand twisting. Storing more energy, recurves increase wood strain. Put another way, storing more energy, recurves need more wood mass to store that energy. Straight bows shoot faster if longer, but the longer a recurve bow the lower the percentage of length devoted to recurve, unless the recurve length is increased, leading to even more tip mass. Fastest straight bows can also be the most durable, because one of the same features making them fast also makes them safe: bow length.

Fastest straight bows are no harder to make than slow straight bows. It's simply a matter of scraping here instead of there. The formula is simple: The Mantra, in italics earlier.

TBB Vol. 1 reported recurves having better speed than straight bows, before the full benefit of reduced outer limb mass was understood.

Straightbow vs Sinewed

Make the best simple straight selfbow you can. Once worked in it shoots, say, 170 fps with a ten-grain/lb arrow. It is easy to make, easy to maintain, physically stable, easy to brace. Make a wood-based bow that gets the best from sinew (highly reflexed and recurved). It shoots very little faster, if at all, requires world-class skill and several times longer to make, is more difficult to maintain, is more susceptible to moisture, and less physically stable and more difficult to brace.

There are reasons to make recurves. For one, they're beautiful. And there's the challenge of mastering the construction of such bows. These alone are reasons enough to make a few.

The bow in America is only about 2000 years old. Possibly many native N. American recurves are design memories of Asiatic composites. Short, long-draw bows need some recurve to prevent the string pulling off the bow at full draw. Contact recurves also reduce stack at full draw, for greater drawing comfort.

Except for the rare exception (the Wilcox Duoflex, for example), wood-based "working" recurves don't really work, in that they don't open up to any great extent. They therefore yield no significant performance advantages over static recurves. If wood-based working recurves are short, and open up enough to matter, they'll break. If enough limb length is involved in the recurve to prevent breaking they're relatively unstable due to twisting. But if they did open up, and did occupy a good percentage of limb length, they would not only yield a contact recurve's normally fatter F/D, the limbs would also become longer at full draw, increasing leverage and lowering string angle, for even less stack and more stored energy. Static recurves cause a bow to have higher early draw weight, storing more energy than a straight bow. Recurves do add mass to the outer limbs, so well-made straight and recurved bows end up performing about the same, the straight bow being much less trouble to make and maintain.

Backed Working Recurves

Such bows can be more durable, but I don't know of one with much string contact to have lasted long if it near fully straightened out. The key here is the amount of strain. A mild recurve has a better chance of surviving, but if mild it doesn't do much, yet still needs to be quite wide in the bending area, raising mass, this wiping out its intended speed advantage, if that was the aim. The Duoflex, a long sweeping deflex/ working recurve design, (see *TBB 3* p.77) is far less strained at any point along the recurve, so is much more durable, but its recurve length creates stability problems. Tillering true working recurves is one of the most delicate balancing acts in all of bowmaking. Any variation of moisture content, any over-straining when braced or drawn, and the house of cards begins to shift. Meanwhile, a simple well-designed ancient straight bow spits arrows year after year with no worry.

When recurves outshoot straight bows it's usually because the straight bow has not taken advantage of its trump card: the ability to have very narrow, very light outer limbs and tips at no sacrifice to durability or stability.

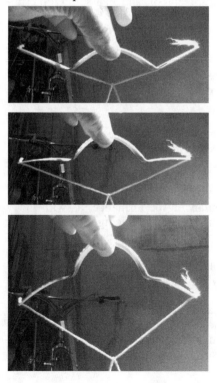

Modeling a proposed design's stored energy without a computer: Cut proposed front view shapes from, say, the bottom of a plastic food tray. Heat and bend to any desired side-view design. Let cool then brace the test bow. Plot its F/D curve with a postage scale and string.

Longbows vs Shortbows

Longbow limbs are their own stabilizers. Longbows store more energy, allow low-stack full draws, and lower draw weight per arrow speed, all promoting more accurate shooting.

One of the cruel realities of bow design is that shorter straight bows can't be as fast per pound as longer straight bows, even at equal draw length. Between 35" and 60" possible performance rises roughly 1 fps per inch of bow length. Cast rises slowly from there to around 68", then only minor improvement from there to 80", and only then if given more elliptical tiller.

Out past 75" the gain is small, ever increasing string mass eating up ever more of length benefits. But let tiller or outer limb mass stray and cast can plummet. If draw length or draw weight is increased then tiller shape can be less strongly elliptical, putting inner-limb wood fully to work.

Short Bow Plusses

Short bows are easier to maneuver in brush or blinds or on horseback. Less wood is needed, therefore staves are easier to find, and the bow easier to make. They're lighter and more convenient to carry. Short bowstrings are easier to make and weigh less and the materials easier to acquire and process. Short bows take less space and are more convenient to carry. They're also quite endearing. A random sampling of Eastern Woodland artifacts reveals average bow lengths to have been 56"; Central and Western bows were even shorter. When bows used for organized war are factored out, aboriginal bow lengths around the world may have averaged in the low 50's, this under real-life, make-meat-or-starve conditions. Steel tools and an assured food supply may be skewing our design criteria when replicating primitive bows.

PLANT BACKINGS

Only man would remake a tree. The easiest way to protect a bow from breaking is with WOOD - wood in the form of a wider or longer bow.

A Bow is Still a Bow Until its Back Breaks

Wood is stronger in tension than compression, so it could be said that wood is naturally self-backed, that if backings were needed trees would have invented them. In this sense, backing is only needed for defective back wood, or rare, tension-weak woods not truly qualifying as bow wood.

The purpose of most backings is to keep a bow from breaking. But backing can also allow designs impossible in wood alone, enhancing performance, as with Perry Reflexing; sinew allowing otherwise overstrained designs; reducing set by stretching easier/farther than the belly compresses; decoration; moisture protection; correcting tiller and hinges; raising draw weight.

Backing is far overused, often taking the place of knowledge, thought and craft. Bowmaking is so much simpler and easier when backing is largely put out of the mind.

For the beginner, backing may slow the learning process - it's a tough call, but maybe a beginner needs to let bows break if they should break. This is valuable feedback. And there's this: a self-bow can be completed in the time it takes to apply a backing and wait for it to cure, and two board staves can be purchased for the price of a typical backing strip.

OK, there is no instructive reason at all to show this photo, but it's just too evil looking not to. That's a slack string, the lemon (citrus) branch naturally bowed. Thank goodness this will allow the bow to be eternally braced - imagine wrestling a string onto that thing every day. With a barely taut string at brace this bow can be drawn to near double the draw weight of an all-else-equal straight version.

Wood-slat Backing

Most wood bowmakers work with wood instead of fiberglass because some kind of internal light turns on inside knowing they're walking in the footsteps of their ancient hunter ancestors. Machined-flat slat bows could not reasonably have existed in pre-civilization eras. Even within this paleocentric view, mainly for reasons of economy, such backing is sometimes a legitimate expedient, just as board staves are.

Backing a Lighter Wood with a Denser Wood

Most tension work is done at and near a limb's surface, so even very thin too-strong backings, if full width, are out of balance with the lighter-wood belly, crushing belly fibers as a result, increasing visible and hidden set. In such cases, thin the backing, but also narrow its surface, creating a trapezoidal shape. By appropriately narrowing a strong-wood backing it can be made to have any desired net tension resistance, lowering the neutral plane, causing the back to stretch and do work, storing its fair share of energy per mass, and reducing belly strain. Trapping will allow backings to be precisely tuned to match the limb's compression wood. Hickory over maple, or even poplar - both can be brought into balance by such trapping.

Bamboo Backing

There are more than 1000 species of bamboo. About .65 SG gross average, some species as low as .50 SG, others to .79 SG. Average bamboo is a little stronger per mass in tension than hickory. A 3/8" full-thickness sample, of the type often used for bow backing, tested at .67 SG. The outer one-quarter exceeded 1.0 SG, surface bamboo reaching about 1.4 SG.

Stretch resistance or stiffness largely parallels SG, and since a backing's surface does most of the tension work, either a thinned or full-thickness bamboo backing has over twice the effective tension stiffness of hickory, and over three times that of red oak or rock maple-like woods. This means that to prevent a bamboo back from overpowering typical belly wood it should be narrowed, not thinned. And ideally in proportion to bellywood SG - only slightly narrowed for Ipe-dense woods, narrowed about half for maple-like woods, and narrowed even more (or a less-dense backing

A trapped bamboo backing by bowyer Richard Saffold, appropriately narrowed over less dense wood. Stronger backings should narrow as the bow narrows, maintaining the same width ratios from grip to tip. The base of the narrowed backing strip should be wider, as seen here, for larger gluing surface.

used) for .50 SG and lower woods. Such narrowing should only be measured at the dense bamboo surface itself, as per a trapezoid shape.

Smaller diameter bamboo's higher crown accomplishes much the same results as trapping. The less dense the belly wood the more crowned the bamboo back can be.

Fiber Backings

Sinew, rawhide, flax, silk and other collapsible backings can't go into true compression, so if thick/strong enough the neutral plane cannot rise close enough to the back surface for the bow to break in tension.

Bow backs stretch about 1% at full draw. Most vegetable fibers, such as flax, hemp, jute and others stretch from about 1.5% to over 2.5%. Cotton stretches about 8%, sinew about the same, silk about 11%.

Linen Backing

Linen (flax) is like wood distilled down to single-duty perfection. Wood does several jobs at once so can do none of them perfectly. Flax fiber's only job is being strong in tension. Because of the spring action of twisted thread or string, combed, non-twisted linen makes a much stiffer backing. But though similar in mass, linen is several times stiffer and stronger than wood, so such a backing can overpower a belly. If managed carefully more tension work can be gotten from linen with far less mass than about any other backing material. To exploit this potential something related to trapping is needed: for example, instead of a full width too-strong combed linen backing apply narrow bands of flax glued to the back, each paralleling the limb's width and thickness taper. By laying down the correct number, thickness and width of such bands a balance of tension and compression forces can be reached. Such a limb will not only be safe, but lower in mass than an all-wood bow.

If twisted threads or strings are used their coiled spring-like nature reduces effective tension stiffness, down to wood's level if given the correct twist. When bracing a freshly made twisted bow string for the first time it lengthens considerably and takes a large permanent 'set'. A bow backing is only asked to stretch about 1%, though, so

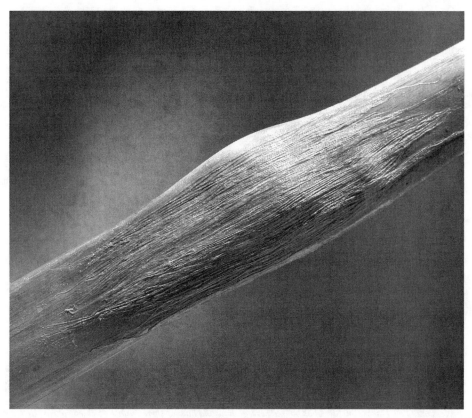

Far stronger than wood or sinew, combed linen makes a first-class hinge patch or spot-problem patch. Feather to zero once a few inches past the danger area.

would take little 'coil' set. So for all but the densest wood twisted linen or linen canvas is likely better than combed.

Linen backings look and are authentically primitive. Flax can be grown and self-processed, or long combed bundles of flax can be purchased from spinning supply shops. If unspun flax is not glued down perfectly straight and parallel it can fail, individual strands popping in succession. Not a nice sound. Linen bowstrings are strained to about the same degree as a well-designed backing, and they last for thousands of shots. Properly glued on linen backing, combed or cordage, seems to last forever.

Flax, hemp, dogbane, nettle, ramie, milkweed, and other similarly strong vegetable fibers all behave much the same. Applied like sinew, they make a bow back almost break proof. About fifty-cents worth of combed flax will do. On a longer straight-stave bow these vegetable fibers are superior to sinew. Sinew is twice as heavy as wood, has very low stretch resistance, and is sluggish unless highly reflexed as on a short horn bow.

Combed linen will allow the clichéd impossible: putting wood back on after too much has been removed. A 30 lb bow can become a 60-pounder. Not much thickness is needed either. About 1/16" of combed flax on a typical limb will do.

Cable Backings

A cable back won't hold splinters down if they decide to lift, but by taking over some of the tension load a cable backing reduces the potential splinter's urge to lift. If applied skillfully cables can reflex a bow somewhat and increase cast. Nylon is a moderately effective imitator of sinew, but being an industrial-age material the bow would no longer be a natural artifact. Nylon is a good proof-of-concept material though. 1/4" to 5/16" is a good starting diameter. Silk is natural, and moderately imitates sinew, and can easily be fashioned into a cable (see *TBB 1,* p. 110).

Sinew is the champion cable backing material, but linen, hemp, dogbane, milk-weed and other such natural fiber cables can serve moderately well if used properly. A linen cable having the cross-section area about one-eighth that of the limb will take over much of the tension load. Linen fibers only stretch about 2 to 2.5%, so they can't be preloaded to nearly the degree sinew can. If the cable is smallish in diameter and elevated at all it can snap. Linen mechanically stacks when approaching its capacity, one more negative compared to sinew.

Professional bow maker Phil Silva has backed several thousand lumber staves with 7 oz. linen canvas. He tests 28" draw bows at 31" before shipping, reporting an insignificant failure rate even when so overdrawn.

Canvas Backings

The strength of 4 oz/yd canvas backing about equals the strength of a bowstring, of about 200 lbs breaking strength. Small compared to the 2000 pounds or more of tension felt by a bow's back. Such a backing would take on about 10% of a 50 lb bow's tension load. It would have to be more than ten times stronger to overpower the belly. These are crude figures, but illustrate the idea. 10 oz/yd linen takes on about 25% of the tension load, so is quite protective, but is still far short of being stronger than the belly.

Being made of twisted threads, fabric has much higher mass per tension resistance than unspun fiber. That higher mass is then doubled because only half the threads are working in tension.

Hemp

Most hemp cordage presently available is crudely processed and made using short fibers. It's quite weak per mass. Well-processed hemp and linen are about equal in strength and elasticity. Linen is likely a touch stronger inherently, but hemp's longer fibers allow less twisting - effective individual fiber strength diminishes with increased twisting.

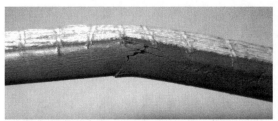

Cotton-string backed fir bow. Cotton pre-stretched to half of breaking strength, saturated with hide glue. The bow took 2.5" of just-unbraced set before breaking, 1" resting set, with the cotton shrinking back toward original length. This backing is quite protective of such light wood, but itself takes working set.

Cotton

1.5 SG, about the same as flax. Unlike all other familiar vegetable fibers, cotton takes large set. Like a stretched cotton shirt, it tends to rebound over time. So resting set looks OK while actual working set is large and cast-robbing. The hope was that hide glue might help here, but it didn't. Linen would tend to overpower the pictured fir belly. Sisal would do a better job on such light wood. Trapped backing would help too.

ANIMAL BACKINGS

Silk

Silk has a lower stretch strength than almost all vegetable fibers. For example, linen has over ten times the stiffness of silk and about the same mass. Wood has over two times silk's stretch strength at half silk's mass. Silk takes set when strained. It has a fairly high final breaking strength, but it stretches about 11% before breaking, compared to wood's about 1%, so unless pre-stressed to near capacity silk's breaking strength is not relevant.

Silk is protective of marginally endangered backs. Where appropriate, silk not only protects, but its natural luster is pleasing to the eye, especially if dyed or painted designs are added. This example, for instance, by bowyer/teacher George Tsoukalas.

Fish Skins

These tend to be weaker than the thinnest rawhide, and attractive coloring and patterns tend to wash out once dry. Sturgeon skin is an exception, and makes captivatingly beautiful backings. John Strunk's sturgeon backed bows are pure art, looking as much like a starry night as a bow back.

Snakeskin

Snakeskins are generally paper thin, doing little to prevent a back from breaking. It does repel water well, so it's sometimes used to protect a sinewed bow from the elements. Snakeskin patterns can serve well as camo; others are captivatingly beautiful and applied for that reason alone, the pictured bow being a good example.

Brazos River snakeskin over Osage, by Dan Walkolbinger.

Gut

Large animal gut can be used as a light backing. Gut is irregular and segmented, but tends to flatten out when elongated. Gut should be stretched considerably before applying. Dampen, stretch and apply as with thin rawhide.

Rawhide

Of all the primitive backing materials rawhide is most often the best choice. In a sense it's tougher than wood itself, but far more elastic. Unlike wood or sinew it's strong in all directions. Unlike some woods it doesn't overpower the bellies of light wood bows. It's not expensive, it's easy and fast to apply, and once in place it's less likely to lift when dampened than sinew. Goat or deer rawhide works well for staves needing light to moderate protection; thin cow rawhide is needed for more serious problems.

Wet rawhide will expand in length about 4%, causing it to do work as it dries, but it can be stretched more than 10% while applying, making it work more, even drawing a bow into slight reflex. Keep the strip full width its entire length when stretching, so narrow portions won't overstretch. If areas of rawhide sound and feel paper-thin try to place them at or near the grip or tip, or anywhere where they'll feel less strain.

Apply before finish tillering. Cut a strip somewhat wider than the bow (rawhide narrows when stretched). Soak thin rawhide until soft and stretchable. Stretch the rawhide as much as prudent before gluing it in place. The stretched rawhide must be set in place and tightly secured at grip and nocks. If using hide glue, and the glue jells before the strip is completely secured in place, heat the fully-bound back enough to momentarily re-liquefy the glue.

If the back is even slightly crowned, simply wrapping it every half inch or so with cloth tape or thick string will hold the hide in place while drying. If the back is flat, an artificial crown of rolled-up cloth will do. Or lay the back down flat on folded bath towels on a flat table and apply weight to the belly.

When hard dry, trim excess hide by working a file at 45-degrees to the back edge. Waterproof with the same material used to seal the bow. Before buying a hide make sure that much of it is a little longer than half the length of your bows. If the bow grip is non-working the rawhide can be butted together at grip center instead of splicing. This allows a shorter hide to serve. Otherwise use V-splices. Rawhide works well on an undulating surface.

Sinew

Given the same just-unbraced side-view profile, self bows shoot faster than sinew-backed bows. Sinew is twice as heavy as typical bow wood, but several times easier to stretch than wood, so sinew backings raise limb mass considerably, but draw weight by only a small amount. When lightly strained, as on a wood bow, sinew reacts more sluggishly than wood. Sinew's best use is allowing short straight bows or reflexed or recurved bows to survive their otherwise overstrained designs. Still, due to its elasticity and low set, sinew is the best of all energy-storing backings.

An elevated sinew cable, being farther from the neutral plane, stores more energy per mass than a conventional backing. But it's very difficult to cause a cable to reduce in diameter from grip to tip, as it must to keep cable mass proportional to limb mass. The elaborate system of knots on Inuit cable-backed bows solved this problem. Another solution is for the cable to run for just a portion-of limb length, as on page 110,

TBB 1, right-side photo. A narrow, thick, sinew ribbon glued atop a high crown may be the best use of sinew on wood. If the bow is flat-backed, crown the sinew where possible, causing it do more work per mass. Let sinew thickness and width parallel limb thickness and width taper.

When backing a crowned-back bow there is no need to apply sinew full width. Only the top of the crown is in danger. Apply a ribbon of sinew about half as wide as the limb. The sinew can be feathered out to zero when approaching the tips, or sooner, saving mass in this relatively unstrained area.

If a back is sufficiently protected with sinew, a bow could be dried and maintained at very low MC, raising not just bow weight but mainly fps per pound of bow weight. Apart from wood being much snappier in compression at low MC, sinew is snappier in tension.

If a bow has taken too much set consider turning the bow around, letting the back become the belly, and sinew backing its belly - now its back. Long bows should be shortened a few inches. Some retillering will likely be needed.

Sinew takes a bit of work to apply, and requires ongoing work to keep safe and dry for the life of the bow. This and the above reasons are likely why Woodland Indians, and most everyone else in the world, rarely used sinew on wooden bows. Sinew-backing of wooden bows was largely confined to very short or highly reflexed bows meant for specialized uses, such as the Plains horse bow and the Pacific Coast bows.

Still, somehow, there is something mighty appealing about a sinew-backed bow, and the recurved and reflexed shapes it permits.

Although making miniature bows can aid big-bow making, a subset of bowmakers, like Joe Prince, left, and Bulgaria's Illiana Vuynova, right, create them just for the fun of it. When shooing 10-grain/lb arrows these tiny weapons broaden eyes at the chronograph.

EFFICIENCY

Straight self bows, designed and tillered to about best present ability, will deliver around 175 fps at 28" with a 10-grain/lb arrow and 3-grain/lb string, about 70% efficiency. But why only 70%? Where does the other 30% of a bow's stored energy go?

Bows would be 100% efficient with either light or heavy arrows, with either light or heavy limbs, if not for limb vibration, hysteresis, string mass, string stretch and a few other less important energy stealers.

Yes, we observe that heavy-limbed bows have slower cast than light-limbed bows. And after measurements and calculations are done we see that ever-heavier arrows raise bow efficiency. It's not arrow weight in itself, though, or limb weight in itself that affects efficiency.

This screams against intuition and apparent experience. More than any other subject, arguments on this point are likely to end in fistfights down at The Bowmakers Bar.

It's important to know why our intuition is in error here, because understanding the true but hidden causes of bow inefficiency can lead to more efficient, durable, comfortable and accurate bows. And it will let us more consistently make near-70% efficient bows - most present wooden bows are in the 60% range.

About 30% of the stored energy in an efficient 10-grain/3-grain straight selfbow is stolen away from the arrow by the following factors and amounts. Even after months of work these figures are still only tentative - guys with put-men-on-the-moon engineering skills struggle to figure out the doings of a simple stick of wood with a string on it. I love it!

Limb vibration......10%
Hysterisis.............9%
String mass...........9%
String stretch.........1%
Other.....................1%

Consider this Thought-Experiment Bow
A bow having absolutely rigid limbs that attach to the handle as if with spring door hinges. Subtract energy lost to hysteresis and the small amount of friction in the springs. And say the bow gods supply a massless, stretchless string. Now, put a one hundred pound weight on each limb tip and nock a 10-grain/lb arrow. From experience with past bows we're certain that cast will be dismal, the arrow barely escaping the bow. Draw and release. The massive limbs only creep forward. However, as the string is pulled taut at string impact 100% of the bow's available energy will be imparted to the arrow. In this case, almost all of it in the last few millimeters of string travel. Due to the lack of limb vibration cast will actually be a little greater that if the limbs flexed normally and had normal mass.

Hard to accept? If so, just ask yourself this: Where else could the energy go if not into the arrow? Not into vibration - the limbs are infinitely rigid. Not string stretch - the bow gods saw to that. Not hysteresis or hinge friction - we've subtracted these already. Aliens didn't slurp it up, nor black holes in space. And energy can't just cease to exist. So regardless of limb mass, there is no other escape route for the bow's stored energy but into the arrow.

Limb Vibration
Yes, limb mass affects arrow speed in real-life bows, but only indirectly, as we see from the thought-experiment bow. Heavy limbs do accelerate more slowly, but Newton says that no matter how slowly they return they must dump their full load of energy into the arrow, or try to. Experiments and calculation by Kooi, Karpowicz, Baugh, Dewey, Case, myself, and others have shown that limb vibration typically accounts for the noted 10% efficiency reduction in a well made bow. And closer to 20% in a poorly made bow.

But how can vibration matter if the arrow is already gone? This post-departure vibration is merely the echo of energy-draining vibration/limb deformation that began before the arrow left the string. Roughly speaking, as the string slows the limb tips when approaching string impact, mid-limb mass resists being slowed, therefore bowing forward, this inertia energy now unavailable to the arrow. Handshock is that inertial energy rebounding. Part of the reason long, stiff outer limbs are more efficient is that they resist that initial bowing forward when approaching string impact.

Light mid and outer limbs increase arrow speed because, having less inertia, they don't bow as far forward when their tips are slowed by the string.

During early and mid inches of return, lighter, faster-accelerating tips cause the arrow to accelerate faster than if on a heavy-outer-limb bow, meaning less energy is left in the bow to cause mischief as the string slams home, attempting to suddenly dump all remaining energy into the arrow. Mischief in the form of string stretch and limb vibration.

Low inertia, light outer limbs and tips are best for light arrows - light limbs dry-fire faster. Lighter tips work better with heavy arrows too, but the difference is less obvious.

Hysteresis

Drop a rubber ball from four-feet high and it might bounce back three feet. Internal friction or dampening has stolen some of the ball's energy. The same is true when drawing and releasing a bow. Design and Performance, *Vol. 1* reported very low numbers for hysteresis. The test method was faulty: I noted a bow's draw weight on the way out, then again on the way back, this taking many seconds, replicating the effect of a truly massively weighted limb.

Suspecting that hysteresis in wood is higher than had been reported, Dick Baugh devised a simple but precise test and got hysteresis numbers of 10 to 20%. To check his results I made a cruder but nearly as precise version of his rig and got similar numbers.

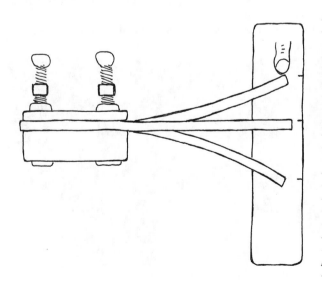

Here's a crude but fairly effective adaptation of Dick Baugh's hysteresis testing setup. Clamp a test slat of wood to an immovable object, with no wood movement except in the overhanging portion. Place a board or such so it almost touches the slat; range-of-travel marks will be recorded here. Mark the slat's position at rest, and mark where it will be pulled. Place a thumb a bit less than an equal distance on the other side of the at-rest mark. Pull the end of the slat precisely to the to-pull-to mark and release cleanly. Repeat, each time moving your thumb closer until the slat barely makes contact. Mark that spot. If the slat is pulled 10" and travels 8" past its resting position to touch the thumb, the sample's hysteresis is 20%.

Later, Steve Gardner and I used a similar test setup and got the same range of numbers. We also noted that when sample tips were weighted, somewhat as a bow limb is by string and arrow, hysteresis fell slightly. It's clear that hysteresis in a freely vibrating sample can be about 20%, but hysteresis is lower in a working bow. The math and engineering explanation is complicated and lengthy, so to save space and to avoid torturing fellow mathlexics, let engineers Dick Baugh's, David Dewey's and Alan Case's agreeing tentative number be sufficient, that number being "about 9%."

That 9% figure will surely vary slightly due to species, moisture content, degree of set, arrow weight, and more. The lab is beckoning…

Hysteresis is possibly greater in compression than tension. If so, then toasting belly wood might lower hysteresis. If hysteresis is greater in compression then a narrowed or naturally crowned back may also lower effective hysteresis, forcing the back to do more of the work.

It seems likely that hysteresis is lower in very dry wood. We know it's higher in very wet wood. Very dry wood also has less mass per draw weight. So if we can conjure up some way to keep very dry wood from breaking, or of keeping just the belly very dry, bow performance could be enhanced.

String Mass

String mass matters because stored energy is used to accelerate it, but unlike the limbs, as soon as the string begins to decelerate, the arrow leaves. The string's frustrated energy is then added to the general tantrum of other left-behind forces. String mass slows a bow as if about one-third of its mass was added to the arrow. Roughly 9% of a bow's stored energy is spent accelerating the string, given a 10-grain/lb arrow and a 3-grain/lb string.

String Stretch

Test: at replicated string-impact stress, a 4x-draw weight string stretched enough to have absorbed about 0.5% of a straight bow's stored energy. The degree of stretch and peak-impact strain was estimated by static measurements. If a dynamic test can be devised this 0.5% figure may shift somewhat.

While string stretch itself withholds a very small amount of energy it facilitates limb vibration to some presently uncalculated degree.

Steve Gardner and The Unmerciful Extractor of Truth. Note the vibrating string, the echo of lost energy.

String Angle and Stack

The angle made by the string and arrow is the important angle. The near-tip string angle is less significant. If limb and string are nearly parallel for a high percentage of limb length then braced string tension is greater, increasing early draw weight.

String Strain

Tie a spring scale into the bowstring. A straight 30 lb bow will read about 42 lbs at brace, about 36 lbs at full draw. A string which break tests at a touch below 60 lbs barely breaks at string impact.

How Does a Heavy Arrow Make a Bow More Efficient?

Heavier arrows leave a bow more slowly. When doing hysteresis tests massively-weighted, slow-moving slats (simulating the effect of very heavy arrows), showed reduced hysteresis (which likely means light arrow should increase hysteresis). Less energy is needed to propel the string slowly. And slower-returning limbs reduce string stretch. And with slowed limb return vibration is reduced. All of these make more energy available to the arrow.

Calculating standard efficiency

1. Measure stored energy: Take f/d reading at each inch of draw. Divide the total by 12 for ft/lbs of stored energy.
2. Measure kinetic energy of the arrow: Multiply arrow mass in grains by arrow velocity by arrow velocity. Divide the result by 450,240.
3. Add two zeros to this figure and divide by stored energy. For typical brace height and draw weight bows this method of noting stored energy will overestimate stored energy by about 4%. To be absolutely precise the force at each end of each inch would be averaged, starting from zero at brace height. For typical bows this work can be avoided by subtracting 4% from results using the above method.

The Most Efficient Efficiency

Standard engineering efficiency - energy in vs. energy out - can be misleading. Standard efficiency is somewhat useful when comparing performance of same-design bows but can be misleading when comparing bows of different designs. At the same draw weight, draw length and arrow weight a less efficient bow can have greater cast than a more efficient bow. For example, a 65% efficient long bow might cast an arrow 165 fps, while a same-weight, same-draw-length short bow at 70% efficiency might cast the same arrow only 150 fps. There are many such examples. Fps per draw weight pound is all that counts to an archer, is precise in all cases, and especially informative when comparing different designs

Factors Increasing Bow Efficiency

Optimum brace height.
Lowest hysteresis wood.
Toasted or low MC belly - this effect still to be tested.
High-percentage stiff outer limbs, for reduced vibration.
Low mass in mid and outer limbs, for reduced vibration and string stretch.
Trapped-backed mid and outer limbs.
Low mass per strength string material.
Low stretch string material.

A Design and Tillering Checklist
for Making Durable, Fast, Wooden Bows

Design and Layout

What do I want this bow to do—what length must it be to do it?

For this wood type, how wide must limbs be for this bow length, draw weight and draw length.

Is the crown too high for the tension strength of the wood and the width of the limb?

What flaws in the stave have to be dealt with?

Is the wood too damp or too dry?

Is there enough stave thickness/width for the grip to be as stiff as intended?

Is the grip wide enough to safely bend as much as intended?

If the bow is long, how much less should it bend near the grip?

If the bow is short, how much more should it bend near the grip?

How wide should near-grip and midlimb be to permit intended tiller shape?

How wide should the outer limb and tips be for intended speed and softness of release?

Is the inner limb, mid limb and outer limb drawn to correct thickness for desired tiller shape?

Are thickness taper lines laid out separately on each side of the limb—to average out any taper flaws?

Floor Tillering

Am I getting intended tiller shape from the very start?

Let me keep this shape as I proceed.

Before first stringing the bow, a 20 lb force against the grip must bend the bow two inches (for a 50 lb bow).

Tillering

Keep intended tiller shape at all stages of tillering.

Keep local thickness taper smooth. No dips, dings, or rises from the intended line.

Repeat, keep local thickness taper smooth; a bow with no weak links is difficult to break.

Make sure both sides of the limb are of equal thickness as tillering progresses.

Check tiller from both sides of the bow; slight limb twist can confuse the eye. Average out any differences.

Does the braced bow have proper tiller? If so, pull it half way to intended draw weight.

Is tiller still proper? If not, make corrections. If so, pull to full draw weight.

Is tiller still proper? If not, make corrections. If so, remove wood generally.

Continue on like this, draw length increasing with each cycle.

Stop one inch short of full draw. Round corners well, sand, shoot in the bow.

True Draw Weight

A given bow will have different weights depending on draw and hold times. Bows drawn and released quickly shoot faster. In other words, fast-pull draw weight is higher. **Draw weight should be determined by exactly replicating the draw speed and hold times when chronographing.** Tempo is important too - a bow drawn slowly during early inches and quickly during later inches will measure higher than if the reverse, even thought total draw time is the same.

If labeled bow weight is taken from a 'cold' bow that weight will be higher than if from a worked-in bow - one drawn and released three or more times. If a cold-weighed bow is chronographed at its lower worked-in weight it will appear to shoot slower than it should for its labeled cold-weighed poundage. Similarly, if drawn and released slowly, then true, moment-of-release draw weight drops farther, efficiency seeming to drop also.

Bow draw weight should probably be determined under conditions of typical use: Worked in - full drawn and released three times or more. As it's weighed, the bow should be first worked in, then drawn to weight at normal draw and release speed, say 2-seconds. Accountants shouldn't like wooden bows.

It's important not to note draw weight on the way back to brace height because this number will be lower, due to hysteresis. If let down very, very slowly the number will be very little different than when taken on the way to full draw, still there will be a small difference. If let down very quickly, hysteresis-induced numbers will be considerably lower.

Announced FPS Numbers are Unreliable

Shooting techniques between individuals can affect arrow speed as much as design. When testing every day, identical fps readings for several shots in a row are not unusual. So chronographed speeds are most valuable when comparing performance between bows shot by the same experienced shooter. Disparity would be reduced with a physical stop on test arrows, uniform time and rate of draw, similarly clean releases, and comparable F/D measuring techniques. Letdown and cleanness of release varies too. In reality, testing standards won't become universal, so reported fps numbers have limited value. Apart from the above, bias can leak in at every possible seam of the measuring, drawing and releasing process. It's not unusual to stand beside a tester and see several points of error, the resulting inflated fps honestly believed and reported; the Other Archer's Paradox at work.

ADDITIONAL THOUGHTS

Best Brace Height

For a 70" stiff-handled bow best speed per draw weight is reached with a 6" brace, measured from the neutral plane. Similar ratios of brace height to bow length are approximately correct for shorter and longer bows.

When Bow Strings Break

A bow is braced with the same string for hundreds of shots, the string gradually wearing out, slowly sneaking up on its breaking point. Finally it breaks. But it baaaaarely breaks. It took 99.9% of the bow's draw energy to break it. Evidence of this: at such times the arrow essentially hits the mark, or the chrono reads essentially the same fps

Yet another reason: Not leaving enough wood width or thickness when filing in an arrow pass. This caption originally sought kinder wording but bowmaker Ken Villars insisted that the hard cold truth be told. An autopsy revealed the wood began separating at that point, the failure widening and propagating tipward, finally breaking at mid-limb.

The Reasons Bows Break

Local thickness taper not perfectly uniform.

Imperfections in wood surface, especially the back.

Bow too short or narrow for its draw length and weight, given the wood species or the particular stave.

Wood too dry.

Wrong tiller shape for the front-view shape.

A hinge in one or both limbs.

A too-high back crown on tension-weak wood.

Split stave: back rings or fibers nicked or cut.

Board stave: back fibers violated, indicated by non-straight back ring lines.

Overstrained or unevenly strained during tillering.

Unevenly strained while being braced.

Overdrawn during use.

Drawn suddenly before worked in.

Premature handle dip or fade.

String break during shot - this seldom breaks a bow.

Knots incorrectly worked or compensated for.

Damaged wood - drying or trauma checks, decay, insect damage, cell collapse while drying, laminar separations between growth rings.

as previous shots. The bow does not break because, except for some vibration energy, the only energy left in it is its brace energy - the limbs are little more tempted to break than if the bow had been braced and the string suddenly snipped in two. Tuukka Kumpulainen of Finland notes that such bow breaks were reported in the English high crown era. This makes sense: the belly becomes a very narrow back once the string breaks, therefore far more likely to break. High brace heights would increase the danger.

True Set
Visible set is lower than true set, the set the bow feels when braced or drawn. When unbraced, a limb's inner wood attempts to straighten the limb, so we never see its true set. This is especially true of bows backed with stronger wood or bamboo.

Arrow Rests and Shelves
Tiller can change on wooden bows over time, ideal arrow-pass position changing with it. Tiller can migrate for many reasons: Should one end of a bow acquire higher moisture content, if stored vertically for a time, for example; or if for any reason one limb is ever strained more than the other, say if braced unevenly at some point. Apart from this, once a bow is finished and shot in it often shoots better from one side than the other.

So it's better not to cut an arrow rest or shelf into the grip. Another option is to place a small wedge of wood, leather or other material against the side of the grip, letting a thin leather grip wrap hold it in place. Just as functional, but easily adjustable. Should the ideal arrow-pass position move over time just reposition the rest. But no arrow rest is needed. Aboriginal archers shoot off of their hands. Simple, primitive, and effective. Plus it's more fun outshooting guys that use shelves. "Shelves are for keeping books on." - Rod Parsons

Nocking Point
Without a fixed arrow rest and nocking point an arrow is nocked in a slightly different place each time, causing linen strings to last longer.

A hunting bow from Mozambique; 64" from tip to tip, circular section, rawhide string, a common African design. From George Nikolov's private collection, Sofia, Bulgaria. Note near identical Anasazi bow nocks, from Native American Bows Arrows and Quivers, Vol 2, page 222; and Navajo nocks, page 216.

Here's a simple way to raise draw weight on any bow in a few seconds. Just tie the string down. Adjust the tie point for desired draw weight.

147

Nocks cut into the back of a limb endanger the bow, unless tip wood is extra thick, in which case extra tip mass is involved.

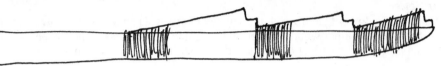

For this reason or that, sometimes you'd like to have a lighter or heavier bow. So file a sliver of bone, wood, antler or horn to triple stair-step shape, sinew that to the back of each limb tip, and you have, for example, a 45 lb, 50 lb and 55 lb bow, or thereabouts. The bow should be designed for the shorter, heavier weight.

Nock Angle

Cut nock grooves at an angle halfway between brace angle and full draw angle. Longer bows have lower angles, at a given brace height.

Handles

Thicker handles require higher brace heights and increased draw length. Limb strain is accordingly greater. All else equal, a stiff-handled bow with, say, 8" of net non-bending grip area, needs to be about 8" longer than a working-grip bow.

Piking

If a finished bow comes in underweight, raise draw weight by piking (shortening) the bow. How much? Tie temporary wedge nocks ever lower till design draw weight is reached. If finish draw weight is about right, but one limb is out of tiller, you might pike just the weak limb.

Kid's Bows

These and other low-weight bows are often harder to tiller than adult bows because they're usually thinner, a same-thickness shaving of wood being a higher percentage of limb thickness than for a thicker limb.

Make kid's bows as much taller than the shooter as they can be happy with. Tiller them to draw 28", but to the shooter's draw weight at the shooter's draw length. Make the bow somewhat whip-tillered.

This length will keep the bow safe when inevitably drawn by an adult, and when braced improperly - the most common cause of broken kid's bows. Kids often grip a bow many inches high or low, and this can break or deform a normal kid's-length bow. The extra length here will allow a bow to grow with its young owner - as their draw lengthens, draw weight increases also. Make a kid's bow limb almost as narrow per pound as adult bows. This keeps limbs a comfortable tillering thickness. A 1" wide kid's bow is a breeze to tiller.

Eight-year-old Jonathan Cisneros, above, inspecting his new gemsbok bow. Most of the bending occurred near the grip, the rest of the limb being relatively straight, so stack was lower than typical for a 41" bow. The string was 90-degrees to the nocks when drawn 23". For kid-pleasing looks the un-reduced ribbed base of the horn rested toward the nocks, so outer limbs were quite wide and heavy. Speed with an 18-grain/lb arrow was 103 fps. This was a relatively thin horn, its 3/8-inch-thick bending area only allowing 17 lbs at 24". Other horns can yield well over 1/2-thickness, allowing bows in the 50 lb range.

Two-year-old Kaylie Hamm holding a bow given to her by her grandfather, Jim Hamm, on the day she was born. Osage selfbow, 45" long, 18# @ 18". This extra length bow will allow her to shoot it for many years, the draw weight automatically rising as her draw length increases.

Ten-year-old Josue Cisneros with his new gemsbok bow, smoothed base ends overlapping at the grip; 45" long, 17 lbs at 24". With narrow ends toward the nocks speed was 116 fps with 18-grain/lb arrow. Automatic perfect tiller due to natural thinning of the horn over distance. Little sister Ashley is packing a self-bamboo bow.

If originally drawn 23" and 26 lb, a couple of years of growth might lengthen this draw to, say, 26" at 32 lb. Should draw weight then be too low an inch can be removed from each whip-tillered end, with no retillering needed - the whip tiller will merely flatten out somewhat, becoming more conventional. If the bow is long enough to begin with, such adjusting can be done several times over the years, no retillering is ever needed. In time, possibly 1/2" or so of length may need to come from one end or the other, to keep tiller balanced.

A typical 35lb/28" bow weighs about:
20" at 20 lb
25" at 28 lb
28" at 35 lb

A typical 45 lb/28" bow weighs about:
20" at 30 lb
25" at 40 lb
28" at 45 lb

Bow similar to the ones pictured may have been the first fumbling steps in horn composite evolution. Cut a straight gemsbok horn in half, lengthwise. Wrap the over-lapped/grip area securely. Done!

Thicker strips from a wider pair of well-curved gemsbok horns. These will allow almost one-half-inch-thick working limbs, and with considerable natural reflex. This will make a legitimate hunting-weight bow, either overlapped and bound together or set onto a wooden handle. The inside curves for a naturally reflexed bow. The outside curves for a naturally deflex-reflex design - wood mounting mandatory at the grip. Horn can splinter in tension if highly strained, so a thin sinew layer, needed only on the crown peak, is the answer. Such bows were possibly the second original step in composite bow evolution.

The Perfect Bow
The perfect bow would be different for each set of conditions. Two guiding pressures would probably apply at all times though. 1) Since longer bows and longer draws are more efficient and more accurate, a bow should always be as long as is practical for given conditions; that might be a very short bow in some cases. 2) There is a draw weight for each archer at which he is most accurate at reasonable hunting distances; this should guide each archer's draw weight choice.

Tillering to Ideal Draw Length.
How fps changes with increased draw length and string follow. Draw weight was adjusted to a constant 47 lb as draw length increased.

The bow: Hickory stave; 61.5" ntn; 1 3/4" at fades, 1 5/8" midlimb. Mild elliptical tiller; 11% MC; 1/2" reflex - 1/4"reflex after being braced; 5 1/2" brace height; flat back; slightly crowned belly; 470-grain arrow.

Draw length	Follow	FPS	Draw weight
18	1/4	122	47 lb
20	1/4	128	
22	1/2	136	
24	5/8	141	
26	5/8	147	
28	3/4	150	
30	3/4	151	
32	1-1/4	151	

By keeping final intended draw weight the same as draw length and set increase, and noting the point at which fps per pound levels off, ideal draw length for a particular in-progress bow can be precisely dialed in. If not the desired draw length the next bow of the same wood can be made shorter or longer. One time-saving option is to start longer than needed, then if the bow doesn't approach tradeoff at desired draw length it can be shortened a bit at a time until it does.

Maintaining final draw weight as tillering progress is ideal Jim Hamm Tillering anyway, so the only additional step here is noting fps as tiller progresses.

Angle of Violation

When it comes to ring violation, what matters most is the angle of fiber violation. When considering violated backs, the angle of violations is more important than its depth. A straight down 90-degree knife cut could be instantly fatal if more than a hair deep. But grain can angle all the way through a 1/2"-thick bow from back to belly over about a length of 20" and remain safe, depending on the species. So, when cutting through back rings, angles of less than that one-in-forty are safe, the limb becoming progressively more likely to break as that angle increases. Before final tillering, if the back has been violated at dangerous angles, it can be made safe by feathering nearby wood to a safe angle, adjusting belly contours accordingly.

Very close-ringed woods such as yew can reveal several cut-through rings while fiber violation angle is quite low and safe.

Bows from Bamboo

Unless the bamboo wall is unusually thick it's best to overlap two billets at the grip. Secured by a couple of rivets made of nails or dowels, the grip is then wrapped with rawhide, sinew or even tape. Overlapping stiffens the midbow and increases poundage per bow length. Such bows can be made in minutes. Even though "quickie" bows, they are excellent in every regard.

With only slightly thicker bamboo draw weight would rise substantially, to 50 or 60 lbs as with the traditional bows of Bhutan. Belly tempering raises draw weight too, and reduces set. When set in place the pictured limbs had 1/2" reflex; presently they're dead straight, and this without tempering. Tillering is automatic if given rough pyramid width taper. Cast equals our more laboriously made wood bows. This design is a good choice for kid's bows: quick and easy to make, and fairly indestructible.

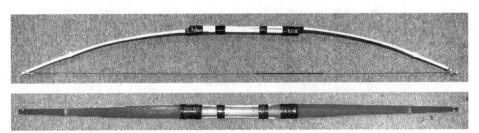

Limbs of this Bhutan-style bow are only 9/32" thick, so for any poundage the bow was made just 54" long and the slats overlapped 12.5". The lignin-rich outer surface as belly, fiber-rich inner surface as back. Wrapping is neo-rawhide (black vinyl electrical tape). Slats were first wrapped at each butt end to prevent slippage, then wrapped at fades and handle to secure the 'splice'. 35 lb at 27"; 1 9/16" at the widest - the grip narrowed for comfort.

Flattening is needed on the concave back edges, sometimes for tillering touchup, but mainly to prevent fibers breaking on the narrow more-strained tops of the concave edges - especially if from less than about a 5" diameter stalk. The consequence of not doing this is seen here.

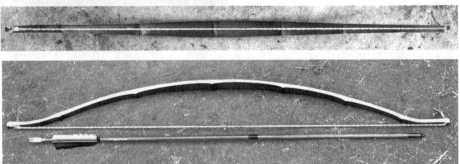

Here concave side ridges were removed, the back perfectly flat; 38" long; 33 lb at 18"; 36 lb at 19 1/4"; Bow mass = 6.5 ounces; 1/4" stringfollow, 1" set; 1 3/8" wide for the center two inches, then relatively straight-line taper toward 1/4" tips, the last several inches kept 1/2" wide. Short, mild heat-bent recurves, to prevent the string pulling off the nocks; 36 lb @ 19 1/4" = 146 fps with 295 grain arrow, 163 fps with 215 grain arrow. Surprising performance for a bow little bigger than its arrow. 24.6 ft/lb of energy stored in 6.5 ounces of bamboo. That's 49.2 ft/lbs from 13-ounces. Not bad.

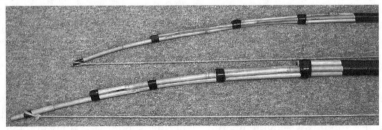

Bamboo pole bows are easy, quick and fun to make, but are not especially fast per pound due to pole against pole friction. Bamboo grown to described custom taper and cross-section would avoid these faults. Estimated mass for such a 60-inch, 50 lb bow: about 10-ounces.

One area of bowmaking satisfaction is imagining and building bows that might have been: An 8' garden-supply bamboo pole. No tillering. Just braced and shot. Explore up and down for a grip position yielding best cast. Butter-smooth draw and surprisingly flawless arrow departure and flight. Only about 28 lbs at 28". Naturally decurved poles would allow hunting weight without pole failure. Possibly such a bow was the first fledgling step toward the perfected asymmetrical Japanese Yumi.

Bamboo is sometimes trained to grow in other than round cross-sections. Place a frame of desired shape over the emerging sprout, and when filled, remove the form. Possibly bamboo could be forced to grow in rectangular or trapezoidal section and with width and thickness tapered limbs. Tiller-grown bow limbs ready to go.

Possibly perfectly straight, smooth, uniform-thickness arrows could be grown in a tube, out of bamboo, other canes, and possibly other woods.

The Flax Plant as Teacher

The drawing and photos illustrate a possible route to the fastest, lowest stack, sweetest shooting straight-stave selfbow design. The lighter and stiffer the outer limb the faster the bow. Making an outer limb narrow and appropriately thick is the means, but if made too narrow, outer limbs bend sideways and even break. Fortunately, nature solved

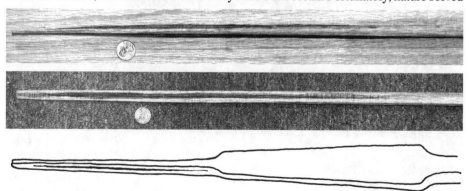

Tests with especially narrow outer limbs show that a flax-imitating cross-section can lower limb mass in that critical area by about one-third, especially helpful when seeking high dry-fire speed, as with flight bows

this problem millions of years ago: A thin layer of very strong flax fiber on each side of the flax stalk to work in tension, a woody core between flax layers to serve in compression. To apply the same engineering to an outer bow limb glue a D-section bead of flax to each side of an extremely narrow and long outer limb, the narrow wood in between handling compression only. Flax is about seven times stronger than wood while only half again heavier. So sufficient limb stiffness would be obtained with very low mass. A similar bead on top of a severely trapped non-bending limb portion would yield desired stiffness with further mass reduction.

Should the limb not be laterally true it could be held in proper position and a touchup wisp of additional flax added. This method may allow limbs with wood width as narrow as 1/8" 2-inches from the nock, 1/4" 8-inches from the nock, and so on, for lowest possible outer limb mass.

This flax-stalk method could also be used to correct more conventional outer limbs that have strayed from true: Bend and hold the limb just past proper position while gluing a corrective flax bead in place.

Being so much lighter than wood, flax would also be a mass-reducing stiffener for the tension side of static recurves.

Flight Bows and Arrows

The route to best flight distance is simple: Strongest per mass bowstrings. Lightest possible outer limbs for high dry-fire speed. Stiff outer limbs for low vibration. Driest possible wood for lower hysteresis and somewhat reduced mass. Lowest drag arrows, made of stiffest per mass material.

Suggested-by-nature specs for farthest-flying natural-materials arrows: Sharp on both ends, as per an elongated wahoo, tuna or mako shark. Barreled shaped, a bit fatter on the front end than the back, the tail end being especially narrow, as on these fastest swimmers. A stay-behind nock, allowing a pointed tail.

For further draw reduction, again, replicate the flax plant, with modifications: Flax fiber is about four times stiffer per mass than typical arrow wood, so again, as on the flax plant, for the stiffest per diameter arrow let a woody center handle compression, a thin layer of flax fiber handle tension.

An ultra high dry-fire speed twin-bow design by Alan Case. A middle string connects the strings of two conventional bows. Depending on the attachment angle of each bow, and their distance apart, the return speed of the center string is multiplied several times. Depending on setup geometry this design can stack abruptly, storing less energy per draw-weight pound, but when shooting very light flight arrows dry-fire speed is king, not horsepower.

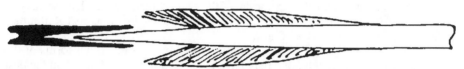

Water is about 800 times denser than air. Shapes fine-tuned over millions of years to travel through water at 60-plus mph are surely the best low-drag shape for any fluid, air or water. The legendary Turkish flight arrows traveled a similar path of evolution.

Stay-behind nocks: This arrow would be too much trouble to make for hunting, but for longer-range target use, and especially for flight shooting, it should yield more level flight and greater distance. The rear of the arrow can safely come to a needle point, for maximum drag reduction, by having the nock permanently attached to the string, the rear point of the arrow resting inside it and slipping free as it leaves the bow. This stay-behind nock would be just deep enough to protect the narrow tail from breaking, and just loose-fitting enough to prevent hangup, and needn't be heavier than a normal nock.

Shape a narrow stiff-wood shaft to an elongated version of the above drawing, which is the elongated shape of fastest fish. Cover the arrow's surface with a uniform coating of long, straight flax fibers set in hide glue. The wider portions of the arrow will hold more total fibers. Coat the surface with additional hide glue and sand to perfection. Dry hide glue is extremely stiff, but there may be stiffer natural materials that are also waterproof.

The bowlista: Adapting the Roman ballista as a hand bow is not too difficult. Pre-stressing of the sinew cables (braided nylon used in this prototype) creates very high early draw weight, for an unusually fat F/D curve.

We're Stone-Age People

There is no need for the Stone-Age to be a museum era. After all, we *are* Stone-Age people. We just happened to be born now instead of then. We have a legacy to reclaim. We can continue innovating, devising all that surely would have come to be, if not interrupted by the upstart Metal Age and all that followed.

Here is a suggested list of the very few new wood bowmaking principles, insights and processes contributed during the last 500 years. Some or all of these may be rediscoveries, but even if so the knowledge has been lost to bowmakers for lifetimes, so they are as valuable to us as if new.

Marc St Louis' belly tempering discovery: Obscure hints exist that forms of this performance-enhancing technique may have been used in isolated places in the past. In any case, Marc's fully thought out and tested invention or reinvention of the process has made it available to present archery, where it is now in broad and growing use.

Dan Perry's Perry Reflexing: Tricking a backed bow into storing energy internally, not just at limb surfaces, in turn allowing narrower, lighter limbs. Backed reflexed bows have existed for quite awhile, but no one seemed to understand that Perry Reflexing had advantages over same-profile non Perry reflexing.

The Karpowicz low-stack design: Outer limbs almost parallel the string at brace. This angle permits higher braced string tension without bending the outer limb, which leads to higher early draw weight, therefore more stored energy and lowering full-draw stack. The reflexed outer and midlimb also straightens and lengthens at full draw instead of shortening, diminishing stack, again increasing stored energy. To affect this near parallel outer limb the bow must be deflexed at the grip, then reflexed near midlimb. At only 51" Adam's pictured bow yields exceptional speed from a short bow, and equals the speed of a well-crafted long bow.

Steve Gardner's tillering-by-mass technique: Allows fine-tuning of bow length and width during tillering for optimum performance with safety.

Comstock/Baker/Hamm's adjust-width-per-wood specific gravity notion: Bowmakers through time adjusted width/length per species via long trial and error. Using density/width guidelines lets the first bow of a new wood, or a light or dense stave of a same species, be safe and efficient, permitting quick and proper use of unlimited wood types.

Jim Hamm Tillering: Revolutionary in a sense, allowing a first-timer or veteran to come in exactly at intended draw weight while never overstraining the limbs. (see *Tillering, TBB 1*, page 257).

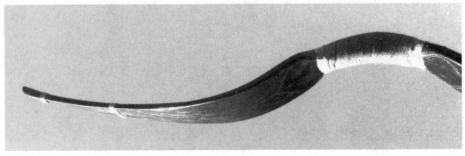

Karpowicz low-stack design.

The Baugh cable bow. By adjusting cable pretension, height, and placement of cable attachment, the shape of its F/D curve can be adjusted. With stiff limbs to quell vibration, and a highly strained sinew cable storing energy, efficiency should be quite high. Having taken his design to this point Dick lost further interest, so it's available to the world for use and modification.

The Baugh Cable Bow: The Baugh Cable Bow is simple and elegant in principle, practical, and primitive in construction, in that it could have reasonably been made in Mesolithic times, notches used instead of hinges. The pictured version is set up as a crossbow, but easily modifiable to a more conventional hand bow. In the photo, note the limbs are non-bending and hinged at the grip. The pre-stressed cable is secured to the grip some distance above the limb, so during early stages of draw the cable would be stretched farther per draw inch than during later stages. In other words, a nearly stackless bow, yielding a fat F/D curve.

A Combined Effort

TBB 1's Design and Performance chapter would not have been possible without the cooperation of a handful of veteran and more recent woodbow devotees. Instead of that original tiny group, hundreds participated here. I regret that space won't allow crediting all who took part, but such would be the literary equivalent of rain falling on a tin roof.

The Bowmakers Bar

For those who haven't visited yet let me tell you about the Bowmakers Bar. It sits on a quiet road out at the edge of town. I'm sure you've seen it many times but just didn't notice. There are high trees behind the place, thickly growing and dark. One day while driving past my eye caught an arc of light against that darkness, the sun shining on an arrow in flight. Looking closer I could make out two archers within the trees. That's how I found the place.

The Bowmakers Bar is open most of each day and late into the night. Over the years bow wood of every description has been planted along the road and out back, especially beside the small creek that angles through the property. Some of the most ancient of these have fallen over time and those near the back of the Bar are often used as benches. There is always someone sitting on one, scraping out a bow. Usually there are several. Newcomers come by often, to sit and watch and listen. A deep cushion of old and new wood shavings covers the ground.

You'll have to bring a bow and show it around. Nothing bowmakers like better than checking out a new bow, asking about every detail of its making, sometimes offering suggestions concerning your next one. There is an informal range outside in the back, a few bales leaning against the trees, the dark earth leading to them well worn. You won't have to wait long before a handful or archers will bound out of the back door, bows and arrows in hand, and a friendly shoot will begin. Feel free to join in. Like as not everyone will want to see your new bow in action. Be prepared for some good-natured ribbing. Even if you didn't buy a bottle of No-Stack fluid offered to newcomers.

I've been visiting The Bowmakers Bar for over twenty years now, the hours spent there among the most rewarding of my particular life. I imagine you'd feel the same over time. If you haven't already, I hope you find your way there one of these days.

FLIGHT BOWS

Dan Perry

Remember the feeling you had when you first saw or drew a natural material bow? Multiply that by ten and you'll know what's in store the first time you watch an arrow launched from one soar completely out of sight. With our competitive and inquisitive nature, testing bows to "see what they've got" was no doubt inherent in bowmaking from the beginning. Shooting bows for distance - flight shooting - was not only a quick and easy way to test a bow's performance, it was so much fun that it became a game. Although it holds additional spice for bowyers, archers soon discovered that some could shoot the same bow and the same arrows much farther than others. So it was not just a test of the bowyer's skill, but also a test of the archer's skill and knowledge.

Understanding how to build a bow and arrows that will shoot farther will enhance your bow building skills for other applications, such as target and hunting bows.

Flight shooting today brings many bowyers together who enjoy not only the competition, but meeting each year to discuss what they have learned and see what is new. The days of tightly kept secrets, which almost doomed the sport a few decades ago, have given way to camaraderie and the sharing of ideas. I have helped bowyers tune arrows and even coached them while they were breaking world records I held.

Here's how the flight shooting game is played. The National Archery Association of the United States of America officially added "Primitive" classes to their flight competition in the late 1980's. These classes were for bows and arrows made from natural materials, and have four separate primitive categories: self bow, simple composite bow, complex composite bow, and Turkish bow. A simple composite bow is essentially a self bow with a single lamination added, a hickory backing, for example. Add another lamination, and it becomes a complex composite bow. A Turkish bow conforms strictly to the form of the ancient Turkish flight bow, a complex composite horn bow shot with a sapier, or hand held arrow shelf, and a thumb ring release.

These classes give a progression of the complexity of bow design, so "pristine" self bows are not competing against horn composite bows. There is also an English longbow class where the bow and arrows must be made of wood or bamboo, though this is not a primitive class as modern strings and plastic arrow nocks can be used. For the most part, it follows the form of the traditional English longbows, a stacked limb cross-section, and no arrow rest on the bow.

There are also weight classes. Bows are weighed in and up to six arrows and an alternate registered before the competition begins. A round is six shots and the farthest arrow is recorded.

Finding places open enough to shoot flight can be challenging. Horn composite bows have recorded distances over 600 yards, and even 50# self bows have exceeded 300 yards. Beaches and dry lake beds are great places for shooting flight. After finding a safe range, with flat terrain and little or no vegetation, a center-line is chosen. A

Finding a place to shoot flight is the first challenge.

shooting line is created by driving stakes into the ground at 90 degrees on both sides of the center line, and stretching a line from stake to stake. The distance of the arrow is measured where the arrow intersects the centerline, not from the archer to the arrow. The idea is to keep arrows as close to center as possible, so accuracy is still involved. A coach is allowed at the flight line who can verbally assist the archer, but may not touch him while shooting. This helps the archer, whose focus is on the tip of the arrow, stay on line.

There are two basic types of flight bows: one for shooting light flight arrows and one for shooting heavy hunting arrows, or broadhead flight. If comparing them to race cars, regular flight bows for shooting light arrows would be the top fuelers of the archery world. Speed purely for the sake of speed! Regular flight bows, while they teach us a lot about the function of bows, are not for deer hunting. The flight bows for hunting weight arrows could be compared to stock cars. Broadhead flight is becoming increasingly popular because of its direct application to hunting bows.

Once the design elements needed for a regular flight bow vs. a broadhead bow are understood, choosing a design for any particular application will be easier. These designs features won't make building bows more complicated, in fact, the more I learn, the more simple my bow designs become. The design elements and principles that make the most difference are subtle. One bow that seems to be nearly identical to another can outperform it by as much as 30%.

REGULAR FLIGHT BOWS
Dry Fire Speed

Dry fire speed is the first essential concept for flight bows. This is the speed that bow limbs return to brace height when drawn and released without an arrow. When I first introduced this concept a few years ago, some bowyers started dry firing their bows to see if they could see a difference. Please resist this temptation, as it isn't necessary. If there was special equipment that could measure this return without an arrow it might be worth the sacrifice of a few bows, but we can understand what is happening without the risk.

In 1992, I built two hickory-backed hickory bows for comparison. They were out of the same board, with the same amount of Perry Reflex (pulled into reflex before gluing). The lengths were 60 inches nock to nock, with draw weights of 50# at 25 inches. One bow was overbuilt in width the entire length of the limb, with 5/8" nocks. The other was built the same width to the fade out, but had a straight line taper to the narrow 5/16" nocks. Using a 500 grain cedar arrow for testing, I was surprised at how close the chronograph readings were for both bows, close enough that it was impossible to be sure my release alone wasn't the difference. When shooting them for distance with the heavy arrows, the bow with narrow light limbs averaged around 6 yards farther than the overbuilt bow. Pulling out the light flight arrows, I tested both bows again. The overbuilt bow shot the light flight arrows 10 to 15 yards further than it did with the heavy arrows, the furthest being just under 220 yards. But the bow with narrow light limbs shot the flight arrows as much as 140 yards further than the overbuilt bow, an amazing difference!

So, what was happening?

Light, narrow limbs allow arrow velocity to continue increasing as arrow weight decreases (or moves toward a dry fire), far beyond what wide heavier limbs can. The dry fire speed of the overbuilt bow was slower as it couldn't get out of its own way. Dry fire speed is different for different designs, so it's essential to learn the design elements that increase dry fire speed.

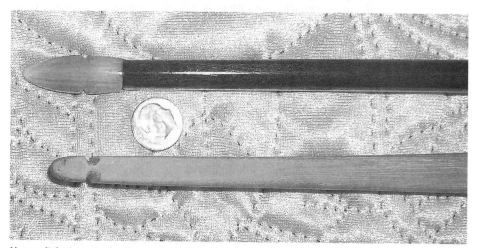

Narrow light tips raise dry fire speed and lower maximum dry fire arrow weight.

The relationship between limb mass and arrow mass is key to building a fast regular flight bow. Length of the limbs is another important design element. I was once asked why I made a bow with long limbs, when only the outer portion was actually bending. I replied that extending the working limbs further apart was keeping the mass of the working limb low, while decreasing the string angle, to gain higher energy storage as well as more comfort shooting. The first six inches after the fades were still stiff, and were really part of the handle section. From where the limb did start to bend, the tiller was normal, not "whipped". If the length of the working limb is reduced and the shorter limbs moved farther apart, less mass is being moved so dry fire speed goes up.

Shorter limbs which work more near the handle can also increase dry fire speed if the mass of the outer limb is kept very low. This is one of the reasons I believe the Turks used horn, since wood could not take the compression of the tight radius in a short, hinged working limb. Their flight bows at full draw were hinged near the handle, the rest of the limb acting as lever, including the short ear.

String weight and diameter also have an affect on dry fire speed. Adding mass to the string is like adding mass to the tips of the bow. Increasing the diameter of the string increases the wind resistance.

This brings up some important points missed by flight archers for years, because we lacked the understanding of dry fire speed.

1) Maximum Dry Fire Arrow Weight. This is the point where arrow velocity gains from reducing the arrow's weight drop off to where they are no longer of benefit, and will be referred to as Maximum Dry Fire Arrow Weight, or Max Dry Fire Weight.

2) Knowing the max dry fire weight of a bow allows us to take advantage of sectional density in the arrow. Sectional density is the mass of the arrow in pounds, divided by the square of its diameter. In layman's terms, with a higher sectional density there is more weight pushing the air out of the way for the same-sized arrow. For example, a golf ball can be thrown a lot farther than a ping pong ball. The ping pong ball slows down much faster because it has less mass to push the air out of the way.

Understanding these elements, and how they relate to dry fire speed, allows bow designs that can do double duty, to a point. The shorter working limbs on a long handle, for example, will serve as a flight bow for both heavy and light arrows.

Mass and Energy Ratios

When comparing a 65 pound bow to a 50 pound bow shooting the same arrow, the heavier bow is about 30% harder to pull but only yields a 10% increase in arrow speed (based on speeds of 150 fps and 165 fps). This disparity is largely because moving the arrow is a higher percentage of the work being done with a lighter bow, which in turn involves workload, bow mass, and energy storage ratios.

If the width of a bow, the weight of the arrow, and weight of the string were all reduced by 50%, the arrow velocity would stay the same. This in spite of the fact that the bow drew half of its earlier weight. But would the velocity of the original full weight arrow be half the original speed, or 50% less? The answer is no, the speed would be higher than 50%. In the lighter bow, a higher percentage of the work being

Brian Perry, aged 14, breaking the 35# English Longbow World Record for Male Youth.

done is moving the arrow, so the lighter bow is more efficient. It shoots the heavy arrow faster than half the velocity of the full weight bow, even though it stored only half of the energy.

An important point should be made about how reducing the weight of a bow affects its performance. It has been said that if a bow is tillered to a lower weight, it will not shoot as fast as it would have if it had never been drawn past the lower weight. Since an archer may want to shoot a bow in a lower weight class at some time, understand that this is only true if the bow is taken down in draw weight by removing wood in thickness. When the weight is lowered by reducing width alone, it doesn't affect performance. If the bow was at peak efficiency at the higher draw weight, it will continue to be at peak efficiency at the lower draw weight. Also, if the bow was safe at its original width, it will continue to be safe at its reduced width and lighter weight, as the way the surfaces are stressed will stay virtually the same.

Energy requirements may be the most surprising aspect about flight bows, as the needs are vastly different between regular flight and broadhead flight.

I once shot a primitive class, complex composite, (composite horn bow) for Harry Drake. When we measured the bow to about 16 to 18 inches of draw, the early draw weight was so low that we calculated that the bow would only draw 35#. When we weighed the bow for the 50# class, the draw weight spiked so dramatically that I shot the bow in the unlimited class, estimating that at full draw the bow drew about 70#.

The bow broke before we were able to plot its force draw curve, but its energy storage was terrible. At the end of the draw, the stack was unreal, close to 7# per inch. The surprise came when the bow shot a Douglas fir arrow 521 yards! I didn't draw the bow to full draw that first round so a record was set at less than the estimated 70# draw. Harry was not happy with shooting it below full draw, so the next round I drew it the full 26". The distance was almost a hundred yards less on average. The bow was breaking down.

An important lesson can be learned from this bow. Pushing the design of a bow past the limitations of the materials is counter-productive. Once the materials begin to break down, the co-efficient of restitution (the speed at which a strained object returns to its original dimensions) drops, and it drops for good. Once the surface of the limbs break down, a plane below the surface becomes the new load-bearing surface, but the mass – the dead weight - between the original working surface and the new plane still has to be moved.

How was it possible that a bow that stored so little energy could shoot so far? The answer is, stored energy doesn't play as big a part in flight archery as we had once believed. That doesn't mean that if this bow had stored more energy, it wouldn't have done better. It means there are other elements at work that are even more important. Not wasting the energy stored by moving additional mass, and leverage, are elements that affect the true key to flight archery, dry fire speed.

Leverage

Leverage may be the most controversial element of bow limb dynamics, since most bowyers I have talked to deny the existence of leverage and gearing in bows. Nevertheless, I will share this study and let others draw their own conclusions.

When I was a young boy, my parents gave building blocks and Lincoln Log sets to us for Christmas. I confess to constructing missile launching devices from mine. My catapults were simple, just the green wood slats over log fulcrums. I would play with

These two 35# bows have one thing in common - they both shoot the same light arrow the same distance! After 100 hours of labor on the cool looking, sinew-backed reflexed recurve, I was devastated when it didn't shoot any further than this 1/2 hour bow from a scrap of hickory. The recurve has a great force draw curve, storing tons more energy. This was my first clue that energy storage was not the only key to the lock. The recurve started its life with longer limbs, and an 18# draw weight. All of the bend was near the handle, so I shortened the limbs, removing the non-working limbs to raise the draw weight. Ironically, I removed the one element it had going for it - leverage. The short working limbs and low mass tips of the straight bow waste very little energy, and increase dry fire speed.

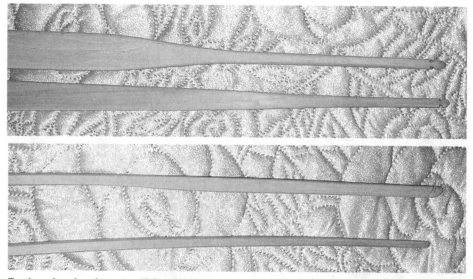

Two bows based on the ancient Holmegaard bow (for more on how to maximize energy storage for this design, refer to Tim Baker's chapter in TTB 3, page 88). The bottom bow in both photos is a 300 yard, 50# hickory selfbow, which broke a world record. Its extreme whip tiller and short outer working limbs store little energy, but are very light and have a good dry fire speed. The top bow in both photos is a 400 yard design. It has the same length working limb as the 300 yard design. It stores a little more energy, even though it has more set and 4# less draw weight. Note that the 400 yard bow's tips are much larger than those of the 300 yard bow. So why is the performance 33% better when it has more mass at the tips? The outer half of the limb is a stiff lever. In the leverage theory, velocity of the working limb is multiplied by the length of the lever, the same way I can throw a dart with an atl-atl much, much further than I can with my arm alone. My arm doesn't move any faster when I use the atl-atl, the atl-atl essentially lengthens my arm, multiplying the velocity. I can use a longer and longer atl-atl to throw a dart faster until the gearing is wrong and becomes slower because the combined weight exceeds the capacity of the energy stored in my arm. There is always an optimum for the work load. Finding that optimum in a flight bow yields the greatest distance.

the length of the catapult by changing the height and location of the fulcrum. As an adult I saw something while watching Turkish flight bows at full draw that brought back those early years. Most of the limb at full draw was simply a lever. The applied force that moved the lever was the tight arch of the working limb.

I saw a connection between the leverage in the catapults of my youth and these flight bow limbs at full draw. My mind began to race through leverage used to launch projectiles of all sorts; atlatls, slings, catapults, trebuchets, looking for connections and common factors. Each of these used leverage in the form of distance from the applied force to accelerate a projectile. Also, it seemed that there was an optimum length for the application. The factors seemed to include the amount of applied force, the weight of the projectile, and the length of the lever (the length of the sling on a trebuchet, the length of the beam of a catapult.) For each, the velocity seemed to increase to a point, then drop back down with added length. In each case, it appeared there was a limit to the length of leverage that a given amount of applied force could move a given weight projectile at increasing velocity.

I had been making stiff, light tips on wooden bows because they were faster, as the stiff tips acted as a lever. The Turks isolated leverage and exploited it in their bows. The distance from the hinged working limb to the nocks is a major player in their

Bows with long stiff tips, left, I refer to as high-gear bows. Bows with a whip-tiller, right, I refer to as low-gear bows.

flight bows, and they used it to optimize the gearing for their war bows. Wood won't hold up to the strain, so they developed the composite bow.

Non-working recurves, siyahs, or light, narrow, non-working outer limbs on straight bows, shorten the working limb and compound velocity. This shortened working limb, combined with leverage, helps with heavy arrows just as with light arrows. If the mass of the outer limbs remains low, dry fire speed goes up, but we also gain by compounding velocity by the length of the lever from the bow tip to the beginning of the working limb.

I coined terms to describe the application and use of these leverage principles. For the longer lever bows that can't move a lot of mass quickly, but have great dry fire speeds due to the lever's compounding of velocity, I call high gear bows. Bows that use less leverage, but are optimized for the heavier arrows I call low gear bows.

BROADHEAD FLIGHT BOWS

Broadhead flight bows have become popular over the last fifteen years due to their practical application to hunting. Heavy arrows require different bow design elements, particularly energy requirements.

When I first began shooting longbows for flight, I proudly brought out my bows and showed them to Don Brown, one of the fathers of broadhead flight shooting. He

Charley Johnson breaking the Men's 35#
English Longbow World Record.

looked them over and asked about the draw length at their draw weight; 50# @ 28 inches. After hesitating a moment, he said "It has been our experience that overdrawing a lighter bow gives us the best distance with longbows." He went on to explain that broadhead arrows were like parachutes, and they needed a long draw. He further explained that since the arrows had so much drag already, the extra length wouldn't have such a negative affect on them.

Many bows later, I understand now what he was saying. The heavy hunting arrows required as much horsepower as could be squeezed out of a bow. The bow had a lot more work to do than a regular flight bow.

Dry fire speed still mattered, but by drawing a lighter bow further, Don was storing more energy.

We also compared a 50# hickory-backed hickory, Perry-reflexed longbow to a 62# reflexed wood and glass laminated longbow. Shooting the same 525 grain, cedar, 28" field point arrows, the hickory bow consistently out-performed the heavier bow by 10 to 15 yards. Don didn't shoot 28 inches out of this bow, even though that is the length written on it by the bowyer. He drew it to 31 inches!

So a dog of a bow - when shooting regular flight arrows at its full draw length of 62# at 28 inches - was suddenly out-performing my other bows when shooting broadheads at 31 inches of draw in the 70# Broadhead class.

These examples illustrate the difference in energy storage between draw lengths.

Early draw weight and less stack at the end of the draw are also important with broadhead flight. Combined with a long draw, bows with these attributes store more energy. By building broadhead bows with narrow, light limbs, less energy is wasted from moving unnecessary weight in the limbs, which leaves more net energy to push the arrow. If the chosen design stores more energy but wastes it by adding more mass at the tips, nothing is gained. Not wasting stored energy is just as important as storing more energy.

Scot Perry, 17, 2006 U.S. Nationals.

MOISTURE MANAGEMENT

Many woods are like sponges, absorbing moisture out of the air, though moisture tolerance is different for different woods. Hickory, for example, is sluggish if allowed to soak up moisture from humid air, yet I have used it to set more world distance records than any other wood.

Moisture management is critical for all wood bows, but especially flight bows. I have seen moisture alone make as much as a 20% difference in performance.

Don Brown kept a light bulb going in a closet where he stored his bows in his California home. Keeping a bow in an air-tight container with silicon packages used to prevent rust on firearms is another way to protect a bow.

There is a fine line between dry enough and too dry. Hickory at 6% may be considered ideal. Hickory at 5% might wind up in pieces. The level to which moisture can be dropped varies greatly with the species. For example, yew seems to tolerate humid climates, but here in the dry desert West becomes brittle at 6% moisture content. In a climate that is very dry, bows can be stored in cool dark place such as a basement.

The finish used will help manage the moisture, should a bow be caught in a storm. Polyurethane finishes work well. In the primitive classes, finishes made from pitches and beeswax will keep a bow safe long enough to be sheltered.

I recommend that every bowyer interested in flight shooting have a moisture meter, as moisture should be one of the first considerations when selecting flight bow woods.

These two 35# longbows are made from very different woods, ipe, above, and eastern red cedar, below. They have the same draw length and are both at maximum strain, just within the limits for the wood, and both have a total mass of just 11 ounces. Don't be afraid to use heavy wood. If built the correct width for the draw weight and length, the bow will weigh the same as a lighter wood.

WOODS FOR FLIGHT BOWS

It's no omission that I haven't recommended a particular wood to use in order to build a world class flight bow. The truth is, the design used and understanding the principles are more important than the wood species. There is such a variation within the same species of wood that it is foolish to decide on just one bow wood based on species alone.

When looking at woods and moisture management, a key factor for wood selection is the climate where it will be used. Dry? Humid? Hot? Cold?

Flight bows push the edge of what a wood can take. They are high stress/strain bows by nature, so a tough wood is required. But tough at what moisture content and what temperature? A flight archer in Finland, shooting on a frozen lake, needs a wood that will hold together in his conditions. A flight archer in the desert west of the U.S. needs wood that can withstand the low moisture contents. A flight archer in England needs wood that will still perform when the weather is always humid. Flight shooters from Finland often use ash. Yew is a proven performer in the humid climates where it grows. Oddly, hickory grows in humid climates, but is an ideal choice for dry climates where low moisture contents can threaten some wood species.

There are some qualities that I look for in a flight bow wood. Density is at the top of the list, as dense, strong wood makes for narrower limbs. Such wood can be stressed more than weaker, less dense wood. This may seem counter productive since one of the goals is making bows low in mass, but because the wood is stronger much less wood is required. When worked down to its breaking point, a dense wood is no heavier than a lighter wood at the same point. I have made 50# draw weight English longbows that weighed only 14 ounces, including the string and handle wrap, and this from wood so dense that it sinks in water like a rock!

If the prospective wood is ring-porous, I want mostly dense summer growth. For example, with hickory I like the spring growth to be mere dotted lines between the dense summer growth rings. For all woods, the grain needs to be straight. Character bows are beautiful works of art, but we intend to torture this wood and can't afford any weak spots. Character bows, with their snakes, knots, and wiggles, also require more mass for the same draw weight.

Steve Gardner, 2005 U.S. Nationals.

I have built flight bows that have set world records from five different species of wood. I have seen flight bows set world records from another two. In order of the most records to the least, they are as follows:

1) Hickory
2) Yew
3) Hard maple
4) Tie: eastern red cedar, hophornbeam, ipe, and Osage orange.

Understanding that I live in Utah, the second driest state in the United States, explains why hickory tops my list. Does that mean it is the best flight bow wood? Not necessarily. It means that it is a good choice for my climate. If I lived in the Northwest U.S., yew may have been my choice. If I lived where Osage was more available, or red cedar, they might get the nod. These are just a small percentage of the woods capable of being competitive in flight shooting at a high level. Greenheart, purpleheart, pecan, mulberry, ash, lemonwood, and black cherry, among many others, will work well for flight bows, so there are a lot of choices. See what is available and make a decision based primarily on climate.

For complex composite bows, horn is needed for the belly, as wood cannot withstand the compression of the tight arc of the bent limb. Water buffalo horn is now available commercially, and can be found online. Sinew is dried and pounded out into fibers to be glued on the back of composite bows, as sinew is elastic enough to handle the tension on the short working limbs. Maple, bamboo, and mulberry have all been successfully used for composite bow cores.

FLIGHT ARROWS

Arrows play a huge role in flight, as they convert stored energy into distance, but often receive the least attention.

Understanding a bow's max dry fire arrow weight is the best place to start. There is no advantage to going lighter than this arrow weight, as the best distances will result from arrows as close to this weight as possible. A higher sectional density traveling at the same velocity will carry that velocity further down range.

In flight archery, there is no correct spine for arrows. This may be hard to believe, but it is true. It all comes down to arrow tuning. Arrows at the same spine, (same deflection with a weight hung from their center at a given length) can behave very differently out of the same flight bow. They wobble or vibrate at different frequencies, for lack of a better term. Getting the arrow's frequency to match the stroke and speed of the bow can be tricky.

So what is my formula? I don't have one! After all of these years, some of the arrows I think are the worst, fly the best. Like building a violin, there are guidelines, but each will have to be matched to the bow.

Similar to group testing arrows, distance testing arrows is always a good practice, but has its draw backs too. If the flight bow design is pushed too far, by the time the arrows are tuned, the bow may be shot out and will have lost its competitive edge.

Cedar arrows barreled by hand.

Moving the brace height up or down can change the "tune" of the arrow. Since this harmonic wobble is affected by differences in the amount of paradox, or deflection around the handle, changing the brace height can bring arrows of the seemingly wrong spine into perfect balance with a bow. Also, changing a string's diameter can change an arrow's tune.

I still prefer the stiffest spine that will fly correctly, as they usually whip less and waste less energy. Barrelled wood shafts reduce weight while keeping enough spine. They whip less and are easier to tune. Many claim that arrows with balance points fore or aft of center are better for different wind conditions, but I like them center-balanced, as arrows balanced in this way have yielded the best all-around performance.

An arrow that wobbles as it rotates loses distance, so good flight arrows do not wobble. I like to heat straighten all of my shafts over the kitchen stove before barreling. After they are shaped, the shafts are spun, standing on their points, and straightened again so there is not the slightest hint of a wobble. This is repeated after fletching. Before registering the arrows at a competition, I always check them again. If they are wobbling, I employ a friction arrow straightener. Mine is a thin piece of polished agate with a small crescent polished into the edge to fit the contour of the shaft, a gift from David "Lynn" Hayes, a great flight archer. With light pressure, stroke the high side of any slight bend in the shaft, and spin it again. Often one light stoke is all that is needed to take out the wobble. Be careful not to damage the wood, use light pressure only. Arrows straightened with this method stay straight an amazingly long time.

The trick with many flight bows is to tune a round of six arrows quickly before the bow begins to fade or break down. While I have had some Perry-reflexed long bows that stayed competitive for four years, most flight bowyers push their bows past the limit. Their bows break down quickly and may be fast, but only for a few shots.

Most of the nocks from ancient flight arrows were three-piece nocks.

The nocks were somewhat bulbous, and of larger diameter than the neck of the shaft. This may have been for nothing more than making sure the nocks were sturdy, however, I suspect that it may have to do with drag.

I also use three-piece nocks, though I have not used bulbous types like those of the Turks.

Sanding tapered flat spots, 3/4 inch long, at a right angle to the grain of the shaft,

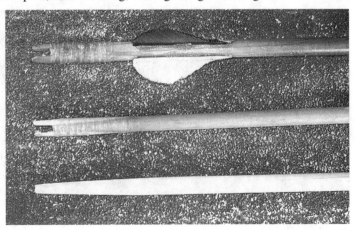

Note the Turkish-style nock of the center arrow, made by adding two wedges of wood.

the thin pieces of hickory are glued to the shaft. I then shape the nock with a fine file and sandpaper. A small needle file is then used to open and shape the nock for the string.

Broadhead Flight Arrows

Many of the same principles hold true for broadhead arrows. They still fly best if tuned to the bow, but tuning is not as critical. There is a great deal of drag on a broadhead arrow. Anything which cuts down the drag increases the distance, so I like dense, small diameter arrows. There has to be enough spine to keep the arrow from whipping coming out of the bow.

The broadhead classes require heavy hunting-style fletching, and feather fletching is required in the primitive and longbow classes.

Choosing the thinnest feathers helps, but my top secret method of getting a broadhead arrow further down field has to do with making the broadhead and the fletching work together to reduce drag, a simple way to gain distance.

A slow-motion video of an arrow leaving a bow reveals an amazing amount of bend and oscillation in one plane, as the arrow paradoxes around the handle. A broadhead is like a canard wing, so if it is placed on the shaft at a right angle to the oscillation of the arrow, it will catch a lot of air and increase drag. If the blade is oriented on the shaft as close as possible to this plane of oscillation, the cutting edge of the blade, or its narrowest profile, is presented to the air. The arrow should stay in the same plane as the oscillation without rotating, which can be accomplished by using a straight fletch, as twisted, or helical fletching, creates a lot of drag. By preventing the arrow from rotating until after the oscillation from paradox has ended, any chance of the blade rotating and catching air is eliminated.

FLIGHT STRINGS

Strings are often overlooked by flight archers, yet they have a measurable affect. When I first started shooting flight in the Primitive Class, I made a silk string. The silk was hard to come by and was dear to me. I was dismayed when it didn't stretch as much as the dacron strings I had been making, and the brace height was higher than I intended. So I didn't twist the string at all. Don Brown noticed this and commented that the un-waxed silk string would spread out like a parachute if I did not twist it. I didn't think it would make any difference, but I was wrong. Strings need enough twist to keep the strands from separating.

Building violins and watching their strings oscillate under tension, I suspect this happens to some degree with bowstrings. Just as arrows oscillate, strings may likewise have movement that causes more drag. If this oscillation could be reduced by using a stiffer string, or by some other method, it might net more distance. For natural strings, I like silk or linen. While I prefer silk for its smaller diameter, I have done just as well with linen, which is a stiffer material.

Strings with less mass, smaller diameter, and less stretch are more desirable, as they waste less energy (also see Strings in *TBB 2*, pg. 187). When building very light endless loop strings, be sure to add more strands under the nock loop serving for additional strength and to help keep the string from cutting into the nocks on softer bow woods. The arrow should not be loose on the string, but should not be too snug. If the arrow will stay on the string without being held, but not move the string when removed, the serving is just right.

Jaap Koppedrayer, 2007 Nationals, shooting one of his Japanese-style bows.

GETTING THE MOST DISTANCE FROM AN EXISTING BOW

To improve performance of an existing bow, a bowyer begins by identifying the bow's dry fire speed and max dry fire arrow weight.

This is best accomplished with a chronograph, as other variables come into play when shooting for distance that can give a false impression of what is happening. This requires help from a spotter. Begin with an arrow that is 10 grains per each pound of draw weight. Have the spotter record only the velocities when the arrow is drawn to the correct length. Over-draws and under-draws should be thrown out.

Average the velocity of ten correct draws. If there was a bad release, be sure to throw it out as it can skew the data. Drop to nine grains per pound and repeat the process. Continue to drop the arrow weight until the velocity gains are negligible. If the limbs of the bow are heavy, it will reach this point at a fairly high arrow weight. If the limbs are light, this will happen at a lower weight and it may be a challenge to find enough spine to continue. If this happens, the arrow is the limiting factor.

A bow with heavy limbs and a high max dry fire weight won't be competitive as a regular flight bow because the dry fire speed is too low. However, this bow has strengths for a broadhead bow. Unless the bow is of high draw weight and a short draw, it is overbuilt and can shoot a longer arrow, storing more energy. Choosing a strong, small diameter string and finding arrows that are well-tuned to the bow, combined with a draw length that is maximum for the bow, will net the best distance.

Bows with medium weight limbs and max dry fire arrow weights in the mid-range might be able to shoot either flight or broadhead arrows. By drawing it to its maximum length, it can still be competitive in the broadhead class. If the higher dry fire arrow weight is viewed as an advantage, the bow might still be competitive in regular flight. By using a dense arrow wood, the sectional density will be higher and maintain velocity better. Again, tuning the arrows for the bow, which cannot be over-emphasized, along with proper string selection, may be enough to put the bow in contention.

With light limbed bows, or high dry fire speed bows, or very low max dry fire arrow weights, finding the right string and arrows is tricky. The bowyer doesn't want to be launching ping-pong balls, but wants to keep the arrow as light as possible to take advantage of the higher velocity. The problem is keeping the arrow spine heavy enough, which requires trying different arrow materials. Match the arrows carefully to the bow, or the arrows will whip when released. The benefits of initial velocity may have to be weighed against a stiffer spine and better sectional density.

Jaap Koppedrayer, shooting an Asiatic composite bow.

Flight bows can be as safe or as dangerous a bowyer decides to make them. I urge erring on the side of caution. I really don't like "one shot wonder" bows on several levels, first and foremost being safety to the archer and the spectators. I feel it's unethical to risk the well-being of others for the sake of an award or accolades.

I feel that a bow should last beyond a single event, or it was never really much of a bow. I take the most satisfaction from a bow I built and used to set several World and National records, and then lent it to a league archer for a season. Afterwards, it was returned to flight duty and set still more records! It was competitive for four years.

LAMINATED WOOD BOWS

Mike Westvang

Laminating different materials together to make bows dates back far into history with influences from the Middle East and Asia. Prior to 1800, English bowyers experimented with laminating yew and exotic woods obtained from their territories, primarily those in South America. Rosewood, snakewood, bloodwood, fustic, and beefwood were backed with lemonwood or hickory.

The hide glue used was susceptible to gathering moisture, however, softening and coming apart. Because of this tendency, the early laminated bows gained a limited following; the universal opinion at the time was that the laminated bow was inferior to a yew ELB due to glue failure. Will Thompson wrote in the late 1800s of laminated longbows available from English bowyers. He also commented that the glue used in laminating the bow softened during the long boat ride to America, leading to a short life before the bow failed.

The laminated wood flatbow is, for all practical purposes, an American bow. Its history is straight-lined from the English longbow, and though examples of laminated wood bows from other countries exist, they appear to have had little or no influence on the development of laminated flatbows.

Laminated flatbows enjoyed a span of only a few decades immediately preceding the Second World War. Some of the finest bows of this era were designed and built by Nels Grumley, who became Fred Bear's head bowyer in 1938. Grumley built four different styles of longbows and static recurves, and later models can be found in laminated as well as selfwood bows. He also backed bows with sinew, rawhide and various woods.

Owens Corning inadvertently changed bows forever in 1941 when it developed a flexible fiberglass cloth that could be used in laminates. It was only a short time before bowyers began using fiberglass laminations as backing on the multilaminate wood bows of the time. Fred Bear applied for a patent in 1946 for the use of fiberglass in bows, effectively ending the development and building of the laminated wood bow.

When talking of all-natural laminated bows, it is easy to get bogged down in the muddy world of definitions. Not all bows fall into a simple category. Some bows, such as a selfbow, are built using a stave. Some have an added backing of hickory or bamboo, while others have induced reflex during the gluing process, known as a Perry Reflex. Still others are backed with sinew or rawhide to add protection or performance. All of these are adaptations of the selfbow.

For the sake of simplicity and to focus this chapter, the laminated bow will be defined as being constructed from three or more layers of basically similar materials, in contrast to a composite, which is made from dissimilar components. Bamboo is "similar" enough that bamboo used with wood is a laminated bow. A sinew-backed, wood core, horn-faced bow is a composite bow.

GENTLEMAN'S TRADITIONAL RECREATIONAL LONG-BOW BY WARING (Elder) OF LONDON
Circa 1790 Ruby wood (pterocarpus santalinus) hickory (hickoria glabra)

Overall length 71 inches

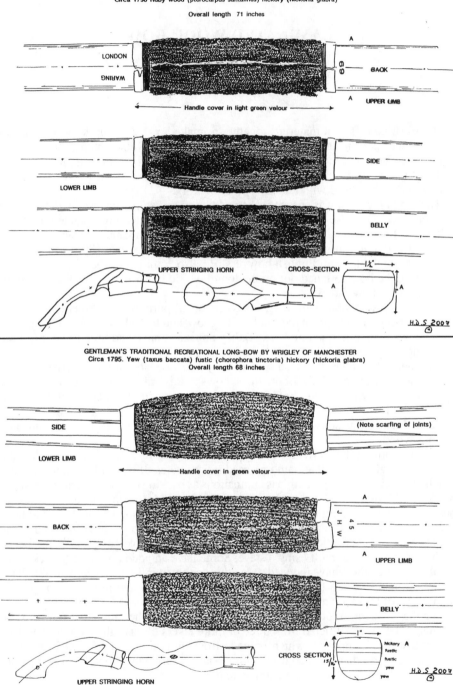

LONDON

WARING

A

BACK

UPPER LIMB

Handle cover in light green velour

SIDE

LOWER LIMB

BELLY

UPPER STRINGING HORN   CROSS-SECTION   1¼"

A

H.D.S 2007

GENTLEMAN'S TRADITIONAL RECREATIONAL LONG-BOW BY WRIGLEY OF MANCHESTER
Circa 1795. Yew (taxus baccata) fustic (chorophora tinctoria) hickory (hickoria glabra)
Overall length 68 inches

SIDE   (Note scarfing of joints)

LOWER LIMB

Handle cover in green velour

BACK

A

J H W

4 5

A

UPPER LIMB

BELLY

1"

hickory

fustic

fustic

yew

yew

CROSS SECTION

15/16"

A   A

UPPER STRINGING HORN

H.D.S 2007

Courtesy Hugh Soar

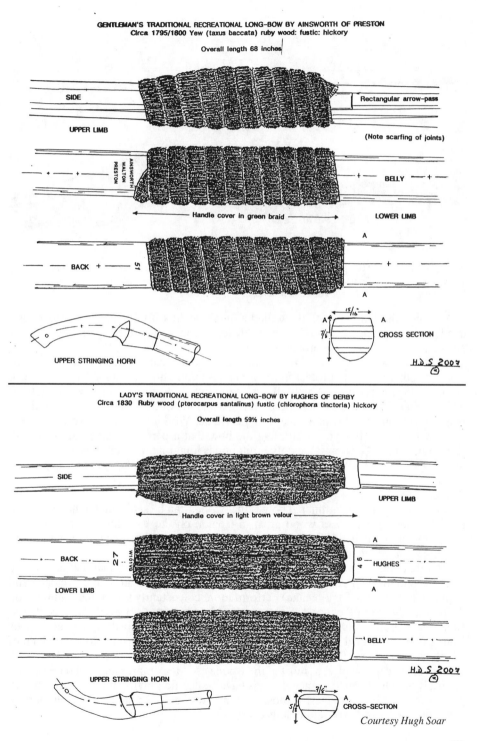

GENTLEMAN'S TRADITIONAL RECREATIONAL LONG-BOW BY AINSWORTH OF PRESTON
Circa 1795/1800 Yew (taxus baccata) ruby wood: fustic: hickory

Overall length 68 inches

SIDE

UPPER LIMB

Rectangular arrow-pass

(Note scarfing of joints)

AINSWORTH WALTON PRESTON

BELLY

Handle cover in green braid

LOWER LIMB

BACK

51

A

A

A

UPPER STRINGING HORN

15/16"

7/8"

CROSS SECTION

H.D.S 2007

LADY'S TRADITIONAL RECREATIONAL LONG-BOW BY HUGHES OF DERBY
Circa 1830 Ruby wood (pterocarpus santalinus) fustic (chlorophora tinctoria) hickory

Overall length 59½ inches

SIDE

UPPER LIMB

Handle cover in light brown velour

BACK

W1010W

27

A

46

HUGHES

A

LOWER LIMB

BELLY

H.D.S 2007

UPPER STRINGING HORN

7/8"

5/8"

CROSS-SECTION

Courtesy Hugh Soar

179

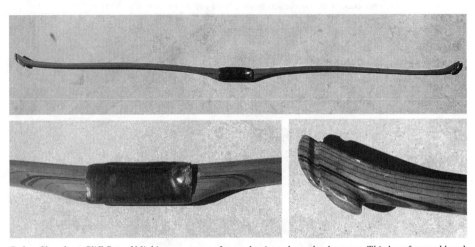

Before fiberglass, Cliff Coe of Michigan was one of many laminated wooden bowyers. This bow featured brush nocks, a hickory backing on three laminations of maple in the limbs, a trapezoidal cross-section, maple and walnut laminations in the handle riser, and Resorcinol glue.

Although the laminated flatbow died a quick death with the advent of fiberglass, this bow has been resurrected in the past fifteen years and is once again being developed and built by bowyers around the world.

A selfbow, whether made from a stave or a board, can be backed with hickory, maple or other woods to protect from failure. As laminations are added, the wood can be bent into tighter arcs, which allows the wood to be formed into configurations which gain efficiency and increase performance. One of the best reasons to laminate is a bowyer can build exactly the bow he wants. Working with a stave to create a selfbow limits the bowyer to building the bow that a particular piece of wood will yield. With laminated bows, the only limitation is imagination. Conjure the bow in the mind's eye and, with a little engineering, build it in a matter of days.

SELECTING THE WOOD FOR THE JOB

An advantage to the laminated bow is that woods can be selected that have specialties. In other words, use a wood great in tension on the back and a wood great in compression on the belly. Core woods can also add to performance if they are light in weight and have adequate stiffness.

Bamboo and pignut hickory work very well in tension with bamboo adding the greatest amount of performance. However, not all bamboos are equal; Madake and Tonkin bamboo (not Tonkin cane) perform more consistently than other bamboos on the market. Some of the woods from bow building history do a great job in compression. Osage orange and yew are excellent choices for almost any design. Other woods from around the world can be used, such as ipe, massuranduba and bloodwood, all of which have produced fine results for many bowyers.

With the exception of yew, most of the woods used in compression that have proven themselves in high performance designs have a specific gravity of .80 or greater. My preference is Osage orange for most of our bows, as it is readily available here in Texas and produces excellent results every time.

Reflex/deflex form.

BUILDING THE LAMINATED BOW

Although the only limitation on a laminated bow design is imagination, one is wise to learn to crawl before running. With that in mind, let's talk about designing and engineering bows.

The first step is to select a shape pleasing to the eye. I have found that the mild reflex / deflex shape works well, and is an excellent place to begin. This is a bow that will retain a touch of reflex in the limbs at brace and tends to shoot fast with very nice manners.

Once a design is selected, choose a process for building. The two most popular are the air hose form used in building glass bows and a jig using C clamps to apply pressure. For bamboo-backed bows, the jig is the easiest beginning method and the easiest to adjust. All that is needed is a straight hardwood 2x4 about 6 ft. long and a few odds and ends of lumber.

The jig we use for our Dryad Hunter has a removable center post 3" high, two mid-limb deflex posts 2 1/4" high, and removable tip curve section of 6 1/2". Screw the center and mid-limb posts and tip curve sections in place, and the jig is ready to use.

I recommend obtaining a length of 1 1/2" wide by 1/8" thick flat mild steel bar stock at your local lumber store to use as a base for the bow. This gives purchase for the clamps and also bends evenly between posts. The most difficult part is acquiring enough C clamps: for a 66" bow it will take two 6" and thirty 3" clamps to do the job properly.

SHAPING THE LAMS

This bow consists of a Tonkin bamboo backing, riser (power lam), an Osage taper and parallel belly lamination, and a set of wedges 12" long and .070" thick at the butt end. Handle and tip overlays are added after the core bow blank has been glued. This 64" ntn, 55 pound bow design uses a belly lam of .180" and a .002" taper with a butt thickness of .190". The riser section is 18" long and .300" thick at the center and tapers to a featheredge at each end. The handle overlay is made of three .300" thick pieces 12" long. All laminations and other parts are 1 3/4" wide.

Shaping and thinning the bamboo is one of the challenges, though anything from simple hand tools to the largest of power tools can be used. After selecting a bamboo plank that has even node separation, lay the bow out on the back of the bamboo using a template. If at all possible, place a node in the center of the bow; this will minimize

Bandsaw the bamboo just outside the lines

Center bow template on bamboo, clamp in place and trace with a dark pencil.

Turn the bamboo on edge and rip it to about 1/8" thick to ready for final thinning on the sander

the number of nodes in the working limb and make tillering easier. The template on this bow is 66" long with a 4" handle and 2" fades. The limbs taper from 1 1/2" at the fade to 1/2" at the tip.

Once the bow is drawn on the bamboo, cut the outline with a bandsaw, leaving 1/8" or so outside the line. Clean up to the lines using a block plane or sander. We use our large edge sander to accomplish this. After working it down, it's time to thin the bamboo for the backing. Using a bandsaw instead of hand tools can reduce the time required for thinning. Cut the bamboo to approximately 1/8" thick.

The bamboo should be reduced to final thickness while keeping it as flat as possible to allow a good glue line. This can be accomplished with hand tools and a toothing plane if power tools are not available. I prefer an edge sander for this job. Take the backing down to approximately 1/32" thick on both edges for its full length. Set aside for use later.

Laminations are easy because they can be ordered from any number of bow supply businesses. Typically, cost is around $20 a set for parallels and a little more for tapers. With a thickness sander, you can make your own with a little effort and save a few bucks.

The thickness sander grinds the tapered lams to match the sled.

For this bow, a set of .180" quarter-sawn Osage parallels and a set of .190 butt thickness .002" Osage tapers is needed. Both sets should be at least 1 3/4" wide and 36" long, free of knots and pins, and have grain running as straight as possible. Keep in mind that the better the components, the better the resulting bow.

After selecting the wood, cut the slats .080" to .100" thicker than required to allow for saw bobbles when grinding. Use a moisture meter before grinding to ensure the wood is dry (10-12% for Osage). If the moisture content is high, place the slats in a hot box for a couple of days at 125 degrees. Check them daily to monitor progress.

Once the moisture content is in the zone, it's time to grind the lams. The parallels are straightforward, but be careful when nearing the desired thickness. Remember that every .002" to .003" is a pound in the finished bow.

Grinding the skive joint using the pattern sander.

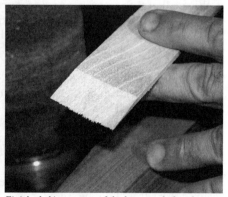

Finished skive on one of the lams ready for glue.

Taking lams down to 1-3/4".

Checking thickness of the belly lam, .020" left to remove to reach the required .180 inch.

The tapers require a bit more care so they'll be accurate. We use a push sled. One can be made by gluing tapers to a parallel hardwood board and then grinding on the sander. First, true the sawn slats to a parallel lamination approximately .050" thicker than the finished taper (in our case that would be .240" thick). Once it is true on both sides, load the lams in the taper sled and run them through the sander. Take off no more than .010" per pass, and rotate the lams from side to side, then once the lam is being ground end to end, turn them over and finish the process. Take it slowly as final thickness is approached.

There are many lam grinding machines available to the hobbyist from a large machine like ours on down to a drill press with a sanding attachment. Riser / power lam shape and length will vary with each design. The one used in this bow is 18" long and .300" thick. It tapers from the center to a featheredge on both ends and is then rounded in the middle to remove the sanded edge. We use a jig on the pattern sander to build these, but they are easily fashioned by hand.

GLUE-UP

When all of the parts are prepared, they are ready to be glued. The laminations are 36" long and will need to be spliced in the middle. The easiest method is a tangent splice, and if done properly, it looks good in the bow. To accomplish this, make a line 3/4" in from the center end of the lamination, then grind an angle from the line to the far edge of the lam. Repeat this with each of the laminations and check for fit. If the fit is good, glue the skive joints using thick Superglue, or cyanoacrylate adhesive, and a couple of squeeze clamps. Set aside for thirty minutes and clean up the excess glue with a sanding block after it's dry.

For a bow with this much reflex, insure the tips hold their shape by adding a reverse wedge to the tips section. We use a 12" taper with a .070" butt made of Osage from the scrap pile, but any hardwood will do the job. It was built using a pattern jig but can be easily fashioned by hand.

Before glue-up, make certain all of the parts are dust free; quick wipe with a tack rag or brush off will do the trick.

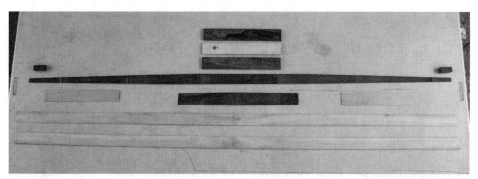

All of the parts ready for assembly. From bottom to top: parallel lam, tapered lam, tip wedge, riser, bamboo backing, tip overlays, and handle overlay lams.

An important aspect of a successful laminated bow is the glue. For an all wood bow or wood and bamboo, it's hard to beat URAC 185 for ease of use and the strength of bond. Another glue that works well and was used on many of the old laminated bows is Resorcinol. Devised as a waterproof marine glue for building wooden boats, it was invented by Dr. Yarstey of Yarstey Laboratories in England in the days before WWII. It was used during the war in the construction of a plywood bomber named the De Havilland Mosquito. It leaves a purple-black glue line. Smooth On is another glue that works well.

Select the glue and read the instructions for use. Multi-part glues need to be accurately mixed by volume or weight to get consistent results. We usually use URAC 185 from Nelson Paints and mix it to a 13 to 100 ratio by weight. Stir the glue until it is smooth in appearance and looks like chocolate frosting. Organize the components on the work surface with plastic wrap under them to contain the glue. I like to use packing tape or masking tape on the belly surface of the parallel lam before gluing to avoid a mess to clean up later. A good progression is to start with the belly lamination, then the two wedges, the tapered lamination, the riser / power lam and finally the bamboo. Apply glue with a brush to each side of the mated surfaces and stack them together until the bow is assembled. Fold the plastic wrap over the bow and snug it up so that no wrap is between the lams. Now transfer the bow to the jig. Align the centerlines and tape the bow into the jig making sure everything is centered. Tape it down to ensure that nothing moves during the clamping.

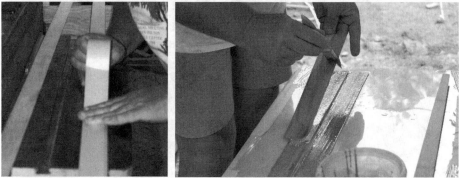

Tape the belly lam to keep the glue from migrating.

Apply glue to all surfaces to ensure a correct bond and glue line.

Tape the bow down to prevent slippage when the clamps are placed

Place pressure plates (we use scrap bamboo) on the bow starting at the center and hold in place with squeeze clamps. Start clamps at the center and place clamps an inch or so apart while working towards the tips. The more clamps used, the better the glue joint will look when finished. Remember when clamping that tight is good, but too tight will squeeze out too much glue, which causes a dry joint and a glue failure. So snug the clamp enough to get *some* glue squeezed from the edges. Work out to the reflex post and add the large clamp at this point. Finish clamping to the tips.

Installed clamps with 1" to 1 1/2" spacing, clamps alternated on each side of the bow. Note bamboo pressure plates to spread clamping force and prevent clamp damage to bow.

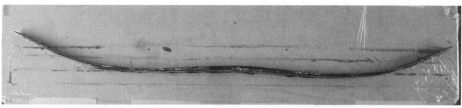

Bow blank right out of the jig.

The finished bow should have around 30-35 clamps installed.Transfer the whole thing into the hotbox, set it for 150 degrees and the alarm for three hours. The glue can be cured without a hotbox by leaving it for 24 hours at room temp (above 70 degrees). Check the instructions that come with the URAC 185.

Use the down time to clean up the glue mess. The brush and plastic tub clean up with hot water before the glue dries. The same brush can be used for twenty or so bows before it starts to shed bristles.

After three hours at 150 degrees, turn off the box and open the lid. Let the bow cool for at least a half hour before removing the clamps. Once all the clamps are removed and stored, take off the tape and gently pop the bow from the jig. Remove the plastic wrap and head back to the sander or bandsaw to trim it up to the profile lines on the bamboo.

Once the clean up is complete, it's time to get the handle section built and glued. The handle will be multilayered, composed of 1 3/4" x 12" x .300" thick pieces of Osage and cocobolo. Three strips will provide the proper depth in the handle. The pieces can bend nicely with the C clamps so they will always fit the handle.

Bow blank and handle lams ready for glue.

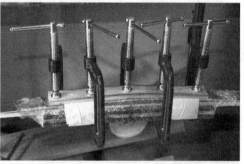

Handle glued, wrapped and clamped. Ready for the hot box to cure glue.

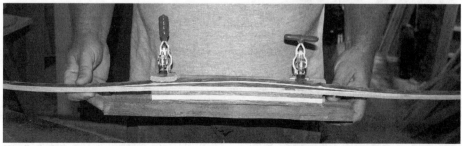

Handle jig for use on the pattern sander.

For gluing, mix up some more URAC 185 and stir it until it's smooth. Use the plastic wrap to keep the glue in place, then glue both sides of each mated piece. Tape the ends to hold in place on the bow until the clamp pressure can be applied. Clamp the center section first and apply enough pressure to squeeze a little glue out at each of the joints, then work clamps out to the ends of the handles. Five or six clamps total will do the job. Back in the hot box at 150 degrees and set the alarm for three hours, or set aside at room temperature for 24 hours. Once the blank is out and cool, it's ready to work.

TILLERING

Start by laying out and filing string nocks. Measure 1" down from the tip and place a mark on the backside of the edge of the bow. Now, using a carpenter's square, measure a 55-degree angle and mark it on the side. Use a rat-tailed file or chainsaw file to cut in the nocks on one side. Flip the bow over and place the file in the nock groove to locate the line for this side. Be careful to align the edges of the two grooves, and they will come in right and regular. True them up on both the back and belly of the bow.

Flex the bow on the floor 15-20 times to bend the limbs before installing a string. Check that the limbs are bending evenly. This bow has a static limb tip approx 7" long, so look to see that it is staying stiff and the rest of the limb is bending well.

Using a stringer, install a string that is 2" shorter than the bow's nock-to-nock length. In this case use a 62" string on the 64" ntn bow. Once strung, measure the tiller to see if both limbs are of equal strength. This is done just beyond the handle section and is measured between the belly of the bow and the string. Anything from equal to up to 1/4" difference at this time would be acceptable. If there is more then 1/4", take ten full-length strokes from the belly of the stronger limb with a cabinet scraper, exercise the limb on the floor and restring. Repeat this process until the tiller is within the 1/4" specification. Be careful, as wood comes off fast and tiller changes rapidly with a sharp scraper.

Jason Westvang floortillering bow. Exercise limbs twenty times on the floor after each change is made.

Once the limbs are bending approximately evenly, it's time to rough in the handle. We use an hourglass shaped (bulbous) handle on this bow, so lay out the shape and use the edge sander to remove material. A bandsaw and hand tools will also accomplish this task. With this style of handle, I like the throat area to be about 1" in diameter and the center of the handle to be about 1 1/4". From the squared handle, use a drawing compass to mark lines 3/8" wide from each side of the handle towards the center. Remove corners identified by the lines. Once the handle is roughed in, tillering continues.

Tillering the laminated bow is usually very easy. The better the engineering, the closer to final tiller the bow will be right out of the form. With the bamboo-backed bows, the area an inch or so on both sides of a node will be stiff and require some adjustment. Also, differences in wood density can require some adjustment. I like to use a cabinet scraper to get the stiff spots moving better. Mark the offending area with a pencil, and remove the marks with ten passes of the scraper. Exercise the bow and reinstall the string. A couple of cycles should have the bow bending in a smooth arc. Draw the bow beyond the braced height one inch at a time on the tiller tree, watching the bend of the limbs. It is important to identify stiff spots and hinges as early as possible and correct them before going farther with the draw.

When the bow reaches 20" of draw with a clean tiller, it's time to start shooting it. I have found through experience that laminated bows with bamboo backings are very resistive to change. Material can be removed and the bow repeatedly floor-tillered, and sometimes the bow will not change. A safe way to ensure the changes are shown after wood removal is to shoot the bow 10-20 times with very heavy arrows at the tillered draw. We use maple arrows that weigh 700 grains to accomplish this, but any heavy arrow will work. Be sure to mark the arrows and only draw the bow to the tillered distance. With this bow, the handle allows it to also be shot with the bottom limb up, which I recommend for half of the shots.

Remove wood from the stiff spots using a cabinet scraper.

Limbs bending evenly. Time to shoot it in.

Bow on the tiller tree, checking the weight and making sure the limbs bend evenly.

Once the tiller shots are down range, check the bend of the limbs again on the tiller tree. Mark areas that are stiff and remove material with the scraper. With experience, the tillering step becomes easier and faster. After material is removed, floor exercise the bow and shoot it again at the new tillered draw length.

Repeat this process until the desired draw is reached. Once a smooth tiller is achieved at full draw, it's time to put the scale on the bow. Weigh the bow to the full draw length (usually 28") and record the results. This identifies the engineered weight for this bow formula and will allow for adjustments to be made in the next bow. Although each bow design is different, a good rule of thumb is to add or subtract approximately .003" to your lamination thickness per pound of draw weight. The bow weight can be reduced as much as five pounds by narrowing the limbs or by trapping the limbs (narrowing the back only). However, the best bows will be the ones that require the least adjustment in width and thickness.

GRIP AND TIPS

The next step is finishing the bow by shaping the handle, adding tip overlays, and an arrow rest.

I like to get the tip overlays fitted and glued at this point, so that when the handle is shaped, I can move right to the tips. For overlays use horn or hardwood. Select the overlay material carefully. If using hardwood, get quarter-sawn with no knots. Horn should be free of cracks or voids. Cut the material 2" long, 1 1/2" wide and 3/4" thick. This will yield enough material so both overlays will match. To install the tips, I like to flatten the last two inches of the back on the sander and glue the hardwood overlay in place using thick Superglue. Clamp the overlay and allow to dry one hour before proceeding.

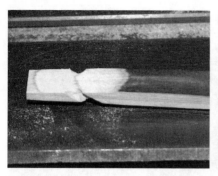

Tip beveled and flattened, ready for gluing the overlay.

Overlay in place, glued and clamped. The Superglue allows shaping within half an hour.

After the glue has cured, the tips are shaped using the flexible rasp (1" strip of 36 grit belting). Use a shoeshine buffing motion across the back of the tip until it is rounded. Then shape the tip end with a sanding block until a bullet shape is achieved. Turn the bow to work on the belly side. Facet the last 6" or so of the bow into the tip with the sanding block. Shape the end of the tip with the sanding block to complete the bullet tip. Then blend the facets from the rectangular limb profile to a round tip using the same shoeshine motion with the belting strip.

The roughed out handle is relatively easy to finish. Using the rasp, knock down the ridges that were formed when it was made eight sided, and radius the belly side to a round profile. This is easily accomplished by using a strip of 36 grit belting. Be careful when blending the ends of the handle into the limbs using the edge of the rasp. If done incorrectly or with too much enthusiasm, a dish can be formed in the limb, which will result in a bow-breaking hinge, so use a light touch when blending and rounding the edge of the handle.

The last step before the bow is finished is installing the arrow pass. Although not absolutely necessary, I find it easier to shoot, as well as more attractive. We like a built-up rest using tooling leather. Get the thickest leather and avoid an oily tan if possible. We buy the thick tooling leather in 12" square pieces from our local leather shop.

Using a rasp to remove faceted ridges left over from power shaper.

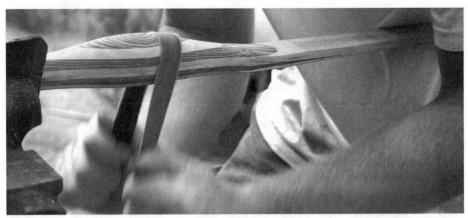

The flexible rasp (sanding belt strip) makes shaping the round belly easy.

To build the rest, simply cut one piece 1" wide by 2" long, and another piece 1" square. Draw a line on the bow 2" above the center of the handle towards the upper limb. Apply thick Superglue liberally to the rough side of the leather, and use it to smear glue on the handle area. Place the leather on the handle and clamp in place. We use a scrap of bamboo and a small "C" clamp. Once the glue is set, remove the clamp and bamboo. Rough the leather with a rasp and repeat the process with the smaller piece of leather.

After the glue is dry, the rough shaping is accomplished with a rasp or sander. Then saturate the leather with thin Superglue and allow to dry. This makes the leather hard and easier to shape with rasp and sanding block so it blends into the rest of the handle. When the rest is shaped, apply a last coat of thin Superglue. The bow is now ready for shooting. I recommend at least fifty shots to ensure that tiller is stable before sanding and applying finish.

Add superglue, then tooling leather, then clamp.

Repeat the process with the second piece of leather.

Finish rasping and sanding the leather, then saturate with superglue and the arrow rest is ready.

Removing tool marks from the edge of the limbs. Don't forget to count the number of passes, otherwise the limb can begin to twist.

FINISHING

The sanding process is simple and straightforward. We use a palm sander for most of the work but a sanding block can also be used. Starting with 60 grit, sand the side of the limbs with ten strokes each to remove tool marks, followed by five strokes on the both the belly and back corners. It is extremely important to count the strokes and keep both sides and both limbs equal. Do not sand the bamboo with 60 grit as it will leave deep gouges. Sand the handle removing all tool marks and any edges left from the facets. Shift to 150 grit paper and repeat the process using five strokes on all surfaces. On the bamboo, lightly sand to remove the shine and the sharp edge of the nodes. 150 grit leaves enough purchase for the sealing coats to bind well.

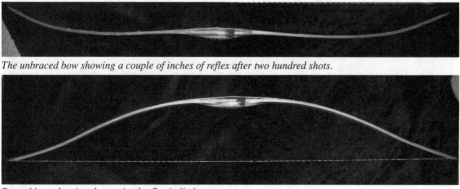

The unbraced bow showing a couple of inches of reflex after two hundred shots.

Braced bow showing the retained reflex in limbs.

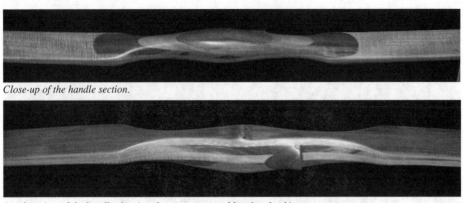

Close-up of the handle section.

Another view of the handle showing the arrow rest and bamboo backing.

The next step is to seal the bow. This can be accomplished with coats of shellac, superglue, or finishes like Thunderbird and Fullerplast. Two or three heavy coats of finish will provide a good seal to the wood and fill pores to allow for a smooth finish. After the sealing coats have cured, usually the next day, sand with 220 grit to remove the shine, while being careful not to go too deep and expose unfilled pores. Wipe the bow with a tack rag or lightly dampened cloth to remove dust to prepare for finish coats.

Usually two or three coats of a spray finish will do the job. If using oil like Tru Oil or tung oil, apply finishes and allow drying according to instructions. Oil finishes are best applied thin and with many coats.

To achieve a non-reflective surface, spray the final coat with a flat or dull finish. Do not use flat for all coats as it has more solids and will tend to color the finish. Another method to dull a bright finish is to hand-rub it with 0000 steel wool or an abrasive pad.

After the finish dries, the bow is complete and ready for many years of service.

Then, it is time to start planning the next laminated bow. For there is always a next one: shorter, longer, stronger, weaker, with more reflex or recurve, selecting a design and woods for ultimate performance, or trying for more interesting color contrasts between the woods. The combinations are endless, and the only limitation is the imagination.

CHARACTER BOWS

Jim Welch

Back when I was making lots of bows professionally, I usually chose a nice straight stave that allowed completion of a finished weapon within a day or two. After making hundreds of such bows over several years, however, using straight staves became like working on an assembly line. They were just flat boring.

I found myself drawn to staves I had first rejected. Soon, I was making bows from staves that had earlier seemed impossible. Character bows may be the ultimate challenge of bowmaking. Flaws, wind, and growing conditions affect how the wood looks and behaves. If it had no character it would be like fiberglass. Now, as far as I'm concerned, the more character the better.

Osage and yew are the classic character woods, because they commonly grow with twists, knots, and, in the case of Osage, thorns. In addition, Osage also tends to have more snakes, or side-to-side wiggles, while yew tends to have more rollercoasters, or back-to-front wiggles. Any wood species can exhibit such character, although perhaps in smaller doses, and anyone making many bows will likely be called upon to deal with such problems.

Paul Comstock once wrote that you can't be a quitter if you want to make wooden bows, and that's doubly true if you want to make character bows.

A bowyer never knows what problem - or combination of problems - he'll encounter. He has to be flexible and not be too tied to pre-conceived ideas about the bow he'll make, never trying to take more than the wood can give. Though he might have planned otherwise, he may have to make it shorter, longer, narrower, wider, with wrap-on nocks, sinew-backed, use half of it for a billet, or heat it and bend it to make it work. With character bows, always be prepared to adopt a fall-back position.

CRACKS

There are several different types of cracks that might be encountered.

Most common are drying cracks, or checks. These usually appear in the ends of staves or in the outer growth rings. Drying checks are one of the reasons for leaving character staves wider and longer than normal. The ends with cracks can be removed. A crack in the outer growth rings can sometimes be avoided by laying out the bow to miss it. If not, these types of cracks tend to vanish if the stave is worked to deeper growth rings.

Another type of crack is a heart check. This flaw can occasionally be found in any wood, but I've seen it primarily in Osage. Osage has a pith in the center of each trunk and limb, into which water will sometimes infiltrate, especially at a fork, causing the wood to rot from the inside-out. These cracks are the opposite of drying checks, as they get worse towards the center of the tree.

If there are too many drying checks or heart checks that can't be avoided, then the fall back position may be to sinew-back the bow.

Drying checks on the back of an Osage stave.

The same checks on the end. Note how they disappear a few growth rings down from the outside of the stave, and can be avoided by selecting a deeper growth ring for the back of the bow.

Though relatively rare, the worst type of crack is a laminar separation, or a separation between the growth rings. It's as if the early wood in a particular yearly ring fails. This seems to be more of a problem with green wood in the northern U.S., where temperatures might get down to 20 or 30 degrees below zero. My guess is that the high moisture content in the green wood freezes and expands, creating a crack between the growth rings exactly like freezing water breaks a pipe.

If such a separation of the growth rings appears while working a stave down to one ring, simply select a lower ring for the back. Bandsaw or scrape the sides to ensure that there are no other laminar separations in the stave. Where one exists there are sometimes several more at different levels. Often a laminar separation is not apparent until the bow is bent during tillering. It then behaves like a glue failure between lamination of a fiberglass bow. The crack shows on the side of the limb, and if it is very deep, in a working area, this is one of the few cases where there is no fall-back position, because it's invariably fatal to the bow. But in the spirit of never-say-die, the other limb may still be perfectly sound and can be spliced to another billet.

A laminar separation on the side of a stave, where the early wood between two growth rings fails.

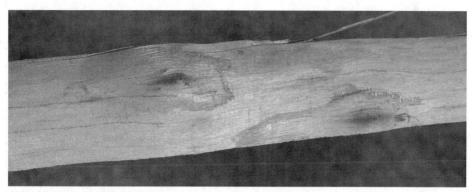

"Islands" of extra wood left on knots.

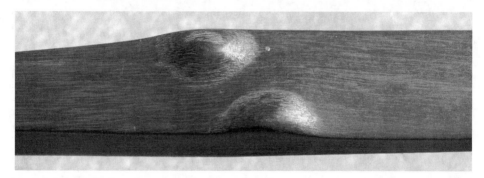

Small islands of extra wood left above the growth ring established for the bow's back.

GROWTH RINGS

The first step in turning a stave into a bow is reducing it to one yearly growth ring, which will be the back of the bow. With white woods this is easy, just remove the bark, and there lies a pristine growth ring. With any wood in which the back of the bow will be an interior growth ring, however, all of the wood above that ring must be carefully removed with drawknife or scraper. To me, this process is as satisfying as following a blood trail to the end; be patient and meticulous.

Taking a thin slice from one end of the stave with a bandsaw reveals the growth rings and their relative thickness. Pick a fairly thick growth ring for the back, even if it requires going down a ways to reach it, but don't take off any more wood than necessary. Also, select a deeper growth ring to get away from drying checks, insect damage, or other problems nearer the surface.

Follow the chosen growth ring wherever it leads, through dips, roller coasters, and over knots. A tree is wise enough to build in extra wood to strengthen an area where a branch or thorn protruded, so follow the growth ring carefully up and over a knot. When a stave has lots of knots, it's fine to leave an "island" of extra wood around each one, which can be removed later. But always keep a continuous thread of the chosen growth ring from one end of the stave to the other, even if it's only by a narrow strip on one side or the other around a big knot. Skipping ahead and failing to keep that constant physical connection will often yield a growth ring above or below the one desired.

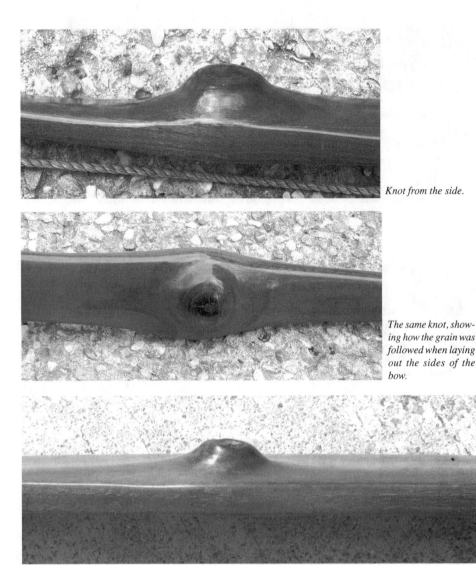

Knot from the side.

The same knot, showing how the grain was followed when laying out the sides of the bow.

A tree usually adds a strengthening lump in the growth ring over a knot.

Once a growth ring has been established from one end of the stave to the other, and it's clear how the bow lies in the stave, extra wood around the knots can be removed. No point in taking a great deal of time and effort working knots or other difficulties that won't be in the bow anyway. All of the extra wood above the chosen growth ring can be removed, but it's fine to leave an extra growth ring or two over a knot as long as the area is not much larger than a quarter. If more is left, say a two inch cap around a knot, then later, when it is well along in the tillering process and bending well, sometimes this extra wood will pop free, creating a hinge in that now too-thin area.

If a knot is soft or otherwise unsound, I usually scrape it out and fill it with superglue and sawdust, then rub the mixture smooth with a latex glove. Let dry 24 hours.

FOLLOWING THE GRAIN

The grain lies at right angles to the growth rings, so it helps to think of the yearly growth rings as the tire and rim of a bicycle wheel, and the grain as the spokes. Wood always splits along the grain, and checks or cracks follow the grain, too.

In bright sunlight, the grain is much easier to see from a low angle at one end of the stave, appearing as scratches in the surface of the back's single growth ring. Position the stave in the sunlight until the grain is apparent.

Starting in the center, draw a pencil line to one end of the stave exactly following the grain. Repeat for the other half of the stave. This will be the centerline of the bow. Refer also to the following section on bow layout to anticipate and avoid problems as this centerline is drawn. The grain will snake between knots, flowing like water around and between rocks in a stream, and should be followed faithfully.

After laying out a centerline by following the grain, it may well be that the tips are out of alignment, or the bow has a pronounced propeller twist. Ignore these issues, for now.

The grain is much easier to see when looking down the stave from the end.

On the back of an Osage stave, the grain appears as tiny, lighter-colored lines.

Properly placing the natural wiggle in this bow's grain made the bow almost center-shot.

Knot avoided by careful layout of the bow. The grain flowed around the knot, which made a snake in the bow.

LAYOUT

Think ahead and imagine where the bow lies in the stave.

Sometimes, with a snaky stave, the bow can be almost centershot if the handle is positioned properly. This makes arrow spine more forgiving, allowing a much wider range of arrow spines and weights to shoot well.

In general, try to layout the bow to avoid flaws such as cracks and unsound knots. It's much easier to leave a problem on the wood shop floor as the stave is reduced than to have to deal with it later. If a problem can't be avoided, it can cause less mischief in a non-bending portion of the bow, between the fadeouts at the handle or right at the tips. I once had a stave with a .22 bullet imbedded deeply in the wood, so I placed it in the handle, and it never caused a problem.

Layout one-half of the bow's design profile on each side of the centerline. This way the bow's limbs follow the grain perfectly. The grain will be cut through as the limbs narrow, of course, but this is of no consequence if the centerline technique is used.

Bow laid out to place cracks in the non-bending riser section near the handle.

Lee Hamm with his snakey take-down bow. The centerline was drawn first, exactly following the grain, then the bow laid out from the centerline.

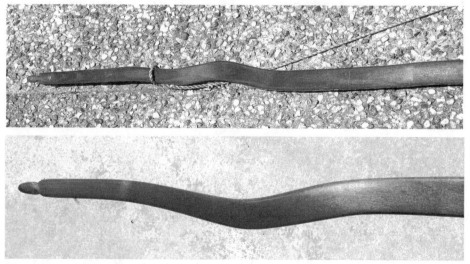

More snakes.

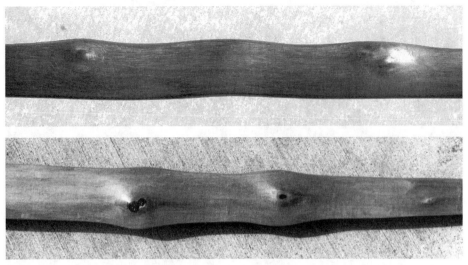

Follow the grain along the sides of the bow, as well.

When a knot is encountered, particularly near the edge of the limb, follow the grain around the knot, and then return to the regular width taper after the knot is passed. This will make a slight lump on the sides of the bow, and a really knotty stave can yield a bow with scarcely a straight line anywhere. Even a huge knot can be compensated for in this manner. The bigger the knot, the more the grain will swell out and away from it as it flows past, leaving adequate wood to carry the bending load as if the knot wasn't there. The same is true for a hole in a stave when a knot, the leftover remains of a branch, has pulled free. Few bows are more impressive than those with silver dollar-sized knots or even massive holes in the limb.

When there is no choice but to position a trouble spot in the working portion of a limb, it's better to position the bow so the flaw is right in the center of the limb. Even a deep crack or enormous knot will seldom cause problems if it's centered in this way. A crack at a bow's tip should also be placed in the center of the limb, then, instead of conventional nocks, use a simple wrap-on nock. When one tip has a wrap-on nock and the other cut-in grooves, a timber hitch is used with the wrap-on nock, whether it's the upper or lower limb, and the normal string loop used with the cut-in nock.

If a crack runs off of the side in a working portion of the limb, and it can't be avoided, then consider backing the bow. A hickory back or a sinew back will cure this otherwise potentially lethal flaw.

Bow laid out so the cracks were in the center of the limb. Note how cracks followed the grain around the knot.

Two bows with massive holes in the working section of the limb. If possible, such problems would ideally be placed in the center of the limb, but if the growth ring was well-worked and the grain carefully followed, even off-center, such awe-inspiring holes wouldn't threaten a bow.

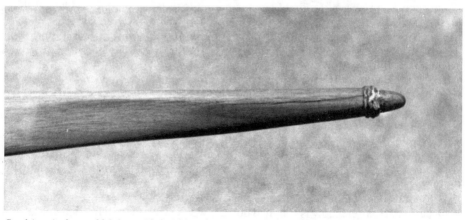

Crack in a tip that couldn't be avoided with bow layout. A conventional nock would have cut into the crack, so a pointed tip and wrap-on nock were used.

When pronounced grain is followed when laying out the bow, often the tips won't line up perfectly with the handle. If badly misaligned once the bow is strung, the handle can simply be shaped to "point" toward the string.

TWISTS AND MISALIGNMENT

A propeller twist occurs when the plane of each limb is twisted, or rotated in relation to the other. I usually ignore such twists up to about 45 degrees or so, as they largely disappear once the bow is strung and have no effect on the shooting characteristics.

More pronounced propeller twist can be adjusted by heating one limb at a time, clamping the handle, and twisting the limb in the opposite direction until it cools. The limbs don't have to be bent all the way back to zero twist, just so they're less than about 45 degrees. Be aware that a limb torqued too far sometimes complains by snapping off, another reason to ignore such a problem if possible.

An option for dealing with a severe propeller twist is to cut the stave in half, then cut fishtail splices positioned to remove much or all of the twist before splicing the limbs back together. Or make a socketed take-down with the same strategy.

When following the grain and drawing the centerline, many times the ends will not line up, causing the string to lay off center on the handle or in severe cases even lay entirely outside the handle. You can bend the handle sideways, which takes a great deal of heat and jigs to hold the limbs. If you use this method, the handle should be bent until the limbs are about 50% past their intended position, as they will return by that amount when unclamped.

Or a much simpler and more elegant solution is to leave the grip wide and thick until the bow is strung during the tillering process. Once the true string position is determined with a strung bow, the handle is simply shaped with a rasp so it is oriented directly toward the string. No heat, no bending, no stress to the wood, and the string alignment will be perfect.

TILLER

Tillering a character bow is often the most difficult part.

Once the bow is roughed out, it's important that both limbs look approximately the same from the side view. If one limb is reflexed, and one is straight, for example, it will be very difficult to judge the true bend of the limbs as tillering progresses. If adjustment to one limb is required, I like to floor-tiller the bow first, as the relatively thin limbs at that stage require less heat to bend. When tillering begins, a little reflex in both limbs is ideal, but it's fine if both are straight.

Occasionally, after a bow is roughed out, the wood in a knot will become loose. Try removing this cone of wood by pushing gently with an awl from back to belly. If the plug of wood comes out, it leaves behind a cone-shaped hole. Such holes will not be

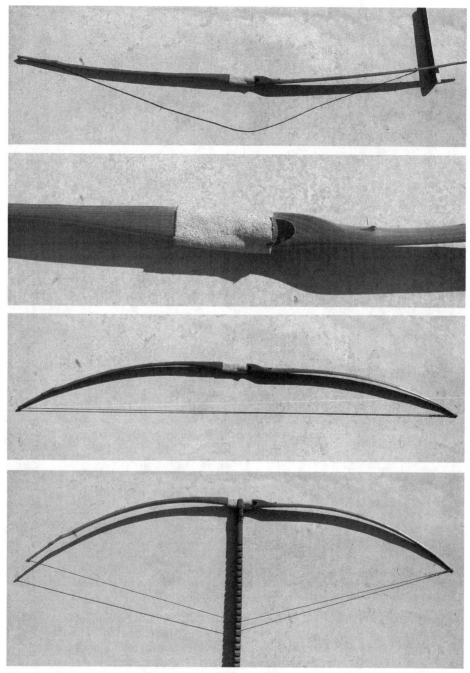

When the limbs are different shapes from the side view, the bow is very difficult to tiller. This reflexed bow was especially tough, as the limbs left the grip area at different angles. Though it looks terribly asymmetrical, both limbs are bending equally and are equally strained.

Such a knot in a stave will sometimes be loose and can be pushed out, leaving a hole.

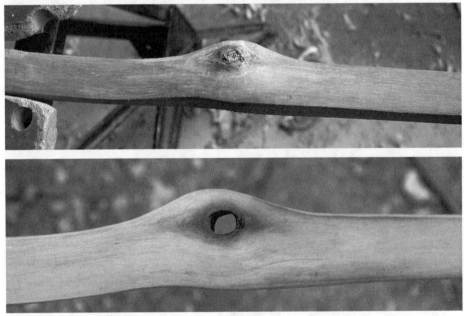

The above two photos show a loose knot in a stave and the hole it left behind.

unsound if the growth ring on the back was carefully worked, leaving behind a bump where the tree added compensating wood for strength. I once made an Osage bow for a customer with a pencil-sized hole through the lower limb. I thought of the hole as a thousand-yard peep sight, but when he took the bow antelope hunting, he reported that the constantly blowing Plains wind whistled across the hole when he turned the bow at just the right angle. He solved the problem by putting a Bandaid over the hole!

Bows with pronounced reflex are easy to make too light. Because of the reflex, they are very difficult to initially string. In the early days I always thought they were far heavier than they really were. Once they were strung, such bows surprised me regularly, as they were often at or even below the desired weight. Now, I string reflexed bows very early in the process, even when they still seem far too heavy.

Once a bow is floor-tillered and strung, pull it only to the intended weight while noting the draw length reached. Never pull the bow more than the intended final draw weight. A bow which will hold together forever at 50# might unravel if you pull it to 70# one time. As tiller progresses, the draw length at a given weight will increase, allowing adjustment to wood removal. When final weight and draw length approach, I like to switch to a scraper and check results often. Don't forget to flex the bow fifteen or twenty times every time wood is removed, even small amounts, so the true bend of the limbs is apparent.

More character-laden holes.

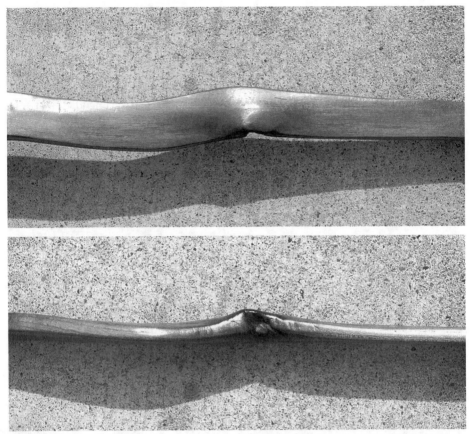

With such rollercoasters or other irregularities, the wise bowyer will use an even thickness taper to insure correct tiller.

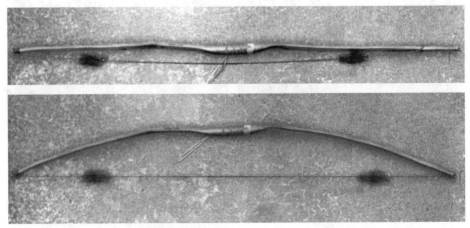

A bow with natural "kinks", which appear to be bending too much no matter how thick. An even thickness taper ensures these areas carry their share of the bending load.

Thickness taper is life. The key to any tillering, and especially character bows, is in having the thickness taper even along the working portions of the limbs. If the taper is uniform with no thick or thin places, then the limbs will bend evenly. They will be too strong when tillering begins, and one may be slightly stronger than the other, but if the taper is even then there will be no hinges or flat spots.

With a character bow, which may well have roller-coasters and other wiggles, the trick lies in keeping the taper even on both sides of the limb and keeping both sides the same thickness. I usually make one pass with a rasp down each side of a bow's limb, sculpting the belly side to exactly follow the back edge while getting thinner from handle to tip, then rasp out the ridge left in the belly. Check often, looking down the side with the eye right above the tip. Make parallel pencil lines on the belly to indicate areas where wood needs to be removed and X's for areas that should be left alone. Check the weight by floor-tillering often, or by checking on the scale once the bow is strung. I always stop an inch short of full draw, say at 50# at 27" for a bow intended for 50# at 28". This extra inch gives a couple of pounds to work with as the bow is sanded and broken in, and it usually settles right on the intended final stats.

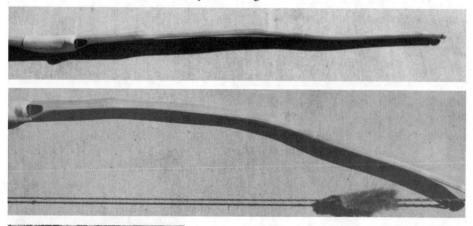

A small area of natural reflex appeared too flat once this bow was strung and drawn, but this upper limb was working correctly.

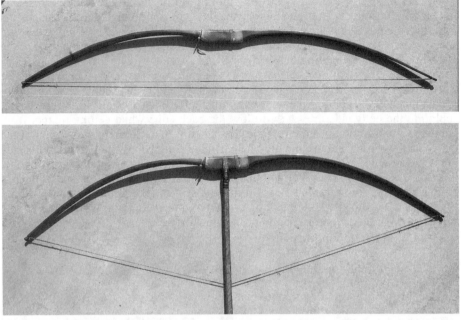

A bow with a propeller twist made by master-bowyer Gary Davis, viewed from one side, both strung and drawn.

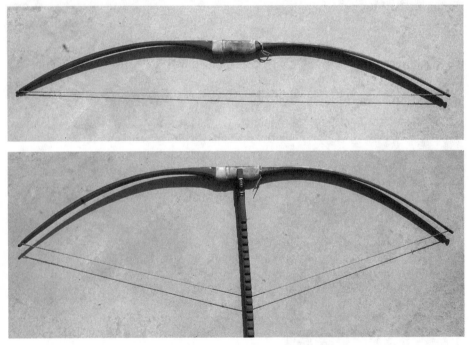

The same bow viewed from the other side. In the photos, each limb appears stiffer, or stronger, when on the right. This is an illusion, however, caused by viewing the edges of the twisted limbs from slightly different angles.

It's relatively easy to judge the thickness taper on the side of a bow compared to judging the true bend of an undulating limb. As it bends, a natural kink in the limb will look as though it is bending too much and forming a hinge, but it will look that way even if the kink is considerably thicker than the area around it. And if that area is thicker and not bending even though it may appear to be, then that's putting more strain on other portions of the limb. So, too, will a little area of natural reflex appear as if it is not bending at all and is a flat spot, and the natural tendency of the bowyer is to thin that area. But that portion of the limb will now be thinner than surrounding areas, and will, in reality, be under far more stress than it should. The only true way to accurately judge the correct bend is by the even thickness taper. An even taper through all those wavy areas insures that every portion of the limb is doing its fair share of the work. Again, thickness taper is life.

The hardest of all bows to judge are those with a propeller twist. As tillering progresses, such a bow will look as though one limb is stiffer than the other. Flip it around, however, and now the other limb looks stiffer. Flip it back, and the first limb is magically stiffer again. The twist will make judgment deceptive. With such bows, pay close attention to thickness taper, as always. When final draw length and draw weight are reached, and each limb has an even bend while performing this alternating "Now I'm stronger" routine, then I call it done.

Make a hundred character bows and no two will be alike.

YOU CAN'T BE A QUITTER

There will be times when you have made a wonderful character bow, having chased a growth ring like a bloodhound, followed the grain perfectly, and tried hard for an even thickness taper.

And it will still break.

Don't throw it in the fire, which will be the natural reaction. Instead, study that broken bow like you've never studied another. Was there a grain violation? Delamination? Maybe hidden damage? Uneven thickness taper? A knot on the back where the growth ring was nicked, allowing a splinter to start? Should the bow have been longer or wider for the wood density and draw weight? Determine how you could have handled a problem differently. You can learn a great deal from a broken bow, sometimes far more than you can from successful ones. Just consider it paying your dues, as all of the 'old hands' have had to pay them.

In the late 1980's, I purchased several Osage staves from a guy in Texas. Most were nice and clean, but one had a couple of huge knots. Now remember that twenty years ago, few of us had any clue how to deal with such problems, so I placed it in the stave pile, where it resided for about a decade. I always wondered if there was a bow in that stave, however, and I finally worked up the nerve, and experience, to tackle it. The resulting bow, *Monkey Butt*, quickly became one of my favorites. In the past ten years, I've used that bow from the reject pile to take numerous whitetails and a bull elk, and few things have ever been more satisfying.

ARROWS OF THE WORLD

Mickey Lotz

Arrow; definition according to Merriam-Webster's Dictionary:
Pronunciation: 'er (") - O, a'- (") rO; Function: noun
Etymology: Middle English arwe, from Old English: akin to Gothic arhwazna arrow,
    1. A missile shot from a bow and usually having a slender shaft, a pointed head and feathers at the butt. 2. An arrow is a pointed projectile that is shot with a bow. It predates recorded history and is common in most cultures.

Most scholars credit the bow as one of the great inventions that helped mankind become what we are today. They seldom seem to mention the arrow, but in fact, one is just as important as the other. Without the arrow, the bow is nothing more than a stick with its ends tied together by a cord. Since the bow and arrow predates recorded history, there is no written evidence of when, where, or by whom they were first put to use. Arrow shafts were made of natural plant and animal materials, which were subject to deterioration over centuries, so none of the original examples have been discovered, having long ago returned to the earth.

The Upper Paleolithic period started around 40,000 B.C., and it was possibly during this stage that the bow and arrow was invented. As it is generally conjectured that fire-hardened wood arrow points preceded bone arrow points, and bone arrow points preceded stone arrow points; it is therefore possible that the bow and arrow were invented far earlier than surviving artifacts would indicate.

However, all this is only archaeologists' speculation, as physical evidence of the arrow shaft, i.e., specimens of wood arrows that survived and have been discovered, can only be dated back to around 10,000 B.C. The oldest surviving specimens to date have come from northern Germany. The arrows were made of pine and consisted of a main shaft and a foreshaft with a flint point.

Arrows dating to 9,500 B.C. have been found in England, Germany, Denmark and Sweden. They were often rather long and made of hazel, Viburnum and chokecherry. Some still had flint arrowheads attached while others had blunt wooden ends for hunting birds and small game. The nock ends showed traces of fletching fastened with birch tar.

Regardless of the exact timing of their origins, invention of the bow and arrow was critical in man's advancement. Use of the bow and arrow certainly made it easier for early man to live, to kill animals for food, and to defend his possessions from others. Compared to its predecessors, the spear and atlatl, the bow and arrow was more compact, lighter, faster to reload, stealthier, and allowed hunters and warriors to carry many more rounds (arrows) with them. Arrows were tipped with light-weight arrow points - true arrowheads, which could be made from smaller pieces of raw material and with less effort than dart points. The arrow itself was a miniaturized version of an atl-atl dart.

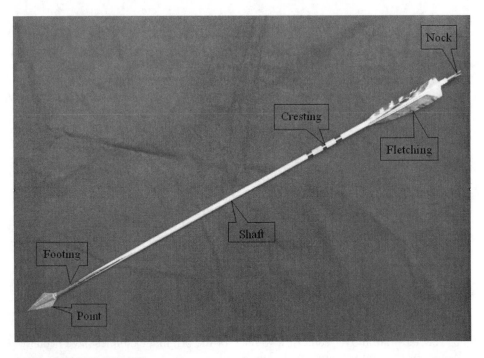

THE ARROW SHAFT

The shaft is the primary structural element of the arrow to which all of the other components are attached. The shaft is generally cylindrical, of some natural material, between 18 inches and 5 feet long, depending on the need of the culture and the materials available. An arrow shaft has to be relatively straight, or be able to be made so, and stay that way or be easily re-straightened. It has to have strength and weight, but remain flexible to recover quickly from being flexed. It also has to withstand repeated flexing without breaking down. Plus, it must be tough enough to withstand multiple impacts with hard objects. The more an arrow shaft material met these specs, the more valued it was, and the more it was sought by arrow makers. Over the centuries, arrow shafts have been made from many different materials, but principally they were made from what was readily available to the arrow maker. This included bamboo/cane/reeds, hardwood shoots, and eventually split timber shafting.

Cane/Bamboo/Reeds

Cane/bamboo/reeds are almost the perfect natural arrow material. There are literally dozens of species that make up this classification of plants, and they grow on nearly every continent. They grow in huge colonies in bogs, streams and riversides and in most wetlands in moderate temperature climates, so it's likely that a ready supply of cane was always nearby. It is self-propagating, so there was a nearly inexhaustible supply. Already cylindrical, it grows in various diameters and lengths, so it was likely a needed size was readily available. Cane/bamboo/reeds were tough, resilient and recovered quickly from being flexed. Cane straightened easily with heat and stayed straight, and also had a natural taper, which was a benefit for clean arrow flight

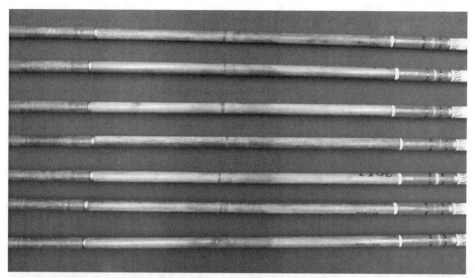

Indo-Persian arrows, showing reed shafting and nodes (Grayson Collection).

Rivercane; raw shaft, straightened shaft, and finished hunting arrow.

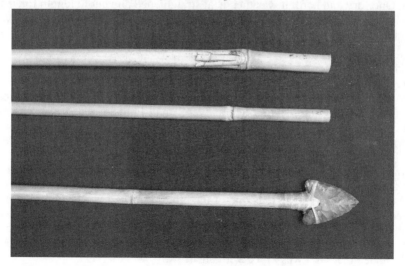

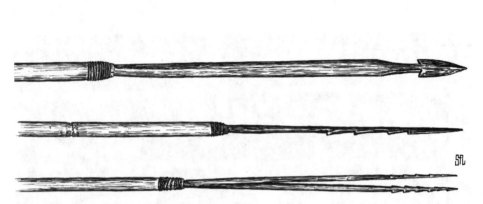

Southeastern US, Chickasaw Indian; phragmites cane arrows, hardwood foreshafts, fine plant fiber cordage wrap (Oklahoma Historical Society Museum).

from various weight bows and handle designs. Its primary downsides were light weight, and the fact that it was hollow. Being hollow, it tended to split if forcefully impacted at either end. One solution was placing the nock just above a node or carving a nock of hardwood, bone, or horn to prevent the cane from being split by the bow string. On the tip end, inserts or "foreshafts" of hardwood or bone were fashioned and inserted to help prevent splitting from an impact against something hard, like a rock, tree, or the shoulder blade of a large mammal. The added benefit of a foreshaft was it also added mass to the light cane arrow, which increased its ability to penetrate. In those areas of the world where bamboo/cane/reeds grew prevalently, most cultures adapted this material for arrow shafting. These include the Africans, Mongolians, Egyptians, Japanese, Chinese, Koreans, natives from the Indian Ocean and Pacific Ocean island chains, and some tribes of North and South American Indians.

All of the cane species were relatively soft when green, but hardened appreciably as they dried out and lost moisture. Cane was cut, gathered, bundled and stored until dry. During that time, it changed from an olive green color to a nice soft yellowish tan color. Once dry and hard, it was then heat straightened and cut to length for shafting. Anyone who has tried cane shafting can attest to its suitability for an arrow shaft material.

Shoot Shafting

Although nearly ideal for an arrow shaft, cane/reeds/bamboo did not grow everywhere. Canes were largely a warm weather plant, so cold-climate cultures were forced to choose alternate materials for their shafting. Nearly as popular as the bamboo/cane/reed shafting were shoot shafts. Shoots were small limbs of various shrubs, bushes and trees, and many hundreds of species were proven to be perfectly suitable. Mesolithic arrows found in England, Denmark, Germany and Sweden, for example, were made from hazel, wayfaring tree (a Viburnum), and chokecherry.

Otzi, or the Iceman, is the nickname of a well-preserved natural mummy of a man from about 3300 BC, found in 1991 in a glacier of the Otztal Alps, near the border between Austria and Italy. He is one of the oldest known human mummies, and has offered an unprecedented view of the habits of early Europeans. Items found with the Iceman included a quiver full of arrows with Viburnum and dogwood shafts and flint heads, an unfinished yew longbow taller than he was, and a copper axe. Ironically, x-rays revealed that Otzi was killed with an arrow.

The advantage of shoots for arrow shafts was their availability in the forested parts of the planet. Wherever a tree, bush or shrub grew, chances were there would be suitable shoots for arrow shafting. Like cane, it was already cylindrical, grew in various diameters and lengths, so varying sizes were available for light-weight or heavy-weight bows. Shoot shafts were tough, resilient; recovered quickly when flexed and withstood repeated flexing. They also straightened fairly easily with heat. Again, like cane, they were naturally tapered, which was a benefit for clean arrow flight. Unlike cane, however, most shoots were not hollow; therefore, they had no need for plugged nocks or foreshafts. Being solid generally made for a naturally heavier shaft, which increased mass and penetration.

The disadvantages of shoot shafts were the effort required to find large numbers of suitably sized shafts in a small geographic area, and although they straightened easily with heat, shoot shafts were more prone to warping due to the hygroscopic nature of

Finished dogwood arrow, shaft scraped and straightened, and raw dogwood shaft.

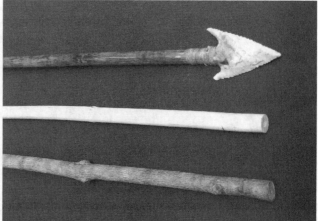

wood and often required re-straightening. Hardwood shoots did not have the naturally waterproof and protective casing of a cane shaft, so to help prevent the absorption of water, additional sealing/waterproofing was required, whether it be rendered animal fat or a shellac of some sort. Shafts left unprotected quickly lost their straightness and some of their durability, particularly in damp climates.

Again, like cane, shoots were relatively soft when first cut. They were then either bundled and set aside to dry, or scraped of their bark first and then set aside to dry. Once dry they became relatively hard. Their bark was scraped off, if not removed initially, and then the shafts straightened with heat and cut to length. They were then ready to be turned into arrows. Some popular shoots for arrows were hazel, some of the dogwoods such as gray, rough leafed, and red osier, sourwood, mock orange, ocean spray, wild rose and several of the Viburnum species.

Split Timber Shafting

Once man learned to fashion metal, particularly into cutting instruments and edged tools, true mass production of arrow shafts was possible. Saws, wedges, and planes allowed the use of split or sawn timber to be made into arrow shafting. The first step was cutting the trunks of straight trees into squares. The large squares were then cut into many uniformly sized smaller squares. The smaller squares had their four corners planed off which turned them into eight-sided octagons. The eight corners were then shaved off making them sixteen-sided, then rounded smoothly with sandpaper or sandstone.

Block of sourwood, four-sided split, rounded shaft, and finished arrow.

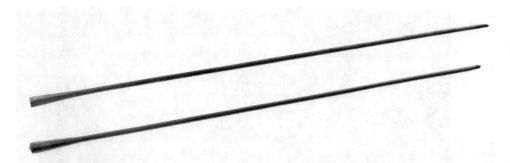

Northeastern Passamaquoddy Indian arrows of split hickory (Peabody Museum, Harvard University).

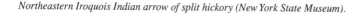

Northeastern Iroquois Indian arrow of split hickory (New York State Museum).

Just as different species of trees had different characteristics, the arrows made from those trees had different characteristics as well. Depending on the species of tree selected, the arrows made from its wood might have been soft, light, warped easily, had poor recovery times, or shattered easily when shot, while arrows made from a different species could be just the opposite: hard, heavy, recovered quickly and tough as an anvil. The trick was finding native species that met most, if not all of the things required in an arrow. For some, that was hickory, or white oak, or Port Orford cedar.

The armies of the English were said to prefer ash for its weight, toughness and ability to carry a large bodkin head for smashing through armor. In any given battle, the English army might have 8,000 archers, each capable of firing ten arrows per minute. Each minute, that would be 80,000 arrows launched toward an enemy. Split timber manufacturing on a large scale made that kind of an arrow resource possible.

Natural arrow shafts, such as cane/bamboo/reeds and shoots, were tapered their full length. Also referred to as "bob-tailed", they were naturally larger at one end and tapered straight their full length to the other end. Once split timber shafting became available, it allowed for other types of shafting to be made. Parallel shafting had no taper, with all sides running parallel to each other the full length of the shaft. Barrel tapered shafting occured where the shafting was thickest in the center, then tapered down on both ends, which reduced mass without reducing spine. Barreled taper shafting was sometimes used for flight arrows to lighten the arrow without reducing spine. Chested or breasted tapered shafts were similar to barreled shafts since both ends were reduced in diameter, but the tapering on the point end was shorter than on the nock end, again improving flight characteristics and fletching wear.

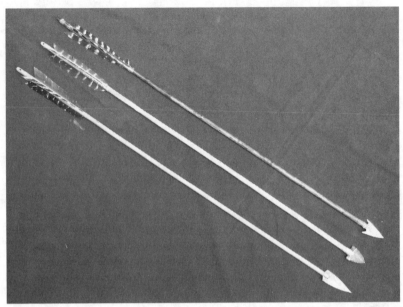

Top to bottom; Finished dogwood arrow, rivercane arrow, and sourwood arrow from split timber.

Of course, bob-tailed or tapered arrow shafting, where the arrow was thickest at one end and followed a straight taper for the entire length of the shaft, just like a natural cane/bamboo/reed or shoot shaft, was made from split timber shafting as well. Tapered shafting improved both flight characteristics and reduced weight and spine compared to a parallel shaft.

Nocks

The nock's sole purpose was to keep the arrow in place on the string as the bow was drawn and released. A nock might have been as simple as a shallow indentation carved into the rear of the arrow for archers using a pinch draw, to a slot cut directly in the rear of the shaft slightly wider and deeper than the diameter of the string itself for archers using a Mediteranean style or three finger under style draw, or as complicated as separate pieces made from hard wood or horn that were then attached/inserted into the end of the arrow.

Japanese bamboo shaft, bone nock insert with golden eagle fletching (Geary Collection).

Top; phragmites shaft with hardwood nock insert. Bottom; Apache, phragmites shaft with nock cut to base of node to prevent splitting, sinew wrapping for fletching gives added strength (Hamm Collection).

Mughal (India) wooden arrow nock, bound with plant fiber cordage (Geary Collection).

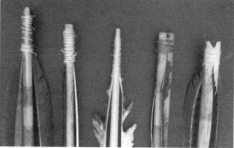

Indo-Persian hunting arrows with highly decorative bulbous bone nocks, painted inside and out (Grayson Collection).

Eskimo/Inuit flattened self nocks, used with a three finger, or Mediterranean, release (Grayson Collection).

Some arrow materials like hollow cane/bamboo/reed shafting lend themselves to nock inserts. Softer woods like pine or cedar also required some sort of reinforcement of hardwood, bone, or horn which kept the string from splitting the shaft upon release. Hardwood such as oak and ash did not need additional reinforcement. To reinforce a nock, most often a slot was cut into the end of the shaft, and a sliver of harder material the same width as the shaft was glued into that slot. The arrow was then rotated 90 degrees, and a shallower slot was cut for the string. When made in this manner, the string actually pushed on the hardwood or bone insert rather than the soft wood itself, preventing the shaft from splitting. Another method of preventing nocks from splitting was to bind the arrow between the nock and the back of the fletch with sinew and hide glue or a tough cord such as silk attached with adhesive, whether it be fish glue or birch tar.

Hardwood insert on self nock.

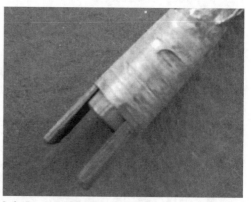

Indo-Persian nock formed by binding flat sticks to side of shaft (Geary Collection).

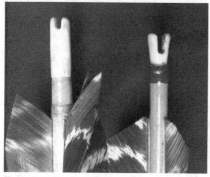

Two types of bone nocks.

African Pygmy hunting arrow, no nock, for use with a flat string, amphibian skin wrap for increased grip (Geary Collection).

West African; shaft bound with plant fiber for reinforcement, five feathers attached with fine plant fiber cordage "barber-poled" through the vanes (Geary Collection).

Inuit arrow; split timber shaft, raised nock with groove, feathers attached with very fine sinew cordage (Geary Collection).

FLETCHING

Located near the rear of the arrow just forward of the nock, fletching provided stabilization by creating drag, which controled pitch and yaw, keeping the rear of the arrow traveling in line with the forward end. Fletching was an important invention. Originally man had only used heavy, short range, slow moving projectiles thrown by hand, such as the spear for hunting and war. Because of the short distances these projectiles were thrown, the dynamics of flight were not important. Once the atlatl was invented, however, and with the increased distances at which atlatl darts could be thrown, fletching became important. This was magnified even further when the fast, light and longer-ranged projectile for the bow was developed.

Fletching has traditionally been made from the wings and tail feathers of various birds. Practically any bird locally available to the arrow maker, eagles, hawks, owls, vultures, crows, guinea fowl, pheasants, chickens, turkeys and geese, have been used for fletching at one time or another. Feathers were the perfect medium for fletching. They were soft, so when shot they folded out of the way of the archer's hand or against the riser of the bow, minimizing deflection. Some were moisture resistant such as goose primary wing feathers due to their high oil lines.

The higher and longer the feather, the more drag it exerted. Fletching size often related to point size. If something large was attached to the front of the arrow, something large was also needed to control the rear of the arrow. Feather size and number

Chinese arrows; shoot shafts, self nocks, eagle feathers attached with sinew (Grayson Collection).

Turkish practice flight arrows; spiral fletching to limit distance, sinew wrapping around feathers. Left arrow has sheephorn nock (Grayson Collection).

could also be used to control the speed and distance an arrow flew. The bigger the feather, the slower the arrow speed and shorter the arrow's distance. As few as one (in the case of a spiral fletched flu flu type bird hunting arrow) and as many as six fletches (also on flu flu's) were used on arrows.

Japanese bamboo arrows; immature golden eagle fletching, gold lacquer over sinew wrapping (Grayson Collection).

223

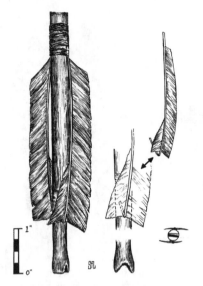

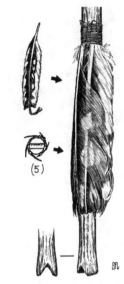

Native American, eastern U.S., two feather fletch which imparted spin to arrow.

Ojibwa split timber arrow, fletched with five flicker feathers (America Museum of Natural History, New York).

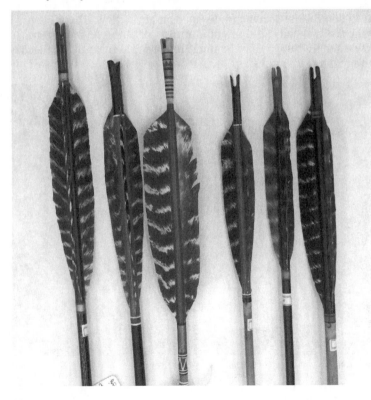

Korean arrows; turkey wing feathers on bamboo shafts. Third arrow from left has bone nock, the remainder have self nocks (Grayson Collection).

Most commonly, three feathers were used, set 120 degrees apart, around the shaft with the cock feather placed at a right angle to the nock slot. Interestingly, arrows from all time frames and cultures almost universally had this fletch pattern. Feathers mounted as such minimized fletching contact with the bow, and therefore lessened deflection.

Fletching could be aligned on the shaft in one of two ways; either straight down the shaft, called straight fletch, or curved around the shaft, called spiral or helical fletch. The spiral mounting forced the arrow to spin as air rushed over it, further aiding in the stabilization and accuracy of the arrow in flight. The larger the object on the point end of the arrow, the more important it be spiral fletched for aerodynamics. Even the earliest primitive arrows showed evidence of being spirally fletched.

Fletching was applied with fish glue, hide glue and birch tar glue, shellac, modern fletching cements and fletch tape, and affixed with no glue at all using several methods of wrapping with sinew or cordage. Feather fletching was shaped in many ways and by many methods. The flu flu arrows were left full height for maximum drag, but others were cut either for asthetics or to achieve certain flight characteristics. The simplest arrows had the fletching cut to shape, or burned off straight across with the hot end of a small stick fresh from the fire. Flint shards, steel knives, choppers and hot wire feather burners have also been used to shape feathers. Parabolic, shield cut, banana cut, and Pope and Young cut were just some of the different modern variations of feathers. The feathers from an arrow used for hunting was typically five inches long and stood three-quarters of an inch high, while the fletching on a flight arrow used in long distance competitions might only be one inch long and stand one-quarter of an inch high.

Feathers, however, were not the only items used as fletching. Some Pacific island and African natives used the leaves of plants. A leaf was picked and a slit made in the shaft above the nock. The leaf was then inserted into the slit half way for a very effective fletch.

ARROWHEADS

Not all arrowheads look alike, are made of the same material, or have the same purpose. The arrowhead was the primary functional part of the arrow, and played the largest role in determining its purpose. Initially, arrows may simply have had the tip of the shaft itself sharpened, however, this must be assumed since aboriginal tribes who have not learned flaking or metal making skills still use this method of tipping their arrows. From the oldest surviving arrow examples, it was evident that it became commonplace for separate arrowheads to be made from stone, metal, horn, bone or some other hard material affixed to the arrowshaft.

We suspect from archaeological digs that the oldest arrowheads date back to around 25,000 years B.C., although the technology to produce stone arrowheads predates this time frame by many thousands of years. We are lucky that even though stone is a natural material, it is one that remains relatively unaffected by nature itself. Where most natural materials simply disintegrate and return to the earth when subjected to heat, cold, moisture and wind, stone is hard enough to withstand these elements. Although bone points might well have preceded the use of stone points, less evidence exists simply because bone is affected by nature's elements and deteriorates. We know, however, that bone and stone arrowheads were also used simultaneously at later times, as were metal arrowheads, once the art of metal working came into existence.

Iroquois Native American arrows; split hickory reduced to leave finished points (New York State Museum).

Wood Arrowheads

Possibly, the first points on the earliest arrows were simply a modification of the end of the wooden shaft itself. By rubbing the end of the shaft on an abrasive rock it could be filed down to a sharp point. Although a point made in this manner would be fairly soft, if held over the flames of a campfire, the wood would be heat-treated, which made it much harder. In the case of tubular cane/bamboo/reed shafting, a piece of wood would be tapered on each end, and one end inserted into the cane with the juncture being bound with sinew or plant fiber. Such pointed heads could certainly cause bleeding wounds, lung collapse, or perotinitus, leading to death of the prey animal. Hardened blunt heads would be used for hunting small game or birds. In the case of cane/bamboo/reeds, the end could be pounded and split into many pieces. A wedge could then be forced in between the pieces, which created a multi-pronged head for hunting fish, reptiles and amphibians. The shafts were bound behind the split with cordage or sinew to prevent further splitting of the shaft.

Apache Native American bird point, four lashed sticks on foreshaft, phragmites cane arrow (Arizona State Museum).

226

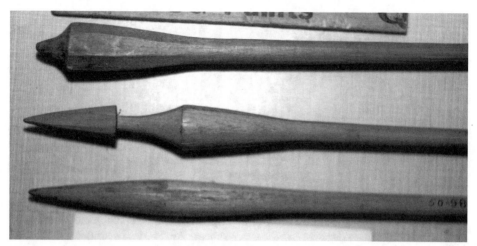

Menominee Native American arrows; split timber blunts, 27 1/2" long (American Museum of Natural History).

Comanche Native American arrows; dogwood with carved triangular points, bark showing on back of points, 25" long (American Museum of Natural History).

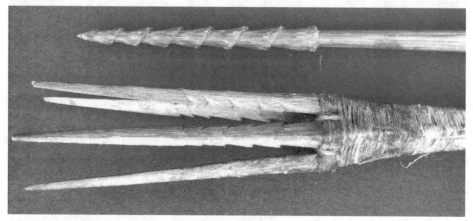

Soloman Islands fishing arrow with wooden trident-style point (Grayson Collection).

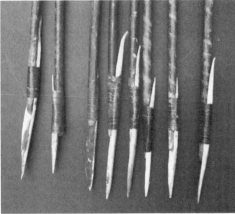

South America, Central Brazil; monkey bone points with bark wrapping (Grayson Collection).

Chinese, Neolithic bone points (Geary Collection).

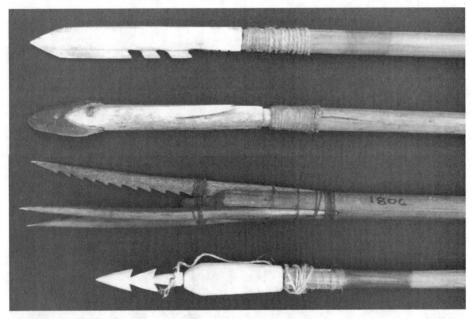

Eskimo/Inuit; Top to bottom, bone broadhead reinforced with sinew; antler foreshaft with copper broadhead; fishing arrow with three bone points set as prongs, reinforced with sinew; harpoon arrow with detachable point, walrus ivory foreshaft, point attached by twisted sinew cord (Grayson Collection).

Bone/Antler Arrowheads

Bone was an interesting and logical next step for arrowheads. It was harder than wood, but softer and more easily worked than stone. Bone arrowheads were most often made from the long tubular leg bones of animals. Once dried and hard, the bone was smashed with a rock, causing them to break and splinter into smaller pieces. Smaller pointed pieces were shaped using flint shards or sanded on an abrasive rock

Choctaw, Native American; antler points (Peabody Museum, Harvard University).

Inuit points, bone and ivory (Geary Collection).

into a useable arrowhead and inserted into the split end of a shaft. The arrowhead was secured with sticky material such as pine or birch tar, then the end of the shaft bound behind the head with either sinew or cordage to secure the head and prevent further splitting of the shaft in case the arrow struck something hard. However, bones were not the only animal products to be used in the manufacture of arrowheads. Arrowheads were also made from antler, teeth, the plate scales of certain fish, and even the barbs from stingrays.

Fox, Native American arrow; split hickory shaft, bone point with incised edges (American Museum of Natural History).

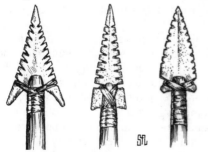

Two bone points, left, (Cahokia Mounds State Historic Site); ground shell point, right, from California coast.

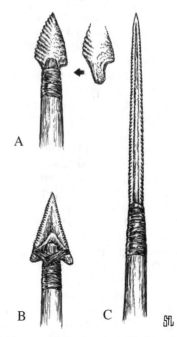

Southeastern Native American; A) alligator gar scale, B) shark tooth, C) stingray barb.

229

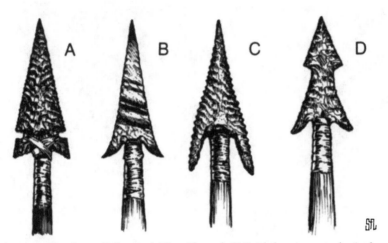

Native American, West Coast; A) Shasta, obsidian side notch, B) Banded agate stemmed point from Columbia River, C) Jasper point from Southern Oregon, D) "Double" arrowhead from Columbia River.

Stone Arrowheads

There were two different techniques used in the manufacture of stone arrowheads.

The first is called direct percussion. Direct percussion was accomplished by directly striking a large stone with a tool such as a hammer stone or large heavy antler billet to knock off large flakes. A flake was then selected and again struck with the billet at specific points to thin the stone to desired thickness. The next technique was called pressure flaking. Pressure flaking consisted of placing a pointed tool such as an antler tine or copper-tipped pressure flaker on the edge of the stone and applying an inward and downward pressure on the tool to remove small thin flakes of the stone. A series of flakes shaped and refined the arrowhead. Once properly thinned and shaped, the head would be very sharp and suitable for cutting and penetrating flesh.

There were hundreds of stone arrowhead designs. The base end was notched, corner notched, side notched, tanged or fluted. Stone arrowheads could be relatively crude or exquisitely made. Once one individual acquired the knowledge to fashion an arrowhead, he, in turn, showed others of his tribe how to fashion that particular style head. This was passed down from generation to generation with everyone in the general area for hundreds of years making the same style arrowhead. Their shape is often characteristic enough to distinguish different groups in terms of their geographical and chronological range.

It is important to remember that knapped projectile points for spears and the atlatl preceded those made for tipping arrows by thousands of years. The techniques and materials used were exactly the same with the major difference being the size of the point. There is much discussion and disagreement by archaeologists on exactly where the line was drawn between an arrowhead and what constitutes a hand-thrown projectiles point. Actual arrow points used for hunting large mammals were often much smaller than what modern man considers adequate for hunting. In fact, many arrowheads identified as "bird points", due to their diminutive size, were actually originally used for hunting large game. Smaller heads penetrate flesh easier, plus it would be easier to stabilize the flight of a shaft with a small point.

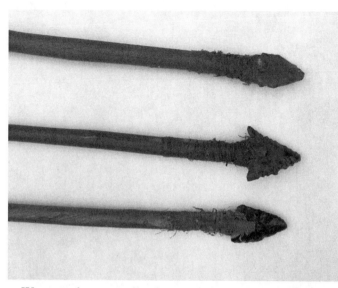

African; stone points attached with sinew, shoot shafts (Grayson Collection).

We must also remember that smaller heads required smaller flakes to produce, or to put it another way, many more heads could be made from a single stone if it were reduced into smaller flakes. Smaller flakes required less work to remove excess material, requiring less effort to make each head. Economy of both effort and resource was always important to primitive man.

Penobscot Native American point, serrated slate (American Museum of Natural History).

Potowotami, Native American; serrated flint point, shoot shaft, (Mills County Museum, Glenwood, Iowa).

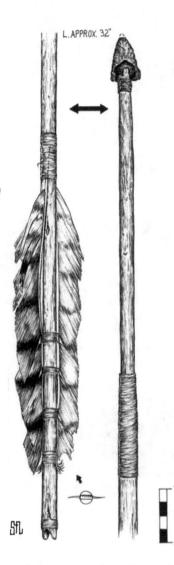

L. APPROX. 32"

Papago, Native American; shoot shaft with hardwood foreshaft, chert point attached with melted pitch and sinew, two hawk tail feathers (American Museum of Natural History).

Although most people refer to the process for making stone arrowheads as flintknapping, many different types of stone were used in making arrowheads including flint, chert, obsidian and practically any other amorphous stone that could be fashioned using flaking techniques. The use of stone arrowheads covers much of man's history and was still in use by natives in North America and elsewhere for thousands of years after metal working came into use. Stone arrowheads were still being used by indigenous people as late as the early 1900s in North America, and are still in use today in South America.

Mounting flaked heads required splitting or cutting a notch in the end of the shafts, securing the heads with some type of adhesive, whether birch tar, pine sap, hide glue or fish glue, and binding with either cordage or sinew.

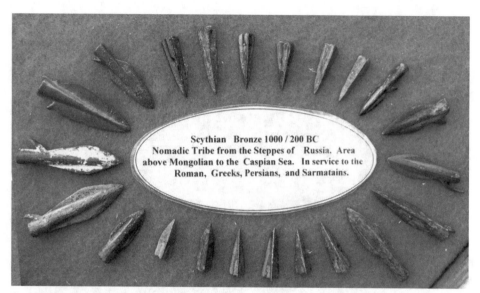

Scythian Bronze 1000 / 200 BC
Nomadic Tribe from the Steppes of Russia. Area
above Mongolian to the Caspian Sea. In service to the
Roman, Greeks, Persians, and Sarmatains.

Scythian bronze arrowheads (Geary Collection).

Metal Arrowheads

The history of metal arrowheads, like that of bone and stone arrowheads, is clouded in that no written record exists explaining or detailing its early development. We know that certain metals like gold, silver, copper, tin and lead were being melted by various civilizations and used as early as 4000 B.C. Although little evidence has been found, it is probably these metals were fashioned into arrowheads and tried at one time or another.

Somewhere along the way ancient people started mixing melted metals together. Bronze was made by melting two metals, tin and copper, and mixing them at a ratio of approximately 10% tin and 90% copper, and a much harder metal, bronze, was created in the process. The use of bronze dates back to around 3500 B.C.

For about 2,000 years, from around 3,000 B.C. to 1,000 B.C., bronze was the most important metal used by people for industrial purposes before the use of iron became popular around 1000 B.C. The Greeks, Romans and Egyptians were all highly skilled metal workers who used bronze for a variety of tools, including arrowheads. The use of bronze spread to central Europe around 2000 B.C. With the advent of molten materials and metal alloys, forms or molds could then be fashioned, and mass production of arrowheads was made possible.

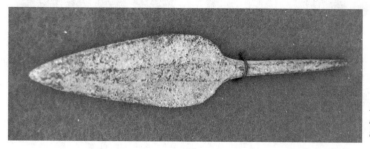

Persian bronze arrowhead (Geary Collection).

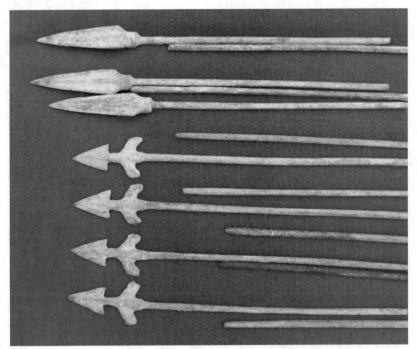

Chinese bronze arrowheads; tanged for bamboo shafts, three-bladed bodkins and double points. (Grayson Collection).

Roman cast bronze arrowheads (Grayson Collection).

Greek/Persian iron head (Geary Collection).

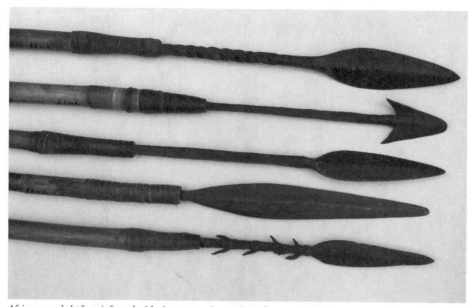

African; reed shafts reinforced with sinew wrap, iron points (Grayson Collection).

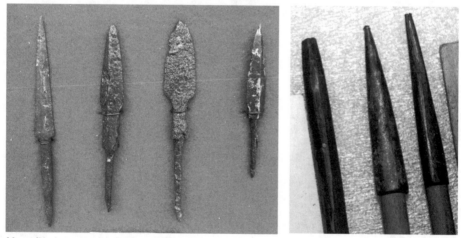

Mongolian iron arrowheads (Geary Collection).

Native American, southeast U.S.; flat copper and tin rolled around cane shafts (Oklahoma Historical Society Museum).

Because the majority of archer civilizations used cane/reed/bamboo arrows, the new bronze arrowheads were fashioned with a long slender tang, which could be inserted down into the hollow cane. They could also be formed with a socket on the back of the head for mounting to a tapered wooden shaft. Up until that time, arrows were used mainly for hunting with minor use in tribal or communal skirmishes, and the same head was used for both purposes. The arrowheads were made quickly and in vast quantities, and the arrow went from a means of gathering food to a method of

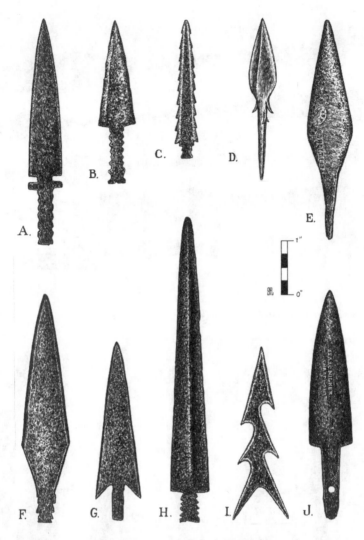

Native American, Great Plains; A, B, F, G, & J) typical iron points; remainder are more unusual.

conquering nations. From that point, arrowheads differed and were classified by design for hunting or combat. Arming large numbers of archers for warfare would not have been feasible if arrowheads had to be knapped one at a time. By making molds and using molten metals, hundreds of designs were made and tried. It wasn't until many years after the Europeans came into North America, bringing metal with them, that the Native American came to value metal heads. They eventually traded for pieces of metal such as spoon handles, knives, wagon wheel hoops, and other flat pieces of iron to fashion arrowheads, or traded goods for pre-made heads called trade points.

As advances in metallurgy produced better and better metals, arrowheads were produced from steel for war and hunting, and brass for archery practice and contests.

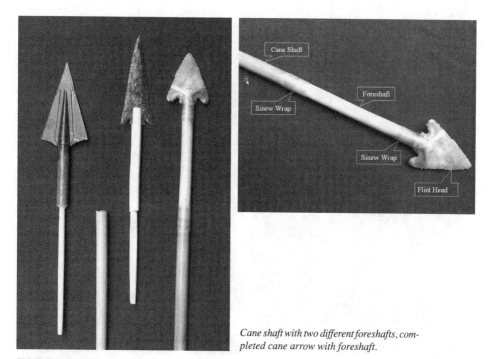

Cane shaft with two different foreshafts, completed cane arrow with foreshaft.

FORESHAFTS

Although some sort of hollow shaft was favored by many civilizations, it was not without its drawbacks. Being hollow, it was light in weight. Early small arrowheads were also light-weight. Light-weight shafts would fly quickly and fly far but carried little momentum, limiting penetration. They would also split easily if they hit something hard, often destroying the entire arrow. Somewhere along the way someone came up with the idea of a foreshaft. A foreshaft was a piece of hardwood or bone several inches long approximately the same outside diameter as the cane itself. One end would be trimmed to fit inside the cane, while the other end was slotted or tapered to accept the arrowhead. The small end of the foreshaft was glued into the cane and the junction wrapped with either cordage or sinew. The foreshaft added weight to the front of the arrow, increasing penetration, preventing the end of the shaft from splitting. Another benefit was that a damaged foreshaft could be removed and replaced without having to make a new arrow.

Native American, West Coast; Shasta compound arrow, shoot shaft socketed to accept foreshaft, obsidian point secured with melted pitch and sinew wrapping.

Native American, Great Basin; phragmites cane shaft, greasewood foreshaft.

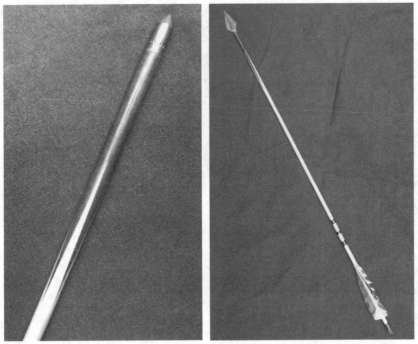

Footed target arrow, showing four-footed splice.   Port Orford cedar arrow with hardwood footing.

FOOTINGS

With split timber shafting, the same problem of ruined arrows from hitting something hard was faced, depending on the species of timber used. However, since split timber shafting wasn't hollow, a foreshaft could not be inserted into the end of it. Arrow makers came up with another solution to overcome the problem; footing. A footing was a short piece of harder wood spliced to the front of a softer arrow wood. With a hardwood footing, an arrow could withstand a much greater impact without damage.

The two different styles of footings were traditionally called two-footed or four-footed. The method of making them was basically the same with the two-footed a little easier to make. The end of the arrow shaft was cut into a wedge and a piece of hardwood cut into an inverted wedge of the same angle. The two pieces were then glued together. The footing was sanded or filed down to match the shaft.

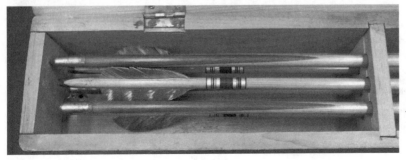

Footed English target arrows; tapered wood shafts with hardwood footing, horn nock inserts (Grayson Collection).

Indo/Persian reed hunting arrows with intricate crests (Grayson Collection).

THE ARROW CREST

Cresting was possibly a means of identifying the original arrow maker or, in later stages of archery, the arrow's owner. Again, like other stepping stones in the development of the arrow, no one knows who first marked his arrows to make them distinguishable from others in his tribe, but it was probably an early development. Arrows took up to half a day apiece to fashion, so a hunter would want them back if it were possible to identify and retrieve them. The ones that weren't broken after a hunt or battle were undoubtedly cleaned and reused. Cresting may have initially come about because one hunter recognized his blood-stained arrow after a successful hunt. It might also have come about to allow the best hunters to claim the best cuts of meats, or to recognize the fiercest warriors of a family or tribe.

Soloman Island decoration on cane fishing arrow (Geary Collection).

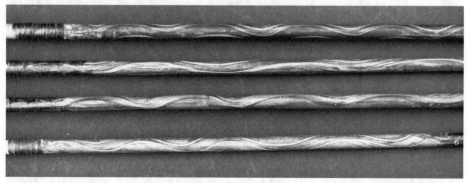

South American, Brazil; painted cresting (Grayson Collection).

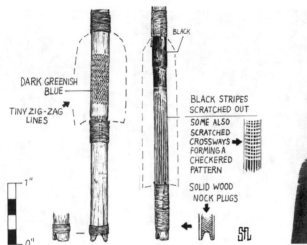

Anasazi, Native American; reed shafts with cresting under the feathers (Arizona State Museum and Favell Museum).

Chinese arrows with natural cherry bark wrapping (Grayson Collection).

Another early cresting may have been painted nocks, or cresting under the feathers, used to identify different types of points in a quiver, for example, as was done on some Anasazi arrows in North America. Cresting bands for identification eventually moved in front of the fletching. From archaeological digs dated to A.D. 200, we know of arrows which had bands of red and black pigment, although cresting was undoubtedly used at a far earlier date. Cresting was created not only with pigments, but with glued-on plant fiber and silk thread, as well.

Throughout time, cresting has ranged from crude to intricate, but in either case its purpose was the same, a method of identification.

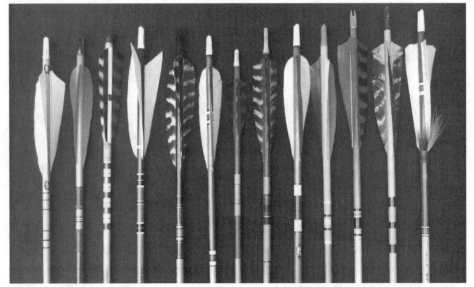

Modern fletching and cresting.

Apache, Native American; white chert point attached with melted pitch mixed with charcoal, then wrapped with sinew (Oregon State University Museum).

BINDINGS/ADHESIVES

Since an arrow was made up of several components, man had to find a way to make the different pieces form a solid unit. Feathers won't stick to a shaft without adhesives or bindings or both. The same goes for arrowheads, whether they are bone, flint, or some type of metal.

Sticky substances such as pine sap and birch tar were likely the first adhesives used. Ancient tribes also discovered the hides, sinew, and other connective tissues from animals could be boiled to remove collagen, the protein in these tissues. The collagen was sticky and useful for holding things together. As early as 1500 B.C., Mediterranean civilizations were using glue made from the air bladders (swim bladders) of certain types of freshwater fish. This glue was said to be moisture resistant when compared to the hide glue made from animals.

Cordage was much easier to obtain. When processed either by stripping, soaking and stripping, or pounding and stripping depending on the plant, the long straight parallel fibers were removed and rolled, reverse-twisted, or woven into cordage. Fragments of fibres, yarns and various types of fabrics that date back to about 8000 B.C. have been found in Swiss lake dwellings.

Cordage made from plants was used for binding foreshafts, wrapping below the nocks to prevent splitting, or binding feathers to the shaft for fletching. Sisal, hemp, flax, nettles, jute, and dogbane were just some of the plants used to make early cordage. Linen, made from the fiber of the flax plant, was the earliest mass produced cordage product, and people were spinning and producing linen by 5000 B.C.

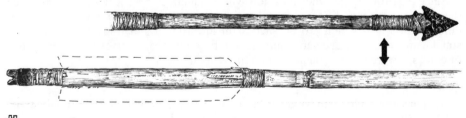

Anasazi, point secured with very fine plant fiber cordage, perhaps cotton (Arizona State Museum).

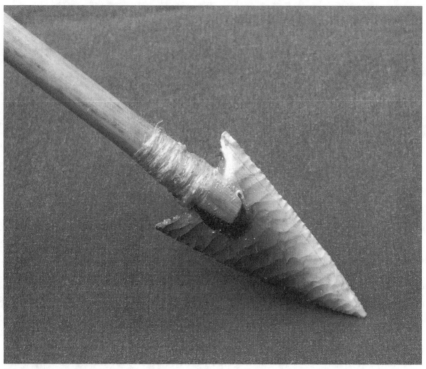

Stone head secured with sinew wrapping and pitch.

Another binding used on arrows was sinew. Sinew came from the leg tendons and from the silver colored membrane which covered the loins or backstraps in an animal. Once removed, the tendons or membrane were set aside to dry. Pounding allowed the dried tendon to be pulled apart and separated. Individual strands of sinew could then be softened by soaking in water or gently chewed, and applied with glue made from the scraping of an animal's hide. While drying, the sinew and the hide glue shrank and tightened, producing a superior bond between the shaft and the arrowhead, feather, or foreshaft. Its only draw-back was susceptibility to moisture, as sinew and hide glue softened when exposed to dampness, allowing the bond to loosen. Sealing with animal fat, beeswax, or pine pitch helped prevent this from occurring.

DIFFERENT ARROWS FOR DIFFERENT PURPOSES

Since the Bronze Age, when mass arrowhead manufacturing became commonplace, the arrow moved into different classifications depending upon its intended use. Specific head designs which proved successful in different situations such as combat, small game hunting, large game hunting, hunting foul, fishing or even archery games or contests, were readily manufactured in great numbers.

War

Man has always lived in bands or family units, tribes, towns and eventually civilizations. Such arrangements were an advantage, as it meant more people to do the work, more people to help hunt and gather food, more mates to choose from, more

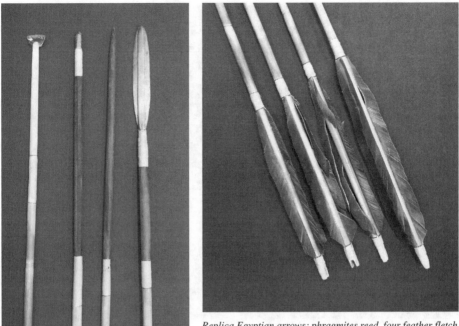

Replica Egyptian arrows; phragmites reed, four feather fletch, bronze leaf-shaped tip with thicker strengthening ridge (Grayson Collection).

opportunity for specialization, and more warriors to defend their possessions. Unfortunately for man, it seemed one group regularly wanted what another group had. A skeleton found in Sicily and dated to 11,000 B.C. had a fragment of a flint arrowhead imbedded in its pelvis, and it is believed that Otzi the Iceman died from an arrow wound around 3300 B.C. Although primitive man no doubt fought it out with sticks, clubs, rocks, spears and the atlatl, it wasn't until the adaptation and acceptance of the bow and arrow that war got really serious.

Chinese Liao Dynasty iron forked arrowhead (Geary Collection).

Japanese "sparrow beak" battleheads on bamboo shafts.

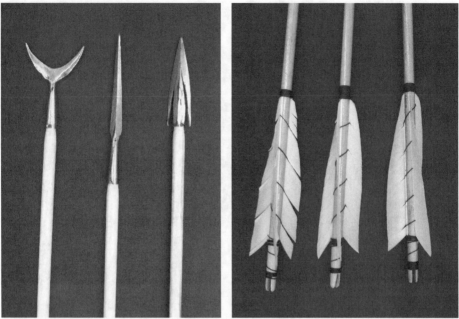

Replica English medieval arrows; hand-forged points – crescent, four-sided bodkin, broadhead; hardwood shaft; self nock; fletching bound with thread (Grayson Collection).

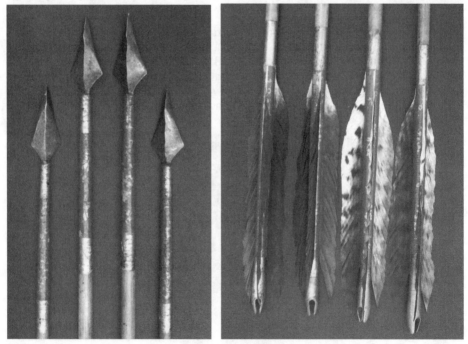

Turkish military arrows; Crimean Tartar- type wooden shaft, hand-forged steel broadheads, sinew reinforced, three hawk feathers, gold painted bands (Grayson Collection).

Surviving examples of Egyptians arrows measured from 34 to 37 inches long, were made from reeds with 8" long hardwood foreshafts bound into the shafts with very fine linen thread, then tipped with flint heads. Fletching was three, three-inch long feathers glued to the shafts with shellac.

In 2500 B.C. the Akkadians conquered Sumaria using infantry archers. All of the great early civilizations, the Chinese, Huns, Assyrians, Persians, Macedonians, Romans, Egyptians, Greeks, Japanese, Parthians, Byzantines and English, to name but a few, used archers to their advantage in warfare.

Although there were many different styles and sizes of bronze and iron arrowheads used in warfare, there were only a few basic types, which were anti-infantry, armor piercing and anti-cavalry. The three styles of head were different in design and intended use. The anti-infantry style arrowheads in general were of a broad two-bladed design, usually triangular in nature with sharpened edges. They were designed to cut unarmored opposing troops, causing massive bleeding. The armor-piercing arrowheads were a three-bladed design, heavy and relatively thin with long sharp points. These were called Bodkin style arrowheads. Less importance was placed on sharpening the blades on the Bodkin style heads as their function wasn't to cut, but to separate and penetrate armor and chain mail and cause deep puncture wounds. Those designed to bring down horse mounted cavalry had large barbs, and were intended to break off when anyone tried to remove them from a horse. This forced them to be pushed through, thus causing maximum damage to the animal. Some called these "swallow-tailed" as they resemble the swept back wings of a bird.

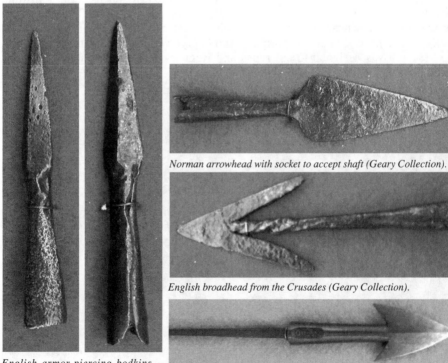

Norman arrowhead with socket to accept shaft (Geary Collection).

English broadhead from the Crusades (Geary Collection).

English armor-piercing bodkins (Geary Collection).

Japanese war point with tang for bamboo shaft (Geary Collection).

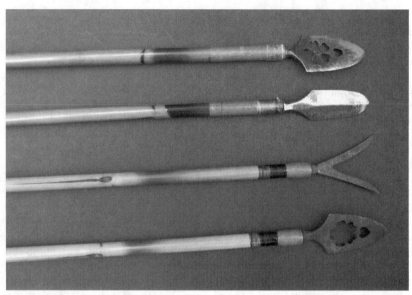

Japanese military arrows; bamboo shaft, steel broadheads, gold-lacquered bands over sinew wrapping (Grayson Collection).

There were other specialty types of arrowheads used in war as well. Whistling arrowheads were used by the Japanese, Chinese, Koreans and Huns. The purpose of the whistling arrowhead was multi-fold; directing troop movement, as a signaling device, and to terrorize opposing armies. Another type of head, called the Half Moon, or Crescent, was designed to cut ropes and riggings on a ship's sail when battles eventually moved to the seas.

VIKING ARROWHEADS
800-1200 AD

Viking arrowheads with sockets (Geary Collection).

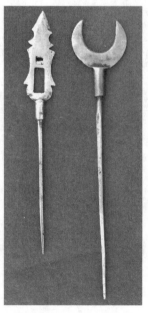

Indo/Persian tanged battle heads (Geary Collection).

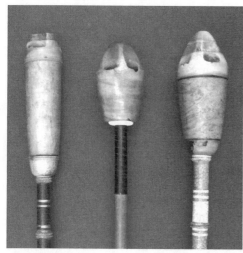

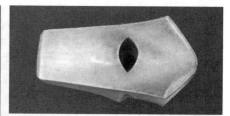

Mongolian whistling arrowhead, four-sided antler (Grayson Collection).

Mongolian whistling arrowheads; sheephorn and walrus ivory, birch shafts (Grayson Collection).

Japanese Samurai whistling arrowhead of bone (Geary Collection).

Arrowheads with tangs were also designed to hold wax, fat or oil soaked rags behind the head which were then set on fire and shot into opposing encampments and supply wagons.

Most civilizations where cane/bamboo/reeds were available used them for shafting. These were all more or less similar to the Egyptian arrows described above, but as metal working became popular around 3000 B.C. the flint arrowhead was replaced in most cultures by bronze, followed by iron.

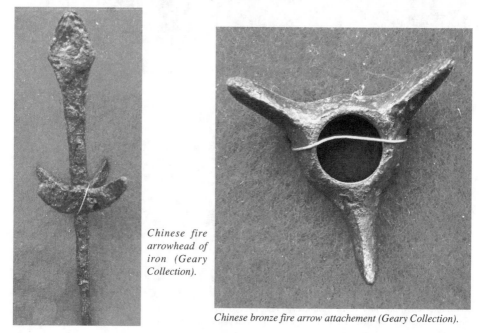

Chinese fire arrowhead of iron (Geary Collection).

Chinese bronze fire arrow attachement (Geary Collection).

247

Once metallurgy advanced to where edged tools could be fashioned, split timber was used for shafting and armies were supplied with hardwood arrow shafts in great numbers. Split timber shafting combined with forged arrowheads was possibly the greatest advancement in mass weaponry for war up until the widespread use of gunpowder. It is hard to imagine just how many arrows, and in turn how many arrow shafts, arrowheads and feathers, would be needed for a single battle, much less a whole campaign. A good archer could shoot between six and ten arrows per minute at a range in excess of 200 yards. It would not be unusual to have 5000 archers in a military division. When the archers got within range of an opposing force, they would fire their first flight of arrows. Before the first volley of arrows had landed, a second was on its way. Before the second round landed, a third was in the air and so forth. Taking the low figure of six shots being fired per minute per archer, a force of 5000 archers could fire 30,000 arrows per minute.

It was reported in 53 B.C. the Parthian archers of Asia carried sixty to eighty arrows apiece and were re-supplied by camel trains as needed. If five thousand Parthian archers shot sixty arrows apiece in a battle, that would total three hundred thousand arrows. Talk about blotting out the sun with arrows. Imagine if a small percentage of those, say one percent, were of the whistling variety. Such death screaming in from above could have been intended to make the opposing force panic, break ranks, and flee.

Big Game Hunting

Hunting large game was not a sport when the bow and arrow was invented. It was a matter of survival, a matter of life and death. The argument could easily be made that hunting was the original impetus for the invention. Early man had been taking

Art Young with a lion he killed with one arrow. In 1925, Young and Saxton Pope went on an African safari to prove to a skeptical public that the bow and arrow was a viable hunting weapon. This photo speaks volumes.

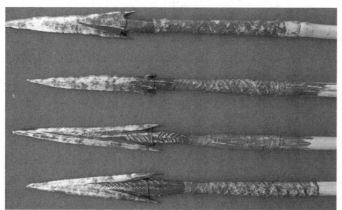

African Pygmy arrows with poisoned heads (Geary Collection).

down big game for centuries with sticks, clubs, and spears, an endeavor fraught with danger. The animals they hunted were large and dangerous, especially when wounded, and in order to make a kill the hunters had to be close. Hand to claw combat, so to speak. Even minor wounds from a tooth or tusk could eventually prove fatal. A family unit could ill afford to lose one or two of its best hunters to dangerous encounters.

The atlatl was a giant step forward in safety for the hunter, and while undoubtedly better than a spear, its range was still less than an arrow. With the advent of the bow and arrow, the hunter could shoot further than with a hand launched atlatl dart with little danger to himself. More importantly, he could carry many arrows, reload quickly, and kill more animals in a herd. With superior tracking abilities, the hunter would simply follow a wounded animal until it died of blood loss or exhaustion.

Although early arrowhead designs could be used for both war and for big game hunting, eventually there came a time when hunting arrowheads followed one path of development and arrowheads for war another.

The first commercially advertised arrowhead for hunting was the Peck & Snyder company broadhead, advertised in 1878 (the same year Maurice Thompson's book *The Witchery of Archery* was published). Advertised as the Will Thompson Broadhead, this head was largely unknown until two of them were rediscovered in the early 1990's. The Peck & Snyder broadhead was very similar to the points traded to Native Americans by early European settlers. This head is now recognized as the first broadhead ever manufactured for sporting use.

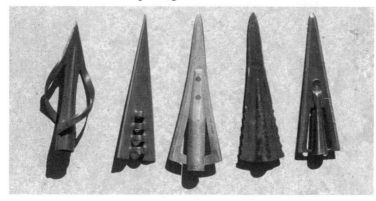

Commercial hunting broadheads from the 1940's and 50's.

A modern footed big game hunting arrow.

The next advertised broadhead was not available until the early 1920's. In 1923-1924, the California By-Products Company of California was contracted by Saxton Pope and Art Young to begin making broadheads to prove the bow and arrow's effectiveness as a hunting implement on their expeditions. No longer able to make enough heads by hand to keep themselves supplied, Saxton and Art provided California By-Products Co. with the design for the heads.

About that time, the Sportsman's Archery Company in Wyoming began producing a large barbed head very similar to the Saxton Pope and Art Young style. Heads of that era are known for their sturdy design, and frequently were barbed since no laws yet existed outlawing them. Early broadheads from the 1920's also included those made by O.A. Norland, Sportsman's Archery, Stemmler Archery, Roy Case, Archer's Co., and Ace. Over the last eighty years hundreds of broadhead designs have been made and tried by many manufacturers. Some proved to be successful, while others simply never caught on and disappeared from the marketplace.

Small Game Hunting

Early man not only hunted the large game animals but smaller game species as well. Rodents, birds, amphibians and reptiles were all hunted for food. The first small game specific arrows were simply the end of the wooden shaft itself, blunted and hardened in a fire. The shock of being hit by the fast flying object was enough to dispatch most small game. Some cultures used large carved wooden blunts as well. Not much evidence for metal blunt heads (until relatively modern times) exists.

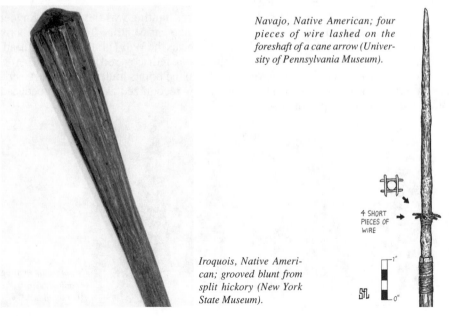

Navajo, Native American; four pieces of wire lashed on the foreshaft of a cane arrow (University of Pennsylvania Museum).

4 SHORT PIECES OF WIRE

Iroquois, Native American; grooved blunt from split hickory (New York State Museum).

Mohave, Native American; shoot shaft, tip reinforced with sinew wraps to prevent splitting (Snider Collection).

Ojibwa, Native American; bone point on split conifer blunt (American Museum of Natural History).

Klamath, Native American; water-skipping duck arrow, showing pitch ring which acted as a hydroplane and made the arrow skip just above the surface of the water.

Creek, Native American; cane shaft inserted into metallic rifle cartridge (Oklahoma Historical Society Museum).

Flu-flus to limit distance when hunting birds or squirrels.

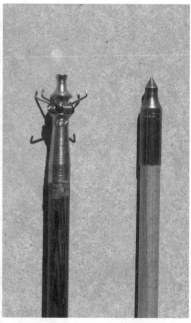

Modern Judo point for small game helps prevent lost arrows by limiting skipping or burying under vegetation. Field point for small game or practice.

English target arrows; tapered wood shafts with hardwood footing, iron points, turkey feather fletch, horn nock inserts (Grayson Collection).

Target Shooting/Games/Practice

Although undoubtedly there were archery games played by primitive man, it wasn't until the invention and widespread use of gunpowder and the musket that the arrow ceased to be of much use in organized military maneuvers. The last recorded major battle in which the bow was used in Europe was in 1644 by the British. Archery was still very popular in England, however, and a different type of arrowhead was developed for sport shooting, as opposed to war or hunting arrows. These were designed for shooting into woven grass target mats so they would cause no damage and could be easily removed. This type of head was conical in shape and had no barbs. Called field points or piles, they were made from brass or steel, and were designed to be fitted onto the end of a tapered mass-produced split timber shaft, rather than hafted into a shoot or cane/reed/bamboo shaft.

Korean target arrows; bamboo shafts, tanged metal points, cherry bark wrapping above points and below pheasant feather fletching (Grayson Collection).

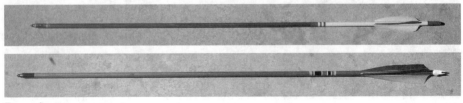

Two modern target arrows.

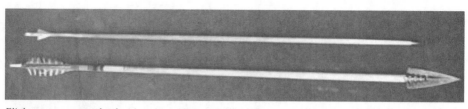

Flight arrow compared to hunting arrow (Grayson collection).

Flight Shooting

Another type of competition was flight shooting, which spawned yet another kind of specialty arrow. For that type of competition, aerodynamics had a dramatic impact on arrow flight. Anything that contributed to drag had to be minimized. Very small diameter arrows were used with barrel or breasted tapers being the norm. Typically, arrows were fletched with 1/2" X 3/8" dove feathers or pheasant tail segments. The smoother and thinner the feather, the less distance-robbing drag it created, but it still had to be large enough for the arrow to fly true, with no wobble.

To reduce weight, some arrows had no points at all, but most were tipped with one-eighth inch brass, steel, tungsten, or aluminum tips for tuning purposes. Arrows could be as short as twenty-four inches but were typically longer, in the twenty-six inch to twenty-eight inch range.

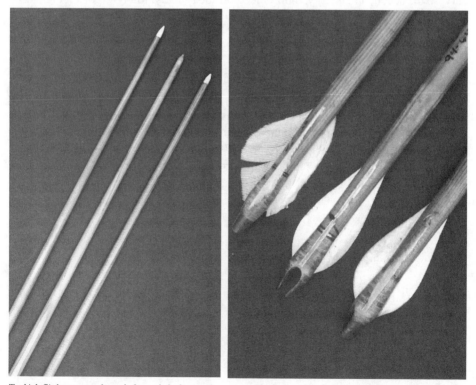

Turkish flight arrows; barreled wood shafts, two have ivory points, one has sheephorn point, bottom two arrows have parchment fletching (Grayson Collection).

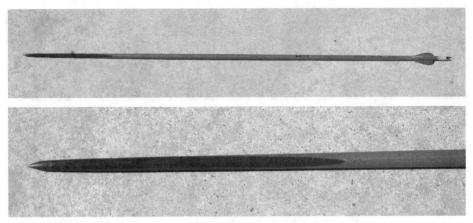

Modern flight arrow by Harry Drake; barreled shaft, hardwood footing, tiny brass point.

The key to flight arrows was having the best aerodynamics, with the smallest dimensions that were still spined correctly for the bow. In theory, one would assume the lighter the arrow, the better, but it didn't always work that way in practice. Speed was needed to fight gravity, but weight along with the best aerodynamics was also necessary, so the speed, and energy, didn't bleed off too quickly. Many flight shooters used Port Orford cedar or bamboo for arrow shafting. In flight shooting, the bow design and state of tune was important, but serious shooters never overlooked well-designed and finely tuned arrows.

• • • •

It is interesting to ponder that for the most part not much about the arrow has changed over time. It's still a cylindrical stick with a point on one end, a nock for the string on the other end, and some type of stabilization set at 120 degrees interval around the shaft just forward of the nock. Whoever originally came up with this magical device could have had no idea what a profound effect his invention would have on the history of mankind.

LESSONS FROM TARGET ARCHERY

Jim Hamm

Bear with me for a moment, kind reader, and I will relate the revolution that took place in my archery world, which totally changed the way I shoot a bow.

Every fall, I used to catch a terminal case of buck fever. I had no trouble getting close to deer, most of the time I just couldn't hit the big ones, and, come to think of it, sometimes couldn't hit the little ones, either. Though I practiced relentlessly and enjoyed some hunting success, consistency at the moment of truth eluded me entirely. Only someone who has worked hard all deer season long, then blown that single three-second window of opportunity, can fathom the resulting frustration.

Also, though having shot tens of thousands of practice arrows over the years, I had less than zero interest in actual target archery. I was a hunter; there was no thrill and no point in shooting a piece of paper with a bullseye on it time after time after time.

Those disparate attributes - getting Ebola buck fever and complete disdain for formal target archery - were forever changed a few years ago by an unlikely event.

My youngest son, Reed, met, dated, and ultimately married a lovely young woman named Mary Zorn.

Now Mary not only fit right into the Hamm Clan, it so happened that she was also the world's best shot with a compound bow. And I mean that quite literally. She was the women's two-time F.I.T.A. (International Target Association) world indoor champion (18 meters), as well as women's F.I.T.A. world outdoor champion (30, 50, 60, and 70 meters), setting a multitude of world records along the way, not to mention repeated U.S. and collegiate national championships. I'll put it this way: Mary is a better shot with her bow than I am with a scoped .22 caliber bolt action rifle, and I'm a pretty fair hand with a rifle.

Through osmosis, over years of studying archery and its history, I had stumbled across a good deal of information about target shooting. Since a real target archer had joined the family, I was motivated to broaden my knowledge and began researching target archery and its origins in earnest. Some of the findings were revealing.

No doubt, shooting contests began shortly after the completion of the second bow ever made, over ten thousand years ago. It's almost impossible for archers to meet without shooting for accuracy or distance or both, using any excuse to watch arrows fly. Any man throughout history who depended on a bow to feed or defend his family would have honed his skill through frequent practice, but formal target archery, as we know it today, is actually a stylized form of warfare and traces its origins to the English longbow.

In 1275, with the longbow firmly established as a crucial battlefield weapon, King Edward I decreed all males over the age of seven should practice archery. Other laws of that era were passed to ensure the availability of a large body of proficient archers. King Edward III, in 1363, made outdoor games other than archery unlawful, and mandated all males between seven and sixty shoot their bows every Sunday.

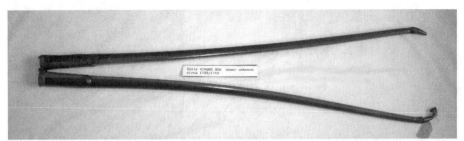

Early hinged 'carriage' bow, circa 1720-1740, yew wood, horn nocks (courtesy Hugh Soar).

Henry VIII (1491-1547) once competed by shooting targets at a distance of 240 yards. Women were shooting, too. Robert Elmer, in his 1926 book *Archery*, reported that Henry's wife, Anne Boleyn, possessed "bowys, arrowys, shafts, brode hedds, bracer, and shooting glove", in 1530. Women were also hunting, as a letter from 1605 mentions deer slain by "honorable Ladies handes."

Though during the 1700's firearms began supplanting bows as weapons of war, interest in archery continued and grew. Royalty supported the organizations that promoted archery. King George IV became patron to the "Royal" Kentish Bowmen. In 1792, he began offering, as a prize, a silver bugle at the yearly archery match, stipulating the distances be 60, 80, and 100 yards, and that either three or six arrows be shot from each "end".

Queen Victoria ascended to the British throne in 1837, and having often shot a bow in her younger years, she maintained an interest in archery and patronized several organizations, including the Queen's St. Leonard's Archers. These formal societies became the domain of gentlemen, rather than the earlier yeoman's archery, and their meetings included the best of food, wine, and entertainment, which often consisted of archery-related songs and poems.

During this time, bowyers specialized in elegant weapons with carved horn nocks, elaborate grips, and beautiful finishes. Some of these bows were "carriage bows", or take-downs with hinges or socketed grips for easier transport. Target weights for men were about 40-45 pounds and for women 25-30 pounds; these relatively light bows had a more pronounced crowned belly, as opposed to the flatter cross-section of the heavyweight warbows of old. With more than 150 archery clubs and societies, some with up to 200 members, more than 50 professional bowyers prospered during this Victorian Era (I was delighted to learn that one of the London bowyers from 1842-1863 was one Robert Hamm).

John Spreat ladies bow, circa 1830. Self lancewood with horn nocks, 59" long, 26#, red velour grip. (courtesy Hugh Soar)

GENTLEMAN'S TRADITIONAL RECREATIONAL LONG-BOW BY WARING (YOUNGER) LONDON
Circa 1830. Self lancewood (duguetia quitarensis. alt oxandra lanceolata)

Overall length 69 inches

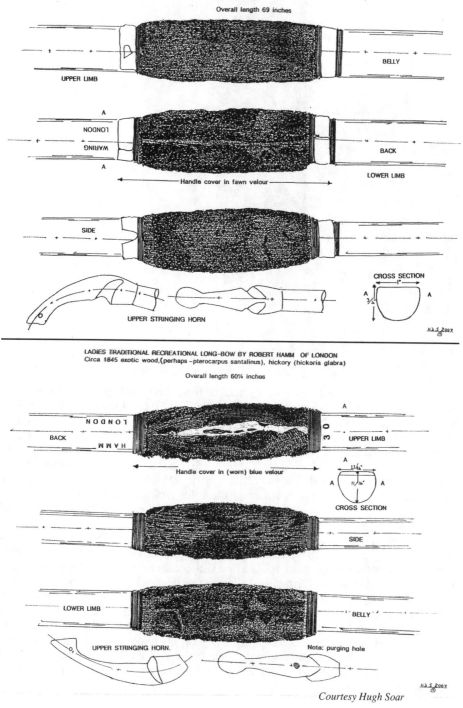

Courtesy Hugh Soar

Peerless Horace Ford, eleven-time British national target champion.

Target bows were, by that time, far removed from their battlefield origins, but they were nevertheless involved in some notable feats. The first nationwide British archery tournament was held in 1844, and five years later, in 1849, Horace Ford won the first of a remarkable eleven national championships in a row, a record that still stands today. In the double York round in 1857, which consisted of 144 arrows at 100 yards, 96 arrows at 80 yards, and 48 arrows at 60 yards - a grueling day's shooting by any standard - Ford shot a world record 1251, a mark that stood unbroken for more than fifty years. Understand he was shooting these long ranges at a target with a gold center ring (scoring nine points) under ten inches in diameter, and his skill seems all the more amazing.

In the United States, a parallel interest in target archery was slowly gathering momentum. For inspiration, these shooters looked to England for yew longbows, which dominated American target archery. The first U.S. archery organization was the United Bowmen of Philadelphia, formed in 1828 with only six charter members. The club grew to over fifty members, but interest waned, and by 1859 they had stopped meeting. The real inspiration for archery in this country came after the Civil War, when Confederate brothers Will and Maurice Thompson used archery skills learned from their childhood neighbors, the Cherokees. They largely lived off of the land in Florida in the years after the war, hunting with their bows, and in 1877 Maurice's book of their exploits and woodcraft, *The Witchery of Archery*, became a sensation that promptly increased popular interest in the sport.

Will Thompson   *Maurice Thompson*

Almost overnight, clubs and societies were formed across the U.S., and in 1879, representatives from the most prominent organizations met in Crawfordsville, Indiana, and formed the National Archery Association, or N.A.A. Maurice Thompson, appropriately, was elected president. The first national tournament was held in Chicago, in 1879, in which Will Thompson won the championship in the double York round. In the next twenty-nine years, Will would win four more national championships, his last in 1908.

Oddly enough, in spite of the Thompson's writings about their Native American-inspired archery adventures, the new American archers largely ignored the Indian archery tradition that surrounded them. Instead, their ideals were the long, narrow, crowned-belly, beautifully finished English-style bows of yew, the prevailing view being that the native bows with wider, rectangular cross-sections from a host of wood species were primitive and second-rate.

Target archery had a firm foothold in the U.S., and many others kept interest alive. Dr. Saxton Pope, Ishi's physician and friend, along with Art Young, were prominent target archers during and after the First World War. Pope even won the 1921 national flight shooting contest. Pope and Young branched out into hunting with their hand-made wooden bows, taking deer and even grizzly bear, and in 1925, took a safari to Africa to test their skill against lions. Pope's book of their exploits, *The Adventurous Bowmen,* is a classic of bowhunting literature and Africana.

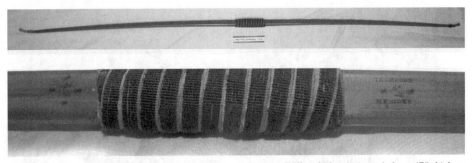

English target bow, circa 1920. Meriden Thompson (no relation to Will and Maurice) man's bow, 47#, hickory back, lemonwood belly, handle covered in green braid. Thompson's forebears were the hereditary bowyers of the Woodmen of Arden. (courtesy Hugh Soar)

Howard Hill was another archer who had a lasting impact on the sport, excelling both at target and flight shooting. He once won an incredible one hundred and ninety-six tournaments in a row, and his uncanny skill and showmanship attracted the attention of Hollywood. His films made him a hero to an entire generation of Americans, and during the 1940's, archery became so popular it was taught in public schools as physical education.

Fred Bear was an archery icon, whose pioneering work with fiberglass laminates before 1950 allowed, for the first time, the mass production of archery equipment. Bear's books and films endeared him to millions of people, who were naturally drawn to his high character and modesty, and of course his remarkable skill with a bow.

In modern times, most archers lean toward bowhunting, though target archery remains robust. At a recent National Field Archery Association (N.F.A.A.) tournament in Las Vegas, for example, well over 1700 shooters participated, not to mention thousands of spectators. The N.A.A., founded more than a century ago, is still alive and well, acting as the governing body for U.S. Olympic archery as well as the highest levels of F.I.T.A. compound competition. Tournaments ranging from local affairs all the way up to those with national implications are regularly held throughout the country.

After witnessing my first big target archery tournament, and watching my daughter-in-law Mary compete, I experienced a paradigm shift that made a couple of things apparent.

First of all, there was nothing boring or easy about pure target archery. The consistency was amazing, as the best shooters were repeatedly hitting a nickel-sized 'X' at eighteen meters. It didn't take a vast leap of imagination to see how my hunting issues would be greatly remedied with even a tiny sliver of their proficiency.

The competitive pressure was intense, building as the tournament neared the end of the second day, and the leaders were neck and neck. Some of the them began wilting under the pressure of shooting three arrows, waiting ten minutes to shoot another three arrows, waiting another ten minutes and so on, all day long. But Mary had toughness under the growing pressure, never losing her composure, never getting rattled, never losing focus, never losing the lead. Long before she ultimately won, it was also easy to see how her incomparable mental game could apply to Jim's hunting.

For too long, I had leaned on the crutch of shooting 'primitive' equipment to excuse poor shooting. But no more. I resolved to learn from Mary, to do whatever it took to revamp my shooting and mental approach to incorporate a target archer's skills.

As it turned out, we learned from each other.

Naturally, right off Reed and I handed her an Osage fencepost, then looked over her shoulder while she fashioned it into a fine longbow. As a gag, Reed and I also made her a bamboo tomato stake bow held together with electrician's tape and zip ties. She was delighted, named it *Bamboozled*, and loved taking it to the high-tech archery tournaments to make the other shooters scratch their heads.

Since I had never shot even a single arrow from a compound bow, I confess I thought it only fair to try her chosen weapon. She provided me with one of her bows, adjusted it for my draw length by doing something to the cams, then set me up with arrows and a trigger release. And, of course, immediately took a blackmail picture of me holding it (as I said, she fit right in around here). In any case, with the sights and trigger release, her bow brought to mind an arm-powered pistol. In my hands it had similar range and accuracy to a pistol, and, I had to admit, was a lot more fun, though my hair stood slightly on end while shooting it.

Besides her mastery of the compound, Mary had also placed in the top ten women in the U.S. with an Olympic recurve, so she understood how traditional bows, and their shooters, tick. To begin my shooting transformation, we talked at great length about the most important aspects of consistency.

The key to being consistent, she advised, was performing the shot exactly the same way, every time. Holding the bow, drawing, anchoring, and releasing in a manner that allowed precise duplication was the key. Proper form had become "proper" because it was the easiest to repeat, shot after shot. Or, as she put it, "we shoot with both feet flat on the ground because it's easier than holding one foot up in the air."

The two most important aspects of form, as expected, were alignment and anchor. Other factors played a role, of course, such as stance, follow-through, and bow grip, but alignment and anchor were the most critical.

Mary Hamm showing proper form; drawing arm parallel with the arrow, feet and shoulders aligned.

261

The alignment issue mostly hinged upon the right forearm (for right handers), be-ing parallel with the arrow at full draw. This was simple, quick to check, and the easiest to duplicate, every time, and when the drawing arm was aligned with the ar-row, shoulders and bow arm tended to be more consistently aligned too.

Anchor was a bit more problematic, as there was not just the factor of where to anchor, but how long to anchor. A consistent anchor yielded exactly the same draw length every time, which gave consistent poundage and arrow speed, the accuracy effects of which were self-evident. It also presented the same sight picture every time, and placed the eye directly above the arrow, which aided in aiming by helping elimi-nate the windage, or left-to-right, factor. Personally, I anchored with the tip of the middle finger of my drawing hand tucked into the corner of my mouth with the bow slightly canted to position my eye above the arrow. At least that was the theory. In truth, I had become a terrible snap-shooter, releasing the arrow the instant, and often even before, I reached full draw, with the expected wild accuracy fluctuations. Mary suggested I shoot into a blank bale at close range, with no target, and concentrate on holding at full draw at least two seconds before releasing. The consistency had to come first, she said; I could always shoot faster if a hunting situation called for it.

So with the basics of good form in mind, I began the process of revamping forty years of erratic shooting, bad habits, and frustration.

After a great deal of reflection, I decided to add to the bare bale routine. I determined to come to full draw, then let down once before every arrow released, and to do so for months, until reaching and holding at full draw was second nature. This drawing and letting down was almost like a practice swing in golf, or swinging a baseball bat between pitches, and combined with not shooting at an actual target allowed me, after a time, to hold at full draw a couple of seconds before releasing an arrow. As holding at full draw became more ingrained, I also focused on arm alignment, and the feel of the shot kept getting better. This feel had little to do with where the arrow struck, but was a combination of rhythm and consistency from shot to shot.

Finally, I felt ready to try a shot at an actual target at close range, ten yards. I stuck to the same routine, coming to full draw, holding, and then letting down once before every "real" shot, when the only thing I would do differently was release the arrow. The arrows were somewhat erratic, complete with occasional flinch-induced fliers, but the form seemed better. I stuck to the regimen, and as time passed the groups began to shrink slightly and the flinches receded.

After practicing the "New Archery" for a couple of months, I asked Mary to watch me shoot.

"Pretty good," she said, after half a dozen arrows, "but your right elbow is a little low."

I shot another arrow.

"Higher."

Another arrow.

"Still too low."

Another arrow.

"You're hitting to the right every time because your elbow is low from the start of your draw."

OK, I thought, raising my shooting elbow still further, to what felt to be an abnormally high level. I drew and released. That arrow smacked the target in the center. Hmmmmm. I tried it again, with the same result. And then again. Dead center.

"Your arm is exactly in line with the arrow now," she said, and suggested I add drawing in front of a mirror to the routine for a while to check alignment. Videotaping myself was another similar tool.

She also recommended I start working on a couple of other things, as well. Follow through the shot, holding the shooting position for two seconds after the arrow struck the target. And upon release, she advised, the hand should travel straight back with no sideways movement. Using tension in the back muscles to pull through the shot helped make the release clean and effortless. If I experienced problems, she also advised, shooting a very light bow for a few days often helped, as the light bow was relatively effortless to draw and hold, which allowed for easy adjustments of form. This ease at full draw also helped develop a near-flawless release, as a stronger bow inherently cleaned up the release as it ripped the string from the fingers.

A clean, accurate release from Reed Hamm; the drawing hand moves straight back and stays relaxed...

I incorporated those new techniques into my shooting, until an emphasis on the back tension and a pronounced follow-through became normal. And occasionally shooting a lighter bow helped groove the form and improved my release. My groups shrank a bit more, though I was still shooting from just one position at ten yards and had plenty of room for improvement. I finally reached a plateau and seemed to stall.

I mentioned this problem to my personal shooting coach. Mary just smiled and said, "Now you're getting somewhere." With these cryptic words, she led me to the next step of shooting well, proper practice.

Practice, she said, begins with a routine. I should choose something simple and natural, but an exact routine I followed before every shot. I decided to take a long breath and exhale slowly though my nose, then focus on the exact spot I wanted to hit, draw my bow while inhaling, and anchor while holding my breath until the sight picture settled down. After a second or two, when I was perfectly still, I would let down. I planned to do exactly the same thing again, starting with the long breath to begin the process, only then I would release the arrow.

"Practice," Mary continued, with just the hint of an unintentional glare, "means not just flinging two hundred arrows. Anyone can launch an arrow. Proper practice takes focus." Her glare was the competitor coming out, the striving for perfection. I wanted that intensity, that glare, so I listened closely.

With each practice arrow, she suggested, focus on the particular form issue throughout the shot, and throughout the entire process. Practice needed to mimic the real deal, whether a one arrow shoot-off for a target championship or drawing on a trophy deer, so I needed to put pressure on myself to make every shot perfect. Concentrate, as the bow reacted the same way every time, the archer was at fault if an arrow went awry. If there was a bad shot, analyze it just enough to understand what went wrong, then promptly forget it and concentrate on the next arrow. Such intense practice takes focus and effort, so I should stop before I got tired, as ten arrows shot perfectly were far better than a hundred shot with abandon.

I incorporated those additional aspects into my regular practice time. In particular, the set routine of starting, performing and completing each shot in exactly the same way worked well, and my groups shrank a little more. But the occasional inexplicable flyer was still disconcerting, and the more I dwelled on the problem, the worse it became. I finally realized I had hit a wall, only this time it was mental, and I asked for more help.

...and tension in the upper back muscles promotes follow-through.

"You're comfortable now with your form," Mary declared, after watching me shoot, "so don't worry too much about it."

"Really? Shouldn't I work on form every time I practice?"

"Sure, but only think about your form at the start of practice. It's more important just to do it the same way every time. The right mental attitude is the crux of shooting, whether your form is textbook perfect or not."

I finally felt ready to concentrate on the most important aspect of target archery or hunting: the ability to perform under extreme pressure, the mental aspect. I asked Mary how she held it all together during an important tournament, where any one arrow out of a hundred could make the difference between winning a world championship or enduring the agony of knowing she choked. How was she able to shoot her best when the stakes were highest?

She answered my question with a question.

"What are you thinking about when you draw on a buck?"

I considered it a moment. "I'm watching his eyes and ears so I don't get busted. Then I try to pick a spot and get off the shot."

"And you're hoping the shot is a good one."

"Right."

She shook her head. "You can't hope for a good shot. You can't hope you don't miss. You have to know with complete certainty that the arrow will go exactly where you want it to before you ever draw your bow."

"Sometimes the deer move," I protested.

"You have no control over that," she said, "but you do have control over making the perfect shot, every time. No doubts."

"Wait a minute, how about in practice? Nobody shoots a bullseye with every arrow, not even you."

"Of course not."

She then explained this apparent paradox.

In order to make a perfect shot, I had to be absolutely confident that I could make a perfect shot. But when my shot wasn't so great? Most people remembered the bad shots, the chokes under pressure, and it sapped their confidence. And that was exactly the wrong approach. A lot of target archers shot very well, missing with only an arrow or two. But that arrow which cost them first place was what they remembered, not the dozens in a row with which they hit the center of the target. It's a dirty trick the mind played, thinking about the small percentage of shortcomings while forgetting the more numerous triumphs, which was something I had to work consciously to change. Once I learned how to shoot perfect shots, my body knew how and I just had to stay out of my own way.

When there was a bad shot, I had to tell myself that it was an aberration and immediately forget it. When I made a good shot, I would tell myself that's what I was capable of doing every time and the way I normally shot. If I was supremely confident the chances of shooting my best were far greater. I would shoot the way I expected to shoot, Mary explained, so don't think about the bad shot I made, intentionally think instead of the ten good shots.

"So you can have it both ways?" I asked, still a bit skeptical, "When you shoot well you expect it and consider it normal, and when you shoot poorly it's a fluke."

"Absolutely," she said.

Then, she did something surprising. She handed me a book, *Golf is Not a Game of Perfect* by Bob Rotella. Noticing my raised eyebrow, she just said, "Trust me." Though I had more than enough bad habits without taking up golf, I tried to read it with an open mind.

I immediately realized the book was not so much about golf as it was how to approach the mental aspects of a physical activity, whether shooting a free throw, swinging a bat, turning a flip, or shooting an arrow. It reinforced what Mary had been telling me about a positive mental framework being the key. It was apparent that her approach was taking her to a Zen-level state of relaxed concentration. I needed some of that; there was no arguing with her results.

I tried to adopt her mental approach, and slowly noticed a difference. I hit the center more often, and my misses were a lot closer. With every good shot, I'd tell myself, "That's exactly what I'm going to do when I get a chance while hunting." I'd ignore the occasional bad shot, thinking, "That's a fluke, that's not the way I really shoot." I was practicing from varying ranges and many different positions, so I told myself that I had shot a hundred thousand arrows over the preceding forty years, and my subconscious mind already knew precisely what an arrow would do at different distances and trajectories. So I just had to have faith and trust my instincts.

It may sound ridiculous, but the more positively I thought, the better I shot. After many months of that positive practice, I was shooting better than I ever had. In one sense, I had talked myself into becoming a better shot.

The next deer season, I had a close encounter with a fine buck, though I never had the opportunity to even draw my bow. The adrenaline tidal wave and the resulting near-paralysis from the instant I first saw him made me seriously question my ability to ever make the shot under pressure. A patient target archer had helped my shooting tremendously, but I wondered whether she could help me with the mental aspect when that once-a-season chance presented itself.

That was the final lesson I had to learn from Mary, and also from an unexpected source.

By chance, that fall I shared a hunting camp with Paul Brunner, aka "Too Short". Now I'm not sure if sitting around a campfire with him was a privilege or some sort of atonement for past sins, but it was never dull. In fact, it was always instructive, especially since Paul was a fine shot and had vast experience bowhunting all over the world, everything from African leopards to Russian grizzlies to record book deer.

Paul - "Too Short" - Brunner, with a well-earned Texas buck. His philosophy at the moment of truth promotes an accurate shot under pressure.

So I asked him how he held it together at the moment of truth. His reply was simple and profound.

Most people, he said, tended to over-analyze a situation, thinking of all possible scenarios when game stood in front of them. The hunter had already done all of the cerebral work in deciding where to sit, what the wind was doing, the rut factors, and much more. Once he was in position and the animal was present, stop trying to predict what would happen, just observe what actually did happen and be ready to act if a chance presented itself.

The more I thought about his answer, the more sense it made. In every encounter, I was constantly trying to out-think the game. "If he turns a little left, I'll have a shot. If the wind swirls he'll bust me. If he takes another step he'll be in the clear. That other deer might get downwind. That brush is in the way. He might see me if I move." After thirty seconds of such rapid-fire internal predictions, almost none of which come to pass, by the way, the mind went into overload and mental breakers started tripping. Far better to follow Paul's advice. Stop trying to predict what would happen, just watch what actually did happen and be ready to act if a chance came.

As profound as Too Short's insight was, I knew there was more to it, that it was only part of the answer. So I explained the recent meltdown with the buck to Mary, who had hunted more than enough to understand the problem.

"That's normal," she said, "same as a three-way tie with one arrow to go during a target championship. Same adrenaline. Same pressure."

The pressure was all external, she said. Don't perceive it as pressure and the pressure won't exist. The deer wasn't putting pressure on the hunter, the shot was exactly like those practiced a thousand times, the pressure was coming from within.

"So how do you deal with it when it comes down to just one shot? What do you think about?"

"Nothing. Not the score or the competition or form or anything else. I just have complete trust I will make a perfect shot, go through my routine, and shoot the arrow."

"But you have to think about something."

She grinned. "To tell the truth, when I compete I'm always singing some internal song. It's just a way to distract my mind." She thought for a minute. "When you see a buck, you might try visualizing the arrow disappearing into his chest, over and over. Give your mind something positive to think about, so there will be no room left for doubt. "

And that was the final piece of the puzzle.

Once in position, I resolved to stop predicting what the game would do. And while I was watching to see if an opportunity came, I would constantly visualize the arrow vanishing into the exact spot I had picked on his shoulder.

The very next time I sat in a stand, I tried this new mental approach and took it even a step farther. With every deer I saw, even the ones I didn't intend to shoot, I constantly visualized an arrow disappearing into the spot I picked, and then, if a shot opportunity came, I would mentally go through my entire shooting routine. Finally, just before dark that evening a spike buck appeared. I decided to shoot him, both to put meat in the freezer and for herd management purposes. When he finally offered a shot at eighteen yards, I almost felt I had cheated. Almost. I had already visualized so many shots, it was like I had been physically practicing the entire evening. The arrow zipped through both lungs in a classic shot, and I watched him crash seconds later less than forty yards away.

The remainder of that season, I fired three more arrows in anger, so to speak, killing another spike whitetail and a cow elk. With the other arrow, I missed a 145" eleven point buck, although to say it was a miss is inaccurate, the arrow went precisely where I intended; he just jumped an instant before I released and was gone when the arrow arrived. I was more than satisfied with the outcome, however, knowing I had made a good shot under pressure even if no blood was shed. Making kills with three out of four arrows that season was a breakthrough.

Today, several years later, my hunting is still being well-served by those foundations of target shooting learned from a champion; good form, proper practice, and the right mental approach. I'm not infallible, by any means. After all, the uncertainty and the variables are what makes hunting with a bow so challenging and so interesting.

But now, unlike the old days, any game animal that allows me to reach full draw within twenty yards is generally making a permanent mistake.

ISHI'S ARCHERY TACKLE

Steve Allely

For traditional archers, the story of Ishi has several facets.

The death of "The Last Wild Indian" in 1916 marked the acknowledged end of North American hunters who lived by their skill with a bow alone. Others would still use their bows in the pursuit of game, but in a dawning technological age there was no room left for hunter-gatherers. In addition, Ishi introduced Dr. Saxton Pope, Sr. to archery. Pope was his physician when Ishi lived at the University of California's Affiliated College Museum of Anthropology in San Fransisco. He also showed Pope much about bowhunting; concealment, close-range shots, calls, and decoys. And finally, of course, Ishi left traditional archery the legacy of his weapons.

His archery legacy actually started several years before he was discovered in Oroville, California in 1911.

One hundred years ago, in November, 1908, a crew of surveyors with packers in rugged Deer Creek Canyon, Tehema County, stumbled into the nearly inaccessible, hidden camp of Ishi and the three other surviving members of his tribe. He called this place "Wowunupo mu tetena", or Grizzly Bear's Hiding Place. The surveyors looted the camp of everything they could carry. Robert Hackley, who was there, would later say, "Among (the artifacts) were a bow, rather thin and flat, with sinew or gut glued firmly all over it's back; a large bundle of arrows including some in various stages of manufacture from simply smoothed sticks to completely finished and prettily decorated arrows; a fish spear; a handful, or more of arrow points, some apparently of bottle glass and others of different material; a basket work tray of the flat type so commonly made by Indians; a quiver ... and other articles which I cannot remember."

Over time, the items taken were scattered among the surveyors and their families, sold, or lost. The bow described above has vanished, a loss for us all, but some of the other artifacts have been acquired by museums. The quiver from the 1908 camp has a noteworthy story. For years, this quiver has been described as a case-skinned otter, fur side out, and that is exactly the way it has been photographed. From Saxton Pope's time until a few years ago, this was universally accepted. The only problem was, the quiver was actually inside-out because the fur was originally on the inside. The fur helped protect and cushion the arrows and their stone points, and the carrying strap was attached to the flesh side, a fact that had been neglected for almost a century. Whether the surveyors or a subsequent owner reversed the hide of the quiver is unknown.

Once Ishi entered civilization in 1911, the last known survivor of the Yahi, he lived and worked at the anthropology museum, recreating and demonstating his native crafts. His bows and arrows began to employ some of the modern materials available: dowels for arrow shafts, commercial paints and finishes for arrows and bows, steel and brass for arrowheads and field points.

Here, then, is Ishi's archery tackle.

A.

Ishi's otter skin quiver from Grizzly Bear's Hiding Place, 1908. Shown as it was originally, case-skinned otter with flesh side out and buckskin sling. Saxton Pope described the quiver as "composed of one full river otter pelt, dispatched by using a toggled harpoon spear ... four punctures in the animal's back show where the toggles had entered and exited." Two of these holes are visible just below the upper sling attachment.

For years, this quiver has been shown in photos in numerous publications with the fur side out, which is incorrect. As early as 1986, Dennis Torresdal of Portland, Oregon had conversations with the author and others pointing out the error. The quiver is now displayed properly. This is how most neighboring Northern California tribes such as the Shasta, Wintu, Achumawi, Hupa, Karok, Yurok, and others used otter pelts for quivers, with the fur side in to protect the arrows and points, and the flesh side out.

Pope recorded that "When on a prolonged hunt, Ishi carried as many as sixty arrows with him, though his quiver seldom contained more than a score. The extra arrows he kept covered with a skin and bound with buckskin thongs, and he carried them slung ... Besides his arrows he carried his bow in the quiver, and slung all over the left shoulder."

Phoebe Hearst Museum of Anthropology, # 1-19566. Purchased in 1914 for the UC Museum collection from Jack Apperson of Vina, California.

B.

Arrow from Grizzly Bear's Hiding Place, 1908. Two piece compound shoot shaft arrow, possibly hazel, 32 3/4" overall with an 11 1/4" foreshaft. Three hawk feathers lashed with sinew. Shaft painted with a red and blue design.

Jack Apperson was a member of the party who discovered Ishi's camp. According to family history, Ishi supposedly shot this arrow at Apperson on that day, striking the underside of his hat brim, narrowly missing him. Interestingly, when Ishi returned to Deer Creek in 1914 with Saxton Pope, Pope's eleven year old son, Professor Waterman, and Professor Kroeber, it was Jack Apperson who provided pack animals for provisions and accompanied the group.

This arrow is now in the California State Indian Museum, Sacramento.

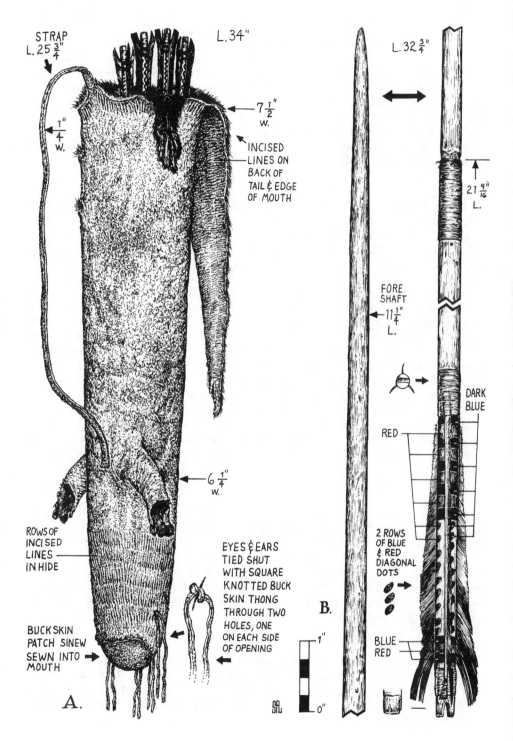

STRAP
L. 25 $\frac{3}{4}$"

L. 34"

$\frac{1}{4}$" W.

7 $\frac{1}{2}$" W.

INCISED LINES ON BACK OF TAIL & EDGE OF MOUTH

6 $\frac{1}{4}$" W.

ROWS OF INCISED LINES IN HIDE

EYES & EARS TIED SHUT WITH SQUARE KNOTTED BUCK SKIN THONG THROUGH TWO HOLES, ONE ON EACH SIDE OF OPENING

BUCK SKIN PATCH SINEW SEWN INTO MOUTH

A.

L. 32 $\frac{3}{4}$"

21 $\frac{9}{16}$" L.

FORE SHAFT 11 $\frac{1}{4}$" L.

DARK BLUE

RED

2 ROWS OF BLUE & RED DIAGONAL DOTS

BLUE RED

B.

1"

0"

Three more of Ishi's arrows taken from Grizzly Bear's Hiding Place in 1908 by Harry Keefer, one of the surveyor team's packers who discovered the hidden camp. Harry's wife, Grace E. Keefer, later gave these arrows to family members Chester and Ruby Rose of Chico, CA. Ruby's nephew, Philip Rose of Richvale, CA, donated these arrows to Chico's Bidwell Mansion Museum for exhibition, but instead the museum placed them in storage. Mr. Rose shared his story with Ishi chronicler Richard Burrill. Through Burrill's lobbying and paper trail documentation, in 2001 these Ishi arrows were finally transferred from storage and put into the permanent Ishi exhibit of the California State Indian Museum in Sacramento.

A.

Turkey vulture feathers on shoot shaft which is slightly barreled. Compound arrow with added hardwood foreshaft.

Pope described how Ishi drilled a socket to accept the foreshaft:

"The other end of the shaft was next drilled out to accommodate the foreshaft. His method of drilling was as follows: Placing a sharp piece of bone, point up, in the ground, and steadying it with his toes, he rotated the shaft perpendicularly upon this point. The motion here was identical with that employed in making fire by means of drill and base stick, the stick being rolled between the palms with downward pressure. The excavation averaged an inch in depth and quarter of an inch in diameter, and ran to a point. During this drilling process, the lower end of the shaft was tightly bound with sinew or cedar cord to keep it from splitting. One end of the foreshaft was formed into a spindle and made to fit this socket, leaving a slight shoulder where the two segments met. Salmon glue or resin was used to secure union, and the joint was bound with macerated tendon for the distance of an inch or more."

This arrow has an amber glass arrowhead with a broken tip and one broken barb. The point, however, is suspect, as the sinew wrapping was applied incorrectly, wrapped on dry over older sinew correctly applied when wet. The arrow is undoubtedly Ishi's, but the glass arrowhead is not typical of Ishi's style and may have been added by some other person.

B.

Compound arrow with slightly barreled shoot shaft and hardwood foreshaft. Feathers largely missing. Point is clear glass, possibly window glass, with portions of one barb tip and base missing. Point attached with pitch and sinew wrapping.

Pope, on the paints Ishi used on his arrows, "The pigments used in the wilds were red cinnabar, black pigment from the eye of a trout, a green vegetable dye from the wild onions, and a blue obtained, he said, from the root of a plant. These were mixed with the sap or resin of trees and applied with a little stick or hairs from a fox's tail drawn through a quill."

C.

Compound shoot shaft with foreshaft. Turkey vulture fletching apparently damaged at some point and repaired, as sinew wrapping now goes over painted cresting. Damaged clear glass point, possibly window glass, broken in two places and glued. Point secured with pitch and sinew wrapping. The tip of the head, one barb tip, and one shoulder tip also missing.

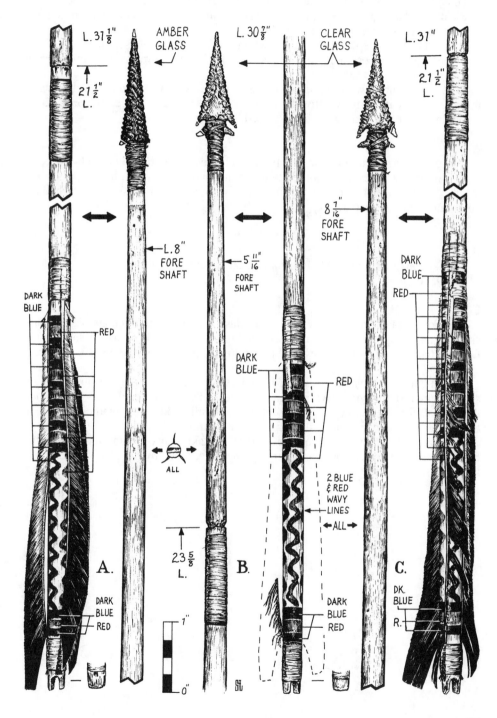

L. 31 1/8"

21 1/2" L.

AMBER GLASS

L. 8" FORE SHAFT

DARK BLUE

RED

ALL

DARK BLUE

RED

A.

L. 30 7/8"

CLEAR GLASS

5 11/16" FORE SHAFT

DARK BLUE

RED

2 BLUE & RED WAVY LINES

ALL

DARK BLUE

RED

23 5/8 L.

1"

0"

B.

L. 31"

21 1/2" L.

8 1/16" FORE SHAFT

DARK BLUE

RED

DK. BLUE

R.

C.

273

Three Ishi arrows, taken by Jack Apperson from Grizzly Bear's Hiding Place, 1908. These match the arrows on the previous page and are part of the same set. These three are now in the UC Berkeley Museum.

Pope, "Of all the specimens of arrows in the University Museum, scarcely any show such perfect workmanship as those of Ishi. His proportions and finish are of very high order."

"The arrow shafts were made of several kinds of wood ... hazel, and this was a favorite wood with him. A native bamboo-like reed was also a great favorite. Dogwood and mountain mahogany he also used."

A.

Compound hazel shoot arrow with hardwood foreshaft, with a dark pitch-like resin visible where the foreshaft is joined to the main shaft. Turkey vulture fletch, sleekly trimmed, attached with sinew wrapping alone without glue. Foreshaft is notched for point but no point present.

#1-19578.

B.

Similar construction to "A", foreshaft notched but no point.

#1-19576.

C.

Compound hazel shoot arrow with clear glass point set with pitch and lashed with sinew. Saxton Pope said there was blood on this arrow, which is perhaps related to the fact that the very tip of the arrowhead is missing. Illustrated as it originally appeared.

#1-19579.

Saxton Pope: "... the feathers were cut with a sharp piece of obsidian, using a straight stick as a guide and laying the arrow on a flat piece of wood. When with us he trimmed them with scissors, making a straight cut from the full width of the feather in back, to the height of a quarter of an inch at the forward extremity."

"Although all men were more or less expert in flaking arrowheads and knives, the better grades of bows, arrows, and arrow points were made by the older, more expert specialists of the tribe."

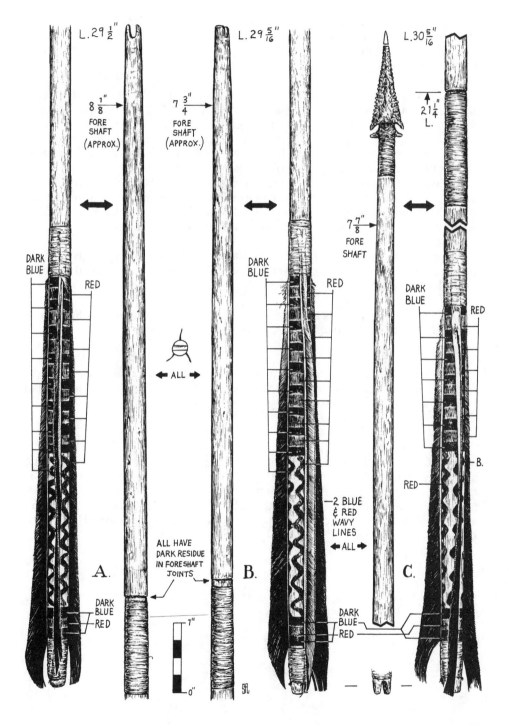

L.29½"

8⅛" FORE SHAFT (APPROX.)

DARK BLUE

RED

ALL

A.

DARK BLUE
RED

L.29 5/16"

7¾" FORE SHAFT (APPROX.)

DARK BLUE

RED

ALL HAVE DARK RESIDUE IN FORE SHAFT JOINTS

7"

0"

B.

—2 BLUE & RED WAVY LINES
ALL

DARK BLUE
RED

L.30 5/16"

21¼" L.

7⅞" FORE SHAFT

DARK BLUE

RED

RED

B.

C.

A.

Part of the set on the previous page, collected from Grizzly Bear's Hiding Place in 1908. Hazel main shaft, probably dogwood foreshaft, resin present at foreshaft junction. Turkey vulture fletch lashed at each end with sinew, no glue. No point present. Hearst Museum.

#1-91577.

Pope: "The first process of manufacture was that of straightening his shafts. To do this he either made a small heap of glowing embers from a fire or utilized a hot stone. He applied pressure with his thumbs on the convex side of any irregularity or bend in a shaft, and holding this near the heat, passed the wood back and forth before the stone or coals. When the wood was warm, it gave very readily to this pressure ... To burn or discolor the wood was evidence of bad technique."

"Smoothing was accomplished by scraping and rubbing the arrow shaft between two pieces of sandstone. He sometimes finished the shaft by rolling it back and forth on the thigh with his right palm while he worked it with a piece of sandstone held in his left hand. By this means he could "turn" a shaft almost as accurately as if a lathe were used."

"...such foreshafts were sometimes added to wooden arrows. They were of hazel, buckeye, wild currant, and perhaps other woods. The foreshaft was normally heavier material than the main shaft."

All of the arrows and bows to follow were made after Ishi was taken to San Francisco in 1911 and began living and working at the University Museum.

B.

Shaft from 5/16" commercial birch dowel. Iron point glued and lashed with sinew. Unidentified black feathers, not buzzard, lashed with sinew at each end and glued to shaft. Cresting of commercial red and green paint. Hearst Museum.

1-225736.

C.

Very long compound arrow over three feet long. Pope mentioned that Ishi made this type for exhibition or gift arrows. Pope also said this is a native bamboo but it is not *phragmites*, and may possibly be some type of non-native cane. Foreshaft from buckeye. Fletch is wild turkey tail feathers, left very long, no glue. Black obsidian point lashed with sinew. Cresting is apparently common water colors. Hearst Museum.

#1-19454.

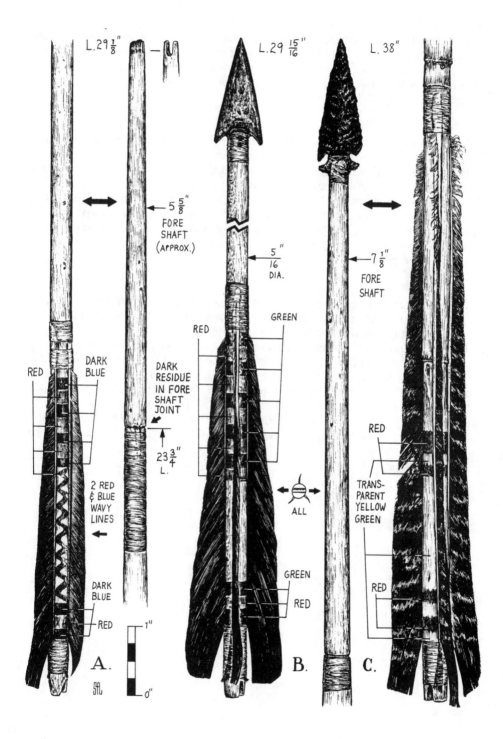

L. 29 $\frac{1}{8}$"

5 $\frac{5}{8}$"
FORE
SHAFT
(APPROX.)

RED

DARK
BLUE

DARK
RESIDUE
IN FORE
SHAFT
JOINT

23 $\frac{3}{4}$"
L.

2 RED
& BLUE
WAVY
LINES

DARK
BLUE

RED

A.

L. 29 $\frac{15}{16}$"

$\frac{5}{16}$"
DIA.

RED

GREEN

ALL

GREEN

RED

B.

L. 38"

7 $\frac{1}{8}$"
FORE
SHAFT

RED

TRANS-
PARENT
YELLOW
GREEN

RED

C.

1"

0"

277

A.

Japanese bamboo main shaft with birch foreshaft. Iron tip with coarse file marks present on surface and along blade edges, point glued and lashed with sinew. There is a dirt stain in this sinew from the arrow having been shot. Turkey tail fletch, glued and ends lashed with sinew. Commercial paint cresting.

Hearst Museum #1-19859.

B.

Commercial 5/16" birch dowel. Hawk feather fletch, glued down and ends sinew-wrapped. This arrow shows evidence of much wear and use.

Brass tubing field point crimped over and glued to shaft. Pope described how Ishi made these: "After some experience in shooting at targets, Ishi devised a substitute for the regular target arrow pile, or head. He made blunt points from thin brass tubing or steel umbrella sticks, cut into one inch lengths. He filed these with deep transverse notches across one end and pounded this portion into a blunt conical shape. These heads he set on his shafts with glue."

Hearst Museum #1-19856.

C.

Long cane arrow, foreshaft of hardwood, probably buckeye. Wild turkey tail feathers, ends bound with sinew, no glue. Cresting appears to be watercolors. Point a grainy dark gray obsidian set with pitch and sinew wrapped.

Pope: "The arrowheads were first set in the shaft by heating pine resin, and applying it to the notched end, then molding it about the base of the obsidian point. When firm, the point was further secured by binding it with sinew, back and forth, about the tangs and about the shaft. Three wraps were made about each notch, and the tendon was wound around the arrow for a distance of half a inch immediately below the arrowhead... A little polish with sandstone gave a fine finish to the binding."

"Such a point has better cutting qualities in animal tissue than steel. The latter is, of course, more durable."

Hearst Museum # 1-19453.

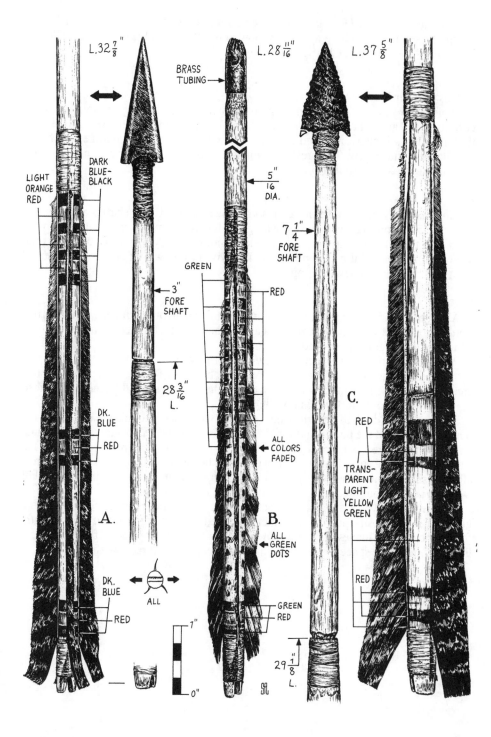

L.$32\frac{7}{8}$"

L.$28\frac{11}{16}$"

L.$37\frac{5}{8}$"

BRASS
TUBING

LIGHT
ORANGE
RED

DARK
BLUE-
BLACK

$\frac{5}{16}$"
DIA.

$7\frac{1}{4}$"
FORE
SHAFT

GREEN

RED

3"
FORE
SHAFT

$28\frac{3}{16}$"
L.

DK.
BLUE

RED

C.

RED

TRANS-
PARENT
LIGHT
YELLOW
GREEN

ALL
COLORS
FADED

A.

B.

ALL
GREEN
DOTS

RED

DK.
BLUE

ALL

RED

GREEN
RED

$29\frac{1}{8}$"
L.

7"

0"

279

Three arrows from Dr. Saxton Pope's personal collection, made while Ishi was living at the museum. These arrows are now in the *Pope and Young Club/St. Charles Museum of Bowhunting,* Chatfield, Minnesota.

A.

This is a bird arrow with a tic tac toe style lattice work for stunning birds. The crosspieces are made from sawn strips of translucent greenish-gray horn, possibly cow horn, and are lashed on with sinew. The 5/16" birch dowel shaft above and below the lattice work is also reinforced with sinew. The fletchings are wild turkey tail feathers attached with sinew. The crestings consist of commercial pigments and are dark blue and transparent reddish-orange.

B.

Ishi made this arrow at the museum sometime after 1911. The shaft is a commonly available 5/16" birch dowel, crested with green and red commercial paints. The point is an iron bodkin-style tip with a brass sleeve immediately behind it to support the shaft and prevent splitting upon impact. The wild turkey wing feathers are attached front and back with sinew wrapping.

C.

Also made of 5/16" commercial birch dowel. This arrow is tipped with a barbed iron blade lashed with sinew. Crestings are red and green commercial paints. Turkey wing feather fletchings attached with sinew.

Pope described how Ishi prepared feathers for fletching:

"In fletching arrows Ishi used eagle, buzzard, hawk, or flicker feathers ... By preference he took them from the wings, but did not hesitate to use tail feathers if reduced to it. With us he used turkey pinions."

"Taking the wider half he firmly held one end on a rock with his great toe, and the other end between the thumb and forefinger of his left hand. With a piece of obsidian, or later on a knife blade, he scraped away the pith until the rib was thin and flat. Having prepared a sufficient number in this way, he gathered them in groups of three, all from similar wings, tied them with a bit of string and dropped them into a vessel of water. When thoroughly wet and limp they were ready for use."

"While he chewed up a strand of sinew eight or ten inches long, he picked up a group of feathers, stripped off the water, removed one, and after testing its strength, folded the last two inches of bristles down on the rib, and the rest he ruffled backward, thus leaving a free space for later binding. He prepared all three like this."

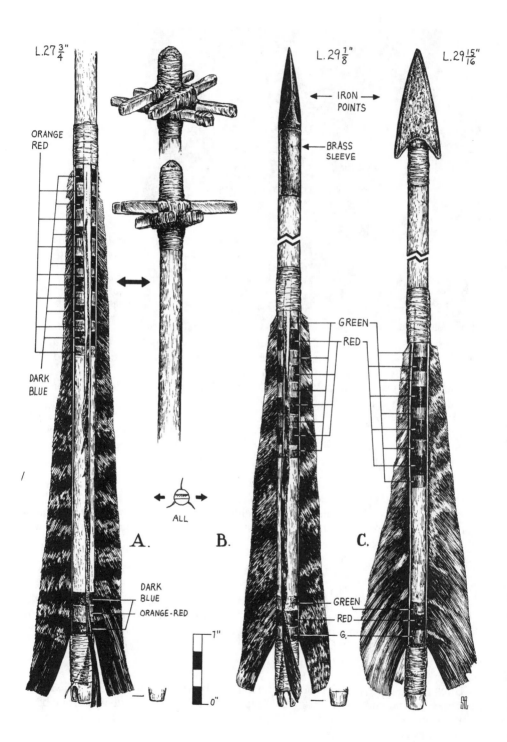

L.27¾"

ORANGE
RED

DARK
BLUE

A.

DARK
BLUE
ORANGE-RED

ALL

B.

1"

0"

L.29⅛"

IRON
POINTS

BRASS
SLEEVE

GREEN
RED

C.

L.29¹⁵⁄₁₆"

GREEN
RED
G.

Ishi shooting at Deer Creek, when he returned in 1914. (A.L. Kroeber photo, Lowie Museum of Anthropology, University of California at Berkeley, #15-5696).

Saxton Pope, "Drawn to the full length of an arrow, which was about twenty-six inches, exclusive of the foreshaft, his bow bent in a perfect arc slightly flattened at the handle. Its pull was about forty-five pounds..."

"He didn't always draw to 26" though, and would vary his draw depending on what he was shooting at and how far."

"It was not easy to extract arrows from the quiver quickly, so it was customary to carry a few in the hand. These, during the act of shooting, Ishi either laid on the ground or held beneath his right arm. Owing to his peculiar method of shooting, this did not interfere when he drew his bow."

A.

Dowel shaft 9/32" diameter, commercial paint cresting. Turkey wing fletching, sinew-wrapped and glued. Black opaque obsidian point, broken between notches (break not shown) and repaired with glue. Point attached with hide glue or pitch and sinew. Shaft apparently sealed with shellac.

Hearst Museum #1-19864.

B.

Commercial dowel shaft, 5/16". Turkey wing feathers, glued and ends secured with sinew. Red and green commercial paint. Black obsidian point, glued with pitch or hide glue, shown restored from slight damage.

Hearst Museum #1-19865.

C.

Birch dowel shaft, 5/16". Black obsidian point lashed with sinew. Crested with red and blue commercial paint. Turkey tail fletching, sinew-wrapped and glued, and beautifully trimmed.

Hearst Museum #1-19866.

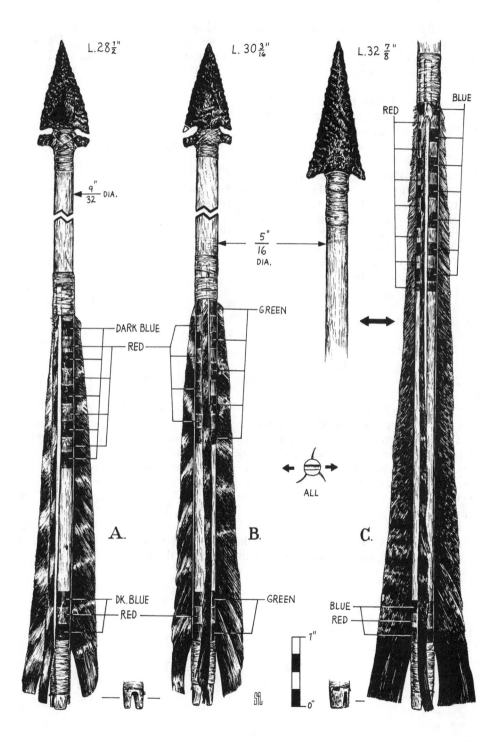

L.28½"

L.30³⁄₁₆"

L.32⁷⁄₈"

9⁄32" DIA.

5⁄16" DIA.

RED

BLUE

DARK BLUE
RED

GREEN

ALL

A.

B.

C.

DK.BLUE
RED

GREEN

BLUE
RED

1"

0"

283

Saxton Pope: "He made them in all sizes and shapes. Large spike-like heads were for gift arrows and war. Medium sized heads, perhaps 1 1/2 inches long, 3/4 inch wide, and 1/4 inch thick, were for ordinary deer shooting, while small flat oval heads were for shooting bear."

A. Clear glass. Hearst museum, # 1-19645.
B. Clear green glass. Hearst museum, # 1-19471.
C. Obsidian. Charley Shewey Collection.
D. Clear glass. Darwin B. Lyon Jr. Collection, Kelly-Griggs House Museum, Red Bluff, CA.
E. Translucent amber glass. Hearst museum, # 1-19642.
F. Translucent amber glass. Hearst museum, # 1-19476.
G. Clear Glass. Lyon Collection, Kelly-Griggs House Museum.
H. Black obsidian. Hearst museum, # 1-19503.
I. Translucent obsidian. Hearst museum, # 1-19510.
J. Clear glass. Hearst museum, # 1-19495.
K. Clear glass. Hearst museum, # 1-19494.
L. Black obsidian. Hearst museum, # 1-21665.
M. Black obsidian. Hearst museum, # 1-19498.
N. Black obsidian. Hearst museum, # 1-19638.
O. Black obsidian. Hearst museum, # 1-19639.
P. Translucent amber glass. Lyon collection, Kelly-Griggs House Museum.
Q. Tinted light gray-blue glass. Lyon collection, Kelly-Griggs House Museum.
R. Opaque white milk glass. Private collection.
S. Yellow tinted clear glass. Lyon Collection, Kelly Griggs House Museum.

Interestingly, two of the points on this page are attributed to Ishi before his 1911 discovery, though the time and manner of their acquisition remains unclear. Points S and Q, at the top of the page, are from the Lyon Collection and very closely resemble the glass points on arrows taken from Grizzly Bear's Hiding Place. D.B. Lyon Jr. was a turn of the century rancher who herded stock in the heart of Ishi's country. He and Ishi had some sort of relationship, as Ishi recognized him instantly when they met again about 1914 and Ishi called him, "Man with dogs!" At that time, Ishi gave him three of his very best glass presentation points, D, G, and P.

Ishi apparently made the more typical Yana-Yahi style points from glass in his aboriginal state, which are much smaller than the Wintu-style presentation points he is best known for when demonstrating flintknapping at the museum.

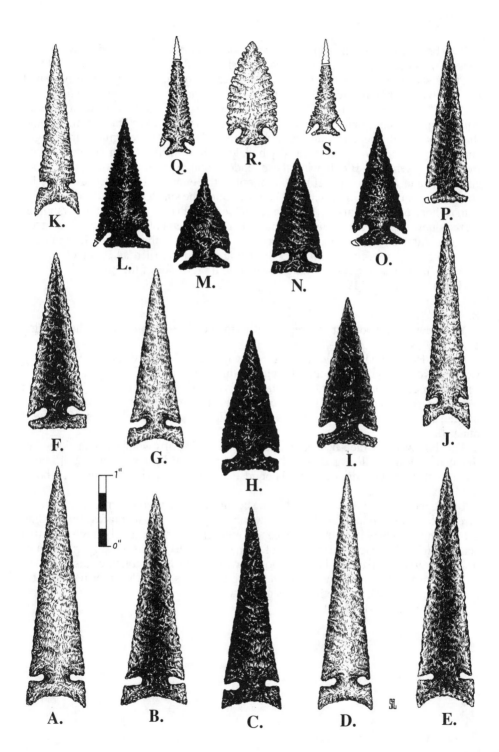

A.

Yew bow, no sapwood, appears to be made entirely of heartwood. Bow sinew-backed with deer tendon, tips wrapped with sinew below nocks. Pope reported that this bow was broken in testing before the application of the backing. Possibly coated with shellac after finishing, as it now has a streaked appearance. Red cloth handle.

Pope: "After being seasoned, he backed it with sinew. First, he made a glue by boiling salmon skin, but with us he was very enthusiastic over our common liquid (hide) glue and disdained the use of hot furniture glue. He applied glue to the roughened back of the bow. When it was dry he laid on long strips of deer sinew obtained from the leg tendons. By chewing these tendons and separating the fibers, they became soft and adhesive. Carefully overlapping the ends of the numerous fibers he covered the entire back very thickly. Having applied the sinew, he bound it on the bow with ribbons of maple bark. After "one sleep" (overnight), he removed this wrapping. As the sinew dried, it contracted and tended to draw the end of the bow into a reversed position. After this had happened he applied more glue to the surface. Several days later, when the backing was thoroughly dry and hard, he filed and scraped it very smooth, filing the overlapping margins level with the edges of the bow."

Hearst Museum #1-19452.

B.

Yew bow from wood cut in Oregon with sapwood present only along the margins of the belly side.

Pope: "He seemed to have no great respect, as the English do, for the white sap wood of yew or cedar. Although he placed this at the back of his bow, he did not hesitate to cut through its grain to attain a symmetrical form, and just as often he would scrape most of it away, leaving only a thin stratum of white at each edge. At the handle, a cross section of the bow was oval, while a section through the mid-limb was much flatter."

This bow was rawhide-backed, made in April, 1915, tips wrapped with sinew below nocks. The handle is a dark red woolen tape spirally wound around grip. Pope reported that this bow drew about 40 pounds, and that it "was one of Ishi's best bows used most at targets."

Bow appears to have been coated with shellac, which has now turned a dark translucent honey-brown and has flaked or worn away in numerous places. Pope: "Ishi showed no tendency to anoint his weapon with grease, nor to apply any protective coat, though later he learned the value of shellac in preserving his backing from dampness. The great aversion he had to shooting while any fog or moisture was in the air rather indicates that his bow was without the coverings of fat, wax, or resin so frequently used by archers in other parts of the world."

Hearst Museum #1-19590.

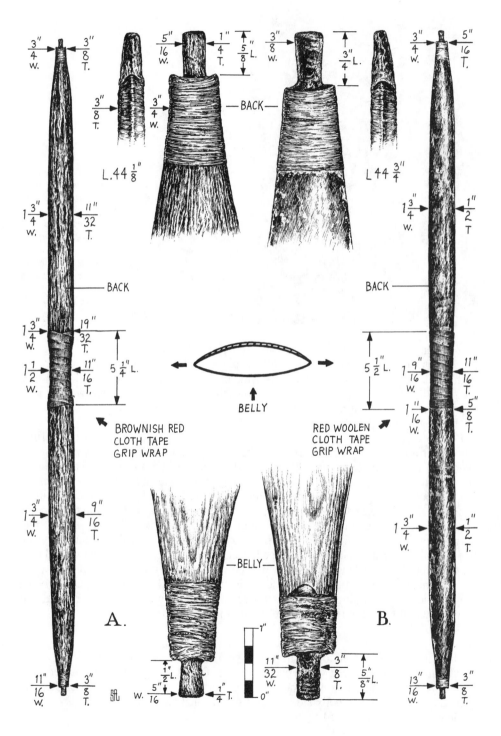

L. 44 ⅛"

L 44 ¾"

BACK

BELLY

BROWNISH RED
CLOTH TAPE
GRIP WRAP

RED WOOLEN
CLOTH TAPE
GRIP WRAP

BELLY

A.

B.

287

Ishi reducing a juniper bowstave. (A.L. Kroeber photo, 1914, Hearst Museum of Anthropology, University of California at Berkeley, #15-5684).

Saxton Pope: "He made bows of many woods while under observation, but upon an expedition into his country three years after his capture he showed us the tree from which the best bows were made. It was mountain juniper. He made a stave from one of these trees on the spot..."

Pope also said that Ishi "...loved his bow as he did no other of his possessions."

A.

Yew backed with rawhide, some sapwood present on belly of bow. Backing has marks from lashing while wet to hold it in place as the glue dried. Rawhide coated with shellac, now yellowed with age. A wide band of rawhide 12 1/2" long encircles the grip, the only one of Ishi's surviving bows that does not have the red woolen tape for a grip. This bow has a linen string.

Hearst Museum # 1-145548.

Pope detailed the making of a sinew string: "The bowstring he made out of the finer tendons from the deer's shank. If fresh, he simply chewed this tissue and teased it apart into threads no larger than floss silk. If dry he soaked it in warm water before chewing it. He then proceeded to spin a string by fixing one end of a bundle of tendon strips to a stationary point and rolling the other end between his finger in a single strand. As he progressed down the string he added more threads of tendon to the cord, making a very tight, simple twist one-eight of an inch thick. When about five feet long, he twisted and secured the proximal end, leaving his twisted cord taut between two points. The last smoothing-up stage he accomplished by applying saliva and rubbing up and down its length. The finished bow string was now permitted to dry. It's final diameter was about three thirty-seconds of an inch. After it was dry he formed a loop at one end by folding back some three inches of string, tapered by scraping, and serving two of the three inches securely with more tendon."

B.

Unbacked ash bow, one of the longer bows Ishi made. According to Pope, it was broken in use, but has been glued back together. The tips might have had a thin rawhide covering at one time, but is now mostly worn away, leaving only a residue and patina, especially on the belly side. Grip is red woolen cloth tape.

Hearst Museum #1-19451.

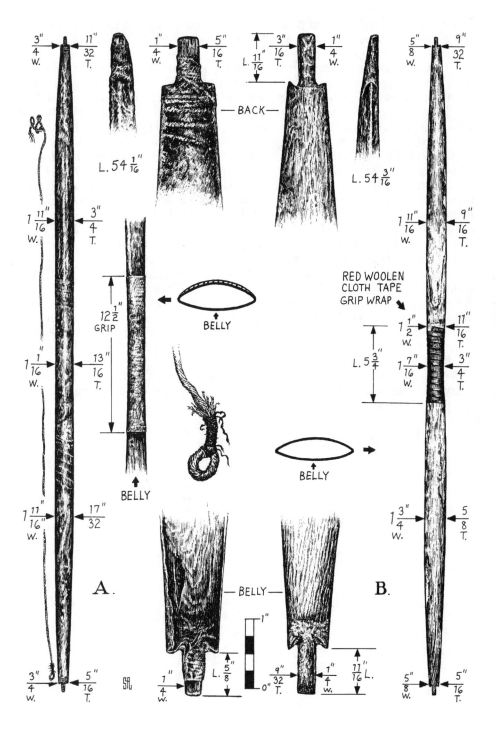

$\frac{3''}{4}$ w. $\frac{11''}{32}$ T.

$\frac{1''}{4}$ w. $\frac{5''}{16}$ T.

— BACK —

$\frac{3''}{16}$ T. $\frac{1''}{4}$ w.

L. $11\frac{1''}{16}$

$\frac{5''}{8}$ w. $\frac{9''}{32}$ T.

L. 54 $\frac{1''}{16}$

L. 54 $\frac{3''}{16}$

$1\frac{11''}{16}$ w. $\frac{3''}{4}$ T.

$1\frac{11''}{16}$ w. $\frac{9''}{16}$ T.

RED WOOLEN CLOTH TAPE GRIP WRAP

$12\frac{1''}{2}$ GRIP

BELLY

$1\frac{1''}{16}$ w. $\frac{13''}{16}$ T.

$1\frac{1''}{2}$ w. $\frac{11''}{16}$ T.

$1\frac{7''}{16}$ w. $\frac{3''}{4}$ T.

L. 5 $\frac{3''}{4}$

BELLY

BELLY

$1\frac{11''}{16}$ w. $\frac{17''}{32}$

$1\frac{3''}{4}$ w. $\frac{5}{8}$ T.

A.

— BELLY —

B.

$\frac{3''}{4}$ w. $\frac{5''}{16}$ T.

$\frac{1''}{4}$ w.   L. $\frac{5''}{8}$

$1''$

$0''$

$\frac{9''}{32}$ T. $\frac{1''}{4}$ w.

$\frac{11''}{16}$ L.

$\frac{5''}{8}$ w. $\frac{5''}{16}$ T.

In retrospect, Ishi's life and passing were like a stone thrown into still water, the concentric circles moving far beyond their origins. He introduced his doctor, Saxton Pope, to archery. Pope and his son accompanied Ishi to his old haunts along Deer Creek, where they hunted and camped for more than two weeks. After Ishi's death, Pope became a proficient target archer and national champion flight shooter, and based upon what he learned from Ishi's patient teaching in the field, he also became a dedicated bowhunter. Pope teamed up with Arthur Young, another student of Ishi's and an accomplished target archer of the day, and they determined to prove that the bow and arrow were still viable weapons for game. They bowhunted in California, Wyoming, Alaska, and ultimately, Africa. Pope's books *The Adventurous Bowmen* and *Hunting with the Bow and Arrow* became archery classics. After Pope's death in 1926, shortly after returning from Africa, Art Young continued bowhunting and giving demonstrations of his shooting prowess around the country. It was at one of Young's demonstrations that a youthful Fred Bear became enthralled with the bow as a hunting weapon, and he ultimately dedicated his life to promoting archery and bowhunting. Bear, along with Howard Hill, Glenn St. Charles, and many others, worked tirelessly to legalize bowhunting and establish separate bow seasons, state by state.

So there are direct links from Ishi, to Pope and Young, to Bear, to St. Charles, to today. The case can be readily made that Ishi, the last flicker of wildness from Native America, directly fostered modern bowhunting. Were it not for the concentric rings that he and his archery tackle began, there might well be no such thing as the bowhunting we currently enjoy. And it's unlikely Jay Massey would have ever written *The Bowyer's Craft,* unlikely Paul Comstock would have ever written *The Bent Stick,* unlikely there would have ever been a *Traditional Bowyer's Bible.*

So in a very real sense, Ishi can be considered a toxophilic forebear to all of us today who craft wooden bows, and particularly to those who seek game with their handmade weapons.

BULLS ON A STICK

Jim Hamm

Chuck Friskie and Matt Rael exercised great self-control, I thought, when we showed them our elk hunting bows. They managed not to flinch. So it's fair to say I liked our guides right from the start.

Jim Welch and I had ventured to New Mexico on a bowhunt for elk, but we were using bows that were somewhat unusual for the uninitiated. These bows we had made ourselves, from a single piece of wood, by hand. Jim's bow reflected his Sioux/Mohawk Native American heritage, and any of his ancestors would have cherished his fine bois d'arc wood bow. My bow was longer and narrower and could trace its roots back to ancient Europe. Both bows were of moderate weight, fifty pounds or so, and we shot heavy wooden arrows in the 600 grain range. Between the two of us, we had made thousands of wooden bows and had hunted with them for decades, so we knew they were just as effective now as they were ten thousand years ago.

But our guides were skeptics. As Chuck examined his bow, Jim noticed his expression, like he was trying not to laugh.

"Those bows will do the job if you just get us in close," Jim said.

"How close?" This was from Matt.

"Well," I answered, "twenty yards is about max. And ten yards is a lot better."

"Don't worry," Jim added, with a straight face, "we're highly trained professionals."

Jim and I, with our love of wooden bows and bowhunting, try to get together at least a couple of times a year, even though we live a thousand miles apart; he in Minnesota and me in Texas. Jim's nephew, Alan Welch, had invited us to New Mexico to his favorite hunting spot. Having hunted the ranch for several years, Alan had taken a couple of nice bulls with his compound bow, but on this trip he was unarmed. He'd come along just to watch the show.

The guides knew what a modern bow such as Alan's would do, but they remained dubious about our tackle.

"Will this thing kill an elk?" Chuck asked, handling Jim's bow like Steuben crystal.

"I suppose," Jim said, "I kill rabbits with it all the time."

"And I killed a deer with mine once," I added.

Alan snorted, our guides shook their heads, and we adjourned to the bunkhouse. Actually, Jim and I had killed dozens of deer with our wood bows, and Jim had once taken a 2200 pound bull buffalo. But neither of us had ever launched an arrow at an elk. From Alan's stories about this ranch, we were hoping to remedy that, but our chosen weapons allowed such limited ranges we knew it was going to take a lot of luck.

We were up way before daylight the next morning. After breakfast, Jim and Alan drove off northeast with Chuck, while Matt and I took his truck to the base of Baldy Peak to our east. Matt explained that the elk were bedding up in the heavy timber on the mountain, then coming down at night to graze in the vast open park fanning out from its base. We stopped in the edge of the forest and gathered our gear with the stars still shining. Hiking parallel to the slope, we began to hear bugling in the distance. A lot of bugling.

"They're already moving," Matt said, then took off at a trot. Though older than him and a flatlander to boot, I managed to keep up without bursting a blood vessel.

When we set up, the woods were just starting to lighten, but there was plenty of light at the "excuse me" range where I would have to take a shot. Matt backed off fifty yards uphill and began cow chirping. Answering bugles echoed. Dark shapes crashed through the timber below. Ten cows and calves headed up the slope twenty yards to my right. Then three young bulls passed thirty yards to my left, well out of range, bugling all the while. More bugles below and a lot more timber was destroyed. I'd heard less commotion at a rock concert.

Watching intently down the hill, I jumped as if electrocuted when Matt grabbed my elbow and whispered, "They're headed around this way. We'll try to cut them off."

We jogged to the edge of the huge park at the foot of the mountain and could see elk scattered out far ahead of us down the slope. I grabbed for the binoculars and focused on the largest group, at least thirty cows. And with them, screaming his brains out, was what appeared to be a fine bull with tremendous mass.

Matt gave a low whistle, confirming my estimation. He took off again, headed through another finger of woods in an attempt to cut off the big bull. The elk were moving fast, but we closed to within two hundred yards before some of the cows busted us and barked out a warning. The whole gang scattered off up the mountain, the herd bull and at least six smaller satellite bulls along with all the women and children, until there wasn't an elk in sight.

Matt sat on a log and I gratefully joined him, glad to give my quivering knees a break. The altitude hadn't been bothering me until I saw that bull.

"Well, that was an interesting morning," I said, careful to keep my voice neutral.

Glancing my way, Matt grinned. "Man, that bull was nice. Lots of mass and a couple of small drop tines. He was old too."

"What I wouldn't give to have a chance at him," I said reverently. But the closest we had gotten was two hundred yards, so he may as well have been in Zimbabwe.

I had hunted elk a couple of times before on National Forest land, and I had seen more elk on that first morning's hunt - fifty or so - than I had in all my other elk hunts combined. While I generally knew what a whitetailed deer or turkey was thinking and what he was doing and why, I considered myself to be an elk hunting rookie. Hunting with and learning from folks who really understood those wonderful animals was one of the main reasons, aside from Alan's stories, that had landed me there on the slopes of Baldy Peak.

We spent the rest of the morning and early afternoon working up through the timber cow chirping and occasionally bugling. We received a few answering bugles for our trouble, but that was all.

The wind picked up all day until it was howling, and I do not abuse that word. But as evening approached, we could hear bugling approaching from uphill. At least we thought it was coming from uphill. With the wind thundering and swirling, it was impossible to tell exactly where they were. We were finally surrounded in the heavy timber with bugles and cow chirps, until they seemed to come from every direction, fading and swelling and then fading again in the buffeting wind. And we never saw another elk.

Frustrated, at dark we headed back down the mountain to find out how Jim and Alan had fared. Over dinner, they reported no bloodshed. But they had seen dozens of elk, several nice bulls among them.

"I was just holding off," Jim deadpanned, "but I guess I'll go ahead and shoot one tomorrow."

"Me too," I said, not wanting him to get too far ahead of me at pestering the guides, "and I know which one I want to shoot." I related the story of the old bull we'd seen that morning.

"OK," Jim said, making a gracious gesture, "you can have that one."

He and I both laughed the hardest, knowing that we would be thrilled to take any bull with our bows, much less one of the bruisers we had seen that day.

The next morning before daylight, Matt and I once again rattled along a logging road in his four-wheel-drive pickup. On the long drive up the mountain, he explained the plan. We would get far above the elk near where he thought they bedded and wait. It might take an hour or even two after first light for the elk to show up, as we would be a couple of miles from the parks below where they grazed at night. Seemed like a good plan to me.

When we finally eased to a stop in a grove of aspens, we could just make out the white trunks. Matt switched off the key and the engine sputtered and fell silent. Elk were screaming right below us.

I just love it when a plan comes together.

Scrambling out of the truck, I grabbed my bow and quiver. Matt hissed, "C'mon, c'mon, c'mon," and took off like a mountain goat down the steep slope, hurtling boulders and logs as he went. Somehow, I kept up with him until he slid to a stop and held up a hand for silence. Two cow elk glared at us from thirty yards away, but turned and bolted up the hill without barking the alarm. Matt was off again, with me tromping on his heels, till he whispered, "set up in there," and shoved me toward a small clump of head-tall spruce trees on the edge of a big open park.

I took cover, nocked an arrow, and could hear elk coming.

The first one was a young 5 X 5, twenty yards away down the hill. He passed behind a big spruce tree, and I came to full draw. He loped into the clear right in front of me, and though I knew I might be kicking myself later for passing on him, I let down the arrow without releasing. Three cows and a spike were right behind that first bull. Then more cows headed straight up the slope to my left, fifteen yards away. Another 5 X 5 with most of the antler on his right side broken off passed in front of me where the first bull had gone. Two more cows followed him.

I could hear a puffing sound, almost like a locomotive, and realized it was an animal breathing hard. And then I could see antlers coming, big antlers, on the same path most of the other elk had taken just below me. Up until then, the action had been so fast that it was like dodging a flurry of snowballs, with no time to think. But the instant I saw him I knew this one was a shooter, and time slowed way down. I must have gone deaf, too, because I could no longer hear his breathing, or the thudding of his hooves, or any other sound.

When he passed behind the large spruce, I came to full draw and waited. I had practiced for months leading up to the hunt, and with every arrow told myself that if an opportunity came, I would make a perfect shot. Even so, when he loped into the clear at twenty yards, I was mildly amazed to see an arrow appear in the bull's side.

I thought then, and still think, that the yellow fletching pointing the way into his engine room was the most beautiful thing I'd ever seen.

He never broke stride, and continued loping over a slight rise in the park and out of sight. My hearing returned and I could still hear labored breathing, only this time it was coming from me. I took a knee, gasping like a beached carp. I spotted Matt, forty yards away up on the crest of the rise to my right, staring intently through his binoculars. He watched a long time, before turning and giving me a thumbs up and a grin.

By the time he eased over to me, I could breath again. Sort of.

"He made it to the timber on the other side of the park, but the shot looks good."

We agreed that the arrow was in the back of the lungs, angling forward and down, and that it had completely penetrated the body cavity.

Matt added, "That's the same bull we saw yesterday morning, the old one with the drop tines."

"No way!" I was suddenly light-headed again. "There's no way!"

"Yep," he persisted, "that's the same bull."

"But we're miles from where we saw him yesterday."

"Well, you said you wanted to shoot that bull, so I thought I'd bring you right up here to him."

I made a rude sound, but Matt's grin just got wider when he realized I really had no clue it was the same elk. We thought the shot had been a good one, but in order to be absolutely sure, we decided to give the bull some time before following. We headed back down the mountain to recruit some loading help.

We arrived back in camp and while munching a quick snack, Chuck radioed that Jim had a bull down. Elated, Matt and I grabbed more provisions and headed back up the mountain.

Jim, Alan, and Chuck were all smiles when we found them. As they led us to Jim's bull, their story tumbled out. They had played tag with the elk off and on all morning. Finally, Jim and Chuck set up in a living room-sized clump of Christmas trees while Alan shot video from a hundred yards away. Chuck first chirped in some cows. The bull soon followed, until he was peering into their clump of trees. Jim reported that Chuck's eyes grew wide when the bull turned his antlers and forced his way into their tiny grove. Jim saw a hat-sized opening and drew and shot in one quick motion. The bull, which was four yards away at that point, turned and ran.

"I'm glad Jim shot when he did," Chuck admitted, "because it was starting to get crowded in there."

The bull was a fine 6 X 7, and the arrow passed squarely through his heart, a superb piece of shooting under the circumstances even from twelve feet away. Jim used the same two-bladed Zwickey broadhead to kill his elk that he used to take his first deer when he was a teenager. I suggested he have that broadhead gold-plated and framed.

Once we loaded Jim's bull, we led them over miles of logging roads to the scene of my encounter. I was still completely confident in the shot, a feeling that grew as we easily followed the blood trail across the grassy expanse of the park. The bull had stopped inside edge of the trees, a fact revealed by a fair amount of blood. But then nothing. Nada. The entire mob of elk had traveled right through there, so there was no hope of trailing him without some blood.

After spending many fruitless minutes on hands and knees trying to discern which direction he had taken, we fanned out through the thick timber. My heart was in my

boots as I replayed the shot over and over, wondering what had gone wrong. But, my growing depression vanished the instant I heard Alan's whistle.

My bull had gone straight uphill from where he stopped at the edge of the woods, crashing after only fifty yards. Matt was quite correct, it was, indeed, the same bull we had seen that first morning, an unusual 8 X 7 with terrific mass and a couple of small drop tines.

Jim and I found that we couldn't stop grinning. Through pictures and handshakes and admiring the latest bull and walking around in a daze, our grins never faded.

"Amazing you could kill bulls like that with just a stick," Chuck said at last.

"There's not enough wood in those bows to boil a pot of coffee," Matt said with wonder, "I would never have believed it if I hadn't seen it myself."

"Oh, we do this all the time," I lied.

"Sure," Jim said with a shrug, "no problem."

Chuck and Matt said in unison, "But we never doubted you for a second," and howled with laughter.

Jim Welch and I have shared campfires for many years, and have bowhunted across a big stretch of country. We've experienced plenty of success, mainly due to pure persistence, but have never seen the equal of that elk hunt. On the way home from New Mexico, we talked about stopping to buy lottery tickets while we were hot, but decided we'd be wasting our money.

We had already won.

APPENDIX I

AWAKENINGS

Tom Mills

This *Traditional Bowyer's Bible, Volume 4,* is being published 16 years after the appearance of *Volume 1.* Tim Baker, Paul Comstock and Jim Hamm are the three surviving authors who, along with the late Jay Massey, contributed to each of the first three volumes. In the following interview, they look back on events surrounding publication of the original series.

• • • •

TM: What was your introduction to traditional archery? What prompted your interest?

Baker: I sort of backed into primitive bowmaking via a lifelong interest in paleoanthropology, specifically after reading Theodora Kroeber's *Ishi in Two Worlds.* This led to a couple of years of being "the only guy in the world" relearning the art of knapping, which led to making an arrow, which led to making a bow. It was quite lame by present standards, still, holding that just finished bow was a SHAZAM moment. No lightning bolt, but I was changed. A happy, eager, obsession had begun.

Comstock: I shot bows with the Boy Scouts and took an archery class in college and there were no compounds around. We used basically straight-limbed fiberglass bows. I later hunted with a compound briefly, but returned to stick bows as soon as I could, because they were my first frame of reference.

Hamm: When I was a kid, maybe seven years old, I saw a diorama in a museum of an Indian crouched in the low branches of a tree with his bow at full draw, an unsuspecting deer walking by. The idea of being stealthy enough and skilled enough to make your own weapon and take game with it plucked a chord in me which hasn't completely stopped vibrating even now, a half century later.

TM: Inspirations?

Baker: An ongoing inspiration is the endless hunt, tracking down the secrets of wooden bows.

Comstock: When I finally understood that at one time bows in the U.S. were mostly or entirely wood, I became obsessed with that idea and wanted to learn as much as I could about this extinct style. Reading Pope's *Hunting With the Bow and Arrow* inspired me to attempt bow construction.

Hamm: I think the primary inspiration for me and others is the challenge of archery. Some feel challenged to see how accurately they can shoot, as attested by the popularity of formal target archery, 3-D shooting, and field archery. For others, it's flight shooting, the challenge of seeing how far they can shoot an arrow. A lot of people take up the challenge of hunting with handmade bows. Many are challenged by how fast they can shoot an arrow, and these folks have done much to hone and improve wooden bow designs. Some like the challenge of creating character bows. These areas can overlap to greater or lesser degrees, but the common thread throughout every aspect is the personal challenge.

TM: Wooden bows practically died out in the 1970's and 80's, what prompted their resurgence?

Baker: All through the fiberglass Dark Ages, a pilot light kept burning - a small number of men, Wally Miles of Oregon for example, continued making and shooting wood. Then there was the enormous silent flywheel of information waiting in dusty woodbow related library books. Jay Massey became aware of both and more than anyone began reigniting the flame with his '87 *Bowyer's Craft*, and by missionary-work talks and demonstrations at glassbow meets. Much of what we have today traces directly to Jay's efforts.

Comstock: The short answer is that thousands were ready to embrace their return. Wooden bows had fallen so far off the radar I think the very mention of them stirred an immediate curiosity. By the mid-1980s there also were archery writers growing openly critical of the compound bow. When good information on making wooden bows became widespread, we had the ironic situation that compounds were old hat, while wooden bows were something new and intriguing. I think we also owe a lot to Jay Massey, who was the first mainstream bowhunter in many, many years to announce in print that he loved wooden bows.

Hamm: There was always an underlying hint of appeal, but back then most people had never even seen a wooden bow, and there was virtually no up-to-date information on how to make them. So only a tiny handful of us were actually making bows. But there was always some scattered interest, fueled mainly by something of a backlash against all of the technology, I think, which had overwhelmed archery and bowhunting.

TM: How did the three of you get to know each other?

Baker: In '88 Dick Baugh (maker of The Bow Scraper) let me know of a new bow book just out, Comstock's *The Bent Stick*. I ordered an early copy, thought it excitingly innovative, and immediately wrote him with sincere praise, a few questions, and somewhat brazenly, a couple of arguments. A return-mail letter openly invited constructive argument, beginning about ten pounds of correspondence over the next few years. Early on he laid down a lubricating ground rule: "We're of no value to each other if we can't disagree." Quite liberating when working to discover and rediscover the true secrets of bows. This became a stated ground rule during later collaborations between Comstock, Hamm, Massey, myself, and others. If memory serves, I believe Jay gave me Jim Hamm's number and suggested I call. Happily, like Comstock, Jim's main impulse was for the truth of things, regardless of what beliefs or conventions must fall. And, like Comstock, he valued and enjoyed robust honest argument. "Recreational argument," as he put it. This began a satisfying time of discovery, knowledge sharing, and joint resculpting of existing woodbow knowledge. All of which kept the Post Office and AT&T deep in the black for the following few years.

Comstock: Tim Baker contacted me by letter and he knew most people visibly active at the time. I ended up communicating with most of them in one way or another, including Jim Hamm. Baker and I ended up sending many, many letters back and forth and talked a great deal on the phone. Some of his letters were 10 pages long, filled with his ideas and stories about bows.

Hamm: Paul, Jay, and I had all written books in the late 80's, and we corresponded pretty regularly. And then Tim called and introduced himself. Jay and I were invited to Michigan in the summer of 1989, to the Great Lakes Longbow tournament, and he, John Strunk, and I gave a presentation on wooden bows to the hundreds of fiberglass longbow shooters. Along with Gary Davis and Chuck Boelter, we were about the only ones there who were making wooden bows, and we were amazed at the reception. Our program was supposed to be forty-five minutes long one evening, but by the time we had demonstrated our bows and answered questions, several hours had passed. Jay and I insisted Paul and Tim attend the following year, and that's where we all met in person for the first time.

TM: Describe that first Michigan meeting.

Baker: I arrived with wood bows, extra staves, and extra tools. I laid out the bows and staves, knocked together a work bench and quietly began making shavings. Within seconds several passers-by stopped to watch. In minutes a throng had gathered. Primed by the woodbow demonstrations the previous year several held split staves and various wood-removing tools. I quickly tillered a bow, as example, then invited all to join in. Staves and tools were shared. More tools and staves arrived. After just an hour or so the now newly experienced began tutoring raw novices. In short, a melee of wood bowmaking began. Comstock arrived from Ohio and joined in as tutor. Jim and Jay left their booths when possible for further support. Gary Davis, a future good friend, arrived with more wood, tools, and a perfect sinew-backed Osage recurve to show. Glenn St. Charles happened by, visibly brightened by the explosion of wood bowmaking energy. He described all this in his future book, *From Billets to Bows*. John Strunk's booth had a three-deep clump of future bowmakers observing his every tillering move. By mid afternoon a small village of beginning bowmakers were at work, all sharing tools, wood, advice and a sudden and near tangible sense of adventure and comradeship. At one point I stopped work to look around and take in the remarkable scene, saying to myself: "Don't ever forget this moment."

By late night when we finally shut down for the day shavings were ankle deep in our 'village.' The next day and the next year and following years were the same. The bowmaking world was in revolution.

Comstock: Before attending, I think I had laid eyes on maybe three other people who had made a wooden bow. There had been days when I didn't think anybody else on earth cared about wooden bows. But within 90 minutes of arriving at the Great Lakes session, I met face-to-face for the first time Baker, Hamm, Jay Massey, John Strunk, and Gary Davis, and their bows. To encounter all this experience, talent and devotion to wooden bows in a single and sudden rush completely blew me away. Also that day, I was electrified to see bows made by Saxton Pope and Arthur Young. It was one of the most amazing days I ever had.

Hamm: I don't think religious experience is too strong a term. Speaking for myself, I was like a parched man crawling across the desert who had finally found a beautiful spring of cool, fresh water. We all stayed up half of every night, elated to have finally found others who understood our molecular attraction to wooden bows. "Cross-pollination" is how someone described our first meetings and the wonderful exchange of information that took place. It was one part discussion, one part argument, one part profound "Ah-ha", and one part tossing good-natured barbs. All I know is I learned a great deal and was eager for much more.

TM: How did the *TBBs* evolve from that meeting?

Baker: Evolve? I think it was more like spontaneous generation. The idea dawned fairly intact in Jim's mind. I think that because he seemed to have kept it to himself for maybe two minutes - he was still on an inventor's high when he began sharing it with us. The multi-author idea felt instantly right and we leaped on board. Of course, as the elaborate scope of the book evolved it became clear how terribly unwise it was, from a business-plan view, for Jim to publish it. Big up-front expenses, and a then tiny and uncertain market. Paul and I feared poor Jim and his shirt would soon be parted. None of us could have dreamed at the time how successful the book would be.

Comstock: My recollection is I was sitting on a lawn chair late at night and Baker came over and told me Hamm had the idea to do it. I believe the rest of us agreed very quickly to participate.

Hamm: Well, it occurred to me in the middle of one of those late-night cross-pollination sessions that we should capture the magic of that broad exchange of ideas and experiences. And so I verbalized the thought and suggested we put together a collaborative book. A serendipitous moment, perhaps, because everyone immediately wanted to be part of it. The idea quickly gained momentum as it bounced from one of us to the next, so there was never a question of not pressing ahead. As Tim later said, "That first volume sat up on the operating table", which pretty well describes the entire experience, as the *TBBs* soon took on a life of their own.

TM: How have your bows changed since you began?

Baker: My first bow was an Ishi design of English Longbow length. The worst of both worlds. It kicked hard and had terrible cast, though at the time it seemed pretty wonderful. Early on I purchased a chronograph and began keeping design and performance stats for each bow made. With this, the features that produce durable, comfortable, fast, accurate bows became quickly apparent. A design mantra emerged from this testing: Make inner limbs wide or long enough to take essentially no set, midlimbs just wide enough to take little set, outerlimbs as narrow as possible for low inertial mass.

Comstock: Well, they're still uglier than sin. Generally they are trimmer and lighter in mass, with less string follow.

Hamm: Over several decades, I've evolved from shorter, sinew-backed bows - sinew was the only way I could get a bow to hold together in the beginning - to long pure self bows. I also make my bow tips much smaller now, the size of your little finger or less; better speed and less handshock.

TM: How does bowmaking compare now to when you began?

Baker: First, instead of a handful, there are now tens of thousands of devout woodbow makers. Next, thousands of them are world-class bowyers. And at least hundreds have a broad encompassing understanding of the material properties and design principles of scores of bow and wood types from various bow cultures from Stone Age times to the present. This condition has never existed before. A true transformation has taken place in the last few years.

Comstock: When I started, trying to get reliable guidance in any form was a very difficult challenge. Today this information is everywhere and I'm glad it is. The general level of sophistication - in understanding and technique - is high.

Hamm: You have to understand that back then, if you were making wood bows you were alone on an island, there was no one else. Since we were isolated in a vacuum the learning curve was flat-lined, and I probably broke a dozen bows before ever launching that first arrow. If I'd had any sense at all, I would have given up (laughs).

Now, I see lots of first-time bowyers making excellent bows, so it's definitely less frustrating now. Lots more fun, too, having others who share your passion.

TM: What are the catalysts for today's huge resurgence?

Baker: At root is the innate, near-mystical, never fully explainable appeal of a wooden bow. The unlikelihood that we can turn a dead stick of wood into this living thing straining to do far distant deeds. Part is the satisfaction of mastering the ever-new challenge of each stave's peculiarities. Part is the sense of natural and proper connection to the organic world. Part is knowing that when tillering a bow we're having the same thoughts our 500th grandfathers had as they tillered their bows - that we share authentic connection to our ancient bowmaking ancestors. There are many such explainable and unexplainable reasons why the bow's appeal would have traction should the catalyst mentioned in your question appear. The catalyst itself was many-faced: Jay's book and the many to shortly follow, for example. Then woodbow-related magazines, physical bow meets, and of course the virtual meets online.

Because *The Bent Stick* opened the door to 'other woods,' democratizing natural archery, I think Comstock was the single most important catalyst. He argues against this, naming Jay Massey instead. But without *The Bent Stick* I know, for one, that I'd have made a few Osage and yew bows then found other interests. I believe this would have largely been the case generally. Jim agrees that without *The Bent Stick* and what flowed from it, *The Traditional Bowyers Bibles* would be a far narrower, much less revolutionary volume. As it is, the *TBBs* have become enormously popular and had enormous influence, arguably becoming the largest single post-Comstock catalyst.

Plain old fate also played a part: Several decades before wood bows were a gleam in Massey's or Comstock's eyes wise forces took hold of a young Jim Hamm, hammering, stretching and molding him to contain precisely the one in several million set of natures needed to produce the *TBBs*. Here was the unusual end product: Someone having a deep love and knowledge of primitive bows, a canny business sense, a nimble open mind, fluid diplomatic skills, the capacity to suppress ego, writing skills, editing skills, publishing skills, the willingness and ability to work more than a year - full-time - on each volume, all these together creating a perfect-storm individual at just the right moment in natural archery's reawakening. I doubt if the planet holds another person with this set of traits.

Comstock: Everyone who has made or shot a wooden bow has contributed to the natural archery resurgence. It is, after all, leading by example and word-of-mouth communication that have fanned the flames. But without question, the greatest path-finder of the resurgence was Jay Massey and his book, *The Bowyer's Craft*. The day this book appeared, everything changed. Before this book appeared in 1987, wooden bows were an essentially invisible and statistically tiny component of the North American archery and bowhunting scenes. Then thousands of us who bought *The Bowyer's Craft* read as Jay described how important wooden bows are. Wooden bows were out in the open again and a long Dark Age had ended.

Hamm: In the beginning there were the publications; individual books from Paul and Jay and others, *TBBs*, *Primitive Archer*, *Traditional Bowhunter*. They all put information in the hands of those who were interested. Today there's also a certain critical mass involved, since there are wooden bows at archery shops, shooting ranges, hunting camps, so anyone with the slightest interest in wooden bows runs into them regularly. And it's easy to find information on the Internet. So a rookie bowyer can quickly find someone to show them the basics of the art. Practically every bowyer knows another within easy driving distance, or can attend a local or regional bowyer's meeting.

TM: Any particular area of interest now? What is your favorite bow these days?

Baker: After making thousands of bows of every conceivable design I've returned to the ancient, elemental, D-tillered longbow. This design has more good features than any other. It's easy to make, it's durable, accurate, sweet-drawing, and when made right and shooting hunting-weight arrows, equals the cast of all but the most difficult to make and unstable exotic designs. If I had to pick just one wood it would probably be elm. Teaching new bowmakers the ropes continues to be satisfying. Nowadays I do this mostly on the *PaleoPlanet* on-line archery forum, and at monthly meets held in the Pasadena arroyo in north LA.

Comstock: Many of the bows I regularly use are backed with hickory.

Hamm: For me, the thrust for archery has always been and continues to be bowhunting. I enjoy turkeys, elk, antelope, and Alaskan game, but above all I dearly love whitetails. Chasing whitetails with a handmade bow is just about the ultimate hunting challenge.

As far as bows, I've shot every type you can make, I guess, from composites on down, but I've finally gravitated to very long selfbows, 72" plus, with a whip-tiller. I like the smoothness and accuracy of the length, and the whip-tiller reduces hand shock and yields excellent speed since the working limb has relatively low mass. I love making such bows from a smaller Osage tree, six inches in diameter or so, with lots of knots and snakey grain and character. It's all good, though, whatever floats your boat, since personal expression is part of the fun of wooden bows.

TM: How do modern bowyers tie into the long history of archery?

Baker: Wood bowmakers today have two natures. On the one hand, by past standards they are essentially bow gods, having a breadth and depth of knowledge no bowmaker could have conceived of in the not too distant past. Then too they are free as no past bowmakers were free. They don't have to make and use bows. Not for food or defense. They make and shoot wooden bows for the innate pleasure of making and shooting them.

Comstock: The near-disappearance of wooden bows was a fluke, a temporary aberration, I think. It was not how things were supposed to be. With the return of these bows, the natural order has been restored. Today's bowyers are carrying the legacy of all who passed before. It is an incredibly ancient fraternity, and we all belong.

Hamm: The nature of wood hasn't changed in the past fifteen thousand years, so bowyers today have a direct link to the past, a time machine. Particularly if they're reproducing a historical design.

TM: It has been fifteen years since the first three *TBBs*, why did you decide to produce another one now?

Baker: Given the general state of wood bowmaking knowledge at the time, the *TBBs* did a surprisingly good job collating existing information, exposing harmful dogma, and expanding the knowledge base. Even after fifteen years, any errors are largely nuance. But during that time scores and scores of subtle refinements and extrapolations of design and materials knowledge have developed. Much of this via discussions on various on-line archery forums. And even three volumes had not covered all that needed covering. Bow woods, arrows of the world, character bows, and flight bows, for example. Then, too, readers were continually asking when a new volume would appear.

Comstock: In the late 1940s, Robert Elmer was asked to update his book written in the 1920s. He said no, it was going to take a new book because of the improvements in technique and understanding. I think the situations are similar.

Hamm: Well, a lot has happened during that time. There are now tens of thousands of new wooden bowyers around the world, and the exchange of ideas and information is at an all-time high, so there have been new discoveries and innovations. Or in a lot of cases old truths have been rediscovered. Either way, guys like Steve Gardner, Marc St. Louis, Dan Perry, Mickey Lotz, Tom Mills, Jim Welch, Steve Allely, and Mike Westvang all have vast experience to share. So Tim and Paul and I talked it over and felt it was time for another volume.

TM: Where do you foresee traditional archery in another 100 years?

Baker: I'm sure I can't do better than Maurice Thompson, "So long as the new moon returns in heaven, a bent, beautiful bow, so long will the fascination of archery keep hold of the hearts of men." He's been pretty accurate to this point.

Comstock: If there is hunting, there will be wooden bows. And the Germans have proved there will be wooden bows even if there is no domestic bowhunting. The spiritual lure and emotional rewards of these bows have taken on a new meaning in the Computer Age. I think the near-disappearance of wooden bows many of us knew will never happen again.

Hamm: Hopefully, the connection will continue, all the way back to that first bowyer sitting in a rock shelter scraping a stave with a flint chip while his stomach growled. With luck, those future bowyers in a hundred years will still be able to pit their bowmaking skills and woods craft against wild game. I hope so, anyway.

TM: Any final thoughts?

Baker: Maybe just an expression of thanks: that the pilot-light handful of bowyers were so completely generous with information; that as our numbers began to grow, primitive wood bowmaking attracted people with similar generous natures, and continues to; that thousands, here and around the world, are effectively a family; that bow gods saw fit to place oracles along the long path - Ascham, the Thompsons, Ishi, Pope, Elmer, Massey, Comstock, Hamm - to name a few; that I was lucky enough to discover this realm, lucky enough to have helped in some small way in its rebirth, and luckier still to be part of this ancient brotherhood.

Comstock: Let me emphasize how pleased I am with the current state of the natural archery scene. It's big and vibrant with many thousands involved, and that's fantastic. I give a standing ovation to all of you who are making and using wooden bows, you who have written about them in print or on the Internet, you who have started websites, you who have put out a video and you who are just getting involved. The widespread popularity of wooden bows has been your creation, the product of your efforts and hard work. If we who got started decades ago tend to go on and on about how rough things were back then, it's just another way for us to say how thrilled to death we are with the way things are now. And my thanks to Jim, Tim and countless others over the years who have let me work with them and talk with them about wooden bows.

Hamm: I've been very fortunate to work with Tim and Paul and Jay and all of the other contributors to the *TBBs*. Jay was a modern-day Saxton Pope, with his writing and wilderness skills and integrity. All of us who make bows today are in his debt. You can draw a straight line from Paul's book *The Bent Stick* to the *TBBs* to today's bowyers.

I refer to Paul as "professor". It aggravates him, which is reason enough to do it, but it's also accurate. Paul doubles as my conscience, never afraid to occasionally say in his loving way, "Hamm, that's pure crap." In my opinion, Tim's chapter on Design and Performance, in *TBB 1*, is the single most important information that has been written on archery, ever. His years of study and making thousands of bows, combined with keen observation and plenty of cross-pollination, for the first time yielded a complete picture of how wooden bows actually tick. Tim is also an all-around good guy; so smart it's sometimes scary, funny, generous to a fault, and loyal. But don't tell him I said so.

Working with those guys has been an amazing experience, one of the highlights of my life.

YOUR FIRST WOODEN BOW

Tim Baker

The following short how-to piece has proven to be unusually successful at putting a durable, efficient bow into the hands of first-time bowmakers. Making it available to novices should ease their entry into this ancient craft.

• • • •

The first thing a newcomer wants to do is make a bow. And that's a good idea. Just plunge in. If you fully study the subject first you'll only understand twenty percent of what you read, and remember ten percent. Instead, just read what's interesting, look at the pictures, then go make your first bow. With that success or failure under your belt the books will make much more sense.

Making your first bow can be a discouraging hurdle. But it doesn't have to be. Following is a 40-50 lb design that is easy and quick to tiller, is durable, accurate, and fast, and costs about six dollars to make.

This bow is the length of your finger-tip to finger-tip wingspan. Its side-view is the 'D' shape of the old English longbow. This design's grip is part of the working limb itself, making the bow easy to layout and easy to make. It stores more energy than shorter bows, draws with little stack, and is more stable and accurate than other designs. It may have a larger number of good features than any other bow type.

These instructions call for a lumberyard hardwood stave. With such a stave it's possible to read this in the morning and be shooting your bow the same afternoon.

If you don't have access to such lumber do this: Cut a straight hardwood tree having a trunk at least wingspan tall. Split it down to four-inch wide wedges, take the bark off without damaging the wood surface. With saw or hatchet reduce the stave to desired length plus a few inches if possible. Reduce it to two-inches wide from end to end, 1" thick at the grip, 3⁄4" at midlimb, and 5/8" at the nocks. Set it horizontally in the warmest, driest part of your house and wait a month. Allow air to move freely over all its surfaces.

Selecting a lumber stave: Use any of the medium-weight or heavier hardwoods. White ash, rock maple, hickory, pecan, mulberry, red or white oak, etc. Select a board whose face displays perfectly straight ring lines, with no meanders, islands or kinks. Pay no attention to ring lines on the side of the board as they can be misleading (see the top photo pg. 32). Although on the rare perfect board ring lines will run straight on both sides and back. Viewed from its butt end, the board's rings can be flat or angle through the board. Beginners should avoid boards having vertical ring lines. You will likely have to look through 50 or more boards to find a sufficiently straight-ringed stave. 1" by 2" by six-foot boards are usually the most economical choice.

Tools: A hatchet and a rasp or knife are all that's absolutely needed to make a bow. But a spokeshave and coarse and medium rasps make the work faster and easier. A block plane is helpful if used carefully. A rat-tail file is helpful when cutting string nocks. A bandsaw saves about two hours of roughing out.

Front-view layout: With a sharp pencil and a straightedge draw the bow 1 3/8" wide from midlimb to midlimb. From there draw a straight taper to 1/2" nocks. Reduce the stave to these dimensions. Don't stray past the line. Create smooth, square sides. Smooth out the slight angle created where the midlimb begins its taper toward the tips.

Side-view layout: Draw these lines on both sides of the stave: Measured from the bow's back, let the center five-inches be 3/4" thick. Moving toward the nocks, let the next two inches taper to 5/8 then to 9/16" at midlimb, then to 1/2" at the nocks.

Reduce the stave to those dimensions. Don't stray past the lines. Let thickness changes be smooth and gradual. Remove the wood from one side of the belly at a time, with the tool at a slight angle, such that when both sides are done a slight crown will have been created along the center of the belly. Then remove the crown. It's important to reduce belly thickness this way. Otherwise at some point you'll dip below the line on the opposite side and ruin the bow. This method also averages out any errors of reduction. It's also easier than trying to remove full-width wood.

As you remove wood down to the pencil lines frequently sight along the length of the limb from a very low angle and make sure your work is smooth and uniform, with no dips or waves or dings. THIS IS ONE OF THE MOST IMPORTANT PARTS OF BOWMAKING - if thickness taper is smooth and gradual it's difficult to break a bow.

Narrow the belly side of the grip just enough to cause a nocked arrow to rest square against the side of the grip. Do this on both sides of the grip. Round all corners of the grip.

Tillering: Cut string nocks in each limb tip with a knife, rattail file, chainsaw file, or something similar, then string the bow with a slightly slack string. Set the center of the grip on one end of a tillering stick - a 30" one-by-three board or similar - and place the string in a notch cut into that board, causing the bow to bend about three inches. Lean this rig against a wall then back up and inspect the curve of your new bow.

The shape you are seeking should not be part of a circle, but more the shape of a satellite dish antenna - an only slightly bending grip, with each portion bending slightly more than the last as you move from grip to mid outer limb. Elliptical tiller. The last ten inches or so should be relatively stiff, only bending slightly. The bow atop page 37 is a good full-draw example.

If your bow does not take this shape, or if the limbs are not curving equally, make pencil marks on the belly where the limbs are too stiff. Remove wood from these stiff areas, first on one side of the belly, then the other, then remove the slight crown created. Do this with long sweeping strokes, creating no dips, waver or dings, frequently sighting along your work, as above. THIS IS ONE OF THE MOST IMPORTANT PARTS OF BOWMAKING.

When the curve finally suits you, brace the bow about four-inches high with a proper-length string and inspect it again. Mark any stiff portions and reduce them as above. When content with the curve, draw the bow to half its intended draw weight, measured by your best guess or a scale. Set the bow on the tillering stick at this length of draw and mark any stiff areas and remove as above. Re-check the tiller, re-mark, remove wood, etc. until perfect curvature is reached.

Now draw the bow to full draw weight. If full weight is reached at, say, twelve-inches of draw you need to remove medium amounts of wood all along the bow's length. Do so by above methods. Check for proper curve on the tillering stick. Correct where needed.

After each correction, pull to intended draw weight a dozen or so times, forcing true tiller shape to reveal itself. Otherwise, the finished bow may well go out of tiller once shot a few times, requiring touch-up tillering, causing draw weight to drop.

Full draw weight will now be reached at possibly fifteen inches of draw. From this point on remove only paper-thin amounts of wood at a time. Pull to full draw weight after each curve check, setting the string into ever farther notches on the tillering stick as draw length increases, but only for a few seconds at a time. Once within five inches or so of full draw inspection time should drop to just a second or two.

This process of drawing to full weight after each tiller check - Jim-Hamm Tillering - insures that you never come in under intended draw weight, the most common failing of new bowmakers.

Continue this process until about one inch short of intended draw length. Smooth all surfaces to your taste, slightly round the corners, and you're done. With use the bow will settle right into its intended weight.

If using hickory, pecan, rock maple, red oak or other equally dense or denser woods, 50 lb is a safe draw weight. Ash or elm will be safe at 45 lb. If birch or black cherry stay at 40 lb. As your tillering skill improves these weight can rise several pounds.

When tillering is near complete, and if the tips are straight - causing the braced string to sit centered over the grip - narrow the last ten-inches of outer limb down to a width of 3/8". This softens any hand shock and increases cast. If the string is slightly off center narrow the tips only on the outbound side. This will bring the string back toward center.

Nock the arrow just above the center of the grip. The arrow will fly more accurately with one limb or the other as the top limb, but this may change over the life of the bow.

This design will yield a durable, efficient bow, which at 50 lbs should cast a 500-grain arrow about 160 fps.

APPENDIX II

CONVERSIONS

1 inch = 25.4 millimeters
1 inch = 2.54 centimeters
1 millimeter = 0.0393701 inch
1 centimeter = 0.3937008 inch
1 foot = 304.8 millimeters
1 meter = 39.3700787 inches
1 mile = 1,760 yards

100 degrees Celsius = 212 degree Fahrenheit
32 degrees Fahrenheit = 0 degree Celsius
Boiling point of water = 212 F or 100 C

1 fps = 0.6818182 mph
1 mph = 1.4666667 fps
150 fps = 102.2727273 mph

1 ounce = 437.5 grains
1 ounce = 28.3495231 grams
1 gram = 15.4323584 grains
1 kilogram = 2.2046226 pounds

Weight of water: 62.4 lb/cubic ft or 1,000 kg/cubic m, or 1 gram per cubic centimeter.

GLOSSARY

Air Dried Wood: Wood that has reached unforced equilibrium with ambient humidity.

Anchor, Anchor Point: A point, usually on cheek or jaw, where the arrow nock or drawing hand touches at each full draw, helping to achieve consistent draw length and aim from shot to shot.

Angle of Violation: The angle at which violated wood fibers approach the back. The greater the angle, the more likely an unbacked bow will break in tension.

Annual Ring: See growth ring.

Archer's Paradox: At release, the string draws the arrow nock toward the center of the handle. This should cause the arrow to deflect well away from the bow, away from the target. Yet the arrow travels where aimed - an apparent paradox - due to the arrow bending around the handle. Correct arrow spine stiffness is needed for best results.

Armguard, Bracer: A shield of stiff leather or other material secured to the inside of the forearm gripping the bow for protection from the released bowstring.

Arrowhead: Attached to the front of the arrow shaft providing balance in flight and shaft protection at impact. Endless varieties, hunting points, war bodkins, field points, and blunts to name a few.

Arrow Length: Measured from the bottom of the arrow nock to the arrow tip, base of the arrowhead, or any assigned point.

Arrow Nock: A groove or notch in the tail end of the arrow shaft sufficient to accept the bowstring.

Arrow Pass: Where the arrow rests against the bow.

Arrow Plate: See Strike Plate.

Arrow Rest: A small protrusion attached to the bow just above the grip to support the arrow.

Arrow Shaft: The portion of an arrow excluding point, nock, foreshaft, if any, and fletching.

Arrow Shelf: A narrow ledge in the side of the bow just above the grip, placing the arrow closer to bow center than an arrow rest.

Arrow Weight: An arrow's total physical weight, usually given in grains.

Asiatic Composite: See Composite Bow.

Asiatic Release: Where the string is drawn with a flexed thumb aided by the other fingers, the arrow steadied by the forefinger.

Back: The side of the bow facing the target.

Backing: Material applied to the back of a bow, usually to prevent tension breaks or to increase performance. Backing can be of wood, sinew, rawhide, silk, plant fiber and more.

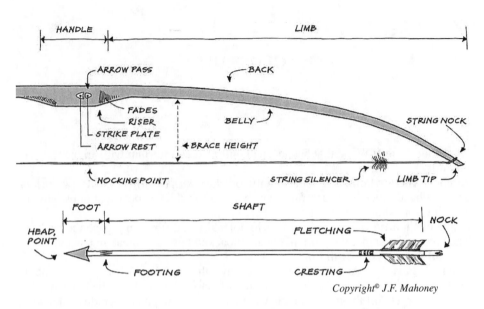

Copyright© *J.F. Mahoney*

Backset: Setback in the handle. Natural, steam bent, or spliced angling of the limbs, placing the unbraced bow tips forward of the grip back.

Bare shaft testing: Shooting unfletched arrows, to adjust nocking point, arrow rest position, etc. for best flight.

Barreled Arrow: An arrow shaft tapered toward the ends from center.

Bast: The fibrous inner bark layer. Some tree bast fibers can be twisted into rope, and even heavy, bulky bowstrings, especially basswood.

Belly: The side of the bow facing the archer.

Billet: One of two short staves to be spliced together to form a full-length stave. Often they are sister billets, taken side-by-side from the same tree to insure similar properties. Billets can permit a bow to be made from otherwise too short or unusable wood.

Bird Points: So called for their small size. But a misnomer, as they yield increased penetration on large game. Easily fatal to deer.

Blunt: A flat-faced arrowhead of rubber, wood or other material, intended for small game at close range. Prevents skin punctures. Tends not to skim under leaves and grass, therefore useful when roving.

Bobtailed Arrow: Widest at front of shaft, tapering to narrowest point at arrow tail. Sometimes known as a tapered arrow.

Bole: A tree trunk or an especially thick branch.

Bow Stringer: A bow bracing aid. Most useful for reflexed and recurved bows.

Bowyer: A skilled bowmaker.

Bowyers Knot: see Timberhitch.

Brace: To string a bow.

Bracer: See Armguard.

Brace Height: On a braced bow, the distance from the bowstring usually to the grip belly, but sometimes measured from the back, the grip belly, or the assumed neutral plane. See Fistmele.

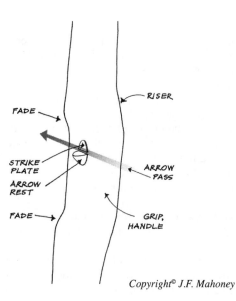

FADE

RISER

STRIKE
PLATE

ARROW
PASS

ARROW
REST

FADE

GRIP,
HANDLE

Copyright© J.F. Mahoney

Brash: Brittle.

Breast: The portion of an arrow that contacts the bow at brace height.

Breasted Arrow: An arrow thickest where it contacts the bow at brace height, then tapering toward the nock, for faster flight and less fletching wear.

Broadhead: A hunting arrowhead with wide, thin, sharp blades.

Butt: A mound of earth uses as a target backing. A target of compressed straw.

Cambium: The thin layer of living tissue between wood and bark, generating both new wood and new bark.

Cant: Angling the bow from vertical to help hold the arrow in place and to aid viewing.

Casehardened: Honeycombed. When dried too quickly, surface wood is considerably drier, harder, and more shrunken than interior wood.

Cast: Sometimes the distance a bow sends an arrow, but more accurately the speed of the arrow leaving the bow.

Checks: Small cracks paralleling the grain, usually from too-rapid drying.

Chrysals: Single or multiple fine rupture lines running across the width of the belly; compression fractures resulting from poor tillering or an over-straining design. See 'Frets.'

Clout Shooting: Shooting for accuracy at a far distant target resting flat on the ground, usually from 160 to 240 yards. Large concentric circles often mark the area, with a small white target at center.

Cock Feather: On a three-fletch arrow: An often different-colored feather to be nocked 90-degrees to the string, insuring that no feather strikes the bow squarely.

Composite bow: A bow whose limbs are made of two or more different materials. Usually a sinew/wood/horn bow, as in Asiatic composite bows.

Compression: The compacting, shortening force felt by the belly as the bow is drawn, exactly balancing the stretching, tension force felt by the back.

Creep: After reaching full draw, forward movement of the arrow before release.

Cresting: Colored bands on the arrow shaft, usually near the fletching, sometimes to identify one's arrows, but often just as decoration.

Crown: The low or high arch on the back or belly of a bow.

Curing Wood: Drying wood.

D-Bow: A working-grip bow that assumes a D shape when drawn.

Deciduous Trees: Trees that drop their leaves in winter.

Decrowning: Flattening the crowned back of a stave. Removing convex wood, most often from a smaller-diameter therefore higher-crowned sapling or branch.

Deflex: A portion of a braced or unbraced bow that angles toward the archer, as in deflexed limbs or tips. Opposite of reflex.

Deflex-Reflex: Limbs first angling toward the archer, then back toward the target.

Density: The weight of a body relative to its volume. The density of wood largely predicts the amount of work a given volume of wood can do.

D-Section: A limb cross-section having a relatively flat back and a crowned, or arched belly.

Diffuse-Porous Wood: Wood with relatively uniform pore structure throughout the annual ring, having no defined early-growth ring, as opposed to ring-porous woods.

Dip, Dips: Where a thicker, non-bending handle dips down to the bending limb.

Draw: Pulling the bowstring to firing position.

Draw Length: Sometimes measured from the base of the arrow nock to the belly of the grip at full draw, but usually measured to the back of the bow.

Draw Weight: Force, usually in pounds, needed to pull a bow to its full draw length.

Dry Fire: Shooting a bow without an arrow.

Dutch Plug, Dutchman: A cylinder of wood replacing a bow limb knot or other defect, usually on the belly side.

Early Wood: Spring growth. The first weak porous layer of wood laid down at the beginning of each growth year in ring-porous woods.

E: Elastic Modulus

Elastic Modulus: The measure of stiffness/resistance to elongation or compression.

Elasticity: See Elastic Limit.

Elastic limit: The percentage of length a material can be stretched or compressed before permanent deformation occurs. For most woods, permitted strain is about 1%.

Elliptical tiller: From a side view, a progressive increase in bend moving from grip to outer limb, extreme outer limbs often remaining nearly straight.

ELB: English longbow.

Endless String: Winding a sufficient number of threads between two nails, or something similar, of desired distance apart. Loops are formed by serving.

English Longbow (ELB): A straight-stave bow, usually man-tall or taller, narrow and deep limbed, often with a crowned belly, the grip often being part of the working limb, therefore not narrowed or appreciably thickened. Most often of yew, but also of other woods. Often with horn nocks. Later versions sometimes have stiff handle sections.

Equilibrium moisture content: Moisture content of wood after drying to balance with surrounding relative humidity.

ERC: Eastern Red Cedar.

Extractives: Compounds deposited in sapwood as it becomes heartwood. The darker color and frequent resistance to insects and decay result from these compounds.

Face: The bow belly.

Facing: Any material applied to the bow belly.

Fadeouts, Fades: Where thicker, non-bending handle wood feathers into wider working limb.

English Longbow-tillered, ELB tillered: An un-narrowed grip, working as part of the limbs. Can be any shape cross-section. A D-bow.

Feet Per Second: FPS. Cast. Arrow speed, generally measured leaving the bow.

Field Archery: Where targets are placed at varying distances in natural terrain.

Field Point: A cylindrical metal arrowhead having a short, convex-sloped point, easily removed from a target, and used for roving and target shooting.

Finger Pinch: When string angle on full-draw short bows is low enough to pinch the drawing fingers.

Finger Tab: Generally a patch of leather worn to protect the string fingers.

Finger Sling: See Sling.

Fishtailing: When an arrow wobbles right to left in flight.

Fishtail Splice: A "W" shaped splice used to join two billets. Also see "Z" splice.

Fistmele: A traditional brace height measured from the bottom of a clenched fist held against the bow's belly to the tip of the extended thumb.

Flatbow: Bows with limbs considerably wider than thick, rectangular or lenticular in cross-section, usually, but not always, shorter than longbows. Medium and lower density woods especially benefit from this design.

Flax: See Linen.

Flemish String: A bowstring, traditionally reverse-twisted of flax or hemp, having a plaited loop at one or both ends. If used with a single loop, a timberhitch usually replaces the second loop.

Fletching: Two, three, or sometimes more feathers secured near the arrow nock to stabilize an arrow's flight. See Flights.

Flight Arrow: An arrow designed for maximum distance; small diameter, shorter, lighter, often barreled, and with small fletching.

Flight Bow: A bow designed for shooting flight arrows to maximum distance.

Flight Shooting: Shooting competitively for maximum distance.

Flights: Individual feathers or vanes on a fletched arrow.

Flu-Flu: Dense, large fletchings, often having six feathers, producing short arrow flight. Used for bird or squirrel hunting, or any aerial target.

Follow the string: See String Follow.

Foot: The front end of an arrow shaft.

Footed Shaft: Footed Arrow: An arrow shaft having denser, harder wood spliced into its foot for durability and better balance in flight.

Footing: Typically dense hardwood spliced into the tip of an arrow.

Foreshaft: A several inch-long heavier material, generally hardwood, inserted into the front of a hollow arrow. Often used with cane or bamboo arrow shafts. See 'Footing.'

Force Draw Curve: Measure draw weight every inch or so out to full draw. Mark these weights and draw lengths on a graph. The area under the produced line represents energy stored by the drawn bow.

FPS: See Feet Per Second.

Fret: Presently used interchangeably with "chrysal". Traditionally frets are larger, and place the bow at greater risk.

Gap: The space between arrow tip and target as seen by the archer at full draw.

Gap Shooting: An aiming method focusing on the visual gap between the tip of the arrow and the target. Gap size is adjusted for target distance.

Grain: Fibers that make up wood. The word is often misused when referring to growth ring lines.

Grains: A unit of measure: 437.5 grains per ounce, commonly used when noting the weight of arrows, arrowpoints, bowstrings, and other light archery-related objects.

Green, Green wood: Unseasoned, wet, usually freshly-cut wood.

Grip: The handle, the sometimes thicker, stiffer, narrower, often non-bending area between a bow's two working limbs. Also, any one of the ways in which a bow can be held.

Group: An archer's pattern of arrows seen in a target after a round of shooting.

Growth Ring: Annual ring: A full layer of wood added to trunk or branch each year.

Handle: See Grip.

Handshock: A harsh kick or vibration sometimes felt by the bow hand and arm upon release of the arrow.

Hardwoods: Non-conifer wood. Hardwood can be light or dense, hard or soft. "Broadleaf wood" is more accurate.

Head: The front of the arrow shaft.

Heartwood: Darker inner wood beneath lighter sapwood.

Helical Fletching: When the feathers spiral somewhat around the arrow shaft, yielding greater rotation in flight.

High-wrist grip: The bow gripped toward the top of the wrist, usually at the base of the thumb and first finger, rather than whole-handed.

Hinge: Excessive bend in one small portion of a bow limb.

Hinged Bow: Related to a takedown bow, but hinged at the grip, limbs folding instead of separating.

Humidity Meter: Measures relative humidity.

Hygrometer: See Humidity Meter.

Instinctive Shooting: Where the archer looks at the target, draws, and releases, with no conscious aiming method.

Interlocking Grain: Alternating left and right spiral grain formed in successive annual rings. Shows a herringbone pattern when exposed at the riser. Makes wood difficult to split, as in elm, for example.

Inner Bark: A more fibrous layer just above the cambium, often a fiber source for cordage.

Kiln Dried: Forced drying with heat and usually reduced humidity, usually to about 8% MC.

Latewood: Summerwood. Wood laid down after early wood. Generally denser as the growing season progresses.

Laminated Bow: A bow made by gluing two or more slats of wood together, often forced into various degrees of reflex or deflex in order to raise stored energy/cast.

Let-Down: See Creep.

Let-Off: Reduction in draw weight at some point before full draw is reached, as caused by string lift-off of extremely recurved or retroflexed bow limbs.

Lift-Off: See String Lift Off.

Limb length: Distance measured from limb nock or limb tip to mid-grip of a working-grip bow, or to the non-bending portion of a stiff-grip bow.

Limbs: The bending portions of a bow stretching from bow center to bow tips in a working-grip bow; on a stiff-handled bow from the handle fades, or where the limbs start bending, to the bow tips.

Limb tip: The outer tip of a bow limb.

Linen: Strong per mass, relatively inelastic fiber from the flax plant, used for bowstrings since antiquity.

Longbow: A straight-limbed, near-man tall or taller bow. Usually, but not always, narrower and thicker in section than shorter bows. See English Longbow.

Loop: The plaited or served end of a bowstring attached to the bow's nocks when braced. Sometimes on both string ends.

Loose: Releasing the drawn bowstring and arrow.

Loose Grip: Gripping the bow lightly enough to prevent the hand from twisting the bow right or left during draw and release.

Mass: The physical weight of a bow, arrow, or other equipment.

MC: Moisture content.

Mediterranean Release: First finger above the arrow nock, two fingers below, with the arrow resting between the first and second finger.

Modulus of Elasticity: see Elastic Modulus.

Modulus of Rupture: The measure of the breaking strength of wood.

Moisture Content: The amount of water in wood expressed as a percentage of its oven-dried (zero moisture content) weight.

Mongolian Release: Typically used on Asiatic Composites using a thumb ring; the string is drawn by the crooked thumb, sometimes aided by the other fingers, with the arrow held in place by the forefinger.

Neutral Plane: The boundary separating tension and compression forces, usually resting about half way between back and belly.

Nock: Arrow nock, the notched end of an arrow. Also, string nock, a shoulder, protrusion, notch or notches on each bow tip to hold the bowstring when braced. Also, to place an arrow in position on the bowstring.

Nock-to-Nock (ntn): Bow length measured from one string nock to the other.

Nocking Height: Zero nocking height would place the nocked arrow square to the string while resting at the arrow pass. Arrows are often nocked slightly above that point on the string, to aid arrow clearance and to prevent feather quills from nicking the hand when using the bow hand as an arrow rest.

Nocking Point: An exact point on the string where the arrow is nocked.

Overbowed: Using a bow too strong for accurate shooting.

Overlay: Wear-resistant material, often wood or horn, usually applied to the back of limb tips to prevent string wear, especially on narrow limb tips.

Perry Reflex: A wood backing applied to the back of a thickness-tapered wood belly while both are held in reflex. The resulting strain at the cured glue line causes additional energy to be stored internally, allowing lower-mass limbs. Named for Dan Perry, who first developed and recognized the principle.

Pike: To shorten a bow, usually to increase draw weight. Sometimes to allow tiller correction.

Pinch: See Finger Pinch.

Pins: Pin Knots. Small surface knots or branchlets, usually elevated.

Point Blank: Where the drawn arrow's tip is viewed directly on the target. Sometimes known as "point-on". "This bow is point-on (point-blank) at 45 yards."

Point of Aim: An aiming method wherein at full draw the arrow tip is viewed against a certain point on the ground or background instead of the target itself.

Porpoising: When an arrow wobbles up and down in flight. Usually caused by an incorrect nocking point.

Power Stroke: Upon release, the distance, from full draw to brace height, over which the bow imparts its stored energy to the arrow.

Primary Release: Where the arrow is gripped between the thumb and first finger.

Primitive Bow: Bows of the types used before metal tools and made of all natural materials. A more severe definition might require use of primitive tools for all stages of construction. Only the tiniest fraction of bows made before historical times are known. Any conceivable design that might reasonably have been made of natural materials by pre-civilized people might arguably be classified as a primitive bow, though possibly with an asterisk because there is no physical evidence of such a bow.

Propeller Twist: A propeller twist occurs when the plane of each limb is twisted, or turned, in relation to the other. Nevertheless, the string often tracks at grip center. Usually from a twisted tree.

Quiver: Any container in which to conveniently hold arrows when shooting and transporting.

Reaction Wood: Abnormal wood in leaning trunks and branches.

Recurve: When a portion of an outer limb curves toward the target, such that at brace height, the bowstring contacts wood some distance before the string nock. See semi-recurve also.

Reflex: Where limbs of an unbraced bow angle or curve toward the target.

Release: The loose. Releasing the bowstring and arrow.

Retroflexed tips: Where tips are angled backward instead of curved.

Ring-Porous Wood: Hardwood species having a light, weak, large-pored, early-growth or spring-growth portion in its annual growth ring. As opposed to diffuse-porous woods.

Riser: A glued-on or purposely-left-thicker grip rising up from the working limbs.

Round in the Handle: A bow whose handle or near-handle wood bends more than it should.

Roving: Shooting at various and random targets in fields or forests, "stump shooting."

Sapwood: White or near-white outer annual rings lying just under the bark/cambium and above the darker heartwood.

Seasoning: Drying, properly removing water from green wood.

Secondary Release: Where the arrow is gripped by the thumb and first and second finger.

Selfbow: An unbacked bow made from a single stave of wood or two spliced billets. Older definitions disallow spliced billets.

Self Arrow: Made from a single blank of wood.

Semi Recurve: A bow whose ends are recurved, but not severely enough for the string to make contact at brace height.

Serving: A protective wrapping around a bowstring's nocking area or loops.

Set: Permanent deflection of the limbs, resulting from compression of belly wood beyond its elastic limit. Set and string follow are not the same.

Setback: See Backset.

Shake: A long deep crack in a bow or bowstave caused by physical trauma or improper drying.

Shooting Glove: Typically a three-fingered leather glove protecting the fingers drawing the bowstring.

Sight Window: An area cut away above the grip.

Silencer: See String Silencer.

Sinew: Tendon. Strong, elastic cords, generally from Achilles tendons, as well as from backstraps lying down each side of the spine, from ungulates such as deer, elk, moose and wild cattle. Long used to back wooden bows and horn composite bows. Useful as thread when mounting feathers and arrowheads, and for making bow-strings.

Slash Release: A near instantaneous draw and release, often seen in flight shooting. Draw weight drops somewhat with slower draws and longer holds.

Sling: A cord or strap attached to fingers or wrist preventing the bow from falling from the hand when shooting with a loose grip.

Smooth: A bow that draws with little or no stack. Sweet.

Snap Shooting: Drawing and releasing in one fast movement without careful aim. Good for a few extra FPS when flight shooting, but reduces accuracy.

Softwoods: Conifer woods. "Softwood" can be misleading as many softwoods are harder and denser than many hardwoods (broadleafed woods).

Spalting: Fungal discoloration forming brown spots outlined by black lines.

Specific Gravity: The ratio of the weight of a solid to an equal volume of water.

Spine: The stiffness of an arrow. Arrow stiffness must closely match the bow in order to fly where aimed, the main factors being draw weight, brace height, and handle width.

Spliced: As when two billets have been joined to form a full-length bow.

Split Stave: A bow stave taken from a tree, as opposed to a board. A tree stave.

Spring Wood: Spring growth. See Early Wood.

Stack: Abrupt increase in draw weight during later inches of draw. Caused chiefly by large differences in string angle at early and later stages of draw. Especially noticed in short bows.

Stacked: A limb cross-section nearly as thick as it is wide.

Stave: Bow stave. A branch, board (board stave), or split section of log (split stave) from which a bow is to be made.

Static Recurve: A recurve which does not significantly open, or bend, at full draw. As opposed to Working Recurve.

Straight-Stave Bow: A bow made from a stave having essentially no natural or induced reflex, deflex or curves. Once tillered and used, a straight-stave bow may show considerable deflex from set.

Strain: Deformation due to stress.

Stress: In archery, force applied to wood, resulting in deformation in tension, compression, or both.

Strike Plate: On a bow, an insert or patch of generally hard material, such as horn, bone or shell, used to reduce wear by the passing arrow. Used particularly with soft woods such as yew. For silence, a hunting bow might use fur or soft leather.
String: The bowstring.
String: To brace a bow. To place the string on the bow.
String Angle: The angle between arrow and string at full draw.
Stringer: See Bow Stringer.
String Follow: Where by set, design, or natural deflex in the stave, an unbraced bow's tips rest some distance bellyward of the back. Usually the result of set.
String Groove: Grooves on the belly of a recurve, which tend to guide the string home upon release.
String Height: Brace height.
String Keeper: A length of string or leather holding the string loop in place when the bow is unbraced.
String Lift-off: During the draw, the string gradually or suddenly lifting off a limb's recurved or retroflexed ends, the bow becoming effectively longer.
String Nocks: Grooves, notches or shoulders at each end of the bow to hold the bowstring. Sometimes fitted with horn or overlays on the back, to prevent wear by the string.
String Silencer: Fur or other material twisted into the bowstring to prevent string twang upon release, often used by hunters. Generally attached about 1/3 distance from tip to grip.
Stump Shooting: See Roving.
Summerwood: See Latewood.
Sweet: Describes either a smooth stackless draw, or a no-handshock release.
Take-Down Bow: A bow that can be pulled or taken apart at the handle for ease of transport.
TBB: Traditional Bowyer's Bible.
Tension: The stretching force felt by the back as the bow is drawn.
Tension Break: When the bow back breaks first, a tell-tale sharp break line on the back, often leaving belly wood directly beneath unbroken.
Thumb Ring: A ring worn on the thumb used to draw and release the string, associated with Asiatic composite bows. In addition to protecting the thumb, it increases draw length to some degree.
Tiller, Tillering: The process of removing wood from a stave such that the bow bends to intended shape, draw length and draw weight. Also, the side-view shape of a drawn bow.
Tillering Board: A broad, sometimes gridded surface, with high support for the bow grip, and a ground-level pulley through which a hook-ended rope can draw the bow varying distances, often with a scale attached, allowing easy and accurate limb shape and weight checks as tillering proceeds.
Tillering Stick: Generally a notched stick on which the bow can be rested with the string drawn to various lengths. Used for judging limb curvature during the tillering process.
Tillering Tree: Essentially a stand-alone tillering board, often portable.
Tillering String: An often longer, stronger string used when tillering a bow.
Timberhitch: An easily adjustable loop knot securing the bowstring to the lower nock. Usually the bottom loop of a Flemish bowstring.

Torque: Twisting of the bow by the bow hand while drawing and releasing, causing arrows to spray right and left from shot to shot.

Tuning: Coordinating placement of the arrow pass, nocking point and brace height for best arrow flight.

Tung Oil: One of the few natural hardening oils, like linseed oil but more protective per number of coats or rubbings. Many coatings will create a relatively sound moisture barrier. From Tung nuts of the Tung tree, native to China.

Underbowed: Using a weaker bow than needed.

War Bow: Designed for war instead of hunting, often having 40% to 100% higher draw weight.

Whip-Ended: A bow that bends considerably in its outer limbs.

White Wood: Sapwood from thick-sapwood trees, such as ash, maple, oak, hickory and others. "White Wood" is also now a vernacular term distinguishing once-traditional bow woods such as yew, Osage and Lemonwood from the once disparaged "other woods." Dark woods such as locust and black walnut are sometimes colloquially included.

Working-Grip Bow: A bow whose handle area bends sufficiently to store a significant portion of the bows total stored energy. A "round in the handle" ELB-like design being the extreme example.

Working Recurve: A recurve which straightens to some small or large degree after string lift-off. As opposed to Static Recurve.

Yumi: Japanese for bow.

"Z" splice: Similar to a "W" splice but "Z" shaped. Slightly less gluing surface, but each splice face is identical, as opposed to the male/female "W".

BIBLIOGRAPHY

Allely, Steve, Baker, Tim, Comstock, Paul, et.al., *The Traditional Bowyer's Bible, Volumes 1, 2, and 3*, Bois d'Arc Press, Goldthwaite, TX, 1992, 1993, 1994.

Allely, Steve, and Hamm, Jim, *Encyclopedia of Native American Bows, Arrows, & Quivers, Volumes 1 and 2*, Bois d'Arc Press, Goldthwaite, TX, 1999, 2002.

Ascham, Roger, *Toxophilus; The School of Shooting*, 1544.

Audubon Society, *Field Guide to North American Trees, Vol. 1 Eastern Region, Vol. 2 Western Region*. Alfred E. Knopf, New York, 1980.

Bear, Fred, *The Archer's Bible*, Fred Bear Sports Club Press, Gainesville, FL, 1968.
   - *Fred Bear's Field Notes*, Fred Bear Sports Club Press, Gainesville, FL. 1976.
   - *Fred Bear's World of Archery,* Fred Bear Sports Club Press, Gainesville, FL., 1979.

Bennett, Matthew, *Agincourt 1415: Triumph Against the Odds*, Osprey Publishing, London, 1991.

Burke, Edmond, *A History of Archery*, George J. McLeod Limited, Toronto, 1957.

Burrill, Richard, *Ishi Rediscovered*, The Anthro Company, Susanville, CA, 1990.

Coe, Cliff, *44 Years Behind the Bow*, Private Printing, 1990.

Comstock, Paul, *The Bent Stick; Making and Using Wooden Hunting Bows,* Delaware, OH, 1988.

Duff, James, *Bows and Arrows*, The MacMillan Co., New York, 1944.

Edlin, H.I., *British Woodland Trees*, B. T. Batsford, London, 1945.

Elmer, Robert P., M.D., *Archery*, Penn Publishing Co., Philadelphia, PA, 1926.
   - *Target Archery*, Alfred A. Knopf, New York, 1946.

Forest Products Laboratory, *Wood Handbook; Wood as an Engineering Material*, USDA Forest Service, Madison, WI., 1999.

Gordon, Paul H., *The New Archery, Hobby, Sport, and Craft*, D. Appleton – Century Co., New York, 1939.

Hamm, Jim, *Bows and Arrows of the Native Americans*, Bois d'Arc Press, Goldthwaite, TX, 1989.

Hansard, George Agar, *The Book of Archery*, Henry G. Bohn, London, 1841.

Hardy, Robert, *Longbow, A Social and Military History*, Bois d'Arc Press, Goldthwaite, TX, 1993.

Heath, E.G., and Chiara, Vilma, *Brazilian Indian* Archery, Simon Archery Foundation, Manchester, England, 1977.
    - *The Grey Goose Wing; A History of Archery*, New York Graphic Society, Ltd., 1972.

Hickman, C.N., Nagler, Forrest, and Klopsteg, Paul E., *Archery: The Technical Side*, National Field Archery Association, 1947.

Hill, Howard, *Hunting the Hard Way*, Wilcox & Follett Co., Chicago, 1953.
    - *Wild Adventure*, Stackpole Books, Mechanicsburg, PA, 1954.

Hoadley, Bruce, *Understanding Wood*, The Taunton Press, Newtown, CT, 1980.
    - *Indentifying Wood*, The Taunton Press, Newtown, CT, 1990.

Hodgkin, Arian Eliot, *The Archer's Craft*, Faber & Faber Ltd., London, 1951.

Hunt, W. Ben, and Metz, John J., *The Flatbow*, Bruce Publishing Co., New York, 1940.

Keasey, Gilman, and Reichart, Natalie, *Archery*, A.S. Barnes & Co., New York, 1936.

Klopsteg, Paul, *Turkish Archery and the Composite Bow*, Evanston, IL, 1934.

Kroeber, Theodora, *Ishi in Two Worlds; A Biography of the Last Wild Indian in North America*, University of California Press, Berkeley, 1961.
    - *Ishi the Last Yahi; A Documentary History*, University of California Press, Berkeley, 1979.

Kroll, Charles, *Fred Bear; Biography of an Outdoorsman*, Fred Bear Sports Club Press, Gainesville, FL, 1988.

Lambert, Arthur W, Jr., *Modern Archery*, A.S. Barnes & Co., New York, 1929.

Little, Elbert L., *National Audubon Society Field Guide to Trees, Eastern Region*, Alfred A. Knopf, New York, 1980.
    - *National Audubon Society Field Guide to Trees, Western Region*, Alfred A. Knopf, New York, 1980.

Massey, Jay, *The Bowyer's Craft*, Bear Paw Publications, Girdwood, AK, 1987.
    - *The Book of Primitive Archery*, Bear Paw Publications, Girdwood, AK, 1990.

Markham, Gervais, *The Art of Archerie*, 1634.

McBride, Angus, and Turnbull, S.R., *The Mongols*, Osprey Publishing, London, 1980.
 - *The Scythians*, 700-300 B.C., Osprey Publishing, London, 1983.

McMillan, John M., and Wengert, Eugene M., *Drying Eastern Hardwood Lumber,* U.S. Dept. of Agriculture Handbook #528, Washington, D.C., 1977.

Nagler, Forrest, *Archery – An Engineering View*, 1946.

Pope, Saxton, *Yahi Archery*, University of California Press, Berkeley, CA, 1918.
 - *A Study of Bows and Arrows*, University of California Press, Berkeley, CA, 1923.
 - *Hunting With the Bow and Arrow*, G.P. Putnam's Sons, New York, 1925.
 - *The Adventurous Bowmen*, G.P. Putnam's Sons, New York, 1926.

Rotella, Dr. Bob, *Golf is Not a Game of Perfect*, Simon & Schuster, New York, 1995.

Rothero, Christopher, *The Armies of Agincourt*, Osprey Publishing, London, 1981.

St. Charles, Glenn, *Billets to Bows*, Private Printing, 1996.

Shane, Adolph, *Archery Tackle*, Bois d'Arc Press, Goldthwaite, TX, 1936/1990.

Soar, Hugh D., *The Crooked Stick: A History of the Longbow*, Westholme Publishing, Yardley, PA, 2004.
 - *Secrets of the English War Bow*, Westholme Publishing, Yardley, PA, 2006.

Starn, Orin, *Ishi's Brain: In Search of America's Last Wild Indian*, W.W. Norton & Co., New York, 2004.

Stemmler, L.E. *The Essentials of Archery*, New York, 1953.

Thompson, Maurice, *The Witchery of Archery*, 1878.

White, Stewart Edward, *Lions in the Path,* Doubleday, Page & Co. New York, 1926.

Traditional Bowyer's Bibles Tables of Contents

INDEX